Chevrolet Corvette
THE OWNERS AND THE CARS

Mario Brunner

SCHIFFER PUBLISHING

4880 Lower Valley Road • Atglen, PA 19310

Other Schiffer Books on Related Subjects:
Air & Water: Rare Porsches, 1956–2019, Saratoga Automobile Museum
ISBN 978-0-7643-6416-7
McLaren: The Road Cars, 2010–2024, Kyle Fortune, ISBN 978-0-7643-6731-1
The Mercedes-Benz G-Class: The Complete History of an Off-Road Classic,
Jörg Sand, ISBN 978-0-7643-6263-7

Copyright ©2025 by Schiffer Publishing, Ltd.
Originally published as *Chevrolet Corvette: 70 Jahre - 70 Storys*,
by Motorbuch Verlag, Stuttgart, Germany ©2023
Translated from the German by Mario Brunner

Library of Congress Control Number: 2024941452

All rights reserved. No part of this work may be reproduced or used in any form or by any means—graphic, electronic, or mechanical, including photocopying or information storage and retrieval systems—without written permission from the publisher.

The scanning, uploading, and distribution of this book or any part thereof via the Internet or any other means without the permission of the publisher is illegal and punishable by law. Please purchase only authorized editions and do not participate in or encourage the electronic piracy of copyrighted materials.

"Schiffer," "Schiffer Publishing, Ltd.," and the pen and inkwell logo are registered trademarks of Schiffer Publishing, Ltd.

Designed by Mario Brunner
Cover design by Jack Chappell
Photos: Mario Brunner
Type set in Steelfish/Times New Roman
ISBN: 978-0-7643-6884-4
Printed in India

Published by Schiffer Publishing, Ltd.
4880 Lower Valley Road
Atglen, PA 19310
Phone: (610) 593-1777; Fax: (610) 593-2002
Email: Info@schifferbooks.com
Web: www.schifferbooks.com

For our complete selection of fine books on this and related subjects, please visit our website at www.schifferbooks.com. You may also write for a free catalog.

Schiffer Publishing's titles are available at special discounts for bulk purchases for sales promotions or premiums. Special editions, including personalized covers, corporate imprints, and excerpts, can be created in large quantities for special needs. For more information, contact the publisher.

We are always looking for people to write books on new and related subjects. If you have an idea for a book, please contact us at proposals@schifferbooks.com.

FOREWORD

As I write this, it is January 17, 2023. Exactly 70 years ago, Chevrolet introduced the Corvette concept to the world at the Motorama car show in New York City.

The first Corvette advertisements urged drivers to "Stop dreaming and start driving," to "Get More out of Life with a Corvette," and promised "The most fun per mile of any car," all of which is still true today. Now, we have introduced the new Corvette E-Ray, which is the first Corvette with electrified AWD capability. I have read about Zora Arkus-Duntov, educated in Europe, who on seeing the Corvette for the first time was inspired to apply to Chevrolet to work on making the Corvette a true sports car to rival the best from Europe. Zora became Corvette chief engineer and later created the first AWD mid-engine concept in 1964 with the CERV II, which achieved a 0–60 time of 2.8 seconds. Our new production 2024 Corvette E-Ray does 0–60 in 2.5 seconds, so Zora would be proud of what we have achieved.

But this book is not about the history of the Corvette. Instead, it is about people and their unique stories. When I met Mario Brunner last summer at the Automotive Hall of Fame in Dearborn, Michigan, he explained his concept of celebrating the 70 years of Corvette with 70 stories provided by their owners. I was most intrigued by the concept, as the Corvette is much more than just a car. The Corvette is fan-based, like a movie franchise or a sports team, and the drivers take ownership and are critical of every change, big or small, because it's their car. Everyone I meet has a story about the first time they saw a Corvette and how they promised themselves that they would get one someday. For some of a certain age, it was the 1963 Sting Ray with the split rear window; for people like me, it was the 1984 Corvette, which brought world-class performance and handling, and for a new generation, it is the mid-engine eighth-generation Corvette that creates dreams.

My father was a fan of sports cars, mainly of European ones; in his travels, he would buy me books and card games featuring sports cars with their country of origin. The only car with the American flag regularly featured was the Corvette, and it became my favorite car. I am one of the fortunate few who was able to turn my love of the Corvette and the dream of owning one into a career, as I have been working for Chevrolet as the Corvette product manager for more than 20 years, creating and proposing plans and strategies for four of the eight Corvette generations. I am most proud of the eighth generation, as it is truly a dream car. It combines the performance and design of a true supercar with excellent handling qualities on the road and the racetrack. And it is also a car that many people can afford. Only the Corvette can do that.

Every year of the Corvette has its own appeal and its own fans. Each Corvette built deserves its own epic story, so thank you for covering the world's longest-running car by documenting 70 of them for the type's 70th anniversary.

Harlan Charles, Corvette Product Marketing Manager ▶

I have been working with—and writing about—American automobiles of the 20th century for more than 20 years.

I have seen hundreds of books that try to explain what a "Car Guy" is. They try to show how someone lives who understands that he can sleep in his car but not race his house.

This book is not one of those. This book doesn't look at just one scene, doesn't offer just one look into another world, doesn't convey just one impression.

This book is the scene. It is this other world, and what one sees and reads is unfiltered and direct, for this book is what happens when a true "Car Guy" by chance is also a capable photographer.

Mario Brunner actually just wanted to buy a Corvette. How, therefore, did he end up in Neil Armstrong's legendary automobile on the runway at Kennedy Space Center? Well, it was just a case of "Car Guys" doing "Car Guy" stuff.

Three of us were there the night Mario met his car—him, Mark Reiss, and me. And I believe that each of us immediately realized that we had stumbled across one of these stories. I could not have foreseen that it would result first in an idea for a book, then a serious book, and ultimately this book, but I knew one thing: one can easily overdo anything one sets his hand to. This is a sentence often spoken by car enthusiasts and perhaps leads them to search for its real meaning.

There is no better place to search for an answer than this book, for what Mario actually had in mind was to tell the history of his Corvette. What he did instead was to tell the story of the entire series through the eyes of their drivers, from that perspective that can only be seen by one who would sell his house and sleep in his car.

If there was ever a book that could take you into the world of a "Car Guy," this is it. Climb in.

Sönke Priebe, Head of Detroit Performance Technologies ▶

CONTENTS

The Magic Number: 285	7
Provocation and Color	11
His Smile and the Car	17
I Actually Never Wanted a C2	21
It's All About Drawing My Attention	25
Legendary Design, Unimagined Driving Enjoyment	29
This Is One Small Step for Man	33
This C3 Is a Work of Art	41
Out of the Garage into the World	45
Two Corvettes, Countless Kilometers	49
When Fascination Becomes an Occupation	53
Anything but Civilized	57
Dad, This Is Dedicated to You	61
A Drifter and His Corvette	65
The Corvette Was Just in the Way	69
25th and 35th Birthdays	73
It's in the Family	77
A Race Team and a Smurf	81
Many Miles, Many Memories	85
Hello from St. Pauli	89
In Memory of a Good Friend	93
Working on Cars to Remain Balanced	97
Sunshine Follows Rain	101
Car Girl Made in the USA	105
More Than a Supporting Role	109
Everyone Knows this Corvette	113
Corvette Made in Germany?	117
The First Car in My Collection	123
Two Owners, Two Colors	127
Corvette in Victory Red	131
Repeated Goose Bumps Moments	135
The Corvette Reporter	139
Two Brothers, One Passion	143
A Corvette for Christmas	147
German-American Love Stories	151
Guest from Monterey in Lake Placid	157
Inspired by Hard Rock	161
Better Than a Mustang	165
One of 46, Blue Instead of Yellow	169
The Miami Corvette Society	173
From a V2 to a V8	177
Silver Surfer on the Coast	181
Black Exterior, Red Interior	185
The Grand Sport Convertible	191
The Grand Sport Coupe	194
Callaway Premiere in Berlin	197
May I Introduce: Sophie	201
Thanks to the Corvette Community	205
Welcome to Paramus Chevrolet	209
A Corvette for Everyday	213
The Red Veteran Vette	217
A Childhood Dream, a Color	221
Band of Corvette Brothers—Part I	225
Band of Corvette Brothers—Part II	228
Boss of Big Blocks	233
More Than Just a Job	239
The Guy with the Corvette	243
Uncompromising Corvette	247
Pegasus and the God of Fire	251
Three Times Corvette C3	255
The Beast	261
A Corvette in K-Town	265
Ride in Peace, John	269
First Car, First Corvette	273
My Absolute Favorite Place	277
I Don't Care for a Yellow Porsche	281
Please, Not a Black Corvette	285
The Shark Has a V8	289
Last Day at Bowling Green	293
Corvette Number 6	297

THE MAGIC NUMBER: 285

To own two Corvettes, a 1953 and a 2020 model, is quite rare indeed. Larry Smith's Corvettes are even rarer. They have the same serial number: 285.

What's your Corvette story?
When I was a teenager, everybody had '55 Chevys, jacked up, with big engines. I had a '57 Ford, the slowest car at school. One day, I came across a 1956 Corvette at a wrecking yard that was a theft recovery. It was missing the transmission and the hardtop. But the price was right, just a few hundred dollars, so I bought it. At my friend's house I found a three-speed transmission from a '55 Chevy. We put it in the Corvette, and we had to make a shift linkage because I couldn't find an original Corvette linkage. I drove the Corvette and I loved it! And I've never been without a Corvette since that day in 1967.

The first new Corvette I bought was a 1974. So Corvettes aren't new to me. I've been around them for a long time. I can't visualize myself without a Corvette. No one can visualize me without one! I have a vintage pickup truck and other cars, and when I show up at a car event with one of these vehicles, everybody goes, "Where's your Corvette?" I mean if it's pouring rain and I am at Lowes buying two-by-fours, they still say, "Where's your Corvette?"

I really like the attention the Corvettes draw. The C8 has been phenomenal. After three years in production, I still take it to the gas station, and someone will turn around and come and look at it. After three years in production, they still ask if this is the all-new Corvette. One day when I first got the car, I took it to a little auto parts store to buy some cleaning supplies. We started talking, and I told them that I had a C8 parked in front of the store. They locked the door, and they all came out to look at the car. They closed the shop!

There are 40,000+ C8 Corvettes in the States right now, but you don't see these cars that much. Many people only drive them on the weekends or to special events. You don't see that many Corvettes at all. Sometimes we spend all day driving, almost to Lake Tahoe and back, spending some time with the Corvette club, and never see another Corvette coming the other way.

I had a 1958 Corvette, and that was the first one that I actually started taking to car shows. It was a really beautiful restored car. It looked like new, and I had basically rebuilt it by hand. You could still go to the Chevrolet garage and buy parts for that car. I bought new bumpers. They ordered them for me, and they came right over the parts counter back then. Back in the day, you saw a lot of C1 and C2 Corvettes at car shows. But now when you go to a Corvette show you see hardly any C1s, maybe a few C2s. The C4, C5, C6, and C7 Corvettes are all over the place right now, and this is why I take my '53 to as many car shows as possible. People have forgotten about the C1, especially the early ones. Don Faircloud bought this car as his second vehicle back in 1963, using it for commuting and picking up groceries. But it was always his pride and joy. I bought the car from him sometime in the 1980s, making me its third owner.

How did you manage to get a C8 with the same VIN as your 1953 Corvette?
I worked very hard to get that particular C8. They were all under wraps, and General Motors was still denying the existence of the mid-engine Corvette. I started at the Corvette museum, trying to find out how I, as a longtime Corvette enthusiast and owner, could get a car with a VIN matching the one of my 1953 Corvette, the car that started it all. Without the '53, the rest of the Corvettes wouldn't be here. The museum didn't know. They sent me to the GM Heritage Center. A very nice woman there told me, "Well, I'm not sure if I can help, but let me check to see what I can do." She came back and said, "I can't help you, but try Harlan Charles at GM and see what he can do for you."

So I told Harlan Charles my story, that I had a 1953 Corvette with the VIN 285 and would love to have a 2020 C8 mid-engine Corvette with the same serial number. And he didn't hesitate! He told me that he would check to see what he could do, and in his subsequent email, he told me that I was on the list for the Corvette. I placed the order with Able Chevrolet in Rio Vista. And then it arrived, and it was a pre-pandemic car. It was built the first week of production and came by rail to California all the way from Bowling Green. We received the car in March of 2020.

What is your all-time favorite Corvette model?
I'm sorry, but I can't choose just one! Let's put it this way: I've owned more than my share of Corvettes. If you put all of them in a bucket, the C8 would be the one that rises to the top. It could be because I've never owned a Corvette with this degree of sophistication. The next-newest Corvette I own is a 1974. I think the C8 is the epitome of Corvettes. There's nothing like it. The '53 is a just '53, a simple car. Driving it is like riding on a buckboard, but it's a driving legend and the foundation of my passion for the Corvette.

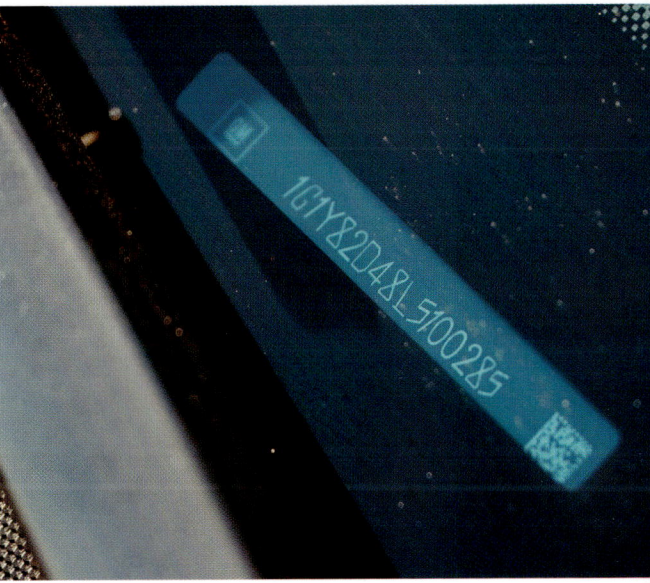

◀ **1953** Corvette C1, **2020** Corvette C8, **Bethel Island**, California, **USA** | November 13, 2021

TO LARRY, CORVETTE MEANS:
MY DRIVING STYLE

Continuous runner. Sixty-seven years separate these two taillights. There was no break between the first one from 1953 until 2020. Production of the Corvette was never interrupted. That's a record that is unmatched, even by that German classic, the Porsche 911.

PROVOCATION AND COLOR

Color choice was a decisive criterion for Frank Otero Molanes when it came to purchasing a C8, the perfect American sports car.

What's your Corvette story?
Fundamentally, I have never borne any grudge against American cars, quite the opposite. I was a big fan of them, particularly in the muscle car field, therefore cars from the late 1960s. At some point, I fulfilled the dream with my '69 Mustang Fastback. I was simply always more of a ball-cap-and-sneakers type than one who wore patent-leather shoes and a floppy hat. For a time, I toyed with the idea of purchasing a Bentley Continental Coupé, one in British Racing Green, but then I asked myself if it really suited me. Actually it didn't; I'm not that royal. I was influenced by Colt Seavers. That's why I thought it was a good thing when at some point my father got a hankering for a Corvette. He actually wanted to buy a C4, then it quickly became a C5. And then the C6 wasn't that far away. It must have been 2010.

It was finally a black C6. The car was registered in my name for the time being, but he usually drove it. It was our fun car. That's how the Corvette theme began for me. At the beginning of 2022, the C8 attracted my attention, and I looked into it more closely. The C8 had been promised in Germany for quite a while, but some time passed before the dealers received the first of these cars. I had studied the details online, and different intrinsic values were assigned to different materials and the LT (Luxury Touring) equipment. It was even possible to obtain belts in various colors, and every imaginable combination could be made. To me, the most beautiful moment in buying a new automobile is configuring it, when one decides how to equip the vehicle to suit one's own tastes. But I hadn't gotten that far yet.

I had always been a fan of light interiors; therefore it was obvious that I would want the interior in Natural Dipped. Light instrument panel, everything in light colors, something not available in most brands of automobile. At some point, I had to see a car like that in the flesh. Up to that point, it was really just the fun of configuring. One Sunday, with nothing scheduled except for lunch with the family, I drove with my father and father-in-law to a dealer here in Hamburg, without telling either of them what I wanted to look at. I went there more on the off chance, but then when we entered the small showroom we saw a red C8. My father and father-in-law stood in front of the car and just wondered what it was. It never occurred to them at first that I was interested in it, because there were all kinds of cars in the shop. I told them that it was a new Corvette. You could see the mid-engine through the glass cover, completely surprising the two of them. Everyone was totally thrilled with the vehicle, with the overall package. And it looked just great in red.

When we were on our way back, I said to my father, "You know what, this will probably be the last naturally aspirated V8 mid-engined sports car ever, so don't we want to buy one? I'll take care of everything, and you'll have to throw the C6 into the deal!" He immediately agreed. Then I considered it for another three to four weeks, thought about exactly what I wanted, and spent a lot of time in forums. There, Natural Dipped is also called "Old Man's Complexion." I didn't care; I liked it anyway.

When everything was decided, I told the salesman that I would like to order. Then I had to go to the dealership. I went there with my wife and daughter on a Saturday and ordered the C8. At that time, they said that I would have to wait a year for delivery. I had ordered quite a few options, plus the best interior, with as much leather and Alcantara as possible. I also wanted a metallic paint finish in Elkhart Lake Blue, an optional rim design, and plenty of carbon fiber interior trim. I left out two options: the front lift and the Magnetic Ride suspension. I deliberately wanted a conventional coil-over suspension.

It took awhile after I placed the order, and the feedback wasn't what one is used to when one comes from the automotive industry and knows what's involved in placing an order. For example, I never got an order confirmation. The car was supposed to arrive in April 2023, but then in September 2022, I suddenly received a call: the car is here.

Indeed, well the C6 hadn't been sold yet. I had also converted my house to a heat pump that year, to ease my conscience, so to speak. On the one hand, you buy a V8, and on the other, you convert your house from heating oil to a heat pump. The fact that the C8 came so early didn't suit me at all at that moment, but somehow I managed to get it together. The day after collecting the car, I wanted to go to an event in Bremen with my father and picked him up in the Corvette in Soltau. Of course, he hadn't expected to see the car yet, so he was surprised and thrilled. The next day, I parked the Corvette at his place in Soltau and didn't see it again for a while. In keeping with our podcast "*zwoaus11*" (two from 11), the C9 was given a seasonal number plate from February to November. It wasn't until March 2023 that the Corvette came to me in Hamburg.

I now have a few ideas about conversions. By way of Steven's C8 forum, I met a few cool people with whom I'm in regular contact, and we play *Grand Tourismo* together online. That means they are all people who have a C8, and of course, we also drive a similar Corvette in the video game. The cool thing about it is that you can assemble the car in the game the way you want it. I took a blue that goes in the direction of my paint job and put the gold BBS rims on it. It's basically similar to a configurator. The C8 community is really exciting, and almost everyone invests in their car again when they have it in the garage. Tires, rims, exhaust system, minor modifications. I'm super happy with the car; it's exactly what I wanted, a dream. Now the C8 has about 870 miles (1,400 km) on the clock, and I turned it up a bit for the first time yesterday, just to hear what was happening. It's quite an atypical sound, atypical when started cold and also at the higher revs; sounds really angry and not so typically deep like a V8. The car satisfies a lot of senses, and you often get a thumbs up for it; I was rather worried that many people would prefer confrontation.

For me, unfortunately, it's a very perfect American sports car, and I say "unfortunately" because nobody here in Germany really wants to hear that. I always thought the Mercedes SL was cool and had already ordered one, but then I canceled it. There were great engines, beautiful interiors, and beautiful colors, and it's my brand anyway. But these real emotions, especially now with the topic of downsizing, I can only muster up if I take the '63 AMG with V8, which is now easily €230,000 or €240,000. You can't even get a naked SL for €100,000. I had put together one for €150,000 with a four-cylinder turbo engine, which is simply not what I expect from such a vehicle. With a car I don't need, it's all about emotion. That is what the Corvette provides.

I met a dentist through the forum who also has a Porsche, a new 718 Spyder. He was at a sports car event last year that Walter Röhrl also attended. Almost all of the participants drove Porsches, but one has a C8. Walter Röhrl drove the C8, then got out and said, "That's the first time the Americans have built a really cool car." That is like an accolade for the Corvette. The dentist then ordered a C8 to go with his Porsche.

◀ 2022 Corvette C8, **Hamburg**, Germany | March 19, 2023

What is the biggest difference for you compared to the C6?
The biggest difference is definitely the sound; it's not what you expect from an American V8, and you have more of a real sports car feel. It's completely different to have the engine behind you. You sit relatively far forward. All the things that go with a mid-engine sports car, you suddenly like. The C8 is also extremely agile, but at the same time very suitable for everyday use with its two luggage compartments.

There are only two opinions about the car, as you can hear again and again in my podcast. But I'm also sure that if Jens [Seltrecht] sees the C8 more often, he'll find it cool at some point. Of course, many people say that this is a car that no one was waiting for. For me, it's the best Corvette ever built. Up until the seventh generation, the developments of the Corvette were always an evolution. The evolution ended with the C7. That was the maximum development stage as far as the front-engine transaxle concept was concerned. With the 755 hp ZR1, there was simply no more.

It's surprising how much better the values of a standard production Corvette suddenly are when you look at the time from 0 to 60, for example. That wasn't possible even 15 years ago with a good 150 hp more power. That's really something.

The quality of workmanship in the interior is also surprisingly good. It's a standard that doesn't have to hide at all. I am very fond of detail because I know from the automotive industry what can be done and how, or what can be done wrong. There is a lot of attention to detail here. The crucial thing here is that I have the feeling that the Americans wanted to say with this car, "Watch out, we're going to show what we can do when we're serious."

What is your absolute favorite Corvette model?
Anyone who knows me knows that I can't commit to one model. I would definitely keep the C8. It's incredibly competitive and somehow fits into my life, where no two cars are the same. I didn't have to buy a car, I don't need the car. It was just this provocation of being different, its unique design and this great color scheme. If it hadn't been for this interior, I might not have become the owner of a C8.

What I would also buy is a late-Sixties C3 with the big block and then either in gold or orange. I could philosophize for hours about the design of the C3, about bumpers that look very integrated, for example. I just find this car totally iconic and still completely underrated.

Birthday present: To mark the 70th anniversary, all C8s from the 2023 model year—including Frank's Corvette, even though it was produced in 2022—are treated to special inserts and lettering.

TO FRANK, CORVETTE MEANS:
AMERICAN WAY OF LIFE

Stingray: The sonorous model designation was only reintroduced with the C7 and has been the name of the entry-level model ever since. But that's also where the similarities between the C8 and its predecessor end. The design of the new mid-engine Corvette is more reminiscent than ever of a fighter jet.

HIS SMILE AND THE CAR

Tammi and Donta Hampton fell in love with the Corvette, and because of the Corvette they fell in love with each other. A true Corvette love story.

What's your Corvette story?
Tammi: The reason I bought my black Corvette is because my husband had one. I was always fascinated by Corvettes after meeting him, especially his yellow 1976 C3. And when he purchased the 2007 C6, I was even more fascinated because it was modern and faster.

So I got one for myself. I bought my all-black C6 because that is my favorite color. And when we went looking for that specific car, I wouldn't accept anything less. I didn't want a black car with red leather seats or a two-tone interior. I wanted an all-black vehicle. So, we found the car that I wanted.

Donta: My first encounter with a Corvette was because of my grandfather, who owned one. He already had it when I was born. So I grew up around the Corvette. When I finished the sixth grade, he let me take his C3 Corvette for a little spin. When I was nine or ten years old, I asked my grandfather if I could have the Corvette when I graduated from high school. I asked him that when I was a little kid, and he said yes.

And so time went by, and finally I was a senior in high school. I was close to graduation, and I never forgot what I had asked him. I held on to that; that was my motivation for graduating. So I approached him and said, "Hey, you remember what you told me when I was a kid? I asked you for the Corvette and you said yes?" He said, "Yeah, I kind of remember that conversation."

Maybe a week before I graduated, he came up to me and asked, "Hey, what do you have in your pocket? How much money?" I said, "I don't know, five dollars?" He had never asked me for money in my entire life, but now he was asking me to give him five dollars. I gave him the money, then he handed over the title and the keys to the Corvette and said, "Don't ever tell anybody that I gave you anything; tell them you bought it." That's how I got my 1976 Corvette C3. Of course, I still have that car, and my grandfather is also in my Corvette club.

That's how my Corvette story began. And of course, later down the line we started the TrendSettas Corvette Club, and we began traveling in the car. So that car is from 1976 and gets nine miles to the gallon. It is not made for the highway at all. I can't pass a gas station with this car. At some point, it was time to get a newer car, something more modern, something with better gas mileage, something that doesn't have to have all its fluids checked every time you go for a ride. So, I got myself a 2007 C6, and I have had that car for ten years now. And I love it. It's my second baby; my first baby is my '76. Because of the story, I will never sell that car. I will keep that car till the day I die.

Tammi: I actually met Donta at a Corvette event, at a party his Corvette club was hosting. A girlfriend of mine invited me to the party, and I was really apprehensive about going. But she wanted me to come with her that night. So I decided to go, and I met Donta.

A nice song came on, and he asked me to dance. We were on the dance floor slow dancing, and we really enjoyed ourselves. Then it started raining. And there are T-tops on his 1976 Corvette, and he had left them at a friend's house. So in the middle of the dance he told me that he was so sorry, but he had to leave right away to get the T-tops for the Corvette. But before he left, he asked me for my cell phone number.

When the party was over, I left and stopped at McDonald's. I was in the McDonalds drive-through, and Donta called and apologized for the emergency with his Corvette and having to leave. He asked me where I was, so I texted him my location. The next thing I heard was that rumbling sound and this beautiful, yellow, pristine '76 Corvette came around the corner. He was on the phone, sitting behind the wheel and just looking at me. He came over and we talked until the sun came out. I knew when I drove away that I wanted to see him again. Because of his smile. And the car. And we have been together ever since.

So, you travel a lot with your cars. Do you travel with all your cars, or do you choose one every time you go on a trip?
Donta: She just recently got her car. The last twelve years, we've been riding together in my car. Driving to car shows; we went to different events all across the states. This year she is driving her car. My car just got a new paint job, so I bring it on a trailer now. We've been doing this for fourteen years together in the same car. We have really spent a lot of time together in the Corvette. And now we are talking on the phone while we are driving. So, we are still together in the cars.

What is your all-time favorite Corvette model?
Tammi: My original love once I got into the Corvette world was the C4. And I wanted an all-white C4 convertible. Since we started traveling in his C6 and I had the opportunity to drive it myself: the C6 hands down. I really love that car.
Donta: The C3. It is my first love. Even today, if I pull the car out of the garage, everybody just gives me the thumbs up. That C3 is my baby, and it always will be.

◀ **2007** Corvette C6, **Detroit**, Michigan, **USA** | September 12, 2022

TO TAMMI, CORVETTE MEANS:
POWERFUL, SEXY, SELF-CONFIDENT

TO DONTA, CORVETTE MEANS:
SIMPLY EVERYTHING

Batman in Detroit. The gray urban canyons of the metropolis form the perfect background for Tammi and Donna's black Corvette and contribute to the cool Gotham City look.

I ACTUALLY NEVER WANTED A C2

The Corvette C4 awakened Peter Guntermann's interest. Years later, there was C6 in his garage, and from then on, several Corvettes of different generations have crossed his path.
What is your Corvette story?

It began around 1990, when a friend of my father's had a Corvette C4. We were visiting him at the time, and he had let me drive the car, told me more about the Corvette and the details. I was a little hooked. During my bank training, I spent three months in the USA in New York, between 1991 and 1992. There I read various car magazines and test drove about ten C4s in total. And what came of it? I didn't buy any of them.

After the three months, I was back in Germany, and the topic dropped out of focus a little. Until 2007. Then a work colleague, who knew that I was interested in Corvettes, sent me a picture of the new C6. I saw the car and was immediately hooked. At that time, GM held so-called "Driving Days." I went to such an event several times before I bought my first Corvette in Berlin. A C6 coupe.

Two years later, I realized that a coupe really wasn't the right thing for me. Instead, I wanted a convertible. Well, then fate stepped in. After a customer appointment, I got into my Corvette, drove off, and accelerated a bit too hard on a wet road. It was a total loss. The insurance company settled the claim very quickly, and I subsequently bought a C6 convertible. I sold it in 2016. She was extremely stable in value, but I had lost a bit of interest in her. On top of that, I had only driven 20,500 miles (33,000 km) in her in the seven years. From today's perspective, that's a lot.

In autumn 2014, I had gone looking for another Corvette in the USA. I had a blue 1972 C3, a 454 convertible, appraised by Greg Picconi, the NCRS Master Judge for 1953–54, locally in the States on Long Island. Joe, the seller, had bought it from the original owner and restored it frame-on within a year. Not a Top Flight car, but a super nice Corvette that I still own. In 2017, I joined the NCRS, the National Corvette Restorers Society. In Germany, by the way, the car was awarded the Second Flight, the second-highest condition rating, in 2018. I just remembered that I almost forgot to mention one car. Before the C3, I had imported a C3 convertible, a 1971 LT-1, from the States in spring 2014. But that wasn't my car—figuratively speaking. Major and minor problems kept cropping up, and so I sold it a year later. Sometimes, it just doesn't fit.

My passion for the C2 began a few years ago on the way to a Corvette meeting in the Sauerland. I followed a Corvette C2 for hours. I had never really wanted one, but after looking at the beautiful rear end of that Corvette for so long, it was over. I had to have one of those!

My first C2 was also in the USA in Florida. Once again, I found a professional who could inspect the car for me on-site. The good man's name was Pete, and he had restored several Corvettes himself, all of which had won Duntov Awards. Pete said I could buy the car without hesitation. By the way, it turned out that Pete and Joe knew each other and had even worked together on a restoration. Such a small world sometimes. After the car arrived in Germany and I drove it for a year, I realized that it wasn't the right car for me. So I went looking in the USA once again.

I found another C2 near Las Vegas via Craigslist. Pete helped me a bit and gave advice. The Corvette had probably been completely restored in Los Angeles in 2011. At the first NCRS Judging, where the car was evaluated in 2012, it got a Top Flight Award. In 2017, the Corvette was bought by the owner before me. He improved the car to get it even closer to original condition. As a result, in 2017 the Corvette received another Top Flight Award with even more points.

Of course, I again went looking for someone who could examine the car for me on the spot. By chance, I came across a chap in Los Angeles who had already evaluated this C2 at the judging in autumn 2017 and awarded it the Top Flight. He just said, "Ah, the car with the over-restored paintwork." I thought to myself, "Over-restored paintwork? Great!" As the judging had only been four months ago, I bought the Corvette blind without any further appraisal. When the car arrived in Germany in spring 2018, I was able to see for myself that everything was as described and promised by the seller. It really was in super condition.

In 2019, my desire for a C6 convertible came up again. I was able to buy a 2013 427 convertible with just 6,300 kilometers on the clock from a Canadian in February 2020, sight unseen, and import it. It is one of 2,552 Collector Editions. Thank God without stripes, but in white, just like I wanted it.

So all of a sudden, I had five Corvettes. But I simply didn't have the time or the nerve to look after five cars. [*Author's note*: There was still a '72 Duntov and an '82 Corvette.] In the end, I decided to sell the Corvette with the automatic transmission and keep my 1967 C2, the '72 C3, and the 2013 C6. A C4 ZR-1 would still be on my wish list, but that would be the end of it; after all, it all started with just one C4 in 1990. Four Corvettes should be enough.

Which is your absolute favorite Corvette model?
If it's just a matter of shape, then the early C3.

◀ **1967** Corvette C2, **Cologne**, North Rhine–Westphalia, **Germany** | September 11, 2021

TO PETER, CORVETTE MEANS:
GREAT LINES, PASSION, EMOTION

Well-toned. The entire body of the C2 looks as if it consists exclusively of well-defined muscles. This is particularly evident in the area behind the B pillar and under the rear window. No car in the '60s had brawnier shoulders.

IT'S ALL ABOUT DRAWING MY ATTENTION

To Brian, who doesn't want his last name to be published, the Corvette is a car to be shared. Taking the C1 out on the road, going to the hardware store, making people smile.

What's your Corvette story?
Corvettes are just iconic cars. I fell in love with the vehicle the first time I saw one. It´s a car that looks like it's going fast standing still; it´s a car that's iconic and has a classic look to it; and it's a head turner. It doesn't need to do anything to draw attention.

I'm not saying that I got it to draw attention. It only needs to draw MY attention. I think for most of us when we like something, whether it's an excellent meal or a nice bottle of wine, it only needs to draw our attention. And I think that's what it was for me.

And it's funny, when I met my wife, we were on our first date, and we were talking about cars at one point, and she had no idea that I owned this car. She told me that the Corvette C1 was her favorite type of car. And I was like, "Done!" That was it! She made me change my will to make sure I left the car to her. So I check under the hood every time I start it to make sure nothing is wired to the starter. Kidding!

My first Corvette was a 1961, which I purchased in 1998 or 1999. It was all I could afford at the time. They say when you buy a Corvette, get the best one you can afford. I bought it from Pro Team Corvette in Napoleon, Ohio. I heard good and bad things about Pro Team, but they treated me fairly, and the salesman's name was also Brian. I didn't pay all that much for it, about $22,000 US. It was a 1961 with a 283 engine. I had some issues with the car, but it was a driver. It was fine for my purposes, and I enjoyed it and had fun with it. It had a Power Glide automatic transmission, nicknamed the "power-slide" because sometimes it would slip out of gear when it was in neutral or in park.

I kept that car for a while and sold it after about four years. I didn't have a Corvette or any kind of classic car for the longest time. I had gotten divorced, and you don't have a lot of money after getting divorced. So in 2012, I decided to start looking for another Corvette.

I ended up working with a guy named Gregg Wyatt out of Atlanta. He had this beautiful 1960. He sent me a number of photos of it, and I had someone go out and inspect it for me. The guy could find absolutely nothing wrong with it. I just fell in love with the car, and I bought it and I've had it ever since. I haven't had any major issues with it, other than the heater core exploding on me. I do the regular maintenance on it myself. I have no talent for any kind of bodywork, but I can do all of the mechanical work myself. I enjoy doing it when I have the time.

It´s not a car that I stare at and rub with a diaper, or a "Trailer Queen." If I park the car somewhere and someone says, "I love your car," I usually tell them to get in it and take a picture. I never yell at people to get away from my car. I don't put "Don't touch" signs on the car at car shows. My philosophy is, don't put your car out there like that if you don't want people to look at it and touch it. Put it under glass and keep it at home. If you want people to appreciate your car, just put a picture of your car out there. I know some people may get angry reading that, but put it in a museum if you don't want people to touch it. I believe people should enjoy it. That's just my two cents. Especially kids, for you are teaching them from a very young age respect and appreciation for these kinds of things. When they see one when they are older, they remember when this guy let them sit in his car and took a picture of them with their dad and the car.

My car is a driver. I take it to the home improvement store, and I might put a piece of lumber in it. I don't abuse it at all, but I use it. I enjoy it. It's not my everyday car, but if it´s the weekend and I am going to run to the hardware store, I'll take the Corvette. Now I'm not going to park it right next to another car. I'll park it a little further away so it doesn't get dinged. Something that drives me crazy is that I will park further away, and then I'll walk out and find someone has parked right next to me at the end of the parking lot. I mean, why did you do that? You've got a hundred other free parking spaces.

I don't think the next generation of drivers sees enough of these kinds of cars to appreciate them. So that's another reason why I get it out there, so they can see it. The question I am most often asked by people is what year it is. Actually they don't ask me; they usually try and guess what year it is.

What is your all-time favorite Corvette model?
The C1 all day long. The 1959 and the 1960 are really my favorite ones.

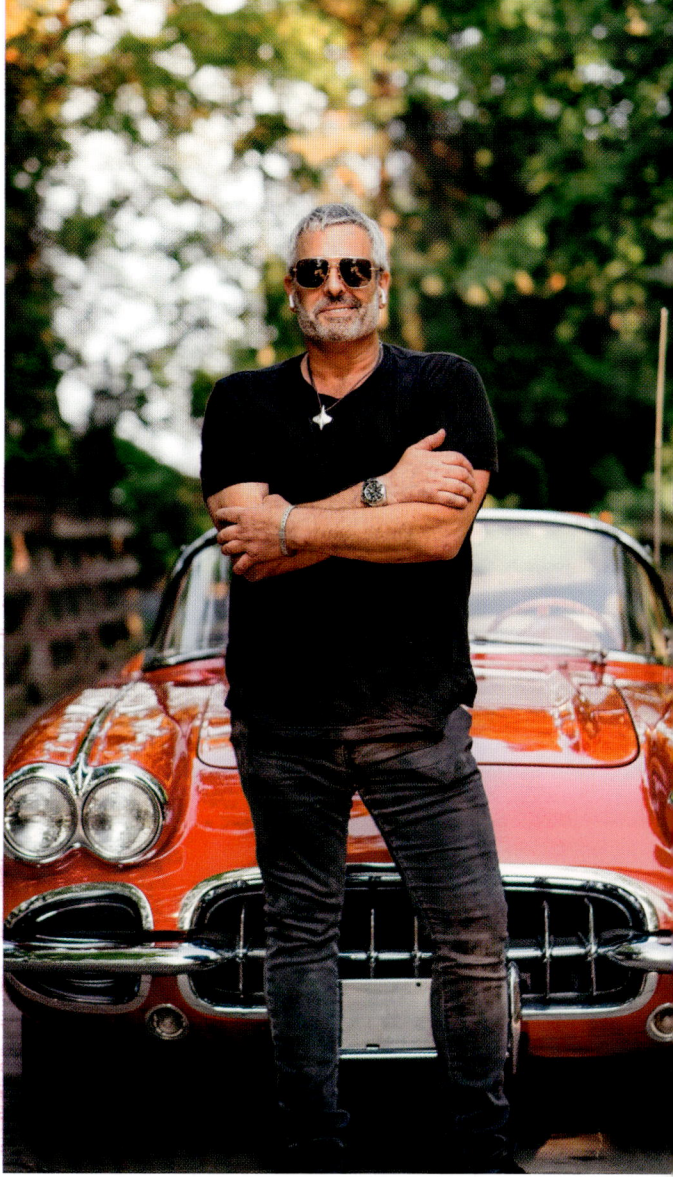

◀ **1960** Corvette C1, **Northbrook**, Illinois, **USA** | September 14, 2022

TO BRIAN, CORVETTE MEANS:
EXCLUSIVE, ICONIC, AMERICAN

Entertainment program. Purchase contracts, invoices, and photos tell a lot about the history of a car. But how many people have sat behind the three-spoke steering wheel and who carved the number into the lid of the ashtray are things the C1 will keep to itself forever.

LEGENDARY DESIGN, UNIMAGINED DRIVING ENJOYMENT

It was rather by chance that Björn Nadler stumbled across the C4 in the trade press. From then on, it was clear to him that he had to own a fourth-generation Corvette.

What is your Corvette story?
I've always fancied the American sports car but never had the desire to own a particular Corvette. Professionally, I am very fond of design, like certain shapes, and simply love all things beautiful. What I particularly like, including when it comes to vehicles, are straight lines. I love cars that simply have an ultra-hard recognition value.

At some point, I read an interview with an automotive expert from the USA about the C4. The man raved about it and said it was one of the most underrated cars. Until then, the C4 had never been on my radar, but the article made me take a closer look at it. From then on, I couldn't get this Corvette model out of my mind. So I started looking for one.

In Germany I looked at several C4s, all of which weren't bad. I wanted a good basis, a car I could drive straightaway. Hardly any car I buy is in the condition I would like it to be in. They are always either optimized or restored by me. Accordingly, I have certain requirements that the cars must meet.

With the C4, I threw everything I had ever thought about a Corvette out the window. I went there to look at the car and knew quite quickly that this was exactly the car I didn't want to buy. Even during the test drive, this attitude didn't change. But I just couldn't say no because I thought the color was so cool. And I couldn't find another one in this color.

I knew when I bought it that it wasn't the C4's original color. What I didn't know was that the color was only available on the ZR1 and only from 1990 or 1991. But I didn't care. To me, it was important that it was an original Corvette color and that the whole car had a stimulating appearance. The rims also play their part in this. They are hard to find in this size; usually you get bigger wheels from later years or they are in poor condition. The overall impression was such that I fell in love with the car. That was the deciding factor for me.

I like cars with patina and cars that are not perfect. Cars in perfectly restored condition are the most boring thing there is for me. I knew what I still had to do on the Corvette. I changed all the fluids and replaced the servo pump. The engine also didn't run one hundred percent smoothly. That's because of the injection nozzles. They needed to be replaced or overhauled. Once that was done, the V8 should have the right pressure again. I would do the rest bit by bit.

After just four months, I already knew that the Corvette was a car I wouldn't sell. It's really rare for me to find a car that I don't become bored with after a while. After twenty years of buying, restoring, and selling cars, I have now found a car about which I can say, "It's exactly mine." It just clicked.

What I didn't take into account when I bought it, however, is how extremely conspicuous a Corvette like this is. That's still something I'm not used to. I really underestimated how people would react to the car when I'm driving it on the road. I have a lot of classic cars, and I'm often on the road with them. Of course, there's the occasional thumbs up. But I've never experienced what happens with the Corvette. Never! No matter where you are, people run out onto the road, brake hard, or drive alongside you and film the car while you're driving.

It's just so much fun to drive the C4. It's different; I've never driven a car like this before. You can sit in the car, drive 250, 300 miles, and get out completely relaxed. You wouldn't guess that from looking at the Corvette.

What is your absolute favorite Corvette model?
It's the C4. Because the C4 really started a design turnaround. I love cars with history, and I love those that have completely shaped a new era.

◀ **1987** Corvette C4, **Neuss**, North Rhine–Westphalia, **Germany** | September 11, 2021

TO BJÖRN, CORVETTE MEANS:
DIFFERENT, CONSPICUOUS, FUN

Underdog. Although the fourth-generation Corvette was built for thirteen years and shaped the children of the '80s, today it is one of the most underappreciated models of the iconic sports car. Yet, its design is simple and elegant, which makes it simply timeless.

THIS IS ONE SMALL STEP FOR MAN

It took Joe Crosby decades to finally own this very special car: Neil Armstrong's Corvette.

What's your Corvette story? How did you get that very special Corvette?
I bought my first Corvette in 1974. I also had a couple of Z28 Camaros and two Chevelles, really bad cars performance-wise. I also had a 1962 Dodge D500. They only made several hundred of them. They were drag cars with aluminum hood, aluminum doors, aluminum trunk, and the 426 wedge engine. The Corvette was the first car I restored. It was followed by another Corvette and then another and another. Each one was reconditioned. Among them were some really awful crates. Abandoned restorations, with boxes full of parts, and no one knew if they all belonged to the car. I bought such cars and restored them to their former glory. Among them was a '64 Corvette coupe that had been sitting in the garage for twenty-two years, more shelf than car. In total, I had 22 old Corvettes. Number 21 was the last one I completely disassembled and rebuilt. Number 22 is astronaut Neil Armstrong's C2.

I saw the '67 Vette in the summer of 1980 on a back county road at a stable where people boarded their horses. Back then, a big block Corvette was worth $1,500. The car belonged to a nice lady named Nancy. She told me that she wanted to sell the Corvette because she would like to buy a minivan to get all her horse stuff into. She wrote her first name and her phone number on a piece of paper. I had two Corvettes at that time, and this was just another old Corvette in Georgia.

At Christmas of 1985, I was visiting my parents in Georgia once again, and I called Nancy. Her husband Dale answered. I told him that I had spoken to his wife about the Corvette four or five years ago and asked him if they still owned the car and if they still wanted to sell it. He told me that he would not sell the car, that he had two little boys, and he would like to do a "father and sons restoration." We went to look at the car anyway. They lived in Alpharetta, which is north of Atlanta. The car was in the basement on jack stands and had boxes piled on it. Dale said the car had been in the basement since September 1981.

He told me that he parked the car four or five years ago, and as I said, the car had become a shelf too. It had boxes on it and was on jacks, and the wheels were sitting in the corner. I said, "Dale, there are two minivans in the driveway. How did you get this big block Vette?" He said, "Well, we had just gotten married and everyone was buying Corvettes, so we were looking for one too."

They got a call from a dealership that had just gotten this car in trade. They drove to see it a few days after Christmas 1967. He almost didn't buy it because it had the big 427 engine. But they made him a good deal. I asked him where he had bought the Corvette. He said, "At Jim Rathmann Chevrolet." I said, "You drove all the way from Atlanta to Florida to buy a car?" He said, "No, I worked for NASA, and I was living in Florida at Merritt Island." He then said the car had belonged to Neil Armstrong. I knew about the astronauts and their Corvettes. He went upstairs and came back down with all this paperwork with Neil Armstrong's name on it. Unbelievable!

What are the chances of seeing this car? He lives 500 miles away from me, the car is in his garage, and nobody knows it's there but him. I asked him what it would take to buy the car. He said that he would not sell it, and he still wanted to restore it with his boys. Every year, when I was up there for Christmas or Thanksgiving, I called him. And every year it was the same "No." One of the times I called him, he told me, "I bought me a jet boat, but the engine is blown. But I have a guy who is gonna come and pull the engine out of the Corvette and put it in the boat." I said, "Dale! Damn! Don't do that! Go to Chevrolet and get a crate engine! Please don't ruin the car." So that was one time the Corvette almost bit the dust.

So every year I got a no. He didn't need the money, and we never even talked about money. Christmas 2011, I was in Georgia again and called him. He told me that he was going to retire in February in 2012 and that he now had all the time in the world to work on the car. I said, "Dale, your sons are grown up and have kids of their own, and the car is still sitting at the same place. You're never going to do anything with that car."

Since the first time we talked, he never called me; he had no reason to call me. Then three months after we talked at Christmas 2011, he called. That was on February 25th, 2012. He asked me if I still wanted to buy his old Corvette because he was never going to do anything with it. I replied, "I've been telling you that for 30 years!" He had bought a new 2012 Corvette, and I was the first person he called about the Armstrong Corvette. We agreed on a price, but I told him if the engine was seized, we would have to renegotiate. He said the motor had been running when he parked it 32 years ago.

The next morning, I took my truck and my trailer and went up to my parents' place. Dale, my brother, and I began preparations to get the car out of the basement at about eight o'clock in the freezing cold. It took us five hours to get all the boxes and the other stuff off the Corvette. You couldn't see the car. You couldn't even walk by. In the end, we got all the stuff off the car and put the wheels back on. I checked to see if the engine would turn by hand, and it did. We tried to move the car, but it wouldn't move! We checked that the car was in neutral, we jacked it up again to check that the wheels were moving, and they were. Back on the ground, the car simply wouldn't move, only the front wheels moved a little bit. The rear end was locked up. I told Dale to get some newspaper. I pulled my truck right up to his house so that the car was behind it. I hooked the car up, and we put the paper under the rear wheels so that they could slide on the newspaper. Halfway out of the garage, we heard a big bang and it started to roll. We finally got the car on the trailer, and I went back home to Florida.

I'd been back a day or two when Dale called me to ask if I made it home okay, and then he said, "Joe, I sold you the car too cheap!" He had set the price, and I didn't complain about it. I asked him why he said that to me. "We left to pick up my new car. The salesman did some paperwork and told us that it is unusual for someone to come in and pay cash for a brand-new Corvette. I told him that we just sold a car this morning." The salesman asked, "What kind of car?" He told him that he sold his '67 Corvette that had belonged to Neil Armstrong. He thought the salesman was going to have a heart attack. The guy at the dealership wanted my name and phone number, but Dale wouldn't give them to him. He wanted to ask me first if that would be okay with me.

The next day, someone from the dealership called me. He told me his name and that he was working for a big Chevrolet dealer, one with dealerships all over the country. The conversation went something like, "We will give you some money and take care of that old piece of crap." I told him he was wasting his time and hung up. The next day, another guy from the dealership called, but it was the same conversation. They talked to me like I had absolutely no clue about the car. At one point I said, "Do you have a pen and paper handy? I want you to write this down. Tell your boss he'll never own this car as long as I have it. Never."

Some people from the Space Museum in Huntsville, Alabama, called me and told me that they would like to buy the car and put it on display in the museum. Two people from the museum came to my house to have a look at it. They took a lot of pictures and examined all the paperwork. I told them on the phone that I would not name a price but that they should make me an offer. I've had quite a few people wanting to buy the car since I've owned it.

I have taken the Corvette to many car shows in many places, and many people have asked questions about it, but nobody ever suggested that I should restore it. They all said they are glad that I kept it the way it is.

◀ **1967** Corvette C2, **Kennedy Space Center**, Florida, **USA** | November 15, 2021

33

I removed the fuel tank and discovered the original tank sticker on it. I cleaned it carefully and took a bunch of pictures of it. When I put the tank back in, I put a piece of acetate over it to protect the sticker. The inside of the gas tank was so clean that I couldn't believe it. I also replaced the two rubber fuel lines in the back of the car, and I bought a rebuild kit for the original fuel pump. I drained all the oil out of the engine, pulled the plugs out, and squirted Marvel Mystery Oil down the holes. I took a pull bar, and over the period of a week, I just keep turning and turning the engine to get oil everywhere. Then I put new filters in and some gas in the tank. I turned the engine for some time without the spark plugs in it to get the oil pressure up. I put it all back together and put some gas down the carburetor, and it fired right up. But instantly, gas began leaking from the carburetor; everywhere there was a gasket, it was leaking. I turned it off and afterwards rebuilt the carburetor too. Now I crank it up once a week and drive it up and down my driveway, just to keep things moving.

When Corvette came out with the mid-engine C8, they asked NASA to let them film a commercial at the rocket garden. GM called me and asked if I could bring my car out to Kennedy Space Center and be a part of this commercial. I got there at 8 o'clock the first day. They had a million dollars' worth of sound and video equipment and a huge tent. That night, they closed the Space Center at 7 o'clock, and they had an invitation-only, high-roller dinner. They had steak, all these fancy drinks, and that kind of stuff. They showed the commercial on a gigantic screen, and I left that night at 11:30.

The second day, all the stuff under that tent was gone, and they opened it up to the public. I was sitting in a chair behind the car because people were asking questions. NASA made a beautiful three by four-foot plaque on a tripod. It told the story about Neil Armstrong and his fast rides. This lady came up to me, and she said, "Are you Joe?" and I said I was. She said, "When I was six years old and my sister was seven, Uncle Dale rode us around in the back of that car, looking out of the window." We talked for at least two hours about the car and her uncle, whom I bought it from. She called me about a month later and said she had family members that would like to see the car again. So they all came to my house, and they got to look at it. They took lots of pictures, and they were all very happy to be with the car.

At another NASA event where I exhibited the Corvette, a person told me that he was friends with one of Neil Armstrong's sons. We talked about the car, and I told him that I had found a little green soldier figure in the car and eyebolts in the back. He called the son, who told him that the little green army figure was definitely his. And he said that his dad had put in the eyebolts so they could tie the car seat for kids down in the back.

A year and a half or two years ago, I got a phone call from a guy who told me that he had been a close friend of Neil Armstrong's. They worked together at NASA, here in Houston and in Huntsville. He was telling me some stories about him and Neil; they did this and that, going out, having a good time. He worked for NASA until he retired. He was probably in his mid-'80s, the same age as Neil Armstrong. We talked on the phone, maybe for thirty minutes, and he asked if he could come by and see the car. I said sure!

The next day, he and his wife paid me a visit, very nice people. I got the Corvette out of the garage, we stood in front of it, and we talked. He was telling me one story after another about Neil and him. You could just tell that he was very genuine about their friendship. There was no question they were buddies. We talked, and he took pictures of the car, I took pictures of them with the car, and I helped him get in and out of the car. And of course, they asked me a hundred questions about the car and what I was going to do with it. I also showed them all the magazines the car had been in over the years. They enjoyed their time at my place. They had been there about an hour and a half, and then they got ready to go.

I put the car back into the garage, and his wife was already sitting in their car. I was walking along with him. About halfway to his car, he stopped and said, "I need a minute." I didn't know exactly what he was talking about. He started to turn around and walked back to the garage, and I followed him. He looked at me and said, "I need a minute." I heard in his voice that he needed some time to himself. I stopped walking with him, and he went to the back of the Corvette. He put both of his knees against the right rear bumper. I could see that he was talking. I stood several feet away so I couldn't hear what he was saying. He talked for about fifteen seconds, and he took two fingers of his left hand; he put a kiss on them and put his fingers on the lid of the gas tank and spoke a few more words. He was talking to the car and his old friend. This was a very special and emotional moment. I like the kind of emotions the car arouses in people. It's more than a car and more than a piece of history.

What is your all-time favorite Corvette model?
Let's just say this '67 Corvette was just a regular 1967 car. I would choose my first, a 1971 454 Corvette.

Many thanks to NASA for the unique opportunity to photograph this special Corvette on the runway used by the Space Shuttle.

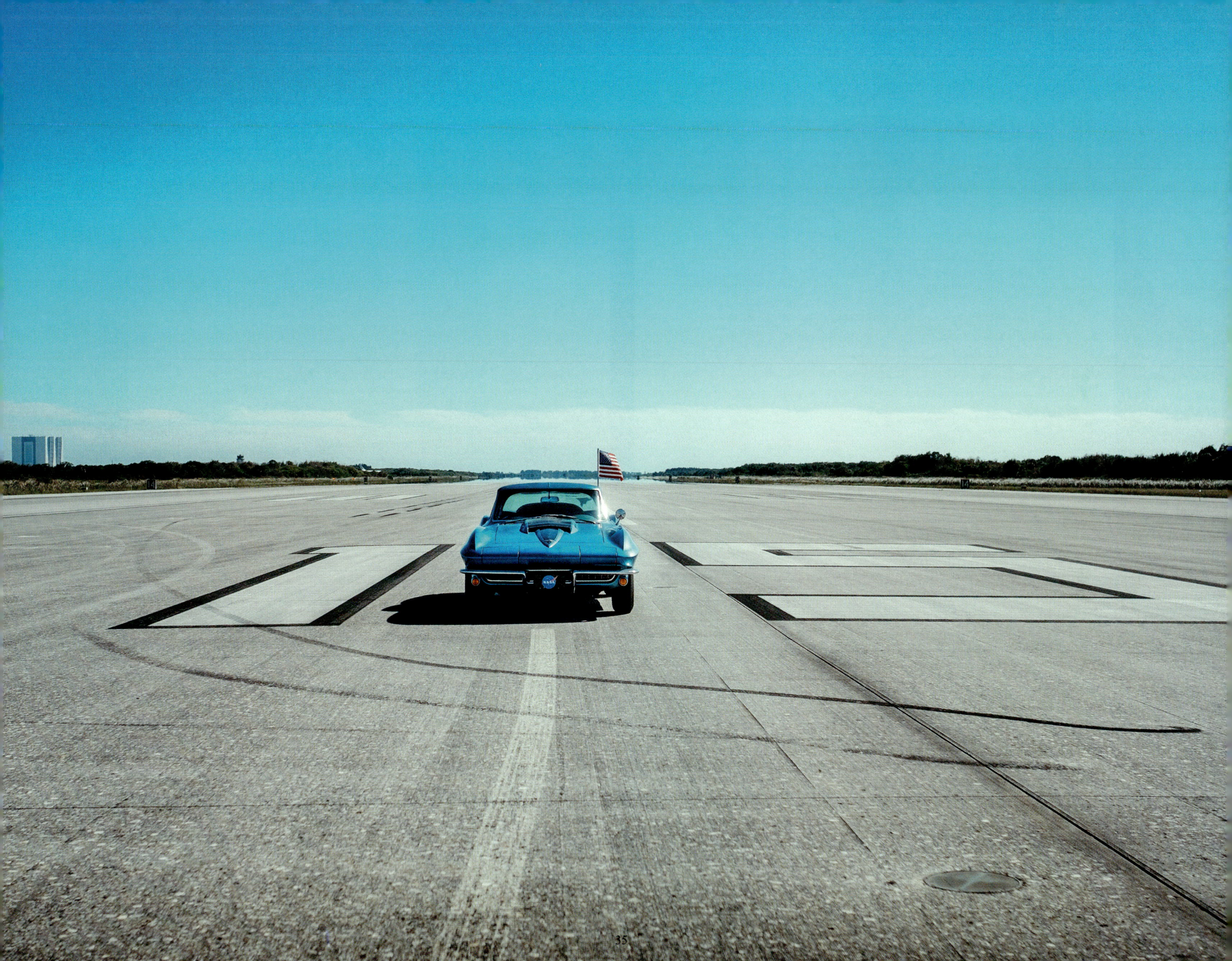

TO JOE, CORVETTE MEANS:
A PIECE OF HISTORY

Ground floor. While Neil Armstrong went to space in a Saturn V rocket, on Earth he contented himself with a '67 Big Block Corvette. The first man on the moon had his coupe for barely a year before he traded it for a newer Corvette model.

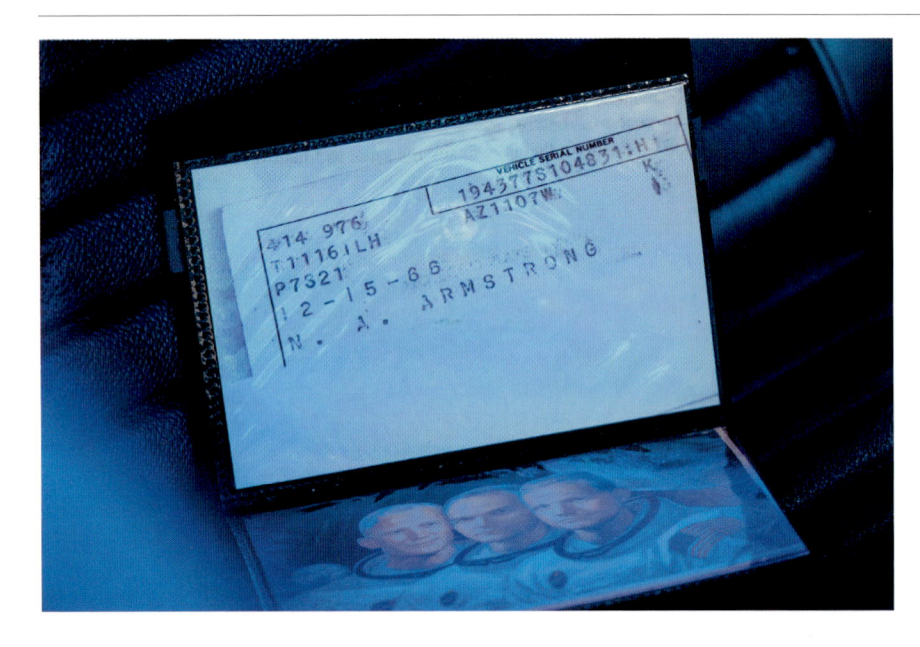

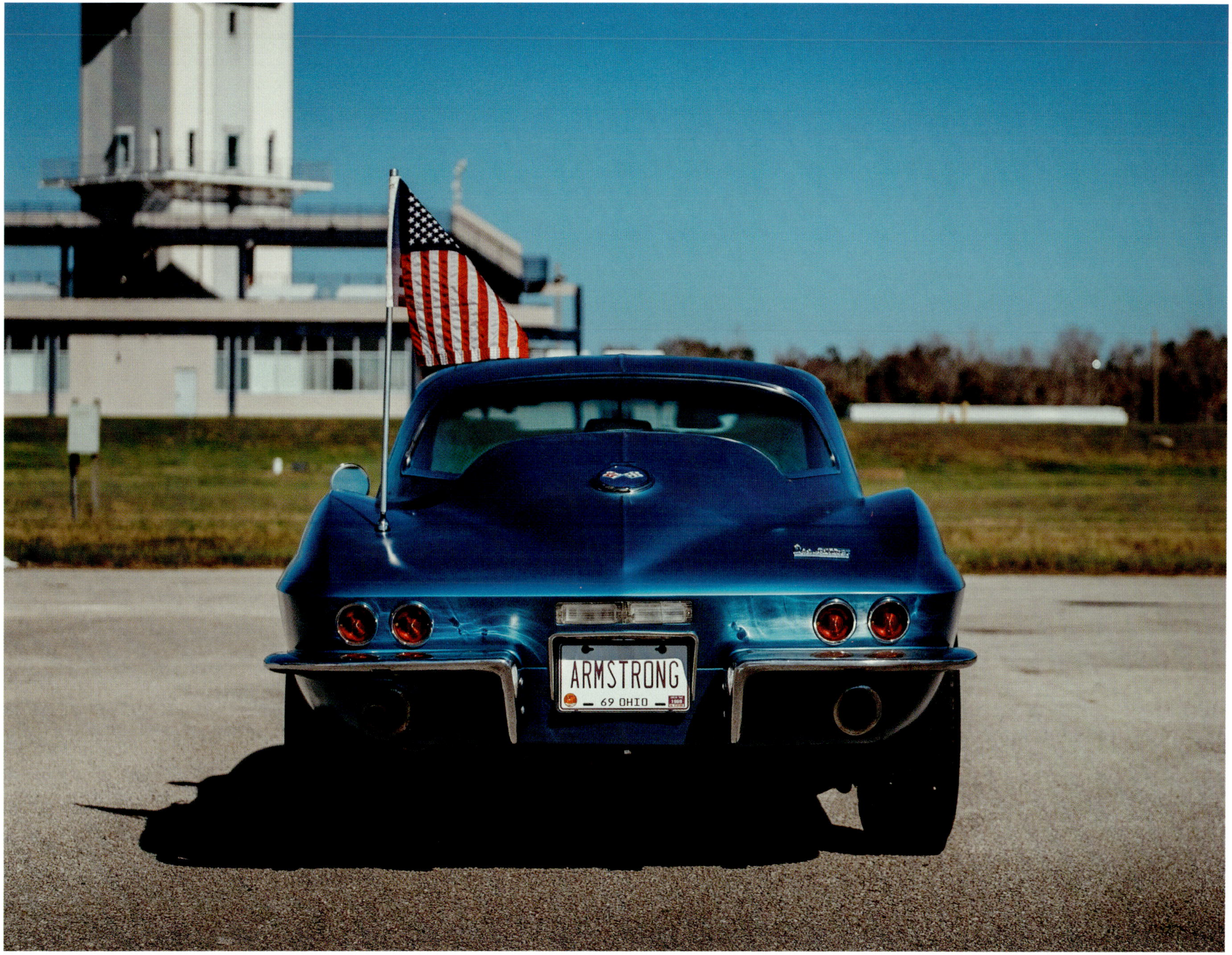
ARMSTRONG
69 OHIO

Untouched. Neil Armstrong's '67 Corvette is completely original, and only absolutely necessary repairs are carried out. Patina was never more important—and valuable.

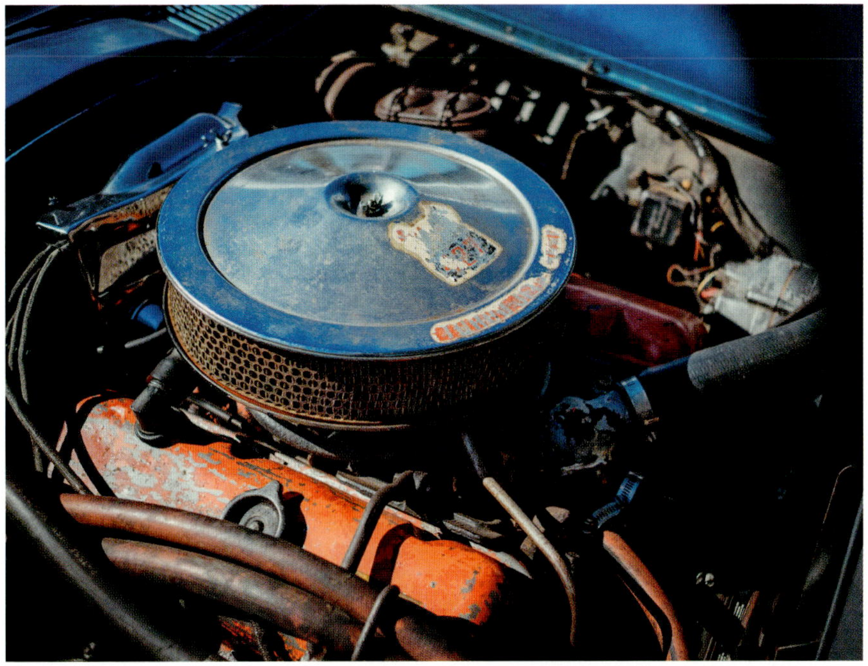

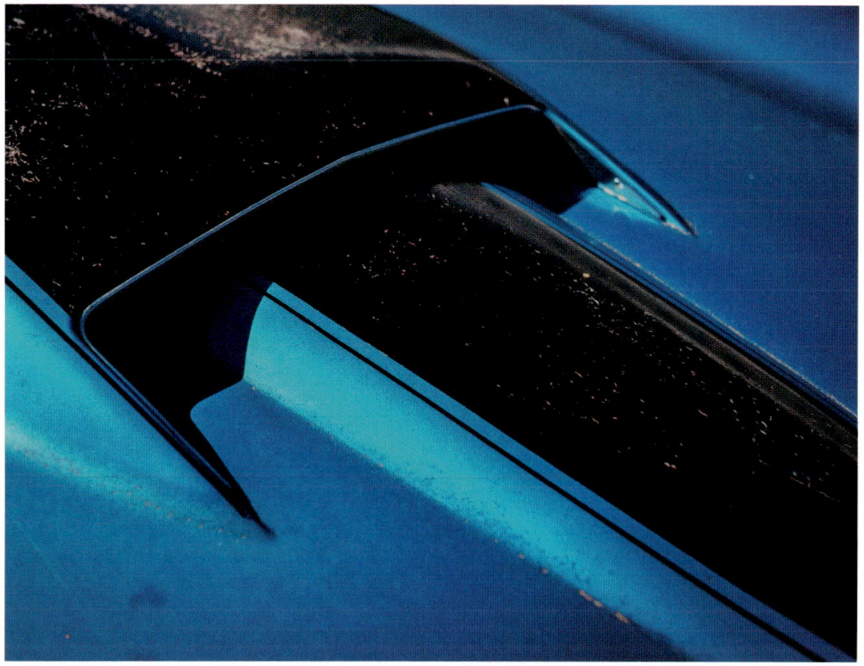

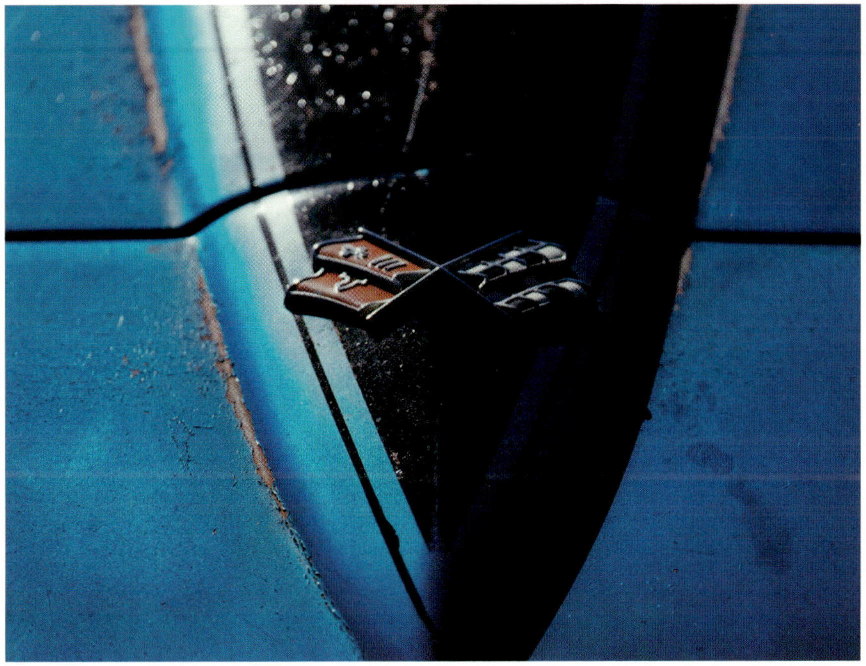

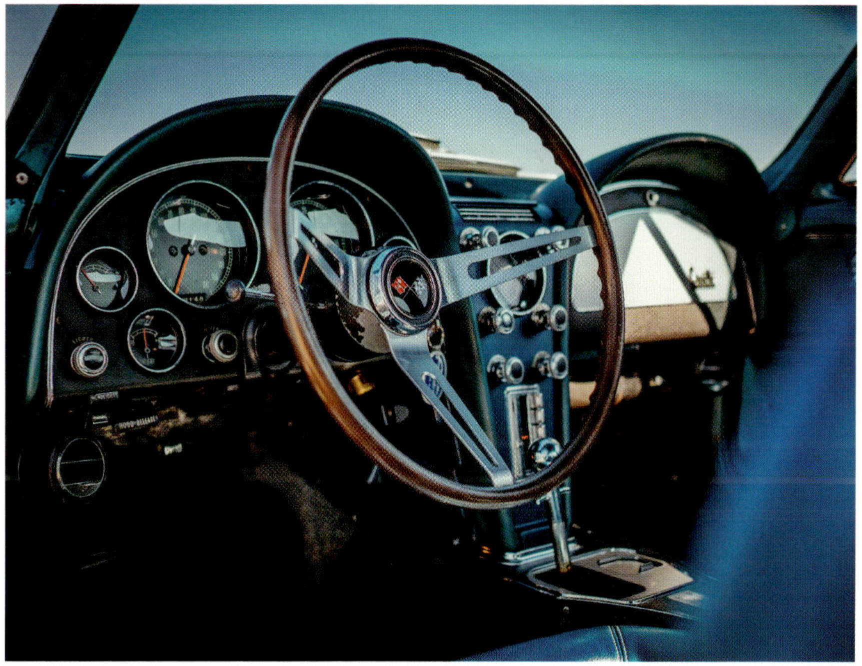

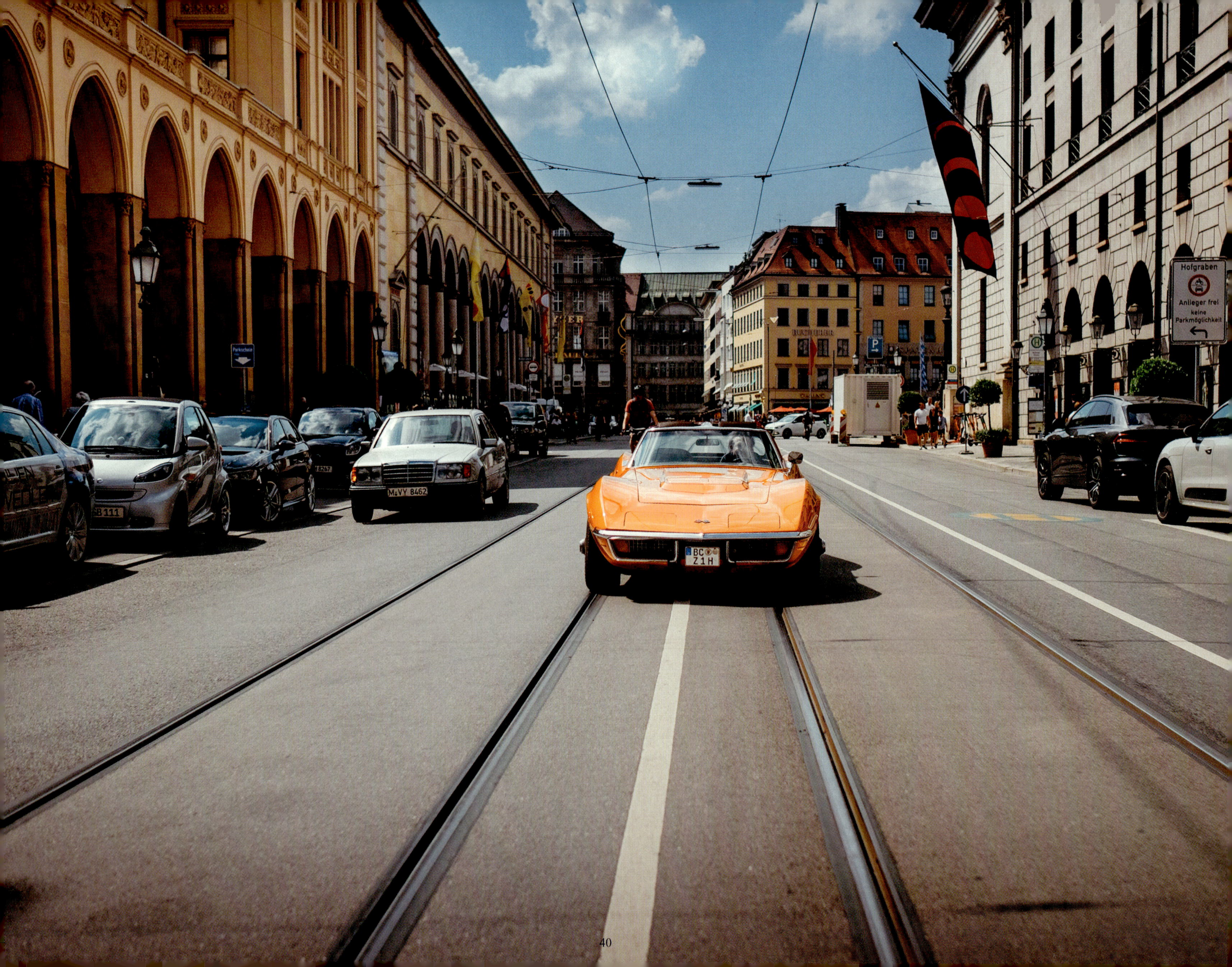
Hofgraben
Anlieger frei
keine
Parkmöglichkeit
M-VY 8462

THIS C3 IS A WORK RT

Rupert Roth lived out a childhood dream and drove a C3 in his favorite color through Munich. His Corvette has also made it into the world of art as an x-ray image.

What is your Corvette story?
As a child, Auto Quartets was one of my favorite games. The Corvette C3 was always one of my favorites. At the time, of course, it was an unattainable dream for me. Today, I think that you should dream as big as you can. So should I have dreamed of a Lamborghini Miura? Actually, yes, but I'm glad I didn't. Of course, the increase in value would have been immense, but the driving pleasure much less so.

My first car was an Opel Manta A. It had a bit of Corvette in it. At the time, the Opel GT, the "German Corvette," was beyond the means of a new driver.

Years later, an acquaintance came by my place with an '86 Corvette C4. The car smiled at me as it sat in front of my flat. I would have loved to drive the V8. The opportunity came shortly afterwards when the owner was out of the country for a few days. He gave me permission to drive his C4 to Italy for the weekend. That was the last straw for me. So I started looking for my own Corvette.

Together with my brother, a mechanic and very car-savvy, I went on the hunt. Without him, I would have become weak at the sight of the first C3. The engine, the smell, the whole package simply fascinated me. My brother was sensible enough to advise me against the car at the time. We looked at around fifteen Corvettes in Germany Austria, Switzerland, and France.

Finally, we found a Corvette in Switzerland, which we then refurbished a little. However, we subsequently sold it. It was a small interim deal, so to speak, so that I could at least drive a C3 for a while.

We discovered my current Corvette in the Netherlands in 2017. Only after buying it did I realize that it was not a normal small block Corvette, but an LT-1. I bought the car with yellow paintwork. After an accident, in which the other party "shredded" the entire side of the car, I had the Corvette painted in Ontario Orange. Today, I am super happy with this color and especially with the Corvette.

You had your Corvette transformed into a work of art by Nick Veasey. How did the collaboration come about?
In 2015, Nick was looking for vehicles via the *Classic Car Magazine* newsletter to expand his collection of classic car x-rays. I volunteered spontaneously and was there in person when my Corvette was x-rayed in Erlangen. I will never forget that day with Nick. As a gesture of thanks, he sent me a life-size x-ray of my C3. In the summer of 2017, I received an invitation to attend the Corvette Summer Festival and the Motorworld Warm-up in Munich. I immediately got the idea of organizing a small exhibition in the coal bunker in Munich. That's how the cooperation with Nick began. Today a passion project has developed under rupert-roth.de; I am, so to speak, the gallery owner for Nick Veasey in the DACH region and bring car collectors together with the artist. In this way, several x-rays have already made it into fascinating car collections.

What is your absolute favorite Corvette model?
It's still the C3 Corvette, but I also think all the other generations are very cool. Similar to the 911 Porsche, you can recognize all the generations. You can recognize the relationship or the origin of the Corvette. It's a design icon.

◀ **1972** Corvette C3, **Munich**, Bavaria, **Germany** | July 23, 2021

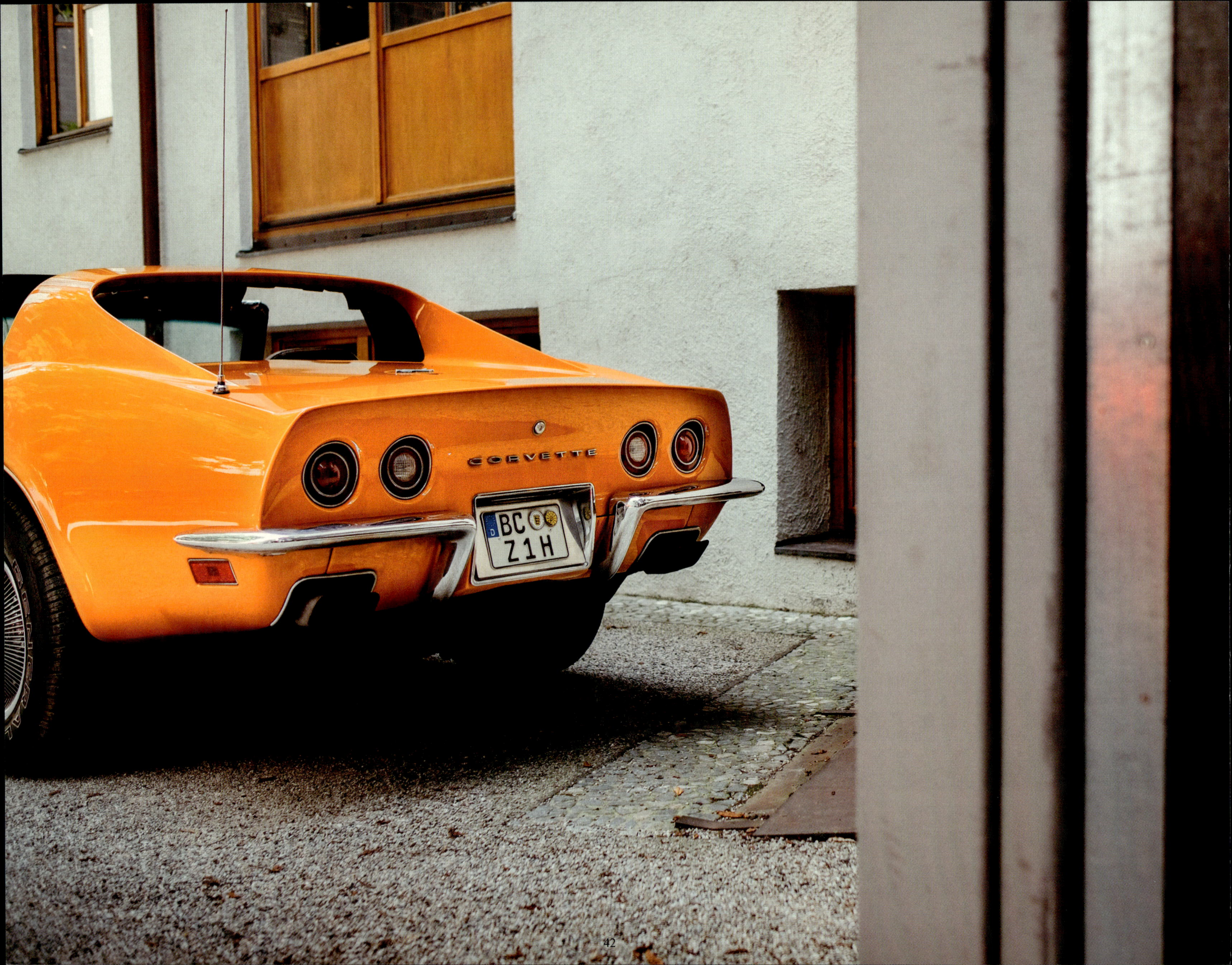
CORVETTE
BC Z1H

TO RUPERT, CORVETTE MEANS:
FREEDOM, SERENITY, BEING IN THE FLOW

See-through copy. Artist Nick Veasey gave Rupert Roth an x-ray of his Corvette on a scale of 1:1 as a thank-you for making his C3 available. Very few vehicle owners have been able to see through their car so precisely.

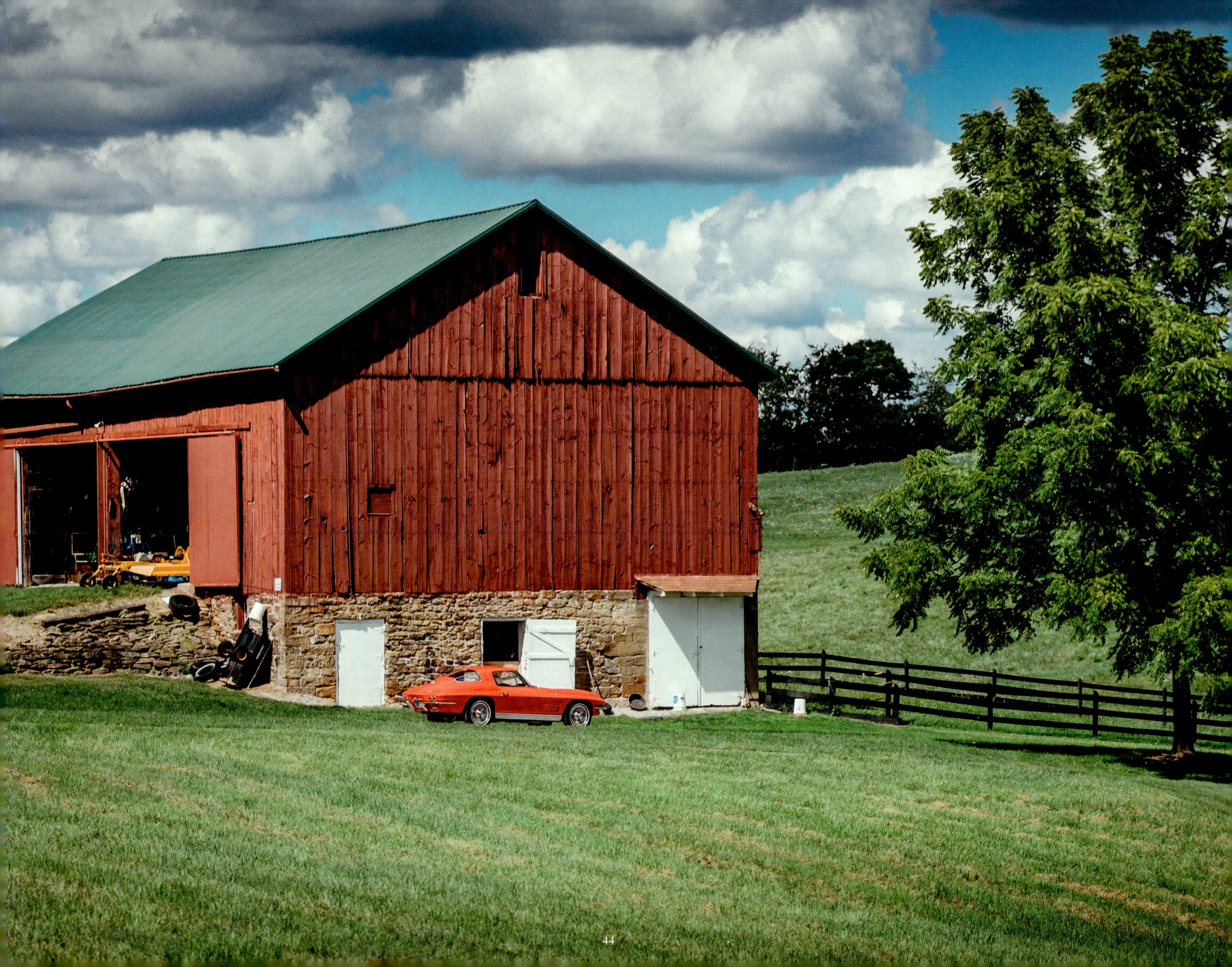

OUT OF THE GARAGE INTO THE WORLD

Corvettes have always been a part of Mitch Hrapchak´s family. Now he is showing the world how he is restoring and building Mid-Year Corvettes.

What's your Corvette story?
It all started when my grandfather decided that he wanted a 1965 Corvette. He purchased a green 1965 convertible from his brother George back in the early Seventies. Life got in the way, so my grandfather parked the Corvette for a number of years. In 1978, my grandmother made a deal with my dad: "If you get straight As and Bs in four years of high school, we will give you the 1965 Corvette or a new 1982 Corvette." The deal was written on the back of an envelope. Luckily, my grandfather didn't get rid of the '65 Corvette or that envelope.

In 1982, my dad received the car; at that time, it was a Cadillac green with gold cobwebs on the hardtop. He completed a minor restoration on it, repainted it a Corvette green, and got it back on the road. Then life happened, and he parked the car for a while.

My passion started from an early age. I was born in 1994, and my dad wanted to restore his car. I was about three years old when we started working on it. We worked on the car every free evening and weekend. We completely restored the car and returned it to its original white color. That car has been in my life for as long as I can remember.

In the early 2000s, we went to Corvettes at Carlisle to see friends who happened to own a red '63 split window. Frank owned the red car as well as a 1960 Corvette Fuelie. Both were stored in the same garage in pieces. His son Greg told him that he should sell one of them to fund a restoration of the other car. I nagged him for at least two or three years to sell me the split window. I nagged him every year at Carlisle and asked him if he wanted to sell me that car. He really liked that we had restored my dad's car together, so he ended up selling it to my dad. We put it away until we got the right garage to work on it. I was in middle school when we got the car.

Around 2008, we started to work on the '63, and my dad made the same deal with me that my grandmother had made with him in 1978. If I completed high school with As and Bs, I would get the car. The biggest difference was that mine was in many pieces, and he got a complete car. We had to put the whole car together, one piece at a time, and we had to find dozens of '63-specific parts for the car. It was an adventure, because '63 Corvette coupes are very unique. Everything is very different from later years—the window trim, the seats, the gauges, steering column, etc. The art of trying to find not just a part, but the right part for it, helped me understand restoring Corvettes.

Working on this car, hunting for parts at Carlisle, and trying to find every required piece for my car turned an interest into a desire. The desire turned into a passion and maybe into a career at some point. The passion kept evolving as the restoration went on. At one point, my friend wanted the red '63 back because it had been his dad's car. But I just couldn't bring myself to sell the car. It is in a home where it's loved, and I know more about the car than anybody. I know every single nut and bolt, I know every quirk it has. It's not going anywhere.

The Corvette community is like a tight-knit family, and having *The Mid-Year Mitch* YouTube channel demonstrated that to me. I am considered very young for this hobby. Whenever you go to a swap meet, many people have had parts for probably twenty or thirty years. They don't want to let them go to some young punk kid. Before I had my YouTube channel, people would either not cut me a deal on parts or they would just dismiss me as if "he doesn't know what he's talking about." Having the channel shows people what I do with the parts, and that has almost earned me a level of respect that I didn't know was possible. It helped show the community that a young guy can be passionate about these cars too. People are almost rolling out the red carpet for me now. It's as if people that I have never met know me and my channel. They want to share car stories, and they immediately trust me. I received hundreds of emails from people who want me to redo their cars for them. I think that is just supercool.

You are thinking about building a 1967 Corvette? What are your plans with that built?
I love having a fully restored car that is perfect in every way that is fun to drive on nice days. But a part of me also wants to build a car I can drive on any day, on a road trip, take it to a track, and take it to an autocross course. I really like the patina scene, specifically cars that have original paint or old weathered paint. I like the survivor car that is maybe a little more towards the ratty side. The challenge of this car is to find pieces that are all Ermine White and put it together. I don't want to fool people and make it look like a barn find, but the car will visually tell a unique story. So, the outside will have weathered patina and the inside will be fully restored in red. I purchased a Roadster Shop Spec 7 chassis to put under the car. I want to have the best technology and still make it affordable. I want to keep it kind of old school and put a 500-horsepower 327 engine that was from the Misfit Split. I will put a Tremec TKX five speed behind it to tame the beast a little bit. The goal of the project is to build something that you are not afraid to drive. It would be cool to have two Corvettes, the beauty and the beast, side by side.

What is your all-time favorite Corvette model?
My favorite generation is definitely the Mid-Year Corvette. I just love the character of the car. I like the color options they had and the lines of the car. But my all-time dream car would be to own a 1953–55 Corvette. If they made one with a small block V8 and a four speed transmission, I would be sold. Maybe one day I will build one of those.

◀ **1963** Corvette C2, **Irwin**, Pennsylvania, **USA** | September 9, 2022

TO MITCH, CORVETTE MEANS:
FAMILY, AMERICAN, DRIVE

Clash of generations. Like many young fans, Mitch Hrapchak was not taken seriously by the old hands at first. Thanks to his YouTube channel *Mid-Year Mitch* and his restorations, the 29-year-old has gained respect in the Corvette scene.

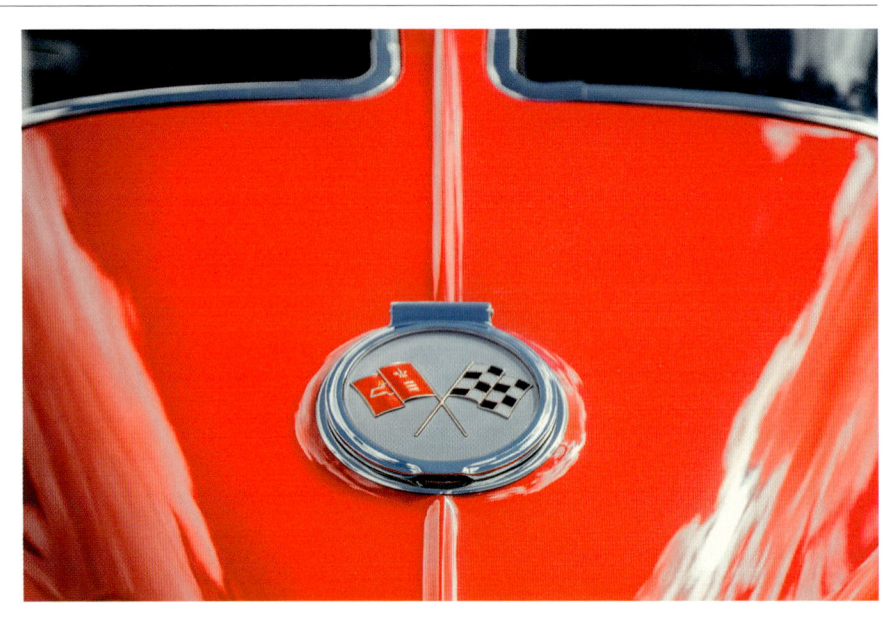

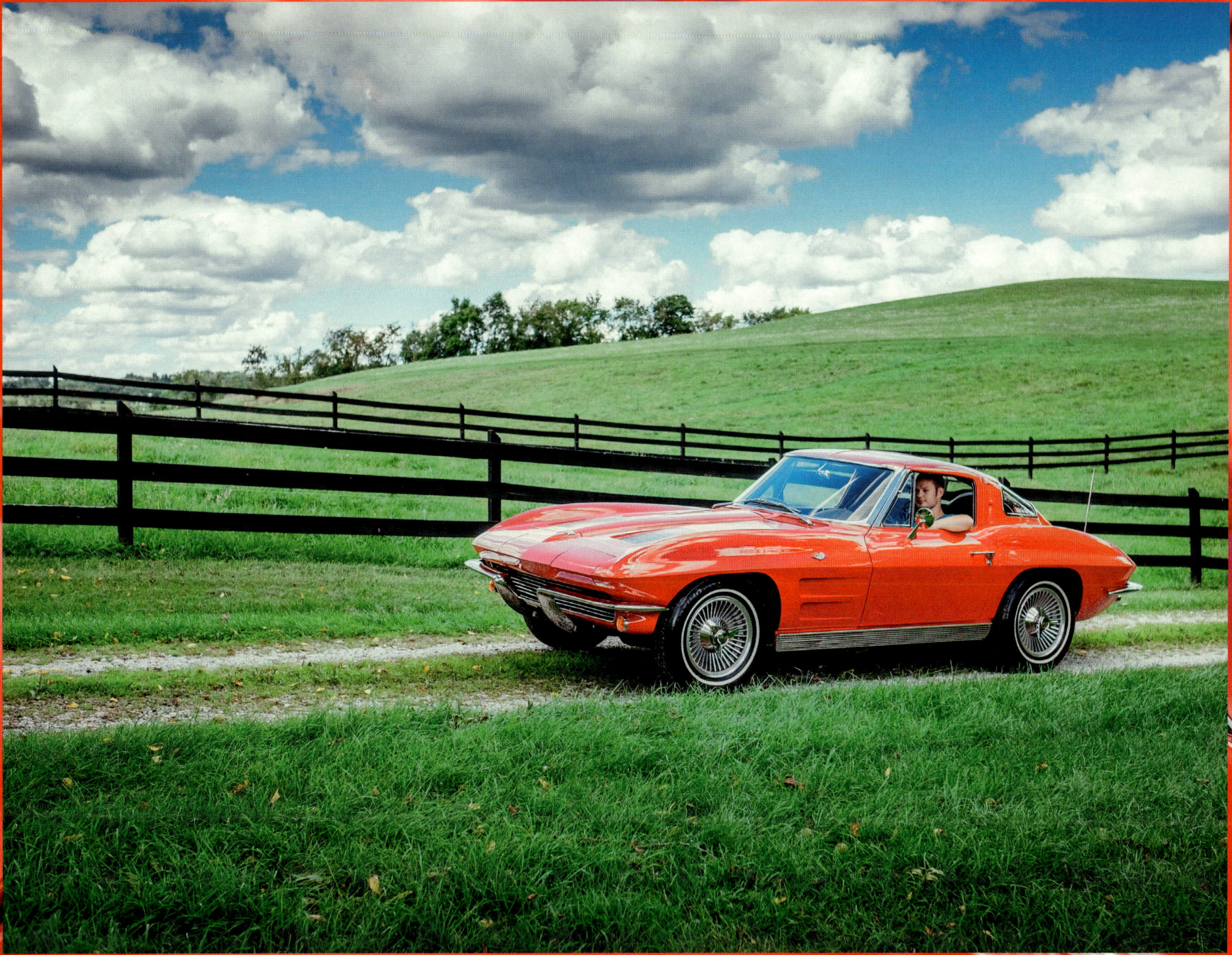

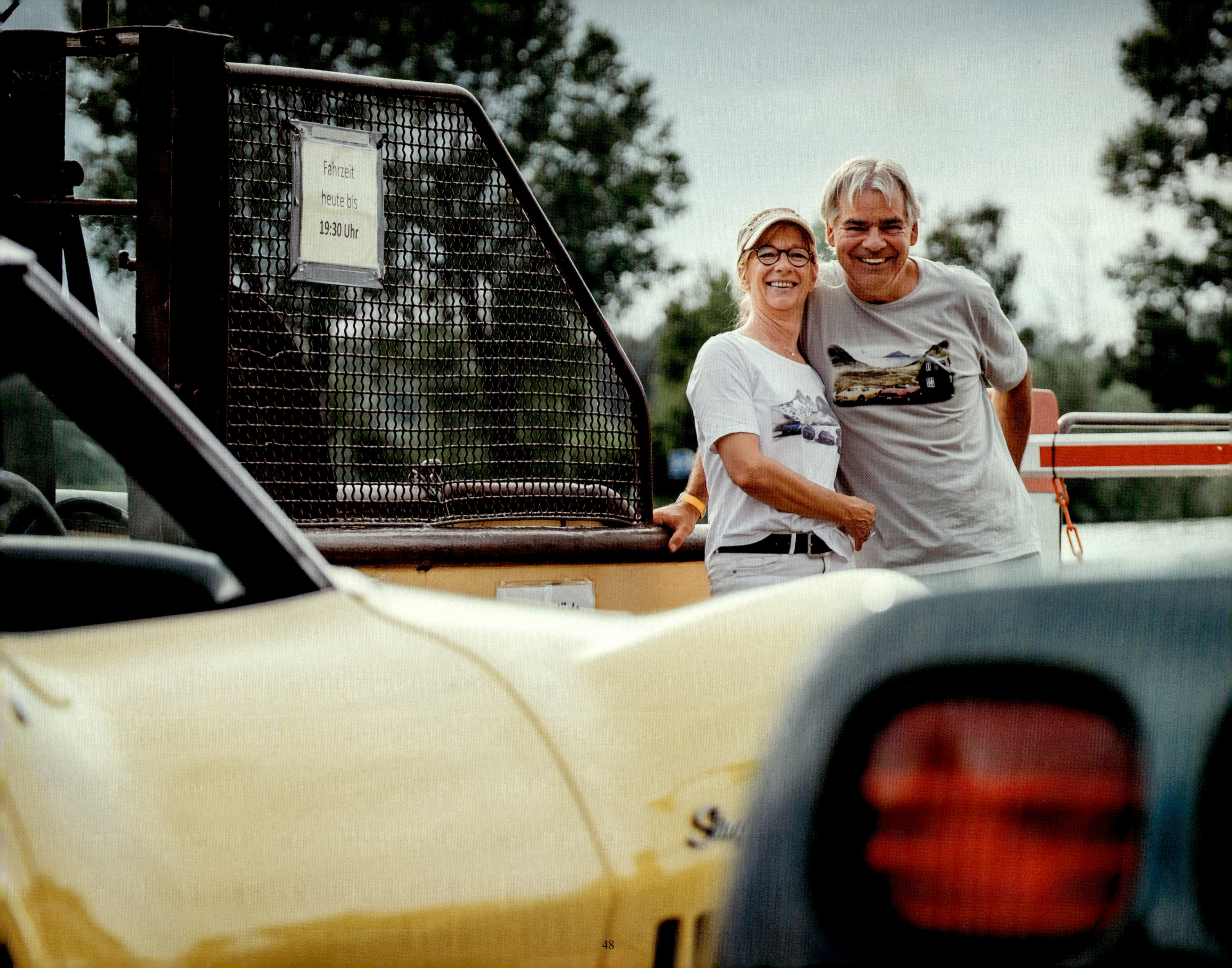
Fahrzeit
heute bis
19:30 Uhr

TWO CORVETTES, COUNTLESS KILOMETERS

Together, Elvira and Frank Romanowsky have covered countless kilometers on the European continent in their yellow Corvette C3 and its green sister.

What's your Corvette story?
Frank: For me it began at the age of 30, or about 30 years ago. Then I had a red C4 with rear spoiler and everything that went with it. I wouldn't say now that it was a pimp's car, but it was something like that. It was also in that flashy Corvette that Elvira saw me for the first time.
Elvira: Exactly. And that was a moment for me when I thought, "Oh, God!" He was immediately out of my league. But then I realized quite quickly that Frank didn't correspond to this feared cliché. But as a woman, blonde to boot, I didn't want to sit in this red, pimped-out sports car. That would have served the cliché to the full. At that time I didn't care much for a Corvette C4 either, as my heart was more for the older Corvette generations. Then when Frank came around the corner with the idea of looking for a C3, I just said, "Sounds good."
Frank: I then spent almost a year searching for a C3 on the internet, but I was unable to find one here in Germany. I then expanded my search to the USA in particular by way of the American Corvette Forum. Twice I had an appraiser in the States look at a Corvette for me. It was really a good idea to use this service, because the cars were basically junk.

I then got in touch with a C3 owner from Florida via the Corvette forum. The exchange of emails was very cordial. He sent me pictures of all the details I wanted to see; by phone he let me hear the engine and answered all my questions directly. Based only on the pictures and our conversations, I then bought the car. After the money hadn't appeared in his account after four days, we discovered that he had sent me the wrong banking details. Fortunately, the money was transferred back to my account, but that had cost nerves. Everything worked out on the second attempt, and six weeks later the Corvette was finally in the port of Rotterdam.

The Corvette has been in our possession since 2010, and it was only with this C3 that we became active in the German Corvette Forum. We quickly got to know other enthusiasts and joined our first tours. The very first tour was the so-called Spätzlesschaber Tour, a day trip through the Black Forest. At this event, we made further contacts with members of the forum who, coincidentally, had also bought their C3 Corvettes that same year, likewise chrome models.

That was the starting shot for further trips. There were major trips throughout Europe almost every year—Italy, the south of France, the Czech Republic, Poland, Sardinia, and Croatia, including a tour of the Dolomites. Then we went to England, Scotland, and Ireland. In 2020, we explored the Faroe Islands with our Corvette. We had originally planned a tour to Iceland, but the coronavirus pandemic threw a monkey wrench in the works. However, the Faroe Islands were definitely a great alternative. We would probably never have done all our tours through Europe if we hadn't met our Swiss friends Katja and Martin.

Did you meet them both by way of the forum?
Frank: Yes, they were also looking for a Corvette at the time and eventually found one. We met in person on the way to a big Chevrolet meet in Switzerland, on the occasion of Louis Chevrolet's 100th birthday. We hit it off right away and have been going on tours together every year since. They plan the trips and we just follow along behind them and don't have to worry about anything. If we still have questions, they tell us to look in the roadbook.
Elvira: You really have to tell how you got the side pipes for the C3. I think it's an interesting story.
Frank: I always wanted a Corvette with side pipes, but unfortunately it didn't happen. In the American Corvette forum, I discovered a post by an older man from Canada who had found original 1969 side-pipes in his barn and was offering them for sale. He had taken the exhaust system off his 1971 Corvette, mothballed it, and forgot about it at some point. I bought the parts from him. He made an extra wooden box so that the exhaust pipes would survive the long journey from Canada to Germany. And they did, arriving undamaged.
Elvira: The seller was really pleased that his side pipes had been brought back to life and had found a worthy car. Later we sent him pictures of our Corvette with the side pipes fitted, which made him very happy. We have already met so many great people with both Corvettes and experienced exciting stories. Even negative events, such as breakdowns, can eventually turn into something positive.
Frank: Somebody always gets left behind in the old crates, and of course we help each other.

How did you acquire your green C4?
Frank: Before the yellow C3, I had a C4, a Nineties model. The car ran really badly. I took it to several specialists, but none of them could fix the problem. So I sold the car to a friend of mine. He found the cause surprisingly quickly: a rag had been left in the injection system at some point. No wonder it ran so badly.

But I always missed the C4 somehow. So I had to get another one. I also wanted another one from 1990 in the color combination of Polo Green with the beige hood. Then I stumbled across our current C4, built in 1990 but already a '91 model.
Elvira: At last a Corvette that I could drive without any problems. With the C3, I always have problems reaching the pedals properly. And I sit so low that I can't really estimate the dimensions of the car. On narrow roads in southern Europe that can be really stressful. And damaging something on the yellow one would be an absolute horror for me. I find the C4 much easier and more relaxing to drive. Ideal for our big tours.

Which is your absolute favorite Corvette model?
Definitely the C3 from 1969.

◀ **1969** Corvette C3, **1990** Corvette C4, **Kollerfähre Brühl**, Rhineland-Pfalz, **Germany** | July 3, 2021

TO FRANK, CORVETTE MEANS:
TINKERING, SUNSHINE, FUN

TO ELVIRA, CORVETTE MEANS:
HAPPINESS, SATISFACTION, FUN

The mile-makers. There is hardly a spot in Europe that Elvira and Frank Romanowsky have not yet explored in one of their two Corvettes.

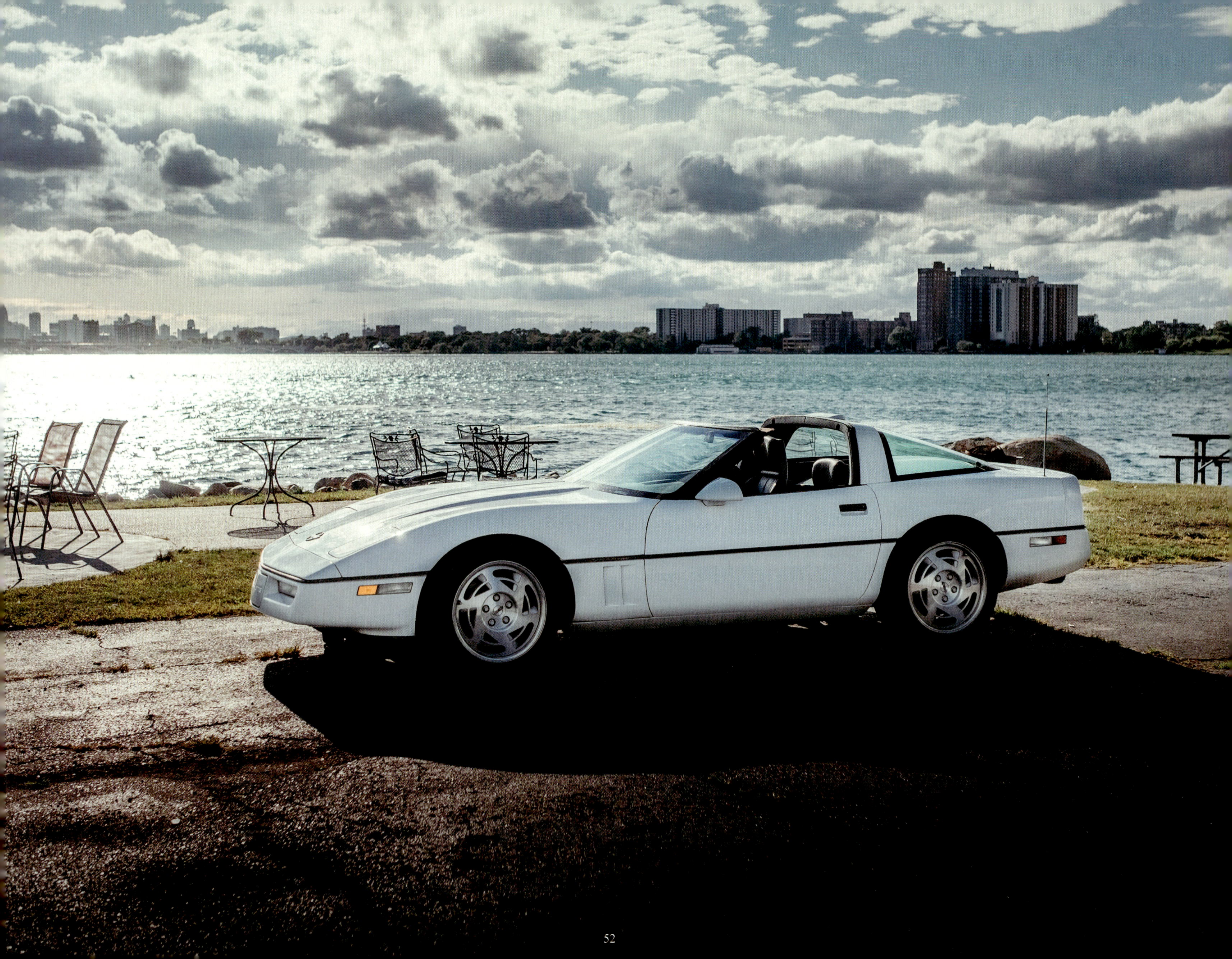

WHEN FASCINATION BECOMES AN OCCUPATION

To Harlan Charles, not only is the Corvette the best two-seat sports car, it is also his occupation and a part of his family.

What is your Corvette story?
The Corvette has always been my favorite car, my whole life in fact. In general, I loved cars from an early age, not just the Corvette. My father used to travel a lot in Europe, and I accompanied him there from time to time. I was totally fascinated by the Europeans' fascination with their sports cars. Everyone knows which country which sports car comes from: Ferrari is Italy, Porsche is Germany, Jaguar is England. In various European books about sports cars, the countries of origin were always given. The only American car I discovered in these books was the Corvette. I thought at that time that it must be something special if it got attention in Europe. So the Corvette became my absolute favorite car. I just thought it was great that there was an American sports car that could compete on the international stage.

So I wished early on that I could work on the Corvette one day. Fortunately, that dream has come true. When I started at GM, the first thing I did was try to find out how I could get my own Corvette. In 1989, I finally bought my C4, model year 1990. General Motors had the following system at that time: one could order a Corvette as an employee, but it had to have been driven 1,000 miles by an executive before you got it. In return, you got thirty percent off the new price. Of course, that's exactly what I did.

I borrowed the car that would be mine from my supervisor for a weekend. Then I drove the Corvette for about 600 miles, so he only had to drive another 400 more miles before I could take possession of it. Of course, my supervisor didn't think that was all that great, but I didn't care. I wanted my C4 as soon as possible.

You have been to 49 states in this 1990 C4?
I have the car to drive it. That's what it's built for, and that's fun. In 1992, I took it on my first major trip across the USA. My girlfriend and I drove to Las Vegas, got married there, and then drove on to Los Angeles. It was our first road trip from coast to coast, east to west. From then on, we drove every year through the States but also to Quebec and eastern Canada. We really saw a lot of the USA in this Corvette. The idea for our ultimate trip came when we thought about where we haven't been yet. Hawaii would be difficult to get to by car, but Alaska is straight overland. That would have to have been around 1997, and the Corvette already had over a hundred thousand miles on the clock from driving to all the other states. So I took three weeks off and we drove all the way to Alaska. At the time, there were no smartphones or navigation systems. We only had classic road maps and a guidebook for Alaska.

By the way, all my trips helped further my career at GM. While working in the Design Center, I created a picture book from some of my travels. I showed them to some of my colleagues and supervisors, including John Cafaro, the Head of Design for the Corvette. I showed it to Randy Wittine, who is in the hall of fame, and a few others. As a result, they suggested me and my stories to *Corvette Quarterly* magazine. So eventually, all the designers who were involved with the Corvette came to know me. When I applied for my current job, it certainly helped. Everyone knew I was a Corvette enthusiast through and through.

I am still very impressed by my car. This C4 is not perfect, but for all the places it's been, going all over the country in bad conditions, on bad roads, it has survived really well. It's not restored or anything; this is just the way it is after all the miles. The car is 33 years old, and it is really a part of my family. I have had so many adventures and experiences with it that it's a very special car to me.

What is your all-time favorite Corvette model?
That's easy. The mid-engine C8 Z06. That's the ultimate. When I was growing up, it was Zora Arkus-Duntov's dream that the Corvette would one day be on the world stage. He was determined to take the Corvette to the next level with the mid-engine design, no more excuses. The way it has been improved, I think it is just getting better and better. For me, the next one is always my favorite Corvette.

It is more than just a sports car; it's a lifestyle, traveling in a two-seat car and finding enjoyable roads to drive. It's just the way you can combine your vacation and fun. The trip is the adventure, not the destination.

◀ **1990** Corvette C4, **Detroit**, Michigan, **USA** | September 12, 2022

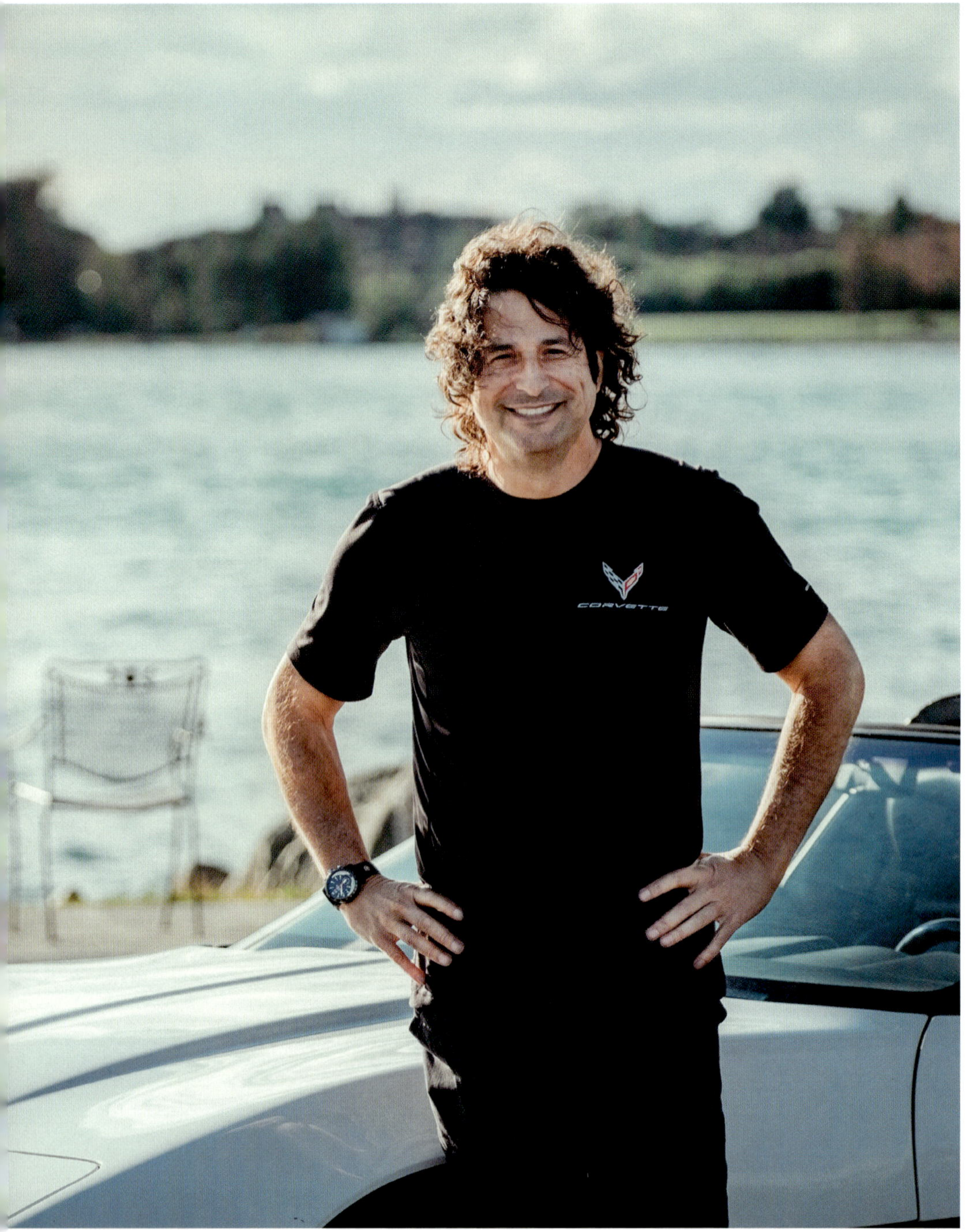
CORVETTE

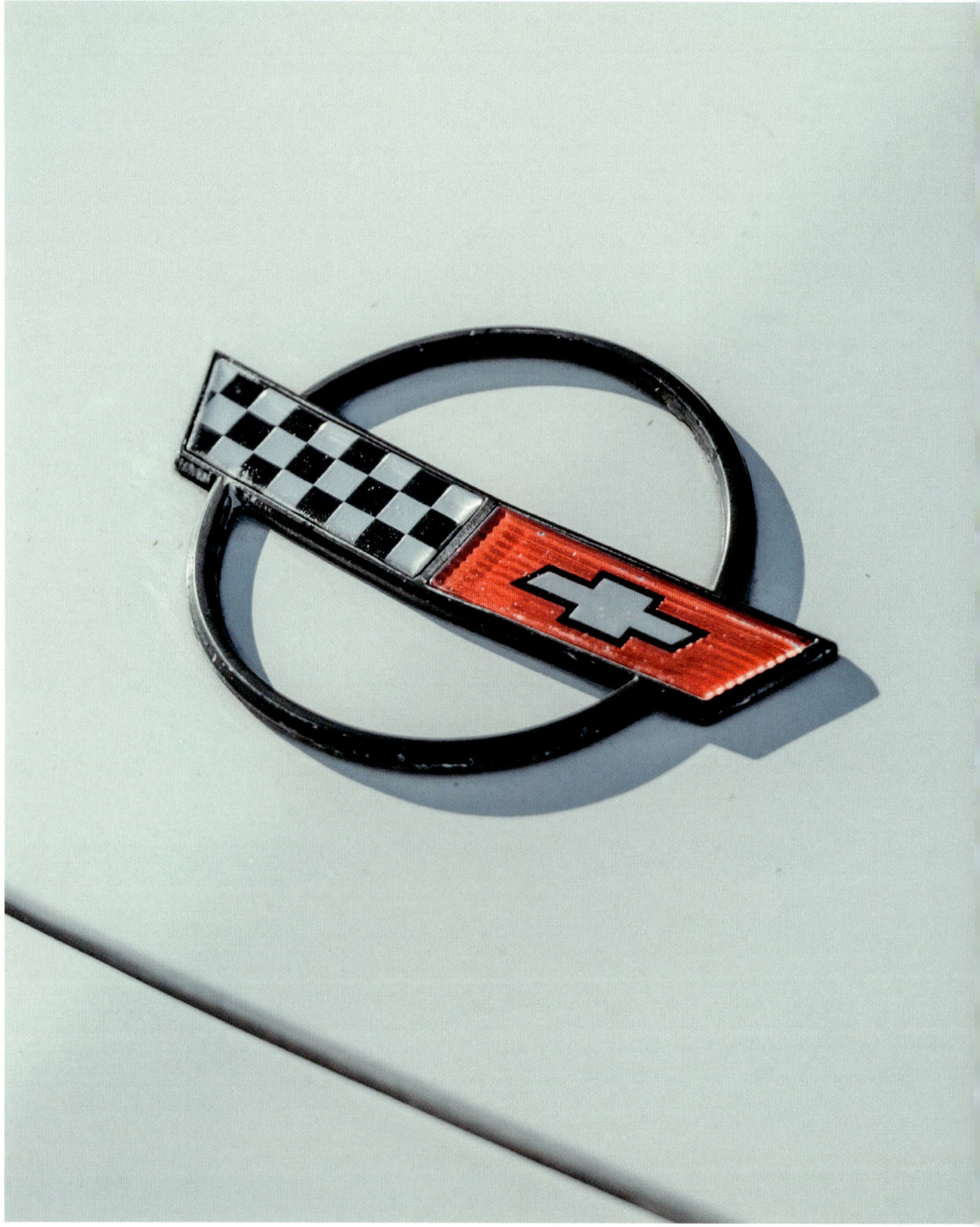

TO HARLAND, CORVETTE MEANS:
DESIGN, TECHNOLOGY, FUN

Motor City on my mind. Belle Isle is in the middle of the Detroit River and serves as a backdrop for Harlan Charles's C4. With the view of the inner city and the General Motors headquarters, it was the perfect location for the Corvette product marketing manager and his car.

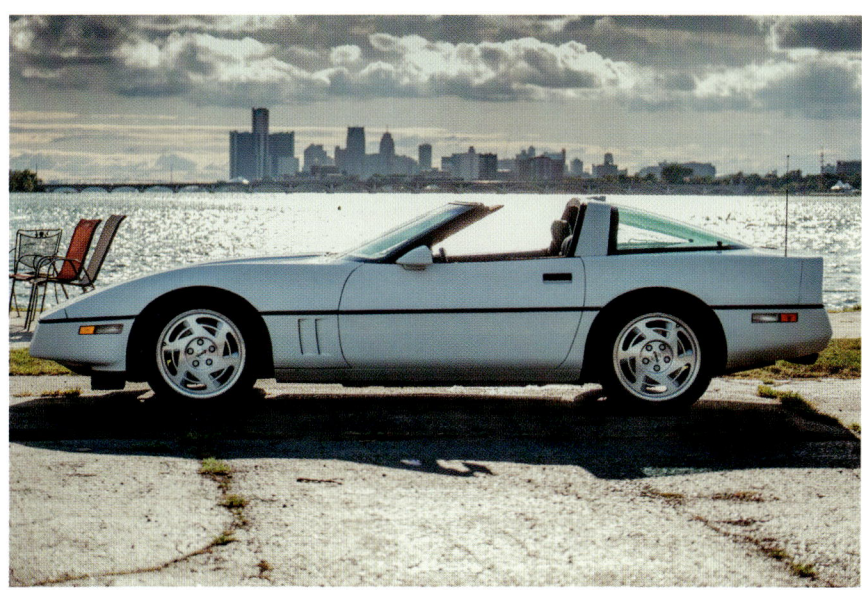

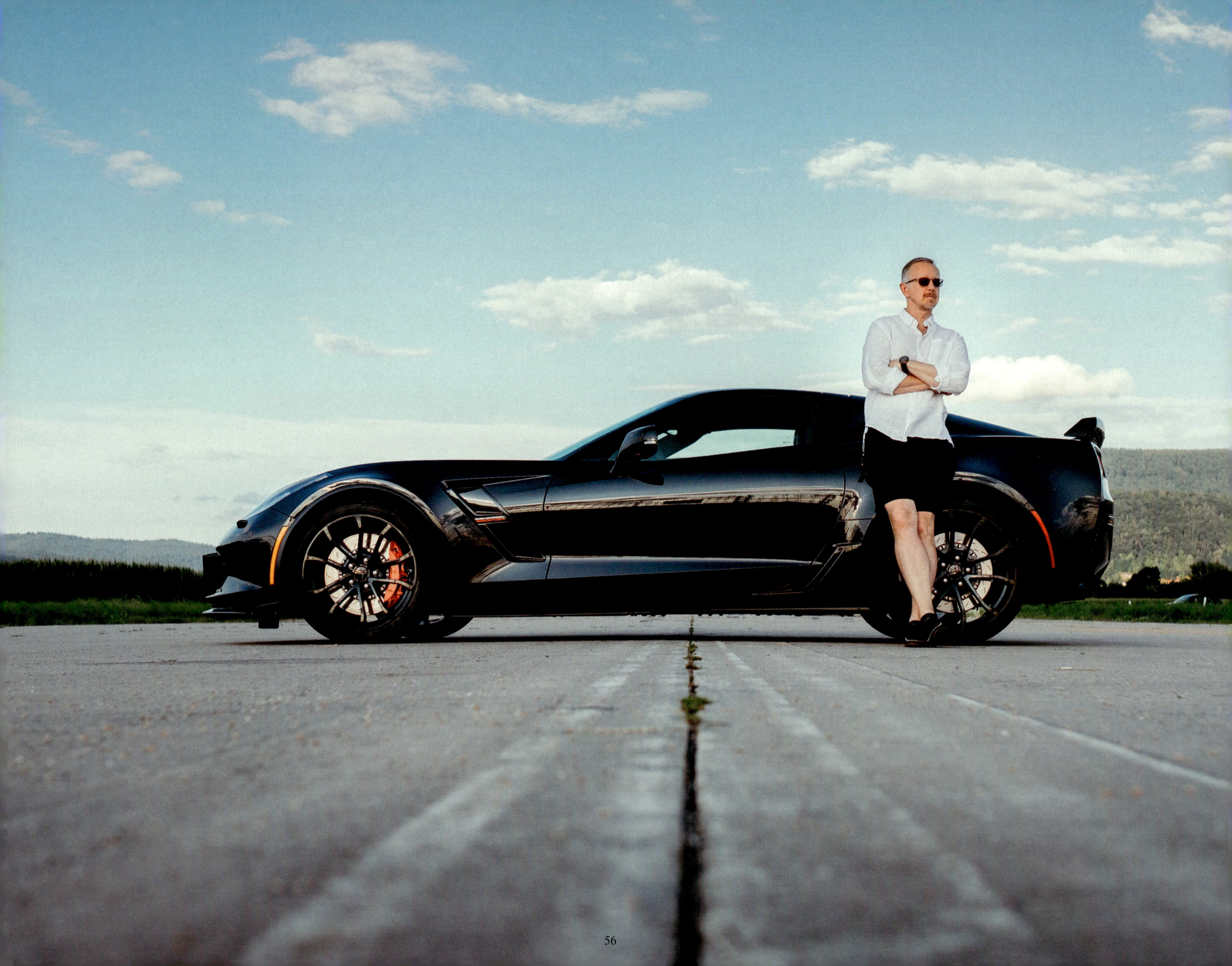

ANYTHING BUT CIVILIZED

Marek Sukiennik is originally from the USA. He now lives and works in Heidelberg and in Germany has fulfilled his childhood dream of owning a Corvette.

What's your Corvette story?
I've always loved driving sports cars, but I've never owned a four-door car in my life. Never. I've never even driven a four-door rental car. I had an Oldsmobile 442, a Pontiac GTA, a BMW M3, a 911 Porsche, and a Jaguar. I've really had quite a few sports cars. My last one was an Infiniti Q60 Red Sport. But Infiniti has decided to turn its back on the European market. So I thought it would be better to buy a car from another manufacturer. The question was: From which one? I always wanted a Corvette, so this time, that's what it was going to be.

When I was a little boy, there were two cars I always wanted, a Ferrari and a Corvette. They were the only sports cars that really fascinated me back then. I have never owned a Ferrari. So I started looking for a Corvette C7 and also found some convertibles for sale. But what I wanted was either a Z06 or a Grand Sport. The Z06 is rare in Germany, and it was almost impossible to find one. So I decided on a black Grand Sport. The Corvette was located near Munich. The seller was the original owner and had purchased the car in 2019 from Karl Geiger in the Bavarian capital.

When my fiancée and I were on our way back from Munich to Heidelberg, at some point on the autobahn she told me that I should take the next exit. So I got into the right lane, right behind a truck. She just said to me, the exit is in three kilometers, not in three meters. I of course took the hint. I overtook the truck, gave it full throttle. The C7 shifted into third or fourth gear; the acceleration was like being catapulted from an aircraft carrier! We flew past the truck and the other cars; it was spectacular.

I also like this brutal acceleration in the Corvette; it is still a real, pure sports car without a lot of frills. My other cars, with the exception of the 442, were more refined, more mature, tamer cars. The 911 and M3 are sports cars too, of course, but they're just more luxurious and a bit more civilized than the Corvette. The C7 just has that big American engine, lots of torque, and makes lots of noise. And that's what I love about the car. The C7 was the first time General Motors put the emphasis on the whole car: the exterior, the interior, and the driving characteristics. Until then, the Americans had focused on one thing above all: straight-line performance.

Which is your absolute favorite Corvette model?
The C1, the C2, or the C7. Those three. The order depends on different factors. I like old cars, and the ones from the Sixties looked really terrific. The design was beautiful, from the outside. Personally, I don't care for the interiors of the old cars. It's not about comfort for me; I have no problem rolling down the window by hand. I just don't like the look of the interior. A mixture of both would be exactly my thing. The body of a classic car combined with a modern interior—just like you now find on restored cars.

◂ **2019** Corvette C7, **Heidelberg**, Baden-Württemberg, **Germany** | July 25, 2021

TO MAREK, CORVETTE MEANS: SOUND, ADRENALINE, ACCELRATION

Reverberator. When Marek drives through the old town below Heidelberg's famous castle, the sound of the 6.2-liter, 466hp V8 meets the historic walls of the university town on the Neckar River. The new and the old worlds rarely collide so directly.

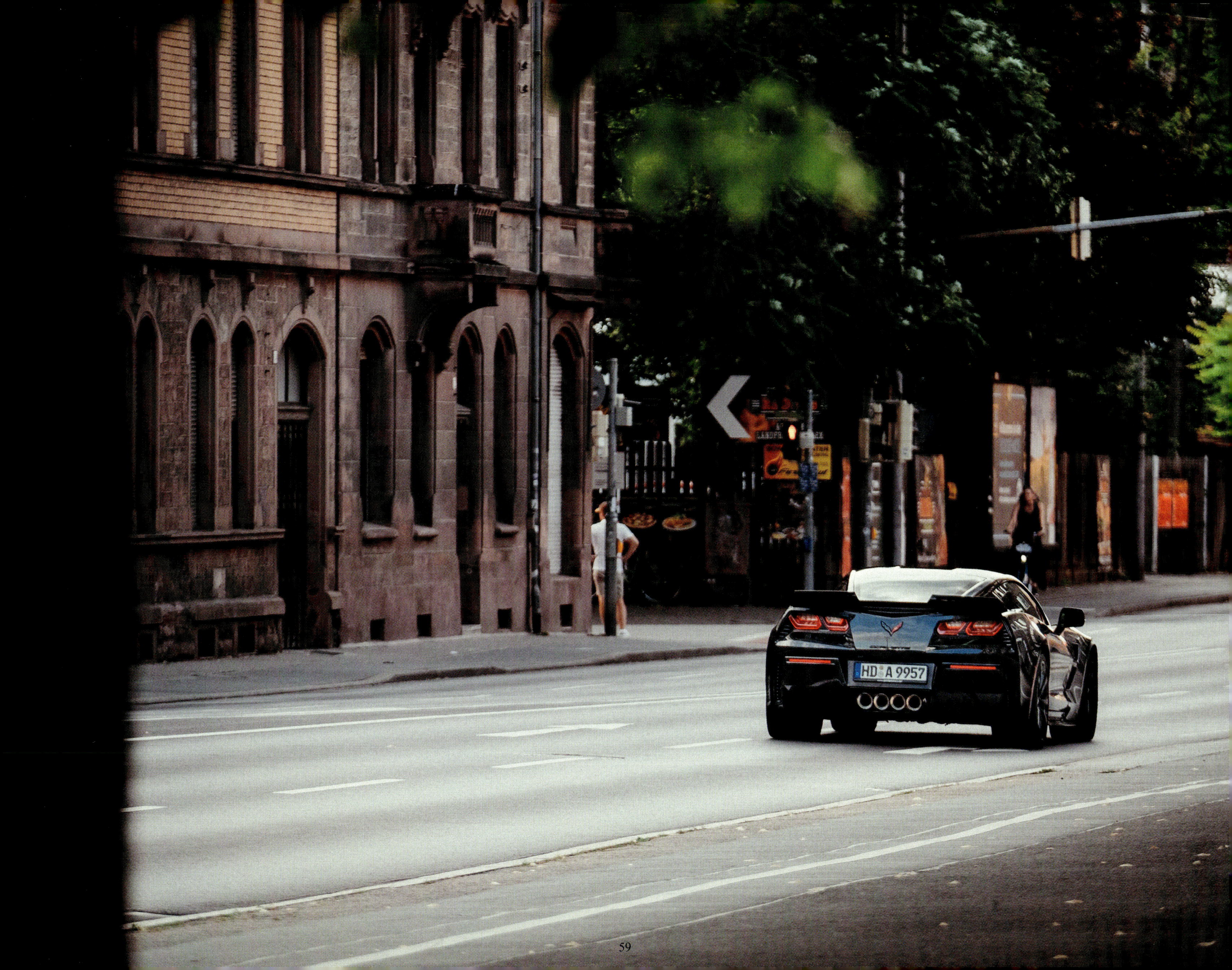
HD A 9957

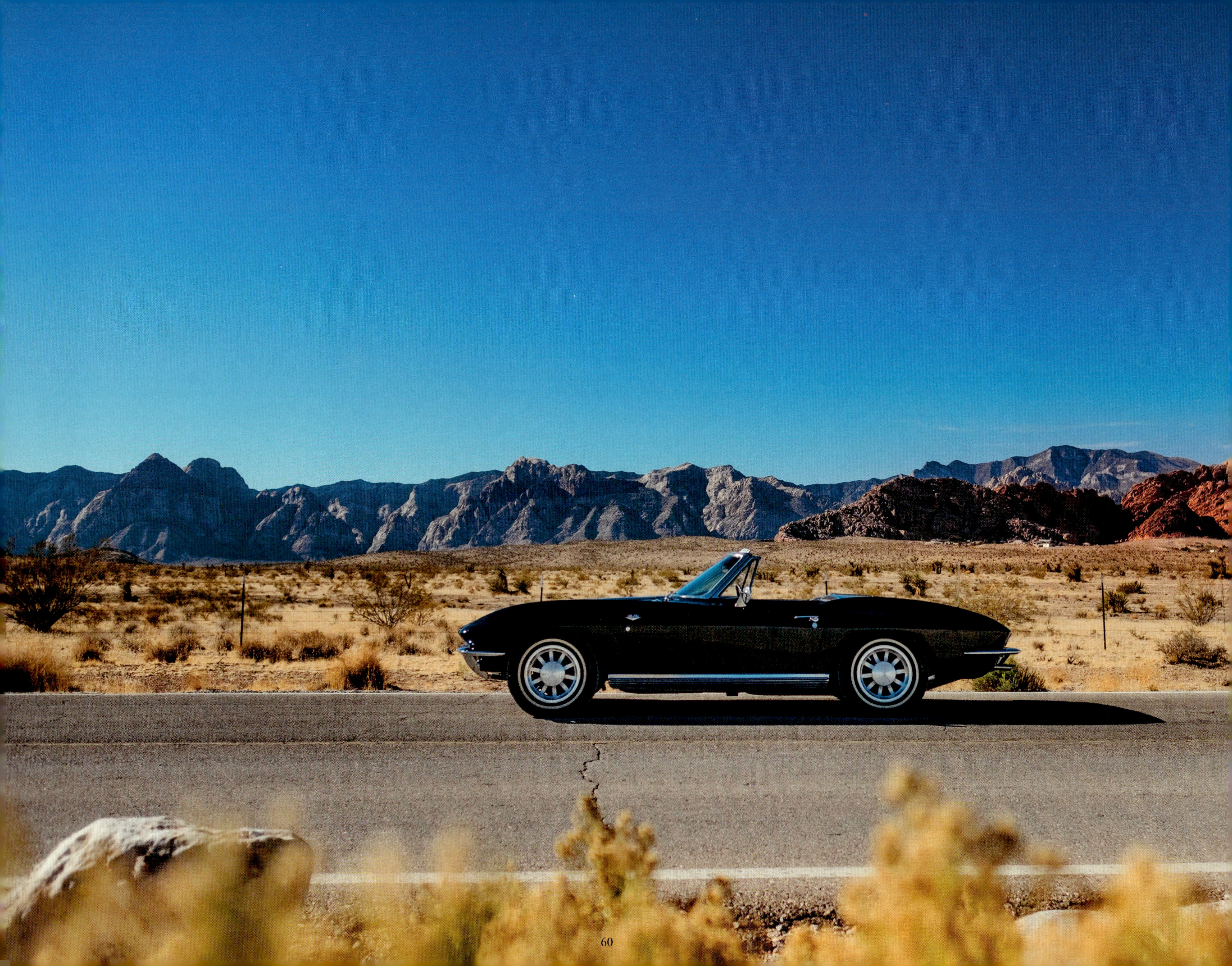

DAD, THIS IS DEDICATED TO YOU

Stephanie Menard grew up in Alaska, and the C2 was part of her childhood. Now the Corvette is taking her back to that time while driving through the Nevada desert.

What's your Corvette story?
My Corvette was passed down by my dad, who bought it from the original owner in Washington State. So my dad was the second owner, and that makes me the third. We had the car my entire childhood, and we grew up with the Corvette. After he got sick in March 2021, he passed the car on to me, because he couldn't drive it anymore. It is a family heirloom, and I don't plan on ever selling this car.

Had you ever driven the Corvette before you took possession of it?
Funny story, growing up my father never let anyone near it, and so we were always the passengers. The first time I drove the car was literally when I had it shipped from Texas, where my parents lived, to my home in Las Vegas. My dad had never let me drive it before that. I always asked him to let me drive the Corvette, but he said, "No, you can't drive it; the car is really hard to drive, first gear is not that easy . . ."

So the first time I drove it I was so scared because of the steering, the brakes, and all that! I stalled it several times at stoplights. The last time I had driven a stick was when I was 17 years old. But it's like riding a bike; you don't forget how to do it. It's a very interesting car to drive. When I got the car, there was a lot of stuff that needed to be done. New battery, new alternator, new spark plugs. There are still a few things that need to be taken care of, like a new paint job. The car has 75,000 original miles on it, so my dad didn't drive it very often, usually on Sundays.

I grew up in Alaska, so the car actually resided in Alaska for over twenty years until my mom and my dad moved to Texas. And so that car is used to driving around in Alaska in the summer months. You see some chips in the paint from the gravel they use to sand the roads in wintertime. My Dad always babied the Corvette and kept it in the garage. He took the C2 to some car shows in Alaska. He loved to collect classics, and when my parents moved to Texas, he bought a beautiful red 1940 Ford pickup truck and took it and the Corvette to some car shows. When my dad got sick, I dedicated my Instagram account to him. My sister inherited the truck, and I drive the Corvette. We have enjoyed taking them both to car shows in Las Vegas.

The car also reminds me of being a kid again and driving with my Dad. The whole experience of it; the sound and especially the smell reminds me of getting in the car as a kid. I was always asking my Dad, "Can you take me to school in the Corvette?" When he did, he'd pull up to my high school and rev the engine, and the kids thought I was so cool. The minute I walk into my garage now, it reminds me of him. It's something that lingers forever. Every time I take it out, I bring his ashes with me, and we go for a drive together. It's a memory that lasts forever.

What is your all-time favorite Corvette model?
Of course, I have to say the '64 Stingray, but I also I like the C1. Especially a red one with the white stripe on the side. That would be beautiful.

◀ **1964** Corvette C2, **Red Rock Canyon**, Nevada, **USA** | November 14, 2021

TO STEPHANIE, CORVETTE MEANS:
BEING A KID AGAIN

Heritage. The Corvette once belonged to Stephanie Menard's father, who drove her around in it as a little girl. Today, she sits behind the beautiful, three-spoke steering wheel and reminisces about a carefree past.

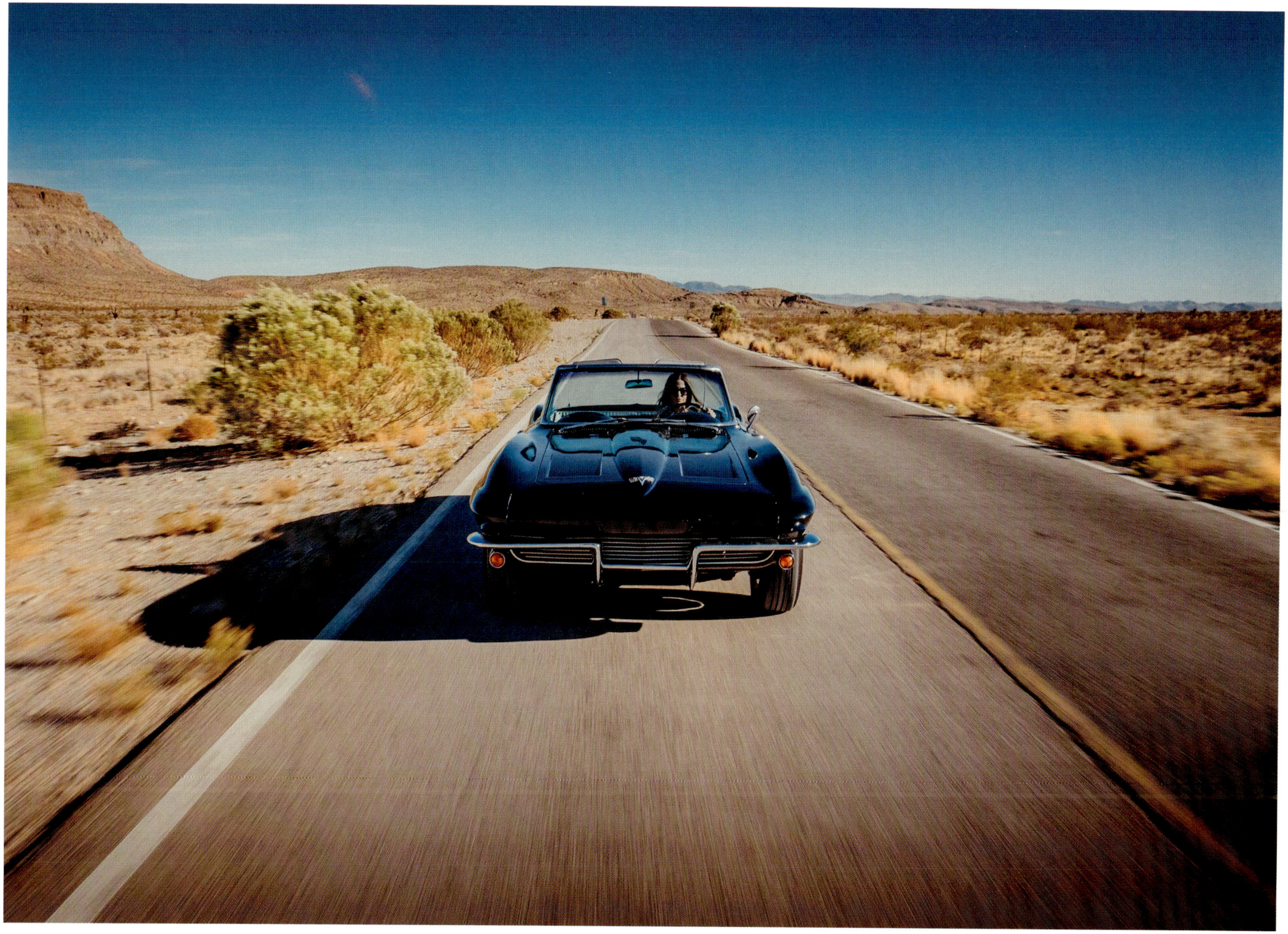

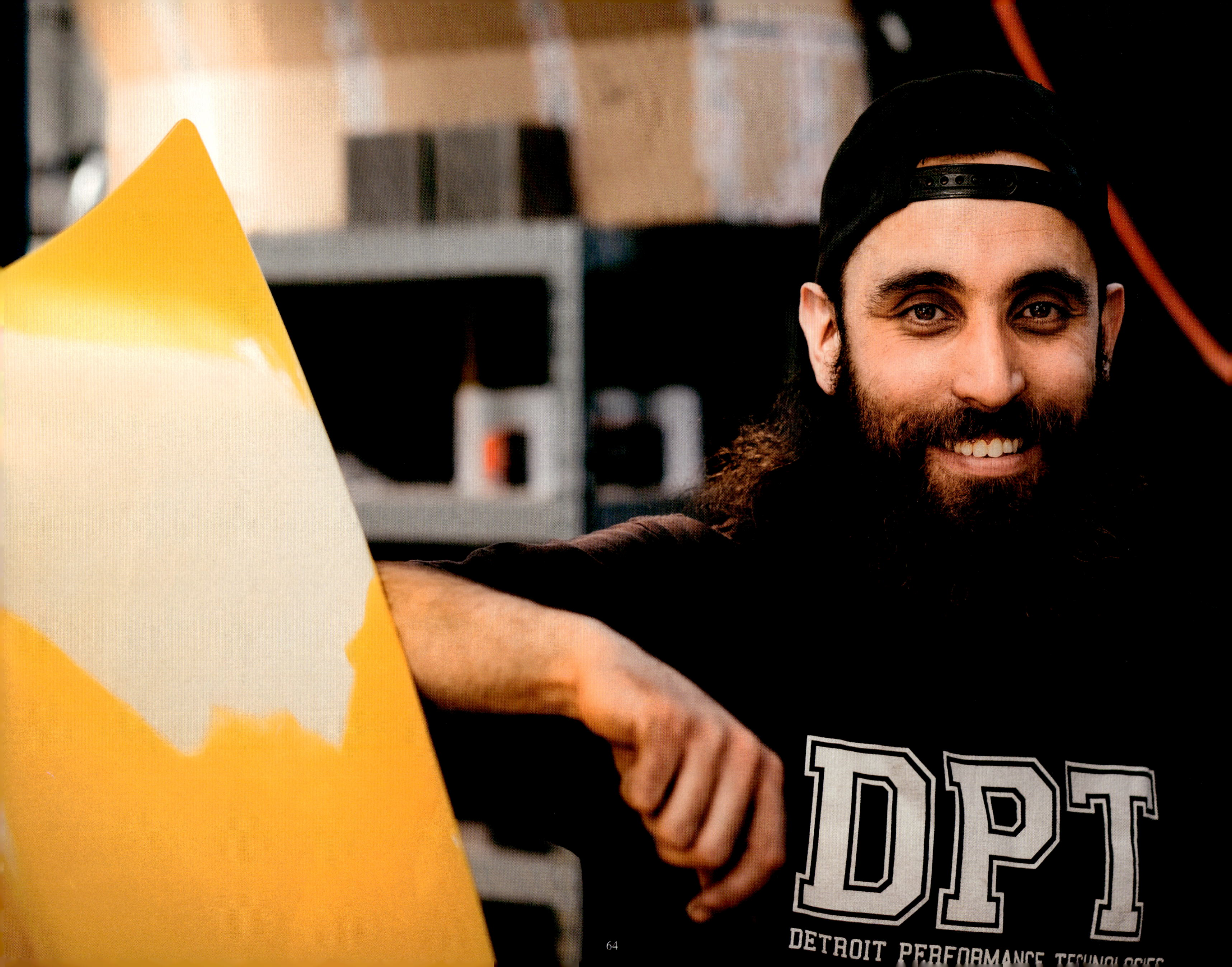
DPT
DETROIT

A DRIFTER AND HIS CORVETTE

A professional drifter, Patrick Wöllper has transplanted an LS engine into a BMW, but on the road, he prefers a yellow Corvette C6. Here he tells us how that came about.

What's your Corvette story?
In my youth, I once saw a yellow Corvette on a Kaba cup. For a long time, I thought it was a C6, but I was so young that it definitely had to be a C5. In any case, it was my first lasting memory of a Corvette. When the C5 Z06 came out, all the reviews of the Corvette really got me excited. What an awesome car! Then the C6 came out, prohibitively expensive for me at the time. After a few years went by and the first sixth-generation Corvettes hit the used car market, I started seriously looking for a C6.

Of course, it had to be yellow. As I said, the Kaba cup had left its mark. Yellow paint, manual transmission, and black leather were a must. The Z06 that matched my search criteria had been decommissioned at the time, and yet the owner still wanted just under €40,000. After corresponding with him for a long time, another yellow C6 crossed my path. And it fit my budget even better. So I bought it. But then the owner of the yellow Z06 contacted me again. He wanted to go abroad, and the only thing he had to sell was his Corvette. The exhaust system was not legal and the lights weren't registered; in fact, nothing about the car was street legal. That's exactly why nobody wanted it.

But I didn't care; I could rebuild everything myself. Its price was better now, but I still didn't have the money; after all, there was already another Corvette in my garage. So I went to my mother and said, "Mom, this is a once-in-a-lifetime opportunity. If I buy the car and restore it, I'll get at least twice as much out of it afterwards. Can you lend me the money?" She loaned me the cash. That's how I got my Z06. I kept both of them, by the way.

However, my first C6 is currently being transformed into a professional drift car so that I can drive it in the European Championship. So far, we've only rebuilt the front axle, installed a hydraulic handbrake, and optimized the suspension. A friend of mine is a model maker, and together with him, I built a spoiler for the Corvette. There's no other spoiler like this one. I told him exactly what I would like. It will be totally cool, and I'm already very excited about how the thing will look on the car.

How did you get into drifting?
After I first got my license, I drove a lot with a friend of mine, and we felt like kings of the road. He had a 5 Series BMW E34 Touring, and I had an ancient C-Class. At a gas station, where we met often, there was a guy with a Ford Sierra with a welded differential, who used it to go drifting from time to time. We thought it was so cool, so one evening we followed him until he stopped. We asked if he could give us a ride. That ride flipped a switch for me; I really wanted to do that too. I had no idea about cars and was in the middle of my apprenticeship as an industrial clerk. After completing that apprenticeship, I began another one to become an automotive mechatronics technician to learn more about vehicles.

I started drifting in parking lots, illegally. First on snow, then on wet surfaces, and then at some point in the dry. Then I went to my first drifting event. I was there with the Sierra owner, so just as a spectator. It was mega; I was so into it. So I went to a drift school. They had events at airfields and driving safety centers, and that's where I honed my skills and got to know my limits better. If I remember correctly, it was at the Anneau du Rhin that I drifted with my own car on a race track for the first time. That was a completely different level, which must have been six or seven years ago.

You installed a Corvette V8 in your drift BMW. How did you come up with the idea?
In Germany, you can find a 3-Series BMW on every corner, so the supply of spare parts is great. The parts and the vehicles too are therefore comparatively cheap. The second car I owned was an E36 BMW, and since then I've driven E36s all the way. I simply have the most experience with the Bavarian brand.

The idea of putting a V8 in a BMW has been a dream of mine for a long time. When I started drifting, I saw a video of an American pro drifter on YouTube. The guy was also driving an E36 BMW, but with a Corvette LS V8 under the hood. A V8, the thing was fast and loud. That's what I wanted, too. I'm just a V8 guy. A six-cylinder turbo or something like that is not for me. In spite of everything, I want to drift with the Corvette in competitions in the near future. There's still a lot of work to be done on the C6, and then I'll have to drive and train with the car for at least a year.

What is your all-time favorite Corvette model?
The Corvette C6 ZR1.

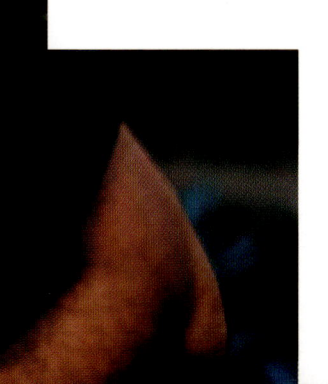

◀ **2008** Corvette C6, **Weinstadt**, Baden-Württemberg, **Germany** | June 11, 2021

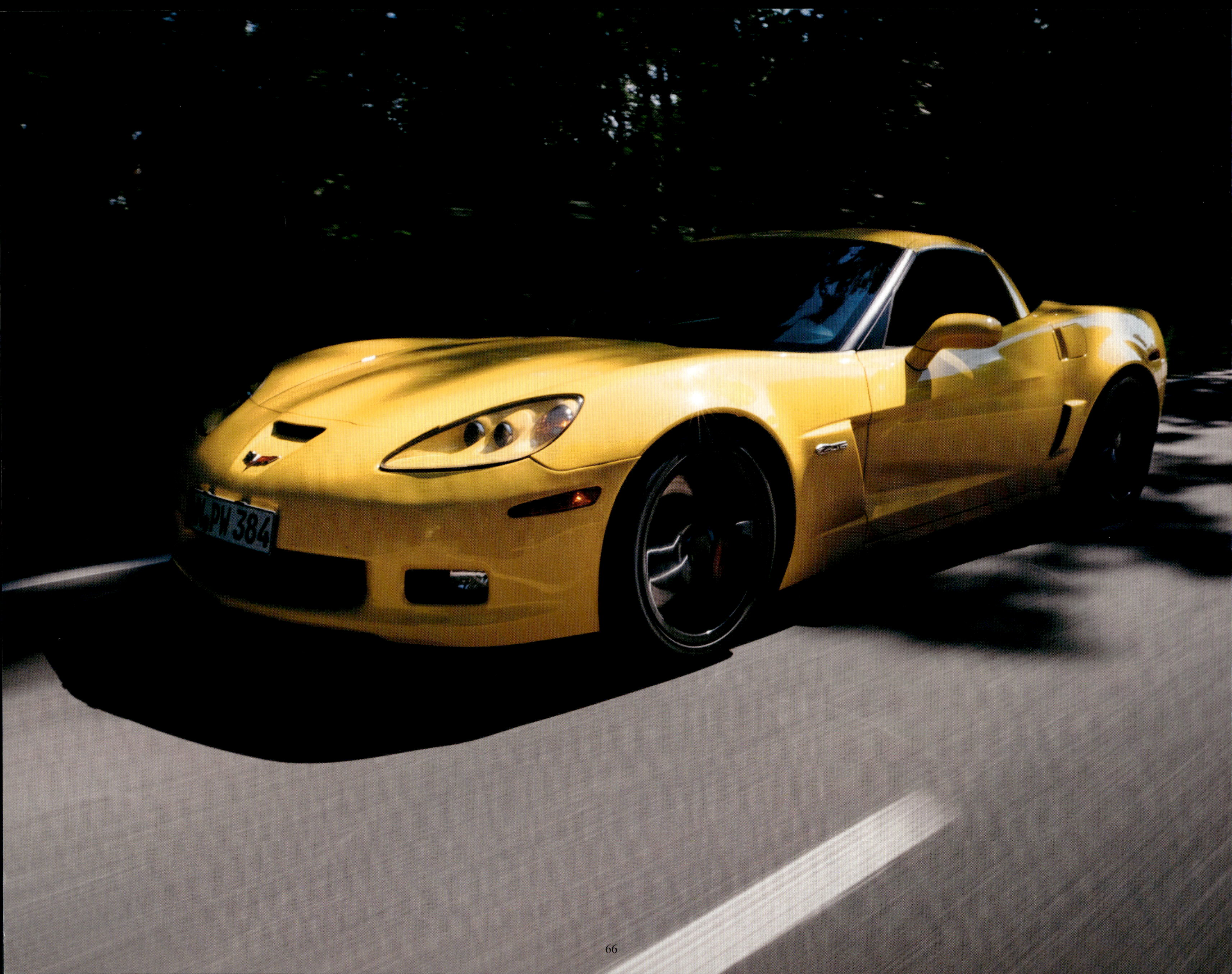

TO PATRICK, CORVETTE MEANS:
SIMPLY AWESOME

Drifty reason. Patrick Wöllper simply enjoys letting his ass hang out in front of an audience. That means drifting in his BMW E36 with its Corvette engine, or in his C6. In addition to the sport of side shifting, he is a mechanic at Detroit Performance Technologies.

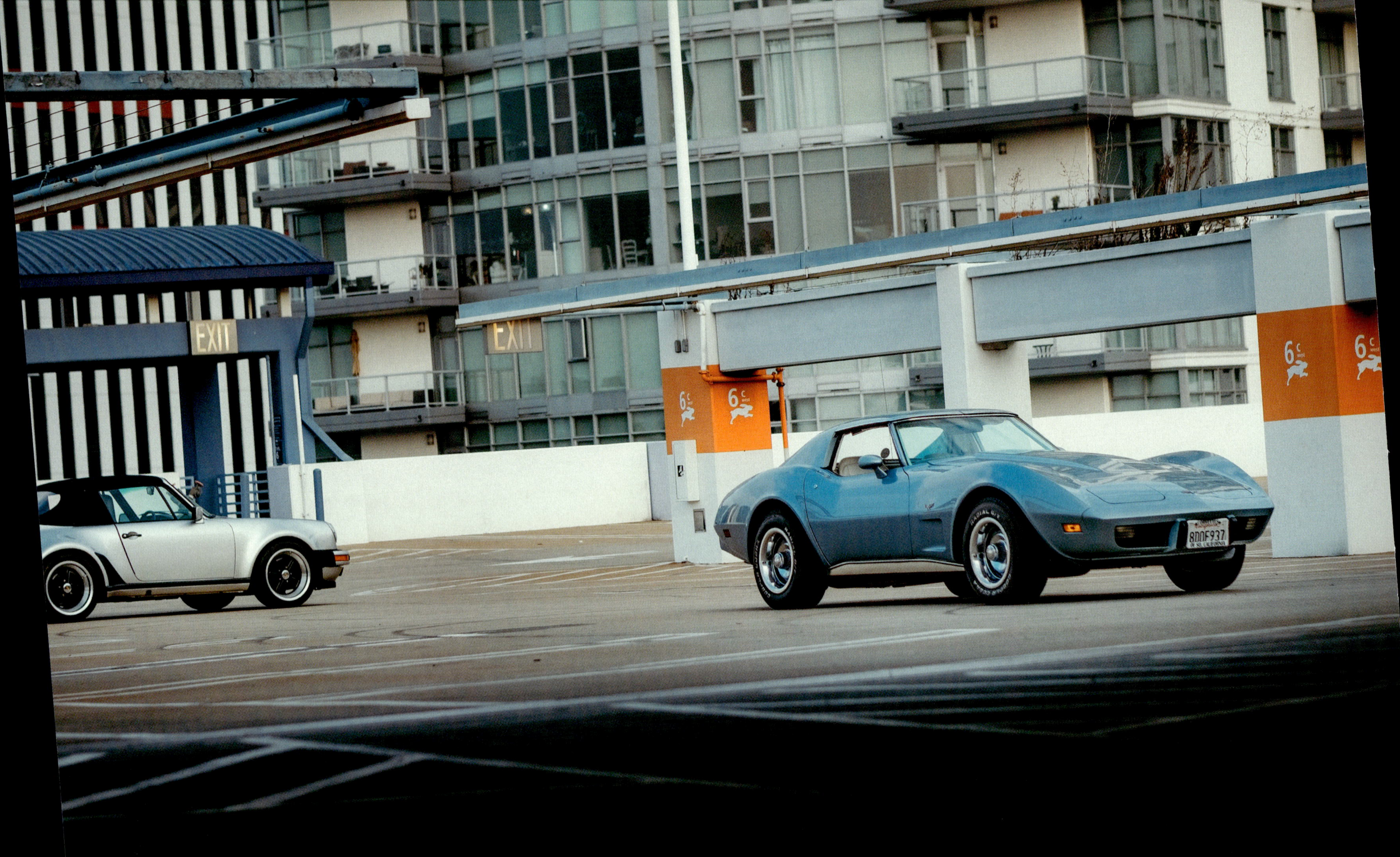
EXIT
EXIT

THE CORVETTE WAS JUST IN THE WAY

Nikola Stanjevich always wanted a Corvette. Not really a 1977, but that's the car that made its way from the East Coast of the USA to Long Beach, California.

What's your Corvette story?
I didn't make the choice to purchase this Corvette. A few years ago, my wife's uncle passed away and his daughter inherited the car. He always had at least one Corvette. The first time I met him, he had a 1963 Corvette Stingray. His daughter posted a text in our family chat group one day and asked if anyone wanted Uncle David's car. She lives on the East Coast, and I live on the West Coast, and because of that, I received the message at 6 a.m. At first, I thought the family would probably respond to the message. A few hours later, I looked at my phone again, and nobody had answered. So, I asked her how much she wanted for the car. She said that she wanted no money at all, but she just wanted to pass it on because it was deteriorating in her garage, and Uncle David would have wanted someone in the family to have the car. So I asked her to arrange shipping and told her I would cover the cost, and a few weeks later, the Corvette arrived in Long Beach.

I had a 1961 MG that I got rid of to create some space in my garage. It was a beautiful car. European cars are very stick-shift oriented, while American ones are not. My kids can barely drive a stick, so it came down to keeping the MG versus getting the Corvette with an automatic transmission. The Corvette won.

I had always wanted to have a Corvette, not necessarily a 1977, but I thought it was a beautiful car. It has the 350 engine. It's completely stock and has power windows and air conditioning, which is just perfect for California. I figured I could resuscitate the car and keep it going. I got the car for nothing, but I had to spend a couple of thousand dollars to get it back to driving condition.

My wife's uncle had been the car's second owner. He bought it from a guy who had it sitting in his barn in Indiana and hardly drove it. When I got the car, it had 30,000 original miles on it. First, I had to replace the front brakes. The calipers were gone because the car had been sitting for a while. I also rebuilt the carburetor, replaced all the hoses, and fixed a couple of other minor things. Then it was ready to drive. I spent a bit more time and money to restore some of its original luster and performance, altogether less than $2,000.

I got the Corvette in 2018 and now it has 45,000 miles on it. I love the car. The color is beautiful, and I love the white interior. Not many Corvettes came with the white interior. When I'm driving, the car feels very powerful. It feels as if the long hood is all taken up by a big, long engine. It's not, but it feels like it.

The story of the Porsche is also interesting. My brother's wife bought the Porsche here in California, and I checked out the car for her and shipped it out to her. She and my brother live in Atlanta. Every time I went to visit him, I had to fix something on the car. So three years later, he asked me if I want to buy the Porsche. I am the Porsche's fourth owner, and it had just 55,000 miles on it. That's how I ended up owning a Porsche and the Corvette.

The way the world is going, every one of our cars will soon be electric. I am thinking about converting the Porsche and the Corvette into electric vehicles eventually. A friend of mine also has a 1961 MG, and he converted his car to electric. And I was looking into that too, but I bought the car for $1,500 and put another $5,000 into it, and it is worth maybe $20,000. I just don't want to spend another ten grand converting it into an electric vehicle.

What is your all-time favorite Corvette model?
It would be the 1963 split-window.

◀ **1977** Corvette C3, **Long Beach**, California, **USA** | November 9, 2021

TO NIKOLA, CORVETTE MEANS: FEELING, POWER, SLEEKNESS

Long-term car. Like the Porsche 911 G model, the Corvette C3 shaped an entire generation during its fifteen-year production run. From 1968 to 1982, boys dreamed of this Corvette, although at that time, the models with the soft bumpers were more popular because they looked more modern.

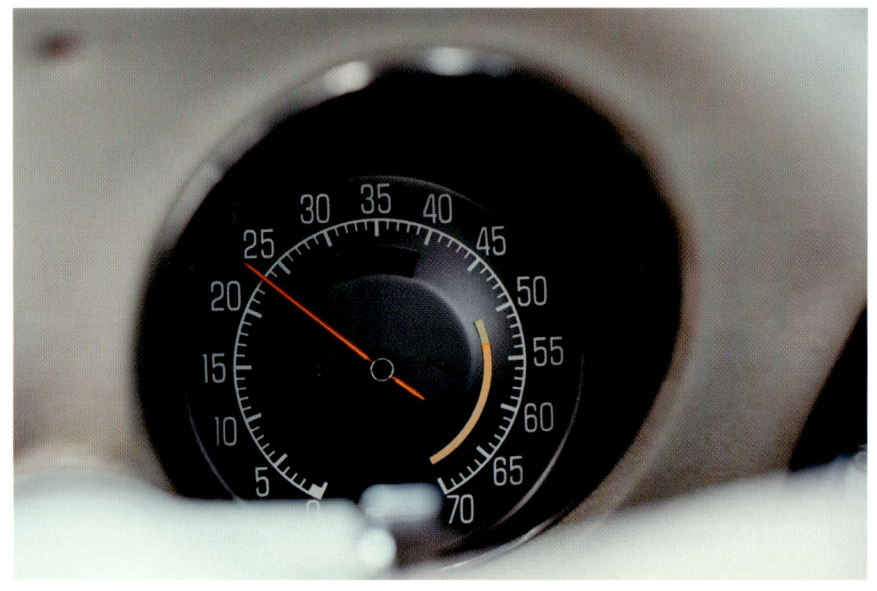

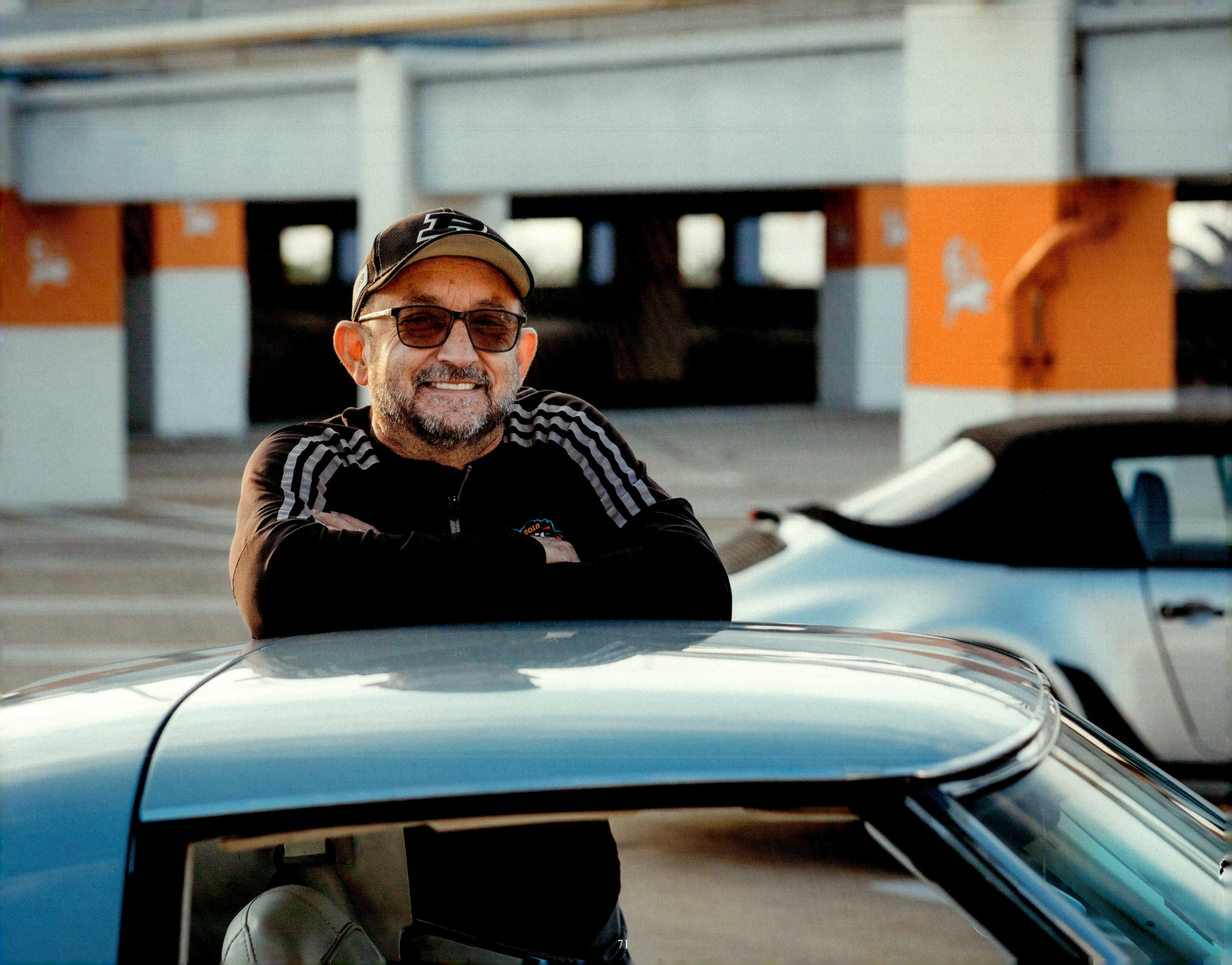

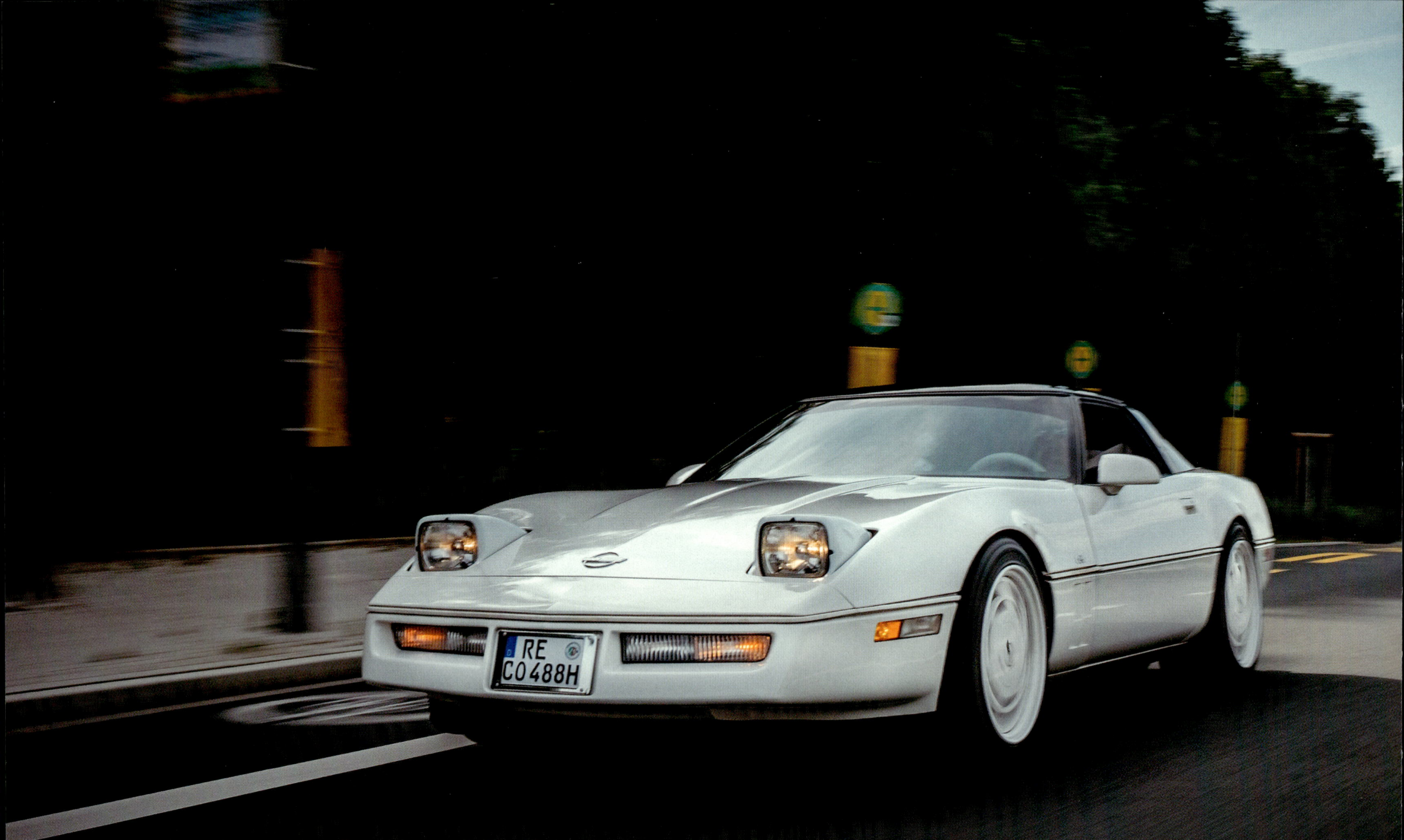
RE
CO 488H

25TH AND 35TH BIRTHDAYS

Everything began with a C6. Now, thanks to Andreas Eilenberg, two rare Corvette special models have found their way to the Ruhr region.

What is your Corvette story?
I will never forget it. My very first contact with a Corvette was through the magazine *Auto Bild*. There was a red C6 on the cover, in a drift with slightly smoking tires. The caption: *Porsche Killer at an Aldi Price!* That made my ears prick up, and I read the article carefully. I liked the car right away, but it was a coupe. My wife and I have been convertible fans since 1988. What I found exciting, however, was that the C6 made it into the legendary "300 Club" without any spoilers. The vehicle registration actually stated 300 kph. Most German manufacturers had limited their cars to 250.

The next day, I found out where I could buy a Corvette, from the larger Opel dealers. So in the fall of 2004, I drove to a large dealership in Dortmund that also had the Corvette in their program. Once there, I had to find out where the American sports car was. Somewhere in a corner in the rear of the dealership, I finally found myself standing in front of the car. I then had to realize that this was not the vehicle I had read about in the test report. I went back to the salesman and told him that I was interested in the C6. He told me that the Corvette in the showroom was a C5. He said that, when the C6 came out the following year, I would no longer be able to buy the car here at the Opel dealership. Aha. This all seemed a bit strange to me, so I waited.

In the spring of 2005, I drove to the Kroymans company in Essen, which was celebrating its grand opening that day. There it finally was, the C6, but it was a coupe. According to one of the salesmen, the convertible was supposed to come six months later. At that time, I still had to sell my wife on the Corvette, and a little later, I took her to a customer event at Kroymans to show her the C6.

Our first test drive was then in the coupe (i.e., the Targa). We just wanted to try it out, because the convertible was also quite a bit more expensive. We asked the salesman to remove the roof parts, and then we headed down the highway in the direction of Düsseldorf. At a certain speed, a very unpleasant droning started. It wasn't a real convertible feeling, so no Corvette for us for the time being. We had to be patient for a while. In August 2005, we ordered our first Corvette. A convertible, of course.

We spent the first two years on the road just for ourselves. Car clubs were not really our thing, but then we saw a black C6 convertible in the city and exchanged greetings. The owner of the black Corvette bought a C3, and he must have known where I lived, because one day he drove it into my yard. We immediately began talking, of course, and he told me about the German Corvette Forum. He also told me about the monthly Corvette regulars' table in Bergkamen and invited my wife and me to join. So we slowly arrived in the Corvette scene, made friends with more and more other owners. And all of them told us again and again that we absolutely had to go to the Corvette meet in Suhl. In 2013, we went there for the first time. We met up with a few Corvettes in Bergkamen and set off in a group of twelve cars. That was really ingenious! With twelve Vettes on the freeway and the country roads, you can't help but attract a few astonished looks.

Because I am used to getting up early due to my shift work, I also wake up early while on vacation or on weekends. In Suhl, it was no different. So I used the time to wash my car. As I enjoy doing that, I began cleaning the windshields of my friends' Corvettes just for the fun of it. And one day, I cleaned the windshield of a C3 Pace Car. The color scheme immediately caught my eye. It was spectacular, this black combined with silver and the red pinstripe, plus the silver interior.

Since the meet, I have delved a little bit more deeply into the Pace Car subject and talked with Anke from our regulars' table at length about it. Anke often flew with her husband to the USA for auctions and knew everything about the cars, which was truly impressive. She gave me all the details. At the time, I didn't know that only 6,502 C3 "Indianapolis 500 Pace Cars" were built, and only 212 of them with a manual transmission. She said that if I could find a shifter with the big engine, I would have hit the jackpot.

So I started looking and found a pace car in the States. I was in contact with the seller for half a year. I wanted to see pictures, of course, lots of pictures. And not only from above. The seller was probably selling the car for a friend, and so every request for a photo or video dragged on, as they had to coordinate every time. At some point the Corvette was sold without me really noticing. So my search went on.

Less than four weeks later, I discovered a C3 in England. It was a car with a traceable history. It had been purchased in 1988 by a couple in Houston, Texas. In 1991, the Corvette came to the UK with 14,000 miles on it. In England, the car had three more owners. The last, from whom I bought the car, had added the Corvette to his collection as an investment only, together with a C5 Pace Car. That all sounded very good, so Martina and I flew to England.

The owner was so nice and picked us up at the airport. Overnight, I read through all the documents about the car, and the next morning, the seller was standing in front of the hotel with his wife and the car. During the test drive, I sat on the passenger side for the first time. With the left-hand traffic and a completely unfamiliar car, I didn't want to take any risks. I concentrated on how the pace car sounded and whether all the gauges were working. Everything was first rate. After about an hour of test driving, I took the car out for a spin in a large parking lot to get the feel of it. We have had the Corvette since December 2015.

So much for the C3, but it didn't stop there. In 2019, between Christmas and New Year, I sat at my computer and read on Wikipedia the history of the Corvette—C1, C2, C3, and then came the C4. Then I found out that there is a younger sister to my C3 anniversary model. Even fewer of the 35th Anniversary version were built than my Pace Car anniversary model—just 2,050 units, and only 180 of them with a manual transmission.

I was totally fascinated and began searching for such a Corvette with a manual transmission. Surprisingly, on an American platform, I quite soon found an ad for a matching C4. The Corvette was at a small car dealership in Santa Fe. The store had mainly European and Japanese cars on the lot.

I immediately sent an email and received a response two minutes later. They answered my every question immediately and in detail and sent me pictures and videos of all the details I wanted to see. That gave me a really good feeling, because everything just clicked right away. On March 6, 2020, I signed the purchase contract, a very good decision. The C4 has resulted in two great friendships. On the one hand, we have become friends with the couple that owned the dealership, Susan and Paul, who have been in well-deserved retirement since the end of 2022, and secondly with the shipper who brought the Corvette to Germany.

What is your all-time favorite Corvette model?
The Corvette C1 or C2.

◀ **1988** Corvette C4, **Recklinghausen**, North Rhine–Westphalia, **Germany** | September 12, 2021

TOP GUN
Original Motion Picture Soundtrack
ORIGINAL MOTION PICTURE SOUNDTRACK
TOP GUN
UP THERE WITH THE BEST OF THE BEST
DANGER ZONE - Kenny Loggins • MIGHTY WINGS - Cheap Trick • PLAYING WITH THE BOYS - Kenny Loggins • LEAD ME ON - Teena Marie • TAKE MY BREATH AWAY (Love Theme from "Top Gun") - Berlin •
HOT SUMMER NIGHTS - Miami Sound Machine • HEAVEN IN YOUR EYES - Loverboy • THROUGH THE FIRE - Larry Greene • DESTINATION UNKNOWN - Marietta • TOP GUN ANTHEM - Harold Faltermeyer & Steve Stevens •
Producers: Don Simpson, Jerry Bruckheimer
CHROMIUM DIOXIDE

CORVETTE

TO ANDREAS, CORVETTE MEANS:
GRINNING, RELAXATION, DRIVING ENJOYMENT

Style icons. While the C3 left its mark on the '70s, the Corvette C4 shaped the '80s. For this decade, owner Andreas Eilenberg not only had the right sunglasses at the ready, but also the right cassette soundtrack in the car.

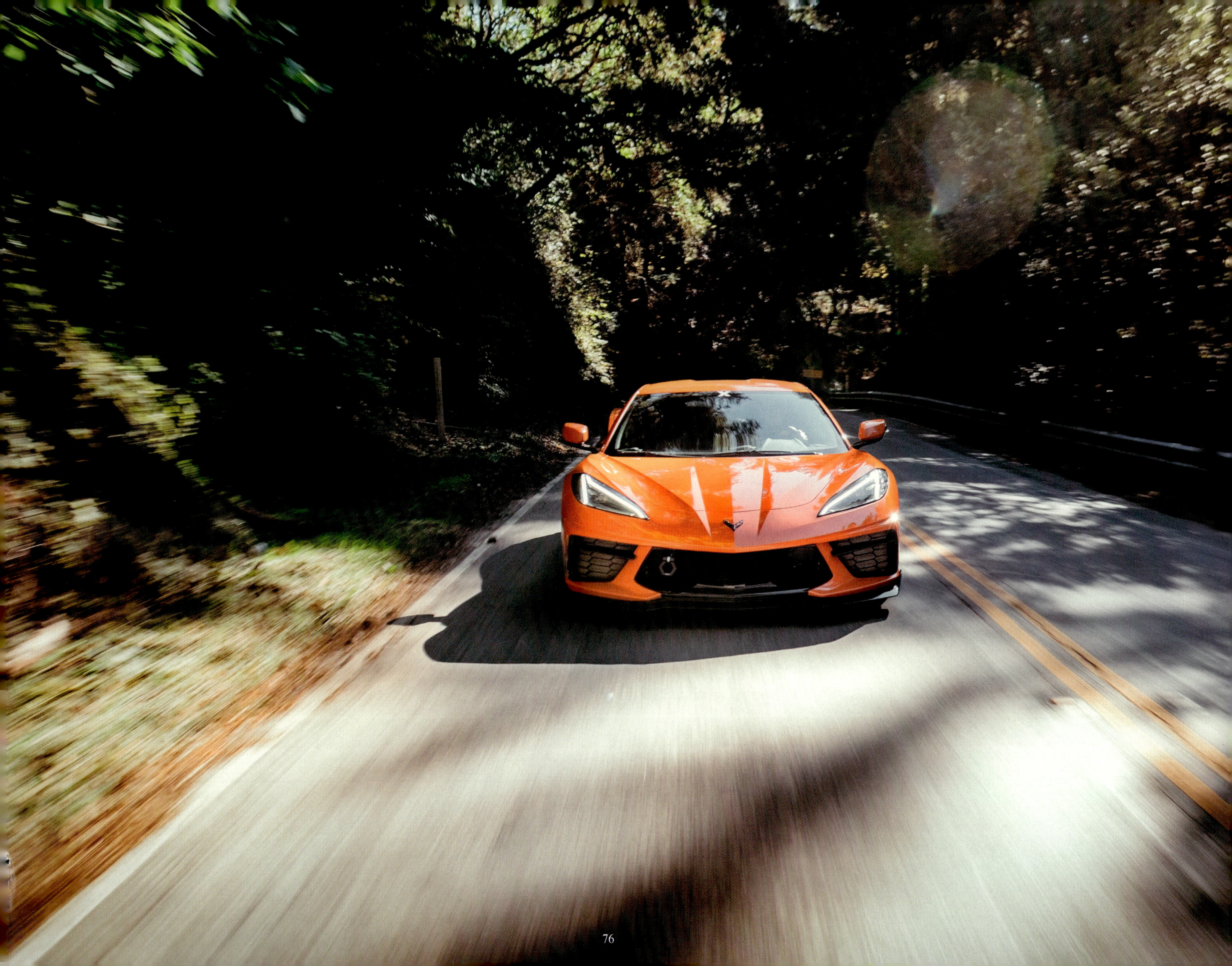

IT'S IN THE FAMILY

Keith Waldorf has been working on cars since his grandfather passed the car gene on to him. His grandfather handbuilt his race cars, and Keith has restored cars with his father and has driven Corvettes since he was old enough to drive. Today, he races on tracks all over the USA.

What's your Corvette story?
In 1935, my grandfather built a race car by hand. It was one of the old dirt track midgets that went around the track sideways. He built the car in the Thirties, hand-shaped the aluminum, built the chassis. He did the whole car and then raced it with a group of guys. World War II happened, and he had to go to war. Some of his guys who weren't in the war took his car and continued to race it. When he came home from the war, he raced that car again in the 1960s. And so cars, racing, and going fast are in my blood. When I was a kid in the 1970s, we went to the races all the time, and I just was really into cars.

Back in the day, we didn't have a lot of money, so anything to do with cars I had to do on my own. I had to get a job, fund it, and do the work myself. I've always been an American car guy. All the exotic cars of the time, like Ferraris and Lamborghinis, were out of reach. So the Corvette was a natural choice. And it was much more of a sports car than the other American options.

When I was 19, my dad and I bought a 1962 340hp Corvette C1 together. We restored and painted it. He didn't like that I always tried to hot-rod it and drive it hard. He wanted to keep it in nice condition. So he came up with the idea that I needed a mid-year Corvette, a C2, to restore for myself. We found a car in Sacramento, California. It was completely original except for the big flared fenders from the 1970s. But the engine was all original, as were the gauges, the seats, the full interior, and the convertible top. Underneath, it was completely original. The car was originally sold in New Jersey and later taken to Manhattan Beach, California. I am the third or fourth owner. I got it in 1991 or 1992 and was on a journey to retore the car.

I took the car apart, stripped it to the fiberglass, and repainted the body. It was supposed to be Ermine White with a red interior, but I preferred Nassau Blue with a black interior. So I went for that color. I still own the car. I've had it for thirty years. That was the first car I restored from scratch by myself. And it sold me on Corvettes.

I love the car, and the look, and everyone who sees it loves it. It's an eye-catcher at every car show I take it to. Driving it with the top down on the back roads with the side exhausts sounds great. You don't break any speed records, but it's just so much fun. I love the car. I will never sell it, and it will eventually go to my son.

A few years later, my passion for Corvettes was joined by my interest in motorsports. At work, I used to race in the simulator with some friends and colleagues. We raced for the best time on the digital Nürburgring, Laguna Seca, and all the legendary racetracks. At some point, that wasn't enough for us, and we decided to race on real racetracks with real cars. Most of the guys were Porsche enthusiasts, by the way.

I bought a 2006 Corvette C6 Z06 for our project. The car was a monster. It had a 700hp LS7 V8! Everything about the car was designed for the racetrack. Its coilover suspension, racing harnesses, optimized brakes, different transmission, and cooling system were all designed by a professional racer. At that time, the Corvette was perfect for the racetrack. I got faster and faster as time went on. In turn one at Laguna Seca, I hit 130 mph at times. All this without a fire-extinguishing system, without a roll cage. If something had gone wrong . . . so I had to take my C6 to the next level or buy a real race car. That's when the C8 came into play.

But there was another reason for my decision to buy a C8: I wanted to try something new. The C8's mid-engine concept is unlike anything I've driven before. When everyone started talking about the new Z06, I thought I'd put my C6 up for sale on the Corvette forum to help finance the new Corvette. Shortly thereafter, GM announced that it would be at least two more years before the Z06 would hit the market. That was definitely too long for me.

Soon afterwards a gentleman from Virginia made an offer for my C6. We went back and forth for a while, but his offer simply wasn't good enough. Then he wrote something interesting: "If my offer isn't high enough, I do have a C8. How about a trade?" And so we reached an agreement. I sold him my C6 and in return got his Z51 Corvette C8 in Sebring Orange. I had never had an orange car before, but the color simply looks great on the C8. As the seller lived in Virginia and I in California, we had to arrange transport. Because of the pandemic, it was difficult to find a shipper, so we loaded the cars onto trailers ourselves and met in the middle, in Amarillo, Texas.

It was a funny situation. Each crawled around the other's car and inspected it carefully. He test drove my car and I his. We also had a small race on the freeway, and my Corvette made the more modern C8 look pretty old. My C6 Z06 was simply incredibly fast. We subsequently exchanged papers and loaded the cars—done! That was in June 2021.

Are you happy with the C8 or do you miss your old Z06?
The old Z06 was difficult to drive at low speeds, and the asphalt here on Skyline Boulevard was not made for the car. The roads here are quite rough, and that is definitely not good for the car's suspension and the racing rims. The Corvette was perfect for the racetrack, but it was not made for casually driving round the neighborhood. I am also a driving instructor for the Hooked on Driving company. The company rents tracks like Sebring, Laguna Seca, and Sonoma Raceway. There the clients learn how to handle their cars on the racetrack. I always had to trailer my C8 to events. Now I can drive my C8 to the events, have fun on the road, and in the evening drive somewhere with my wife to eat.

That is my Corvette story. We have a C1 in the family, we have my C2, we had a C3, we have a C6, a C7, and now a C8 with the mid-engine. Zora Duntov wanted a mid-engine Corvette in the 1950s, and I think it's cool that now we finally have one.

What is your all-time favorite Corvette model?
That is really a good question. The C2 is simply one of the most beautiful cars ever made. But the C8 is so powerful and simply a super total package. I would say the C2 and the C8.

◄ 2020 Corvette C8, **Skyline Boulevard**, California, USA | November 12, 2021

TO KEITH, CORVETTE MEANS:
THE AMERICAN SPORTS CAR

Driving machine. The roads south of San Francisco, around Alice's Restaurant in Sky Londa, are an Eldorado for every car enthusiast. Winding roads lined with old redwood trees offer ideal conditions for experiencing the potential of the mid-engine C8.

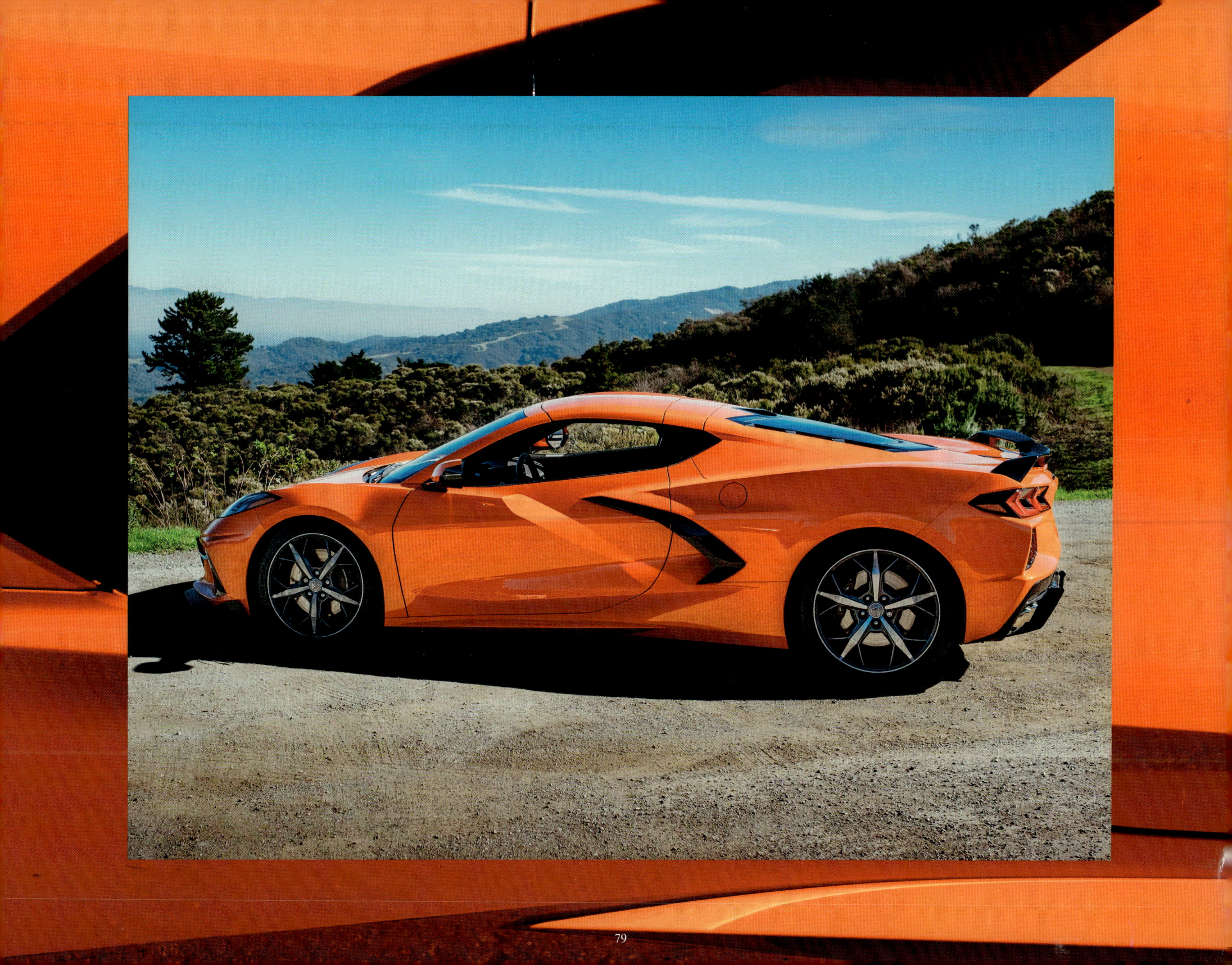

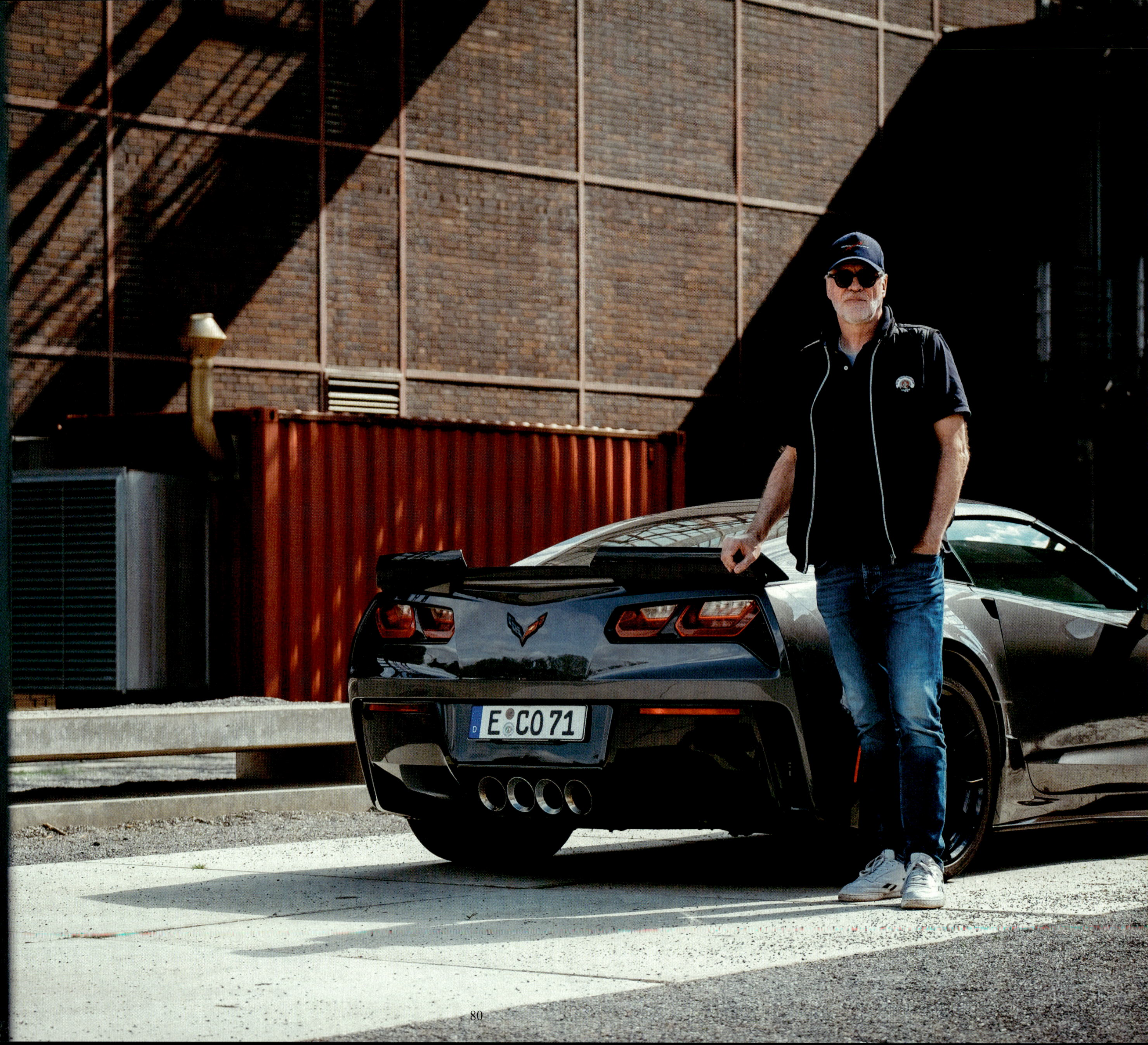
E CO 71

A RACE TEAM AND A SMURF

Martin Budde had to get used to the blue interior and exterior of his Chevrolet Corvette. In the meantime, however, his C7 is adorned not only with blue "hash marks," but also with the signatures of a number of successful Corvette racers.

What is your Corvette story?
It began for me in 1990. I was an appraiser in an office in Castrop-Rauxel and had a special customer in Essen. The head of the company had many cars and always drove a Mercedes SL. When he heard about the Corvette C4 ZR1, he was very interested and, in no time, imported one from Canada. It was metallic dark green with leather the color of cognac. A dream in my eyes! He climbed into the car and made a circuit. Afterwards he said, "The Corvette is too hard for me, too loud; I don't want it."

I was in charge of his fleet at the time, and he told me to take care of the Corvette, to drive it until he decided what he was going to do with it. After six months, the car was sold to the Corvette Center in Mörfelden. I was very sorry to see the car go. That was my unintentional entry into the Corvette scene, so to speak. I knew that I would eventually have one of my own.

After having several SLs and Porsches for a few years, I bought a gray Corvette C6, a special Performance Edition model, in 2011. Until 2017, I drove it without any problem, had no trouble with the engine or anything like that. She was just a lot of fun to drive.

When the Corvette model year change took place, my good friend Edgar Fiebig, himself a C7 driver, drew my attention to a new model in Mönchengladbach. So we went there, and there was a metallic gray Collector Edition Corvette in the showroom. When I saw the interior, I almost fell over with shock. Horrible blue leather everywhere. I said, "You can't do that to me; it's a Smurf car!" Incidentally, I have a little Smurf in my glove compartment, a gift from the originator. But the far bigger problem at the time was that I couldn't really sit well in this car.

Two weeks later, I was shown a vehicle whose seats had been modified so that I could fit without any problems. That had probably been ordered by a customer who was also a bit taller. So the argument of the lack of space suddenly fell away. Two days later, I signed the contract for the blue C7. In the meantime, I have grown to like the Tension Blue color. It just makes the Corvette a little different than the other C7s you see.

Immediately after my purchase, I was invited by the *Autosalon am Park* to a race event at Zandvoort. Included was access to the paddock and the Callaway Competition tent. We were even able to spend the lunch break with the drivers. I sat with Daniel Keilwitz, who unfortunately couldn't drive at the time because he had broken his leg. During lunch, I had an idea. I asked Daniel if he would autograph my car for me. He said he wouldn't sign a brand-new car, that I was crazy.

I then talked to team boss Ernst Wöhr and asked him to round up his guys so that they could all autograph my Corvette as well. He liked the idea, and the team's drivers all signed, one after the other. On the right front Daniel Keilwitz and Erst Wöhr, and on the left Jules Gounon and Renger van de Zande. Incidentally, this team ended up winning the 2017 GT Masters.

These signatures are now constant companions on my tours. Just last weekend, I was on the road with 22 other Corvettes in Alsace. For me, the C7 is a real Grand Tourismo. I have driven many fast cars, but none was as honest in its handling as the Corvette. It is absolutely my touring car. I will definitely keep my C7; the C8 is not an option for me. I test drove the new one, and yes, it is a perfect car, no question. But I just miss that nice long hood when looking forward. That to me is part of the identity of the earlier Corvette.

I've been thinking about a C2 coupe for a while now, though. That's my dream of a Corvette. I'm even thinking about getting one with an automatic because I want the car for cruising. Edgar, who brought me to the C7, has been trying to get me a C2 for four years. I was close to buying one once. The Corvette was in Cologne, a red one, with automatic transmission, power steering, air conditioning, brake booster; everything was in it. But we could not agree on the price. It just wasn't meant to be. My motto: "I don't go looking for a car; the car must find me."

What is your all-time favorite Corvette model?
The C2 coupe is my favorite. Silver-color exterior, red interior, with knock-offs on it. That's wonderful.

◀ **2017** Corvette C7, **Essen**, North Rhine–Westphalia, **Germany** | September 12, 2021

TO MARTIN, CORVETTE MEANS:
FASCINATION, HISTORY, SERENITY

Blue man! All 935 examples of the Collector Edition C7 that were built wore plain metallic gray on the outside and bold Tension Blue on the inside. It's their feature. At least for Martin, it took some getting used to at first. Today, he celebrates it with his color-matching Smurf.

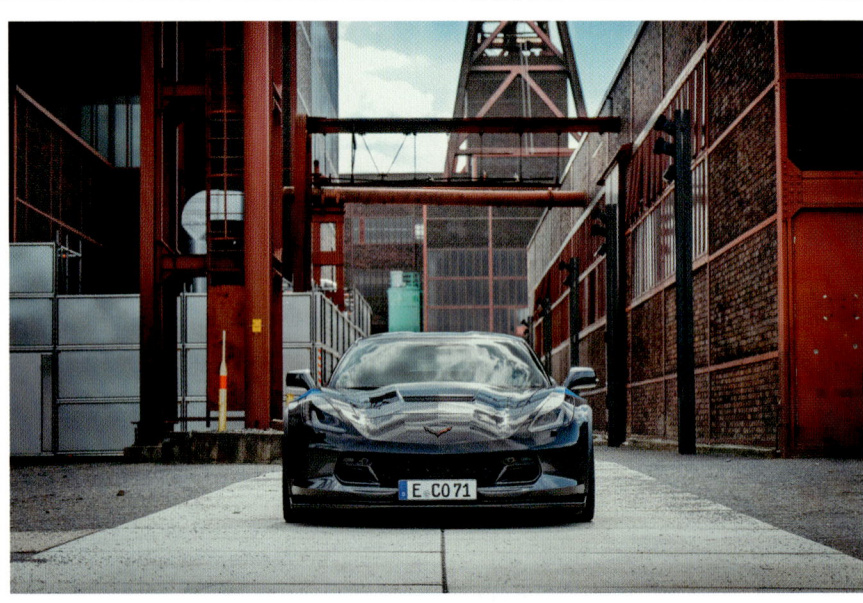

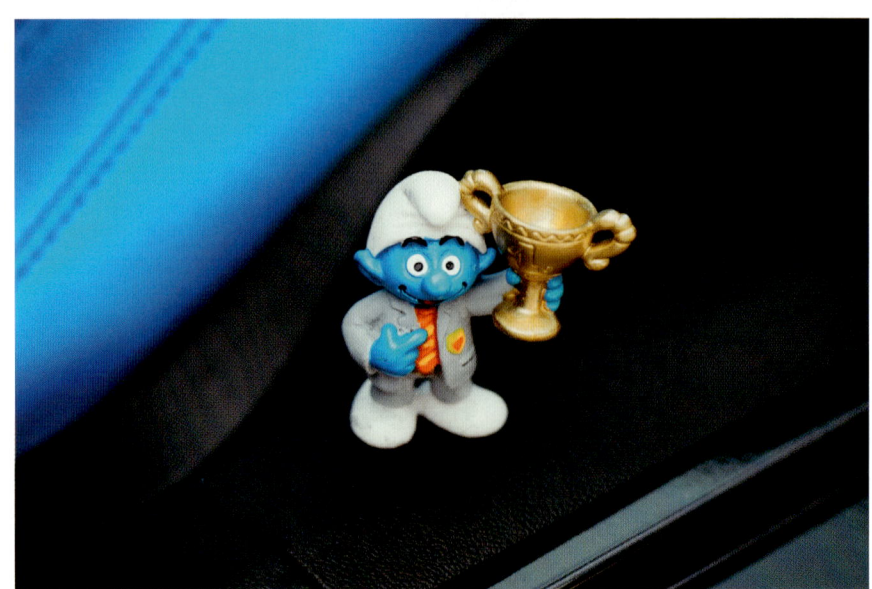

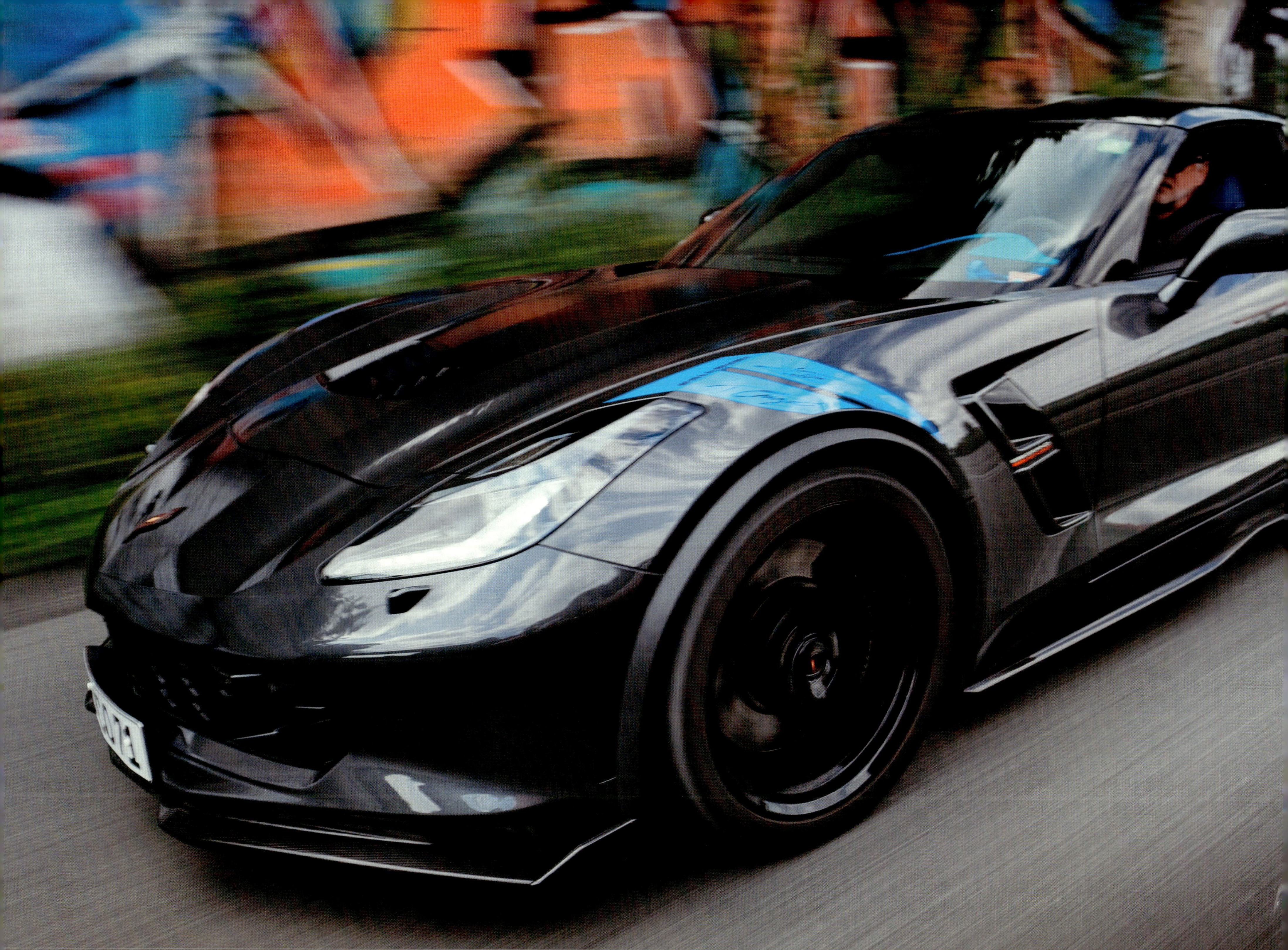

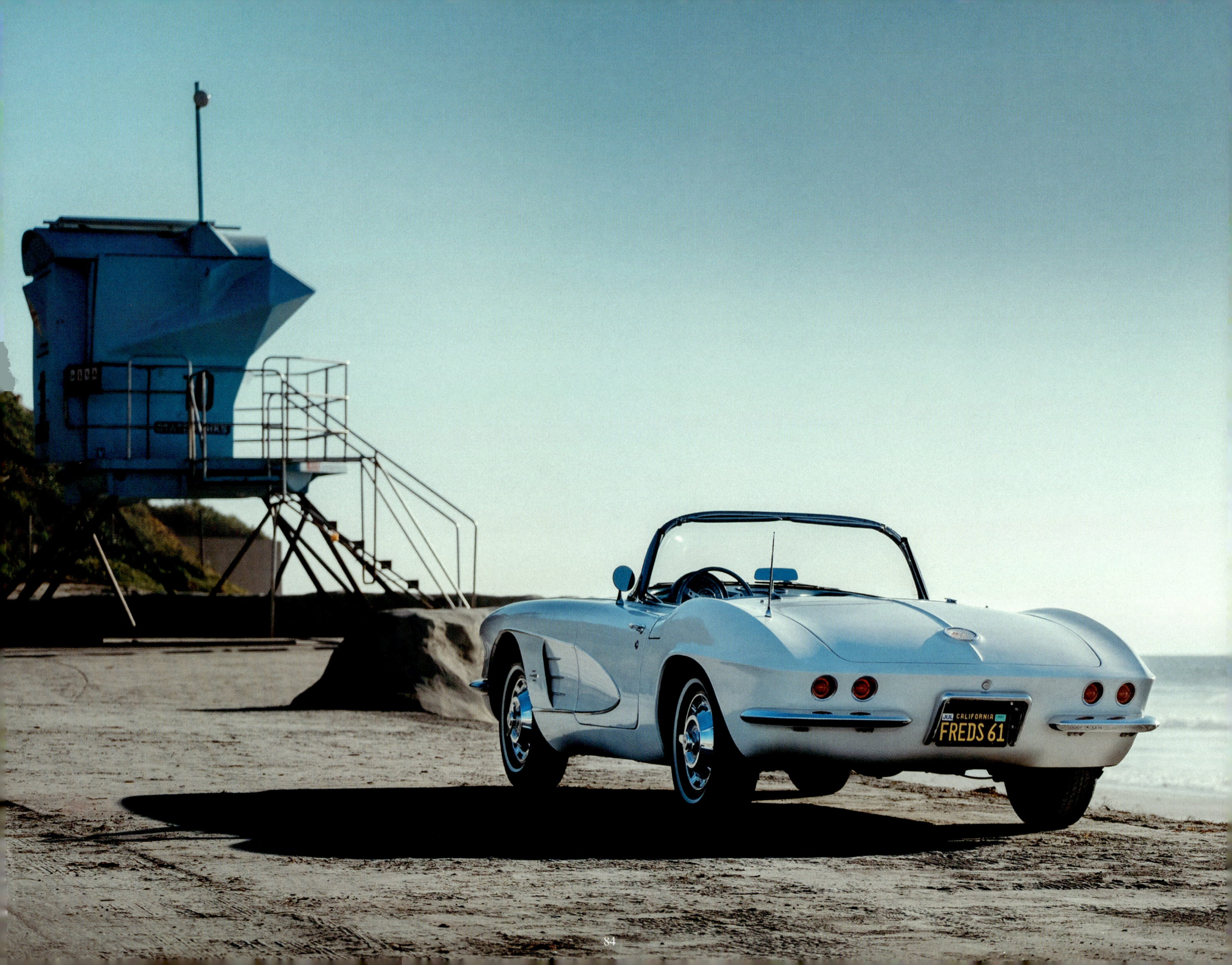
CALIFORNIA
FREDS 61

MANY MILES, MANY MEMORIES

Fred Kokaska's father bought a brand-new Corvette when he was eighteen years old. It now has more than 100,000 miles on the odometer and is still owned by the family.

What is your Corvette story?
I never went looking for the Corvette; the Corvette chose me. My father bought it new in 1960. He was then 18 years old and in the US Air Force. His grandfather helped him finance the car, for the price was far too high for a teenager. He drove the Corvette a lot, putting more than 100,000 miles on it, mainly between Mississippi, where he was stationed, and Chicago, where he lived.

He married my mother in 1964, and they had two children. Having a family changed the life of my father, who was also a pilot. As he got older, his interests turned more toward aircraft, and at some point, we acquired a small four-seat aircraft. As a result, the Corvette moved into the background. It was stored in a garage and remained there for more than thirty-five years.

My father died in 2011. While sorting and clearing out his things, we came upon his Corvette. As my sister had no interest in cars, my mother asked me if I wanted it. At the time, however, I had a 98 C5, was self-employed, and had two small children. I told her that I had no time to worry about the car. After a few beers with a good friend, he said that if I sold the Corvette I would regret it for the rest of my life. He was right.

The Corvette was in a really bad state. It was home to rats, the tires were flat, and the engine hadn't been started for years. But it was fun to work on the car. I got the engine running and restored the interior. The trim parts had to be re-chromed. This was done by a long-established business that had been around for some forty years. Chuck Smith, a local hotrod legend, overhauled the carburetor. The Corvette was already looking very good. I was also assisted by my son, who was twenty years old and interested in cars. He helped me by taking on several smaller projects. I hope that he will one day take over the Corvette when the time is right. He's definitely enjoying himself.

While restoring the convertible, I also took apart the small glove compartment between the seats. I planned to repaint it. On the inside I found a handwritten note—"Carol" next to a telephone number. As my mother's name was Carol, I asked her directly what she knew about it. She remembered writing down her number in the glove compartment when she met my father and was still in college. That must have been in 1962 or 1963.

But that is only one of many things that happened to me during the restoration. At some point, someone said to me, "You will never drive the car more than ten miles at a time." I thought to myself, Why not? My idea was to one day drive the Corvette along Route 66. In the beginning, I still had too many minor problems, and the car was not reliable enough for such a trip. But last August, after working on the vehicle for ten years, I finally drove it across the USA from San Diego to Carlisle in Pennsylvania, of course to take the C1 to the legendary Corvettes at Carlisle event. The car covered 6,000 miles during the trip. We drove down Route 66, spent the nights in old hotels, ate at old diners. We covered an average of 500 miles per day. On the last day it was just 100 miles from Amarillo to San Diego. Stupidly, we drove into the remnants of Hurricane Ira. It rained like crazy, water ran into the car everywhere, and the small windshield wipers were completely inadequate to deal with the cloudburst. That was rather scary, but nothing happened. One really does make such a trip only once in one's life.

What is your all-time favorite Corvette model?
I love every generation of the Corvette, but of course, my favorite is my C1 with all the history connected to it. As well, its design is simply timelessly beautiful. I still have my C5, which I bought new, because I like it so much. I am also on the waiting list for a Corvette C8 E-Ray. I'm very excited about that.

◀ **1961** Corvette C1, **San Diego**, California, **USA** | November 10, 2021

TO FRED, CORVETTE MEANS:
CONNECTION, PRIDE, MY FATHER

Hello, sunshine! When Fred Kokaska's father met his future wife and mother of his children in 1962, she left her name along with her phone number in the glove compartment. At the time, the Corvette was only a year old. Today, it is still family-owned and resides in California.

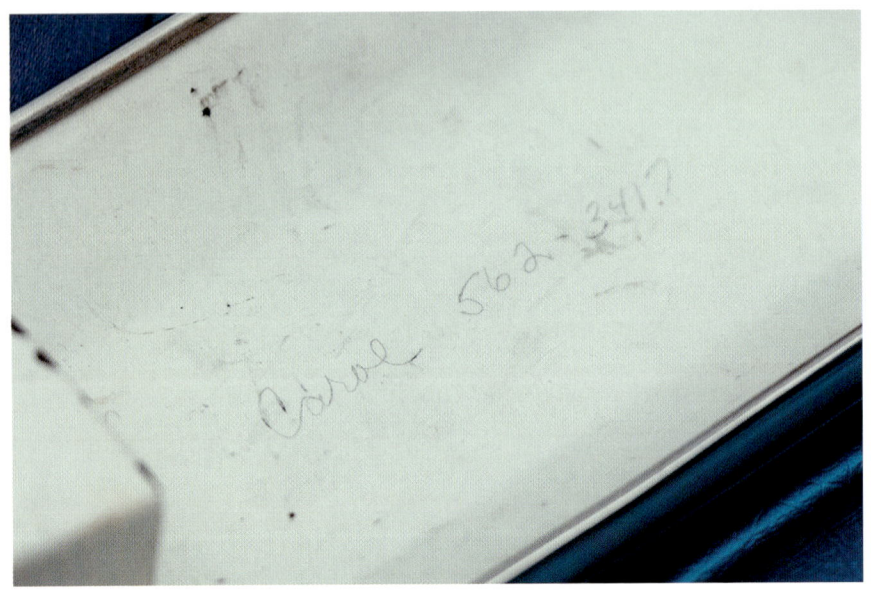

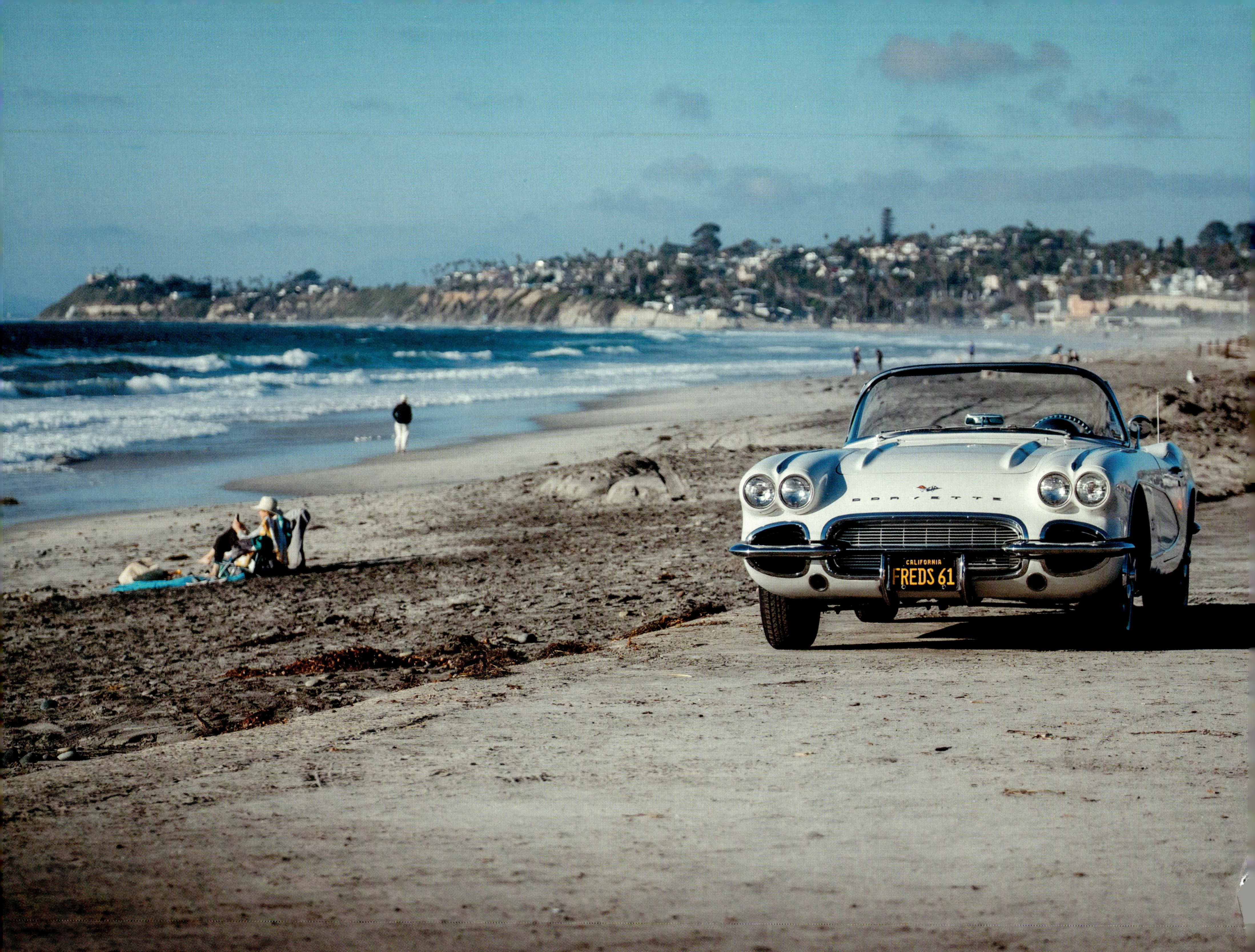
CALIFORNIA
FREDS 61

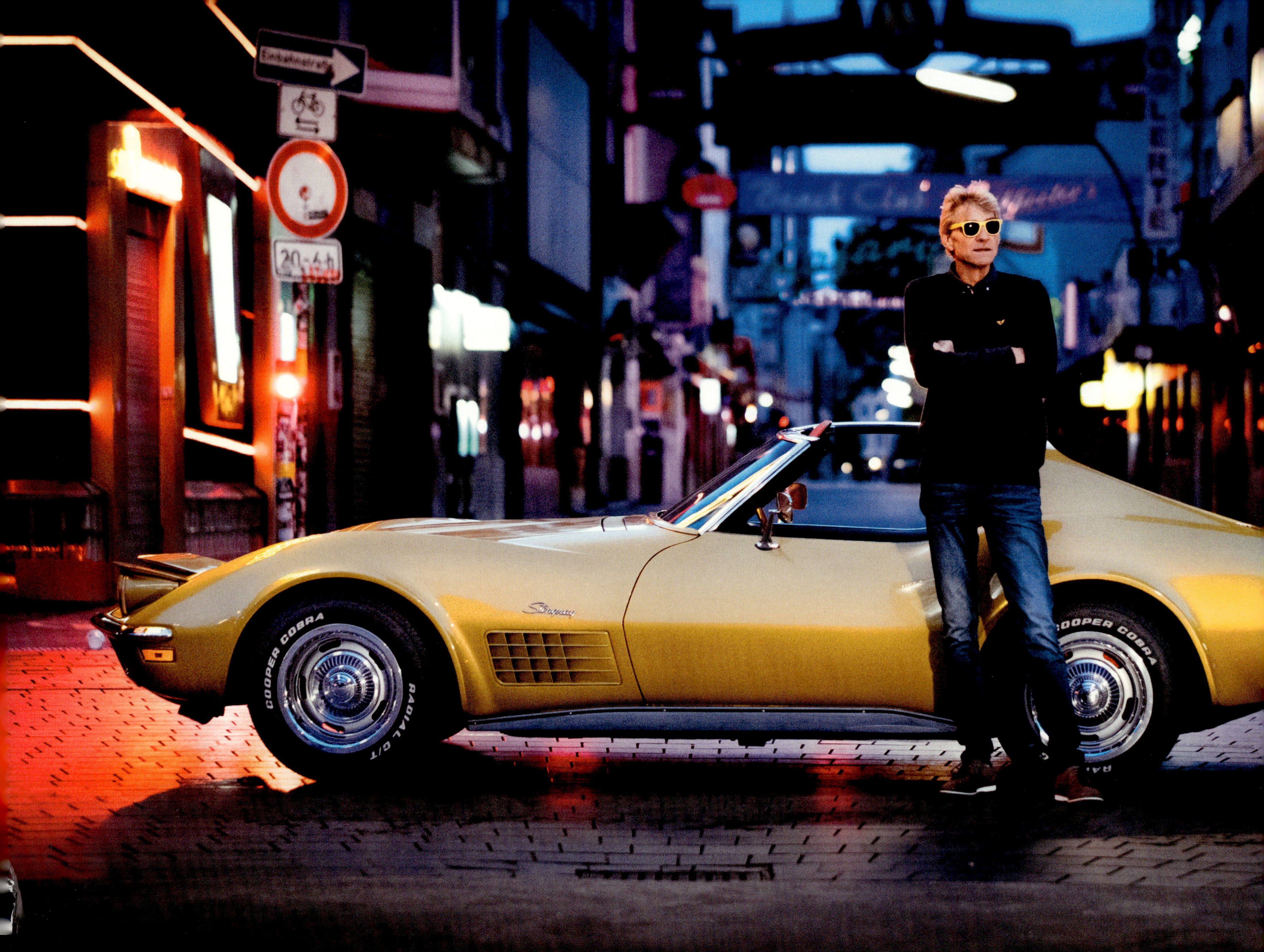

COOPER COBRA
RADIAL G/T
COOPER COBRA

HELLO FROM ST. PAULI

Ulf Jörgensen wanted an extraordinary Corvette. He achieved this wish 100% with a C3 in the rare color War Bonnet Yellow.

What is your Corvette story?
I previously had a 1971 Plymouth Barracuda, which began the V8 saga for me. At the time, I had already been to many auto shows. I always liked the old Ford F-100, beautiful pickup trucks. But I was simply too tall for that vehicle, and the pedals were too close together. And if I wanted to take my son, who is also more than six feet tall, with me, a truck like that would be somewhat cramped. Then I saw the Corvette C3 at a show. From the front, from the back, from the side, actually from every viewpoint, it simply looked sleek, cool, and sporty. Then there were the beautiful details, the pop-up headlights, and the hidden windshield wipers, simply mega.

There were, however, major differences between model years of the C3. Models with and without chrome bumpers, with and without glass top, and so on. I liked the early models until 1972 with the chrome front and rear bumpers the best. They were of course also the most expensive of the C3 Corvettes. How could it be otherwise?

So I went on the hunt for a third-generation Corvette. In 2015, I found what I was looking for, and since then, I'm very happy that I chose the Corvette. It is in original and good condition and has never let me down until now. I also really liked the War Bonnet Yellow color right away. I would never have taken a white, black, or even a red Corvette. I wanted something out of the ordinary and got that with my yellow-gold C3.

Not many Corvettes were made with the War Bonnet yellow color and a leather interior, which is why from the beginning they were especially well cared for, driven little, and displayed at many car shows. There is currently 50,000 miles on the car's odometer. At some point, the C3 was exported by a gentleman from Finland and arrived in central Europe. He had never registered the Corvette, and with its red Finnish license plate, it was driven only a little. A Harley dealer from Celle finally brought the C3 to Germany, intending it for his daughter. The good man had two or three other American cars, and at some point, he decided to sell them all so that he could acquire a C2. Consequently, the Corvette ended up on the internet, and it was there that I found it.

I arrived on the scene two days after I saw the ad. I took with me a friend who did a lot of work on American cars and therefore knew a lot more than I did. My expert's opinion was very important to me, and I can only recommend this to everyone. He found nothing negative about the vehicle, and I immediately made a down payment. As the Harley dealer had also not registered the Corvette, I became the Corvette's first registered owner in Europe.

What is your all-time favorite Corvette model?
That is definitely the C3. The C2 is not quite to my taste, and the C1 is a little too expensive for me. If my Corvette-owning days should come to an end, which I hope they won't, I don't know what else I would buy. The C3 is already my perfect car.

◀ 1971 Corvette **C3**, Hamburg, **Germany** | August 6, 2021

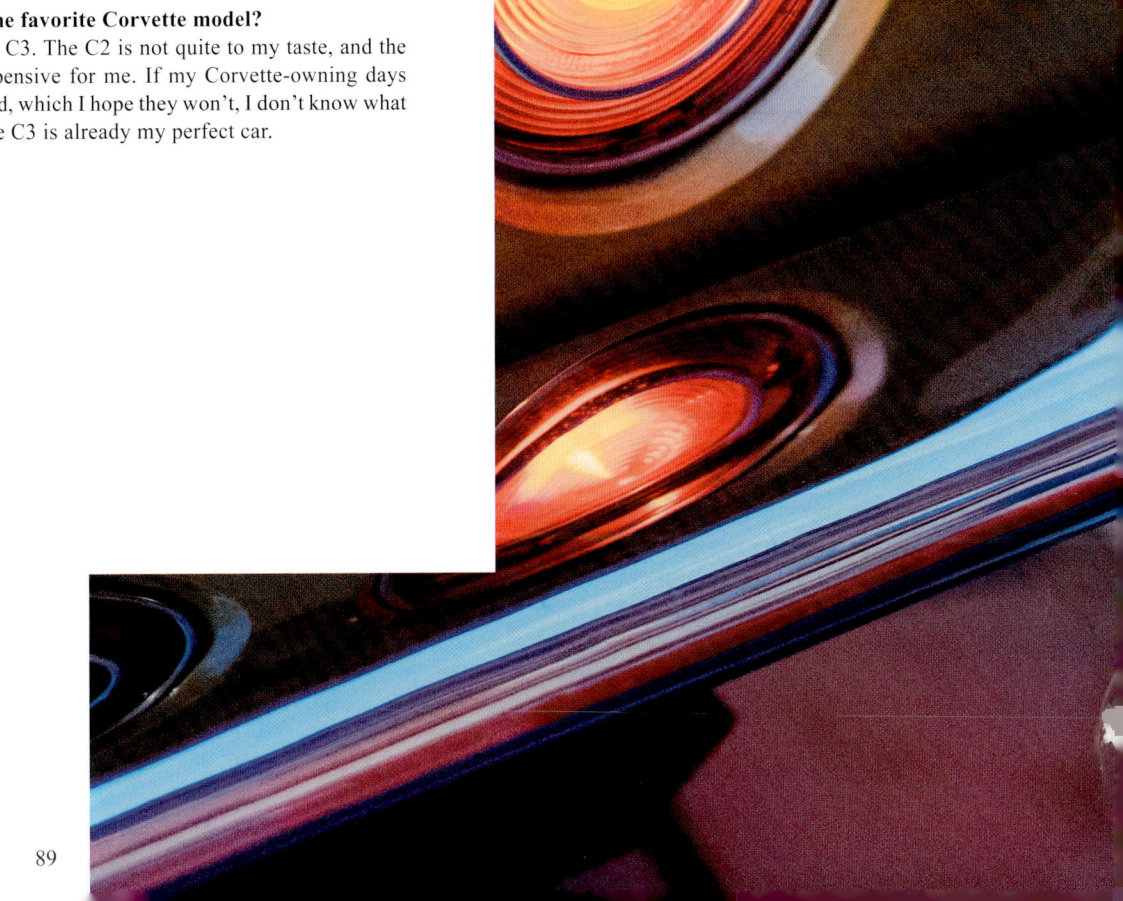

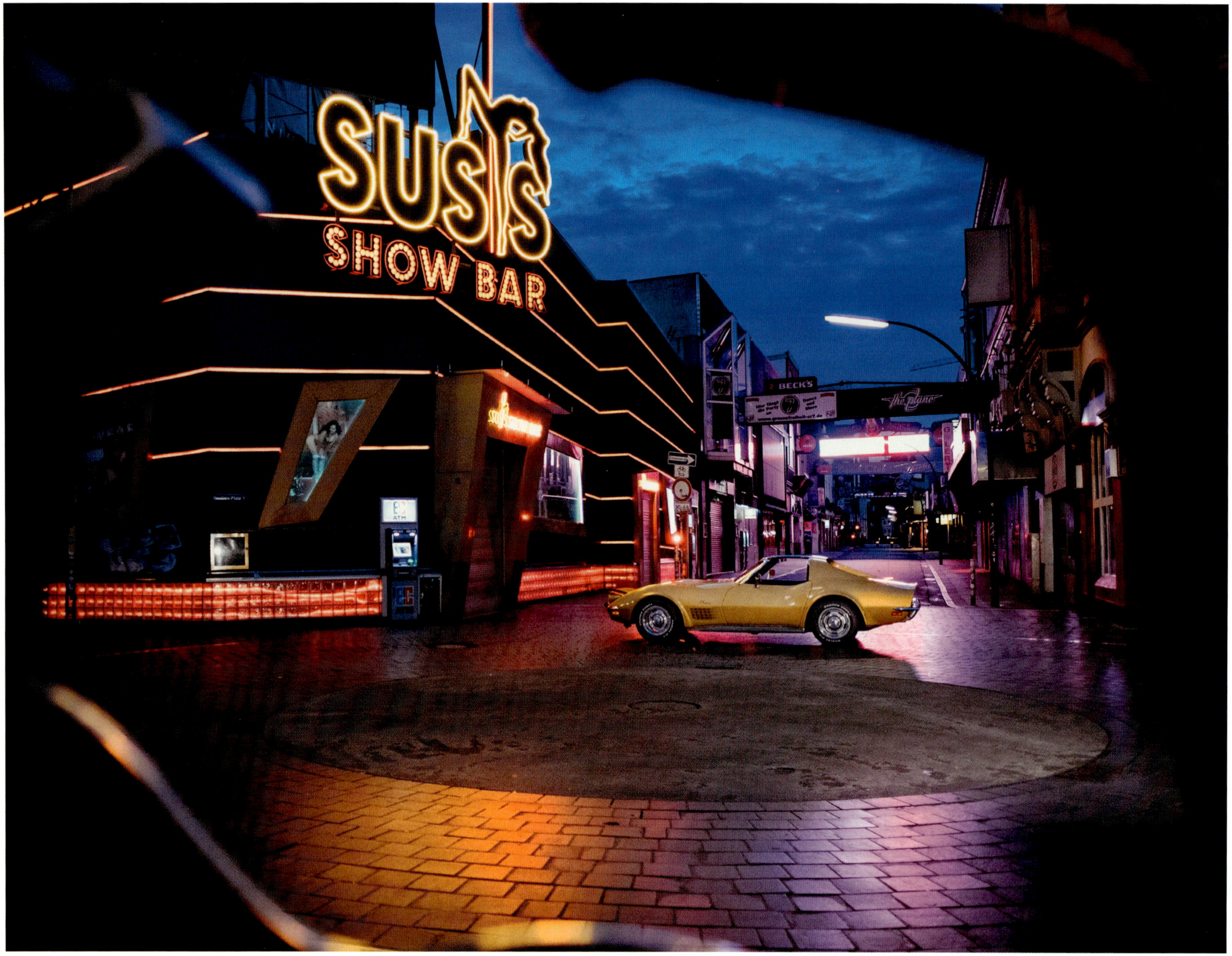
SUSI'S
SHOW BAR
BECK'S
ATM

TO ULF, CORVETTE MEANS: EMOTIONS, FREEDOM, FUN

King of the Kietz. In the 1970s, the third-generation Corvette was one of the dream cars of local hoodlums and small-time gangsters. In Germany at least, the C3s had a semi-seedy reputation and weren't a rare sight in St. Pauli either.

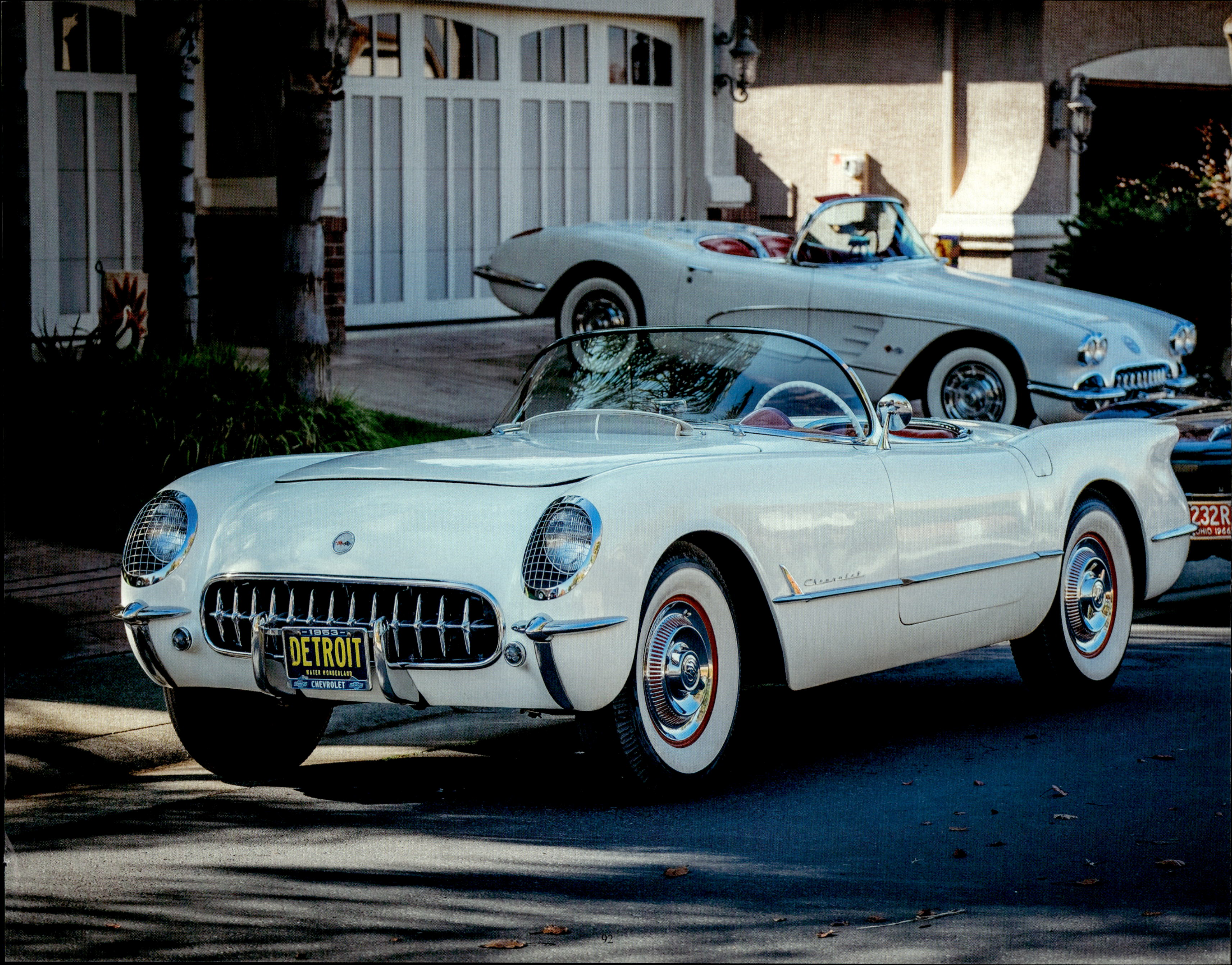
1953
DETROIT
WATER WONDERLAND
CHEVROLET

IN MEMORY OF A GOOD FRIEND

When Brian Martin worked for GM, he never dreamed that he would one day own a Corvette himself. Today he calls three of the old sports cars his own, including a legendary 1953 C1.

What is your Corvette story?
I was born in Dearborn, Michigan. Detroit was the center of the American automobile industry, and many friends and family members worked for the Ford Motor Company. A lot of people I knew drove Mustangs or other cars from Ford. I rarely saw Chevies. In my youth, however, I occasionally saw a Corvette on the road and thought, "Oh my God, what it that?" I was told that it was the first true American sports car. From then on, the Corvette had me under its spell.

I graduated from college with a degree in business administration and got the opportunity to work for General Motors, for the Chevrolet Motor Division. I was in my early twenties and completely fascinated by cars. The best thing: my employee ID card also gave me access to Chevrolet's archives. While on my lunch break, I often went to the basement and looked through the collection of documents. I enjoyed looking at the countless original documents concerning the history of Chevrolet, and of course, the papers on the history of the Corvette were of particular interest.

During my time in Chevrolet headquarters, Roger Smith was the head of General Motors. He lived in Bloomfield Hills, Michigan, and occasionally visited our office in Warren. If I overheard that Roger was coming to see us, there was a good chance he'd pull up in his 1953 Corvette. In that case, he would park it in the executive parking garage. I would look each time to see if I could spot his Corvette there. Every time I saw it in the garage, I was fascinated by that incredible car.

A few years later, I was working in customer service and was friends with a supervisor who was about to retire. He had an original hood emblem from a '53 Corvette on his desk. On his final day he said to me, "Boy, I know you love the '53 Corvette," and he gave me the tag. I could hardly believe that I owned a part of a '53 Corvette! The idea of someday owning a Corvette myself, let alone three of them, including one from the first model year, was completely absurd at the time. By the way, I still have the emblem that was given to me at that time.

A second is on my +5' Vette. How I got it is both sad and beautiful. I was then living in Chardon, Ohio, and was driving my +5' C1. Parked in front of a small ice cream parlor was a yellow 1965 Chevrolet Impala SS. An older couple was sitting beside it. I stopped to have a closer look at the car and entered into conversation with its owners, Denny and Ruth Burdick. Denny liked my Corvette, but he observed that the early models were not very well made. His father had been manager of a Chevrolet service department, and I told him that I had run the field service department of a car dealership. We spoke for quite a while, and he invited me to come and take a look at his old Corvette. When he told me that it was a +5', I was speechless and assured him that I would visit him.

About two weeks later, I was standing in front of his garage, and he opened the door. Before me sat a 1953 Corvette C1, covered and on GoJacks. I asked if I might have a closer look at the car and walked into the garage. I had my doubts that it was a real +5'. He pulled off the cover, and it was definitely one of the 3,640 examples from the first model year. I opened the driver's side door and the serial number confirmed it: number 133. When I saw it, I really began to tremble! That was a very special day for me. I told him that I would feel honored to help him in case he ever needed to repair anything on the vehicle or even just clean it. From this developed a close friendship. We often went to old timer meets together and talked about Corvettes.

Twenty years later, in June 2020, Denny unfortunately died. His family called and said that they wanted me to have the car. In December 2020, I bought the +5' from them. For me, it is a privilege to own one of the very first Corvettes, and I feel honored to continue living my friend's dream. The car really meant a lot to Denny and Ruth. It was important to them that the C1 would go to someone who would treasure it and not simply sell it off at auction. They wanted a true Corvette lover to have it, and they knew that I was the right one. There were a few things on the car that Denny wanted to repair—the broken antenna cable, for example. I have already taken care of everything he always wanted to have done. I know that he is looking down at me and saying, "Everything done right!" I appreciate very much the fact that Ruth Burdick and her children left the car to me.

I love the 1953 Corvette. It is the unique vision of Harley Earl, the father of the Corvette, and the first American sports car. A child of the "everything is possible" spirit of the postwar years in America. The boys came home from Europe and the war and wanted to enjoy their lives. Harley Earl knew what made a sports car and convinced GM to take on the competition from the Old World. The most beautiful thing about the +5' is that it is so pristine and uncomplicated, just the original. Harley Earl saw a market for so elegant and special a car, and it became more than a piece of technology. He made it into a work of art with performance. People wanted the Corvette because it was more than just a way of getting from point A to point B. The Corvette embodied an attitude towards life, travel, fun.

What is your all-time favorite Corvette model?
I love the car that started it all, the C1. It's fun just to look at the vehicle, to maintain it, or to drive it.

◀ **1953** Corvette C1, **1959** Corvette C1, **1966** Corvette C2, **Rocklin**, California, **USA** | November 13, 2021

TO BRIAN, CORVETTE MEANS:
ELECTRIFYING, AMERICAN, BEAUTIFUL

Six-cylinder. Anyone who thinks that real American cars all have V8s is mistaken. The history of the Corvette began in 1953 with the legendary Blue Flame straight-six, which, thanks to three Carter flat-flow carburetors, produced 150 SAE horsepower.

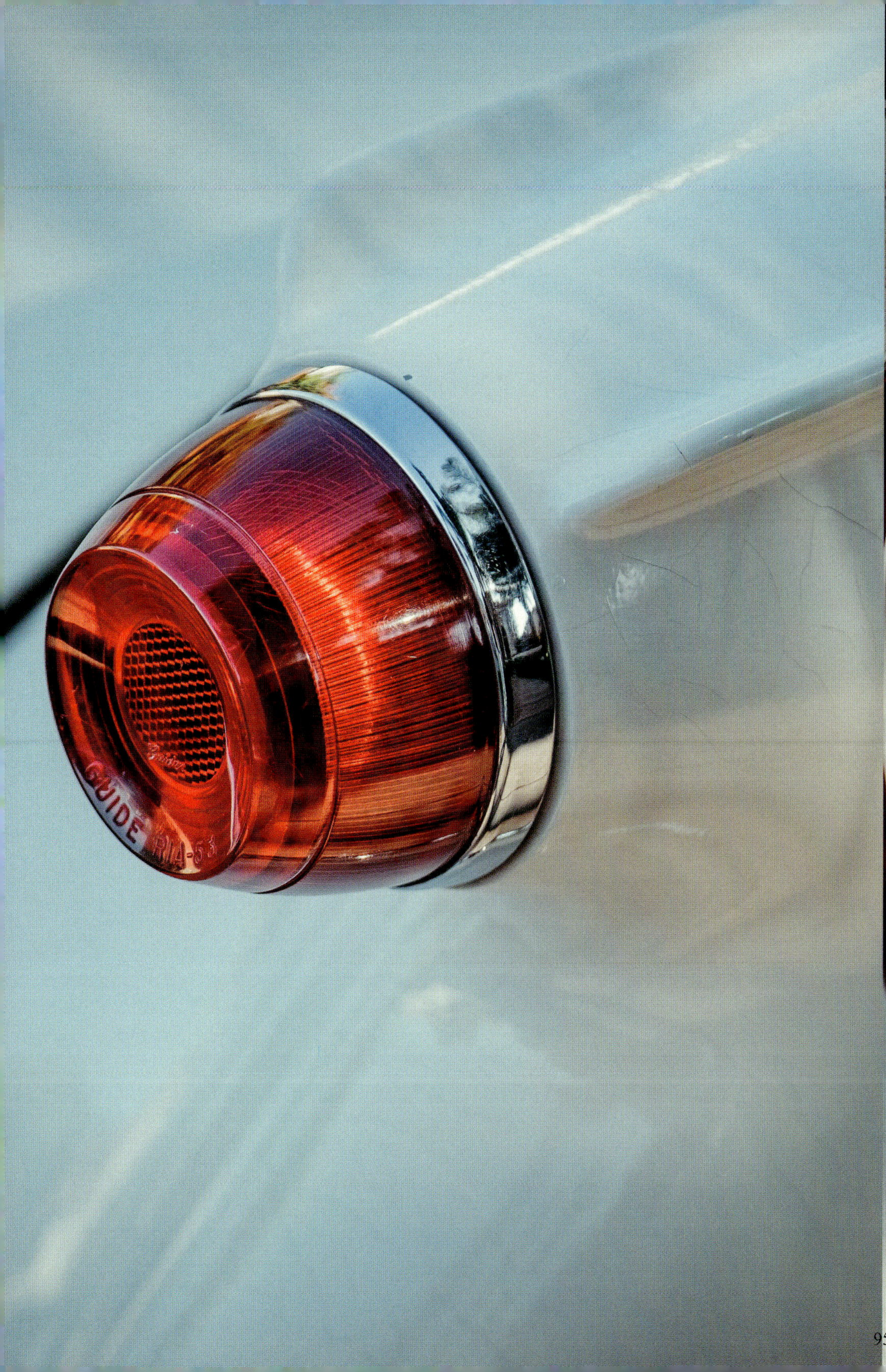
GUIDE
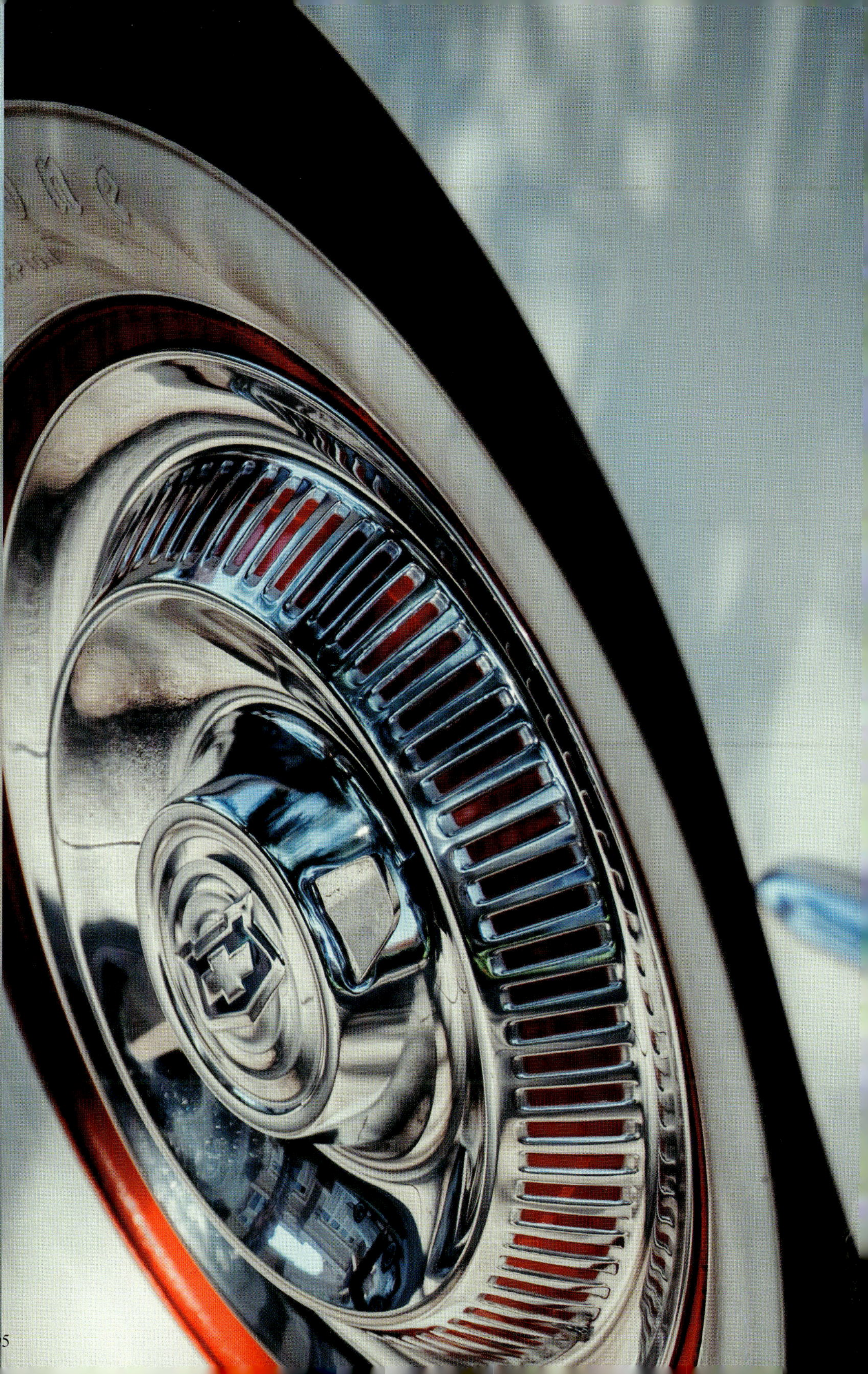

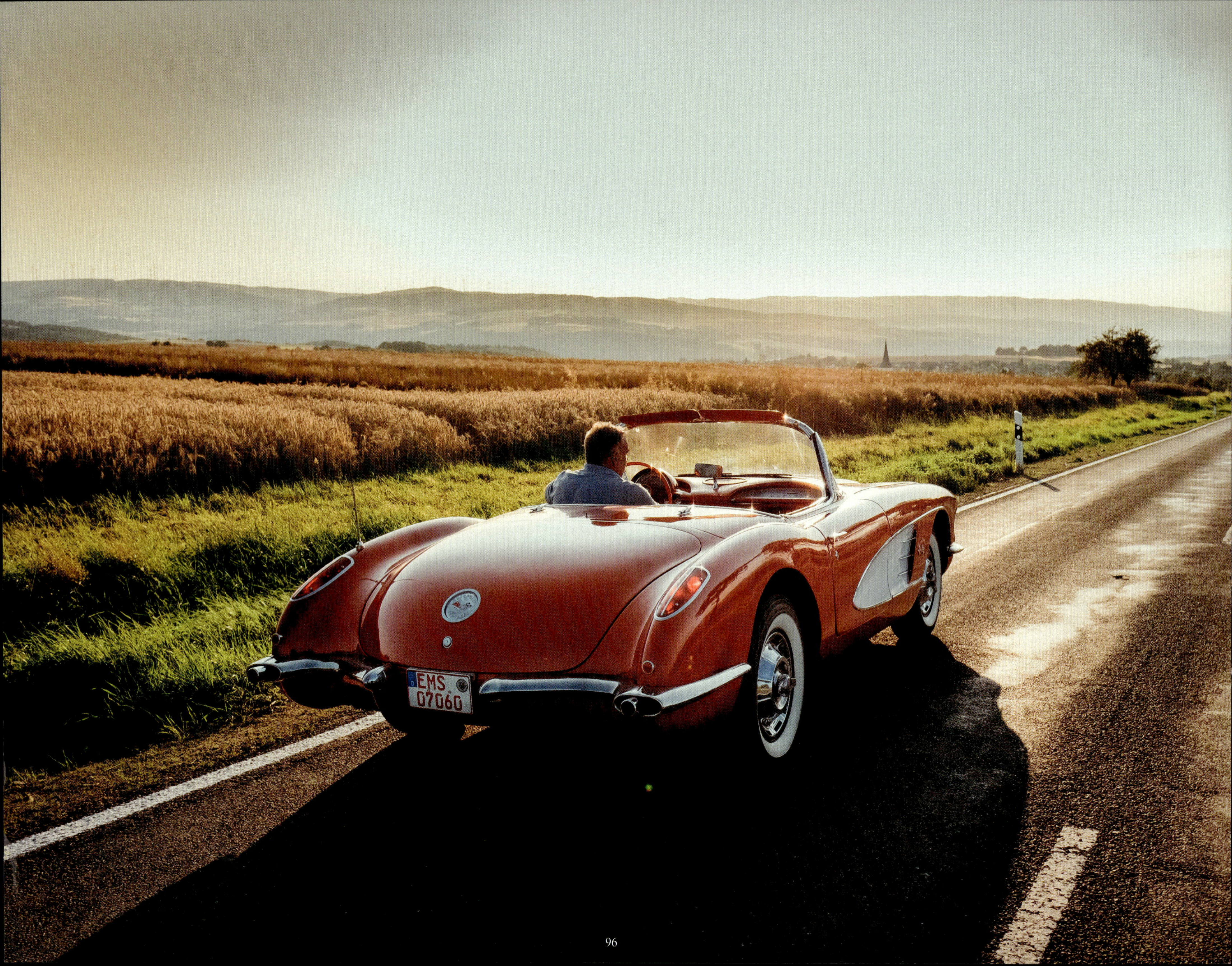
EMS
07060

WORKING ON CARS TO REMAIN BALANCED

Michael Dahlen bought his first Corvette, a red C1, with no idea of what he was getting himself into. It was the start of an intimate relationship that is still far from over.

What is your Corvette story?
I've always been car crazy, always had several different cars. Today, for example, I also have my '89 VW Corrado. I simply have always had a thing for special cars.

At some point, I decided that I wanted to buy a classic car. The first thing that came to mind was a Mustang. Then I looked around for other cars in the same price range. My red C1 was at a dealership, and I just bought it, completely clueless. I really knew nothing about the Corvette; went there thinking the car was made of sheet metal and found out that the body was made of plastic. So it was all new to me.

From then on, my affair with the theme continued to develop, and I bought one after the other. In between there was also a Mustang, but then I went looking for my next Corvette. I always keep my eyes open for cars that I like.

I'm self-employed and usually work seven days a week. When I need a break from the daily grind, I turn off my cell phone and go to the garage to work on my cars. Of course, I also like to drive, but not 100- or 200-kilometer tours. I like to cruise around the local area. For fun, and to see if the car still runs as it should. If not, I have something to work on again.

By the way, I bought the garage here because of the Corvette. I had another workshop, and suddenly there were four or five cars in it, some of them on lifting platforms. Then the red Corvette was added, and I just didn't have enough space, so I had to get something new and bigger.

How did you get your green C3?
My focus with the Corvette wasn't really on the C3 at all. I was thrilled with the C1 right from the start. Such a cool car; you just can't get more Fifties than that. But as time went on, I found the early C3 chrome models more and more interesting.

I found the C3 at a dealership in Pennsylvania and did not buy it until 2020. The color in particular excited me. What I didn't expect at all was the Corvette's exciting history. It was purchased new in New York in 1972 by a lady, the only previous owner. I found the original bill of sale, the handwritten purchase order, both window stickers, all the invoices, and insurance certificates. There are also invoices from 2014, which is basically when the car was turned upside down once and re-registered. In all those years the Corvette was only driven 24,000 miles. The car was a real stroke of luck you don't find that often.

Still keeping an eye out for other Corvettes?
Yes, I would like a gold C3 with a beige interior. I keep looking in the US and Europe, but unfortunately there are few good vehicles on the market. A dealer friend is rebuilding a C3 right now, so maybe that's just the Corvette for me. I still have a bit of room, so we'll see.

What is your all-time favorite Corvette model?
I like the C2 convertible best.

◀ **1960** Corvette C1, **Loreley**, Rhineland-Pfalz, **Germany** | July 21, 2021

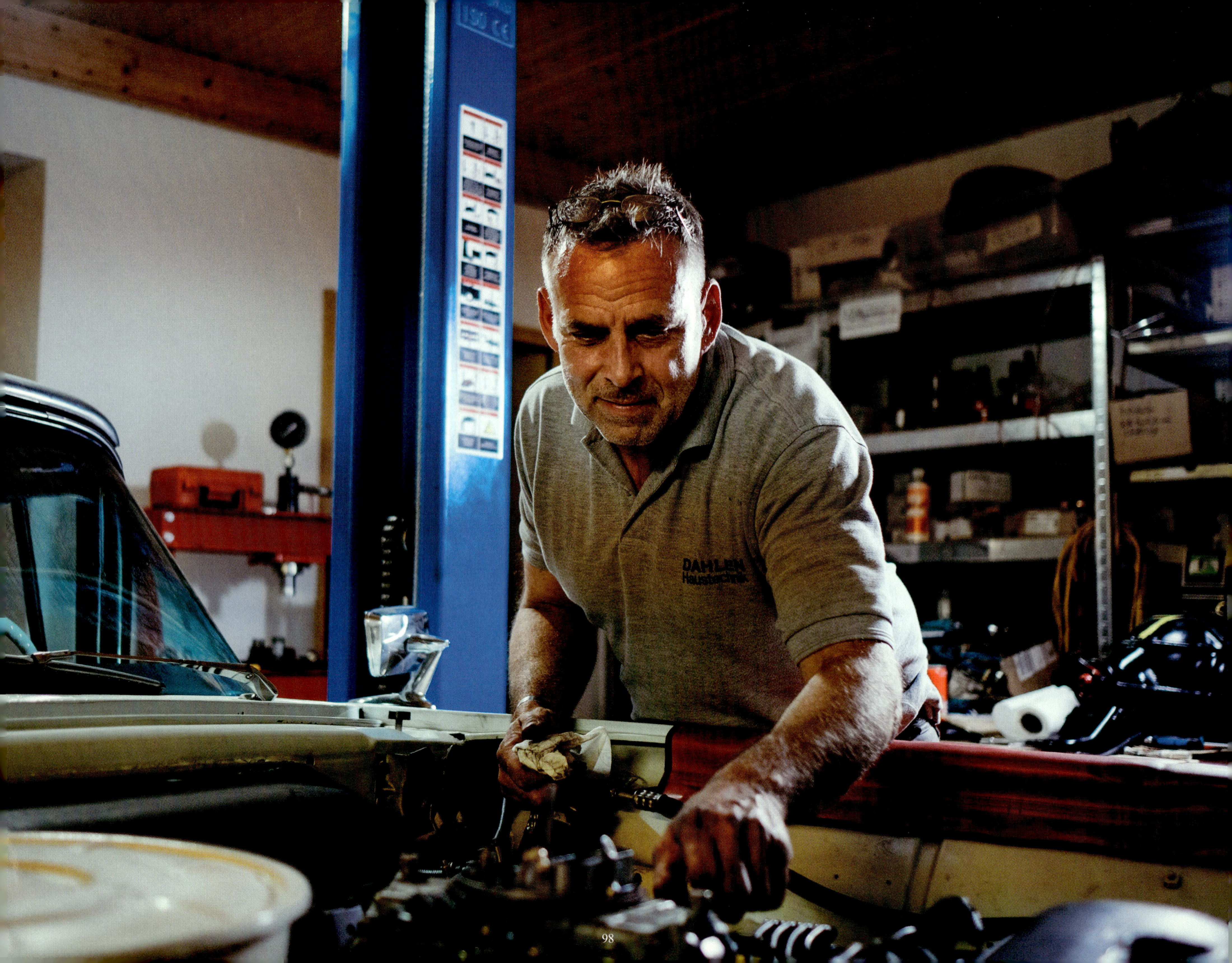
DAHLEN
Haustechnik

TO MICHAEL, CORVETTE MEANS:
RELAXATION, CRUISING, LOOKING

Flag alphabet. From the beginning, the Corvette logo was decorated with two flags. This has not changed to this day. The black-and-white checkered flag stands for sportiness, while the red flag bears the Chevrolet bowtie as well as a fleur-de-lis from Louis Chevrolet's family coat of arms.

▲ 1960 Corvette C1, **Loreley**, Rhineland-Pfalz, **Germany**

99

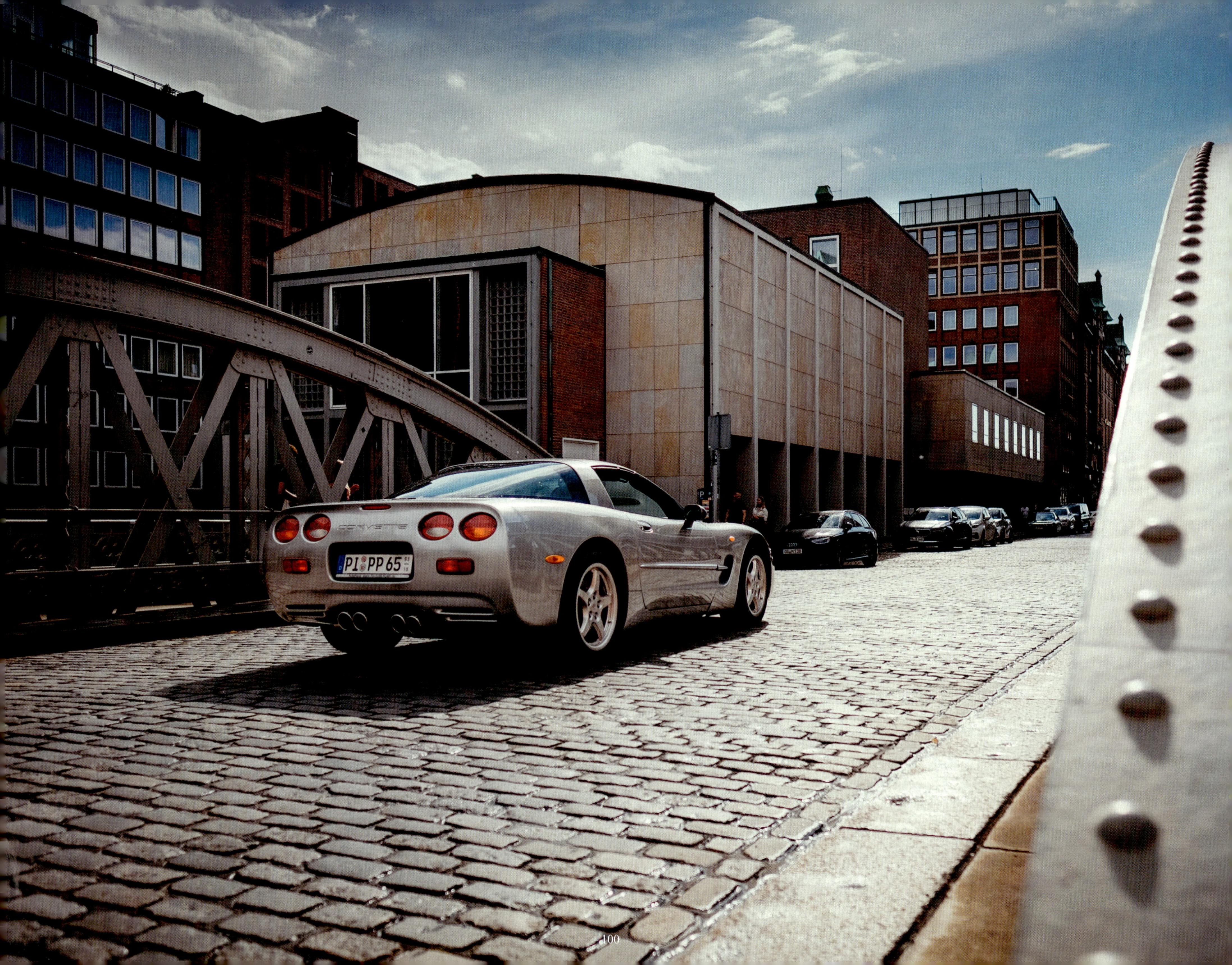
CORVETTE
PI PP 65

SUNSHINE FOLLOWS RAIN

Long before he was old enough to obtain his driver's license, Philipp Ressel was active on the Corvette forum and completely fascinated by the American sports car. Then in 2019, he fulfilled his childhood dream.

What is your Corvette story?
For a long time, the Corvette has been my personal dream. I was roaming about the Corvette Forum when I was still in school and did not have a driver's license. A nice gentleman from the Corvette club here in Hamburg took me with him to a forum meeting, even though at that point, I neither had a Corvette nor the financial means to buy one. The whole thing was only possible because various users in the forum very kindly convinced me that I was welcome there even without a Corvette and that my arrival and departure had already been arranged. That was an unforgettable experience, through which I was drawn even deeper into the scene. I rode in more Corvettes that weekend than I could have ever dreamed of. I've liked sports cars in general since I was a kid, but the Corvette in particular just did it to me. I love the American eight-cylinder. A V10 or V12 is also nice, but to me nothing beats a V8. The sound is simply indescribable.

When I started working, the time had come to look around for a Corvette. I had saved up some money during my studies and decided, together with my wife, to buy one. There was no rush, but maybe a good offer would appear. The first two attempts didn't work out. One was snatched up from under my nose, and the seller and I disagreed on the other. In the meantime, we had bought a house, and after that, the topic of a Corvette fell asleep a bit, but not for long.

In 2019, a C5 was offered for sale in the forum at about half the usual market value. On the one hand, this was because the vehicle registration had been expired for nine years, and on the other hand, because it had been sitting outside for seven years without moving. The color was not my cup of tea, and the circumstances of the sale in combination with the price were quite questionable. The owner, however, was known to some users in the forum from the old days, and he was at the same time incredibly honest about defects and possible deterioration caused by its inactivity. He sent me pictures of every part of the car, even of those that a seller might not want to show. It was a risk to buy a car in that condition, but the offer was just too good, the timing was right, and it was an EU model, which was also quite important to me. So without prior inspection, I drove almost 300 miles to Bonn with a borrowed tow truck and brought it home to us in the north. I remember fondly how I kept looking at the Corvette in the rearview mirror on the way home.

As expected, the neglected car needed some attention. For a month, I took care of all the existing problems myself. I brought the brakes up to scratch and went through the interior three times with a wet vacuum and lots of shampoo until the musty smell finally dissipated. Fortunately, in the forums you can find instructions and pictures on how to work on your Corvette yourself, which made it relatively easy for me. By the way, the C5 was built on July 21, 1999, in Bowling Green. Two days later was my sixth birthday. That's kind of a cool connection.

Meanwhile, I am very happy with my Corvette. Of course, the car is twenty-two years old and has already run 125,000 miles (201,000 km) in its life, so every now and then a little something can crop up. Like the windshield wiper that quit working today. But I'm rarely mad at her.

What is your all-time favorite Corvette model?
That is the C6 ZR1. I would also have liked to have had a C6, but I am very happy with my C5.

◀ **1999** Corvette C5, **Hamburg,** Germany | **August 5, 2021**

TO PHILIPP, CORVETTE MEANS:
ATTITUDE TOWARD LIFE, SPORTINESS, JOY

Orphan. The Corvette stood motionless outdoors for seven years until Phillipp Ressel brought it back to life in 2019. In painstaking detail, he removed the moisture and musty smell from the interior, overhauled the engine, and restored it to its former glory.

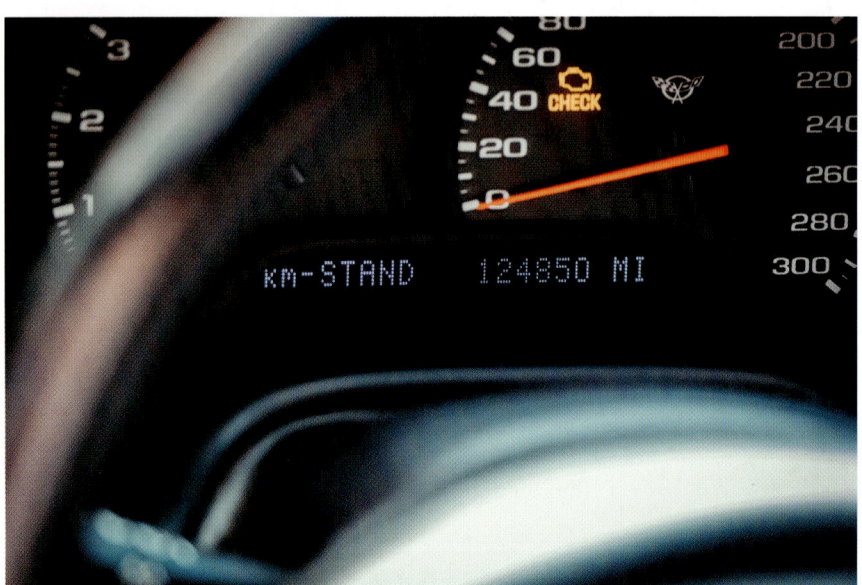

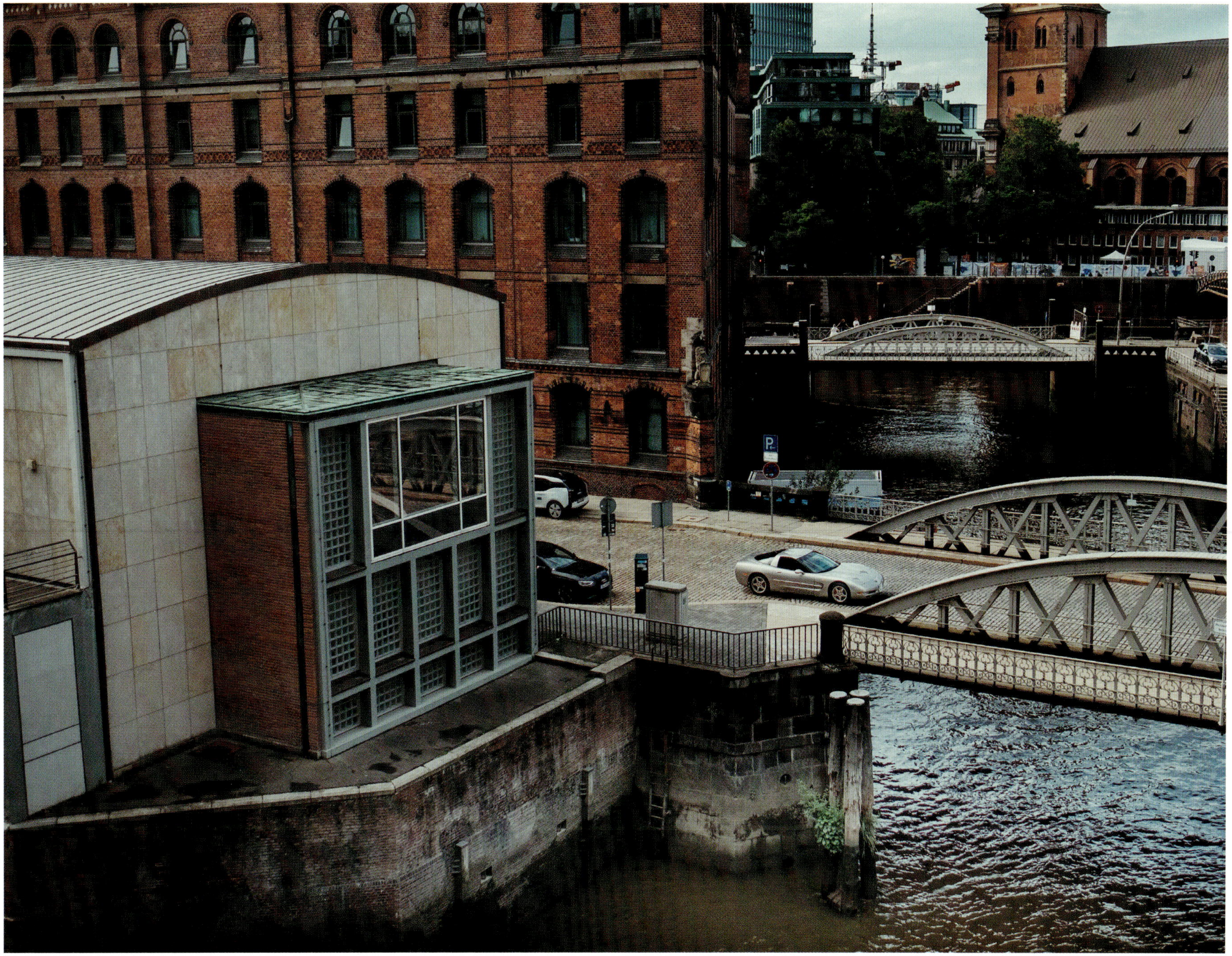

SHIPPING
AND
RECEIVING
SPLASH MURALS
MALEKE
CARIRIANNA
QUINION
CEDRIC R
ASIA
KEVIN
KATIE
.R

CAR GIRL MADE IN THE USA

The first car that Mary Macionski ever drove was a '67 Corvette convertible, but even as a child, she was already a true car girl.

What is your Corvette story?
I was young then, still in elementary school. One Sunday while on our way to church, I noticed a car driving in front of us. It looked different than any of the others on the road. I asked my father, who then worked for the Cadillac division of General Motors, what kind of car it was. He replied, "That's a Corvette Stingray." I then said, "Papa, I love that car." It was a fire-red split-window 1963 coupe. A few years later, I saw a 1967 Corvette in Sunfire Yellow, and from then on, I liked yellow Corvettes best of all.

The first Corvette I ever drove was a silver 1967 convertible. I was in college, and a friend of mine let me drive it. He was also a big Corvette fan. I remember well how exciting that short drive was. The second Corvette, which I occasionally drove in the years between 1989 and 1992, was a red C4 convertible.

One night during the Woodward Dream Cruise, my friend Rick and I drove around for a while in his red '62 Corvette. (I attended the Dream Cruise every year, beginning with the first one in 1994.) We were just driving around, and he asked me, "When are you going to buy your own classic car?" I told him I had never thought about it, whereupon he asked me what kind of vehicle I would choose if I were to buy a classic car. "It would either be a Cadillac or a Corvette." He looked at me and said, "Get a Corvette."

In the evening, we met Rick's friend Mike, who had a red split-window coupe. He told me that his mechanic Marc had a '76 Corvette that he wanted to sell, but only to someone who really appreciates the car. To a Corvette enthusiast, in other words. Half an hour later, said mechanic appeared, and Mike introduced us. Naturally, I had to ask him about the color of the car. Yellow was the answer. I had taken the bait.

The owner of the yellow Corvette owned a garage in my hometown, two miles from my house. After the Dream Cruise, I drove by his place to have a look at the C3. It was a day like today, warm and not a cloud in the sky. I took the car for a short test drive. It was the third Corvette I had ever driven. My heart beat faster; it was such fun to drive it. I came back from the test drive, and the owner looked at me and said, "The car suits you. It's you." I gave him a check for $100 as a down payment. We agreed that I would pay him a certain amount every month until January, when I received my bonus. The company I worked for postponed the bonuses until April. Fortunately, that was no problem for Marc. I called him on April 18; it was time to finally pick up my Corvette. I bought the C3 at the end of 2002, and in 2003, I was finally able to collect it. That day, however, I had no one who could drive me to the garage. I therefore put on my roller skates and got to the meeting place that way. Of course, I returned in my bright yellow Corvette.

Since then, I have been to many great car shows here in Michigan in my C3 and, for twenty-nine years, also to every Woodward Dream Cruise. I am simply a car girl. By the way, a very funny story happened to me once at the Dream Cruise, about ten years after I bought the Corvette. I parked not far from the parade. There were about forty other classic cars in the parking lot, with people walking across the lot and marveling at the old cars. One man came up to me and said, "I love your car; I love that yellow 1976 C3. A while back, I was going to buy a Corvette just like it from a garage in Oak Park." I looked at him and said, "That's the exact car you wanted to buy. I got it from Marc, the owner of the garage."

When I'm on the road with the Corvette, I get the "thumbs up" from all kinds of people. Kids, women, men, no matter what age. They all love my Corvette. I'm approached at traffic lights and at the gas station; people want to know what year it was built, how long I've had it, and so on.

By the way, my uncle worked for Chevrolet. In 1968, Chevrolet introduced the new C3. When he visited us at my parents' house one Sunday, he pulled a piece of paper out of his shirt pocket. He unfolded it and showed it to me; it was a technical drawing of the new Corvette design. He said, "I know you think the Corvette is great; this is what the new models will look like." So I saw the third-generation Corvette before it was officially introduced. And now I even own one.

What is your all-time favorite Corvette model?
Still the C3. Some of my friends have already suggested that I should buy a newer Corvette. But it would be very difficult for me to part with my C3. With the car, I can participate in any kind of car show, but with a new Corvette I would have no chance at the classic car meets. I get invited to events and shows because of the C3. Many people have new Corvettes, but you don't see the classics that often.

◀ *1976 Corvette C3*, **Detroit**, Michigan, **USA** | September 13, 2022

TO MARY, CORVETTE MEANS:
THRILLS, EXCITEMENT, ATTENTION

Pop art. The Motor City is not just gray; it can also be very colorful. Just five minutes outside of downtown Detroit, there is plenty of colorful graffiti, which made the perfect background for Mary Macionski's yellow 76 Corvette.

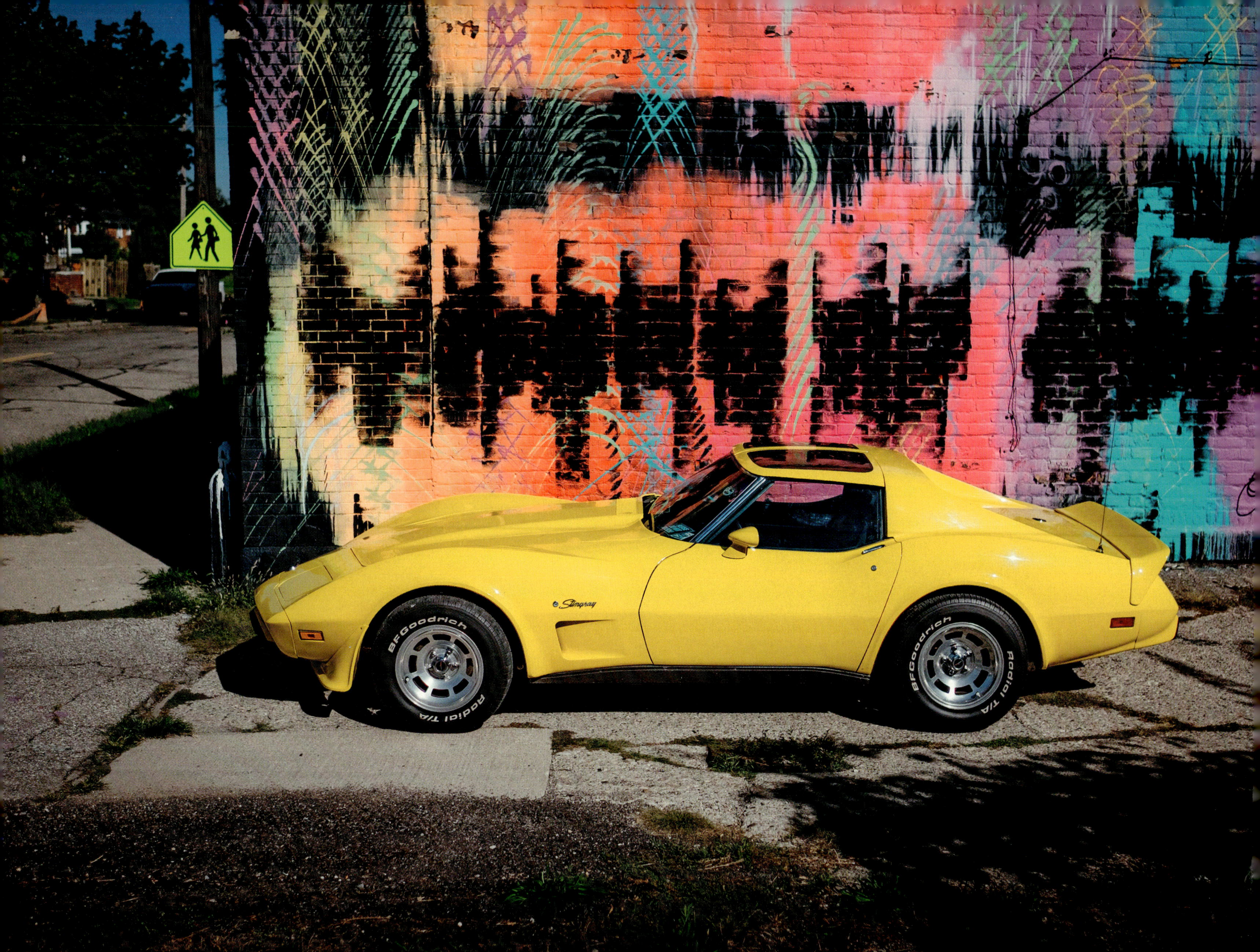
Stingray
BFGoodrich
Radial T/A

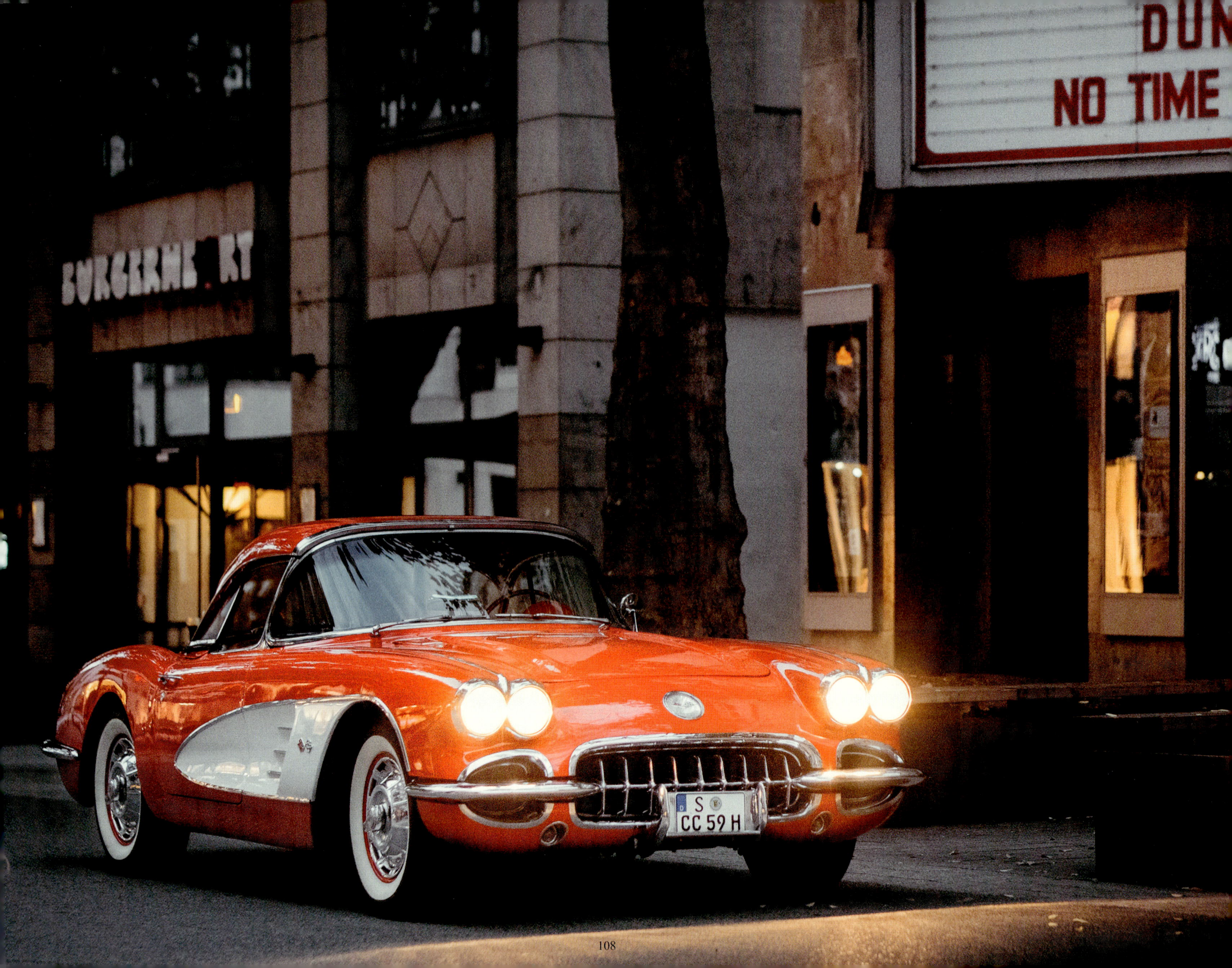
NO TIME
S
CC 59 H

MORE THAN A SUPPORTING ROLE

Grace of Monaco—**this Corvette played a supporting role in the movie. After its Hollywood career, Elmar Hartmann brought it to the Swabian capital and gave it a leading role.**

What is your Corvette story?
The Corvette has always been a childhood dream for me. After all, these are cars we played with as children. In the past, of course, you were very far away from fulfilling such a wish. But with age, after a few things in life have been settled, the realization of such a dream comes within reach.

At some point, I began looking seriously for a Corvette and dealing with the subject in detail. I clicked through the internet and read through various classic car magazines. For a while, I also flirted with a C3 but always came back to the C1. The design is simply incredible.

During my research, I quickly discovered that the market for good C1 Corvettes is quite limited. I didn't really want an automatic. I wanted something simple and was always looking for a C1 with a three-speed manual transmission. There was a Corvette that I really liked in Monaco. Not exactly around the corner, but the Côte d'Azur is always worth a trip, and so I flew there. The test drive, my first time behind the wheel of a C1, took place in sophisticated Monaco. The seller, a Swede, was really super nice and serious. In 1988, the Corvette had come from the USA to Sweden and was also registered there for some time. I didn't know until then that the Swedes are so crazy about American classic cars and that there is such an active scene there.

With my impressions from Monaco, I flew back to Germany and first went to a specialist garage for advice, including on the subject of the vintage car registration. The guys in the workshop offered no reasons not to buy the Corvette. So I went on to the next step—I had to convince my wife. In this I was successful.

Finally, I rented a trailer and with my wife drove to Monaco to pick up the Corvette. That was a great trip. An absolutely lasting impression! After all the business had been taken care of, we drove through all of Monaco with the seller and his old Buick convertible. Then we pulled the trailer with the Corvette through all of France and back to Germany. This trip gave my wife a completely different relationship with the car.

When the weather is fine, my wife often says, "Today is Corvette weather. Come on, let's take her for a drive." We are both really so happy with the car. And we get so much positive feedback wherever we go. That is really unique—a really sympathetic figure.

And your Corvette played a supporting role in the movie *Grace of Monaco*?
Yes, it was this very car. I have a letter confirming the car's supporting role, and I also have pictures in which you can see the C1 on the set in front of the casino in Monaco. The movie *Grace of Monaco* was released not long after we bought the Corvette in 2014, so it was a very special experience for us to see our own car on the big screen, even if it was only a brief glimpse.

Did you know that the car had had a role in a movie before you bought it?
No, I only found out over the course of time. I don't have many documents about the car that could document its complete history. This makes the story all the more exciting, of course, and makes the C1 something very special to me.

What is your all-time favorite Corvette model?
As far as the design is concerned, the C1 is of course the absolute winner. I also find the C3 very exciting, a very striking design. But I wouldn't trade.

◀ **1958** Corvette C1, **Stuttgart**, Baden-Württemberg, **Germany** | October 17, 2021

TO ELMAR, CORVETTE MEANS:
DRIVING EXPERIENCE, LIKEABILITY FACTOR, DESIGN

Hollywood star. Elmar Hartmann's '59 C1 played a supporting role in the movie *Grace of Monaco*, but Chevrolet's Corvette is generally a popular guest in films or TV series like *Stingray* and *Riptide*.

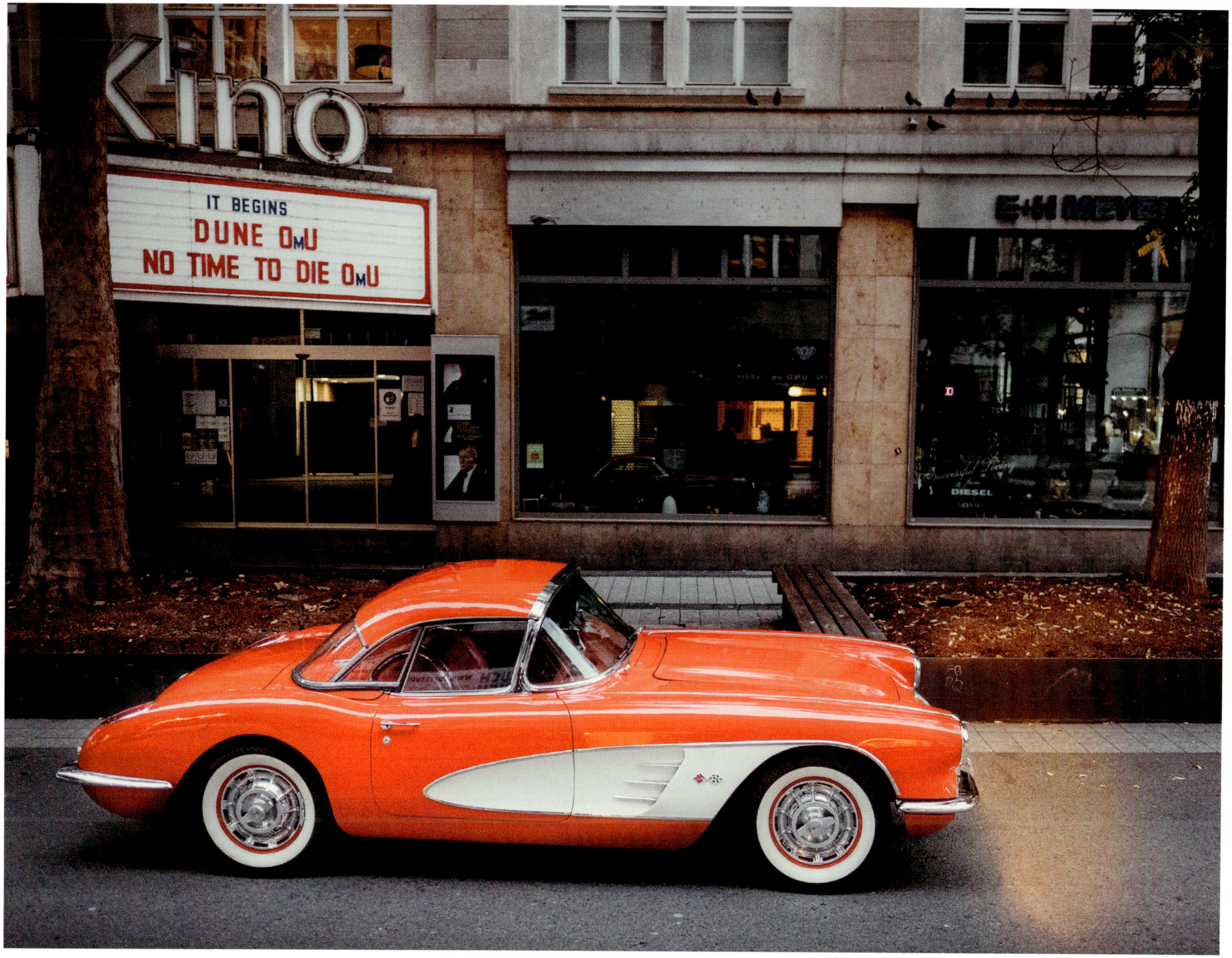
Kino
IT BEGINS
DUNE OmU
NO TIME TO DIE OmU
E+H MEYER
DIESEL

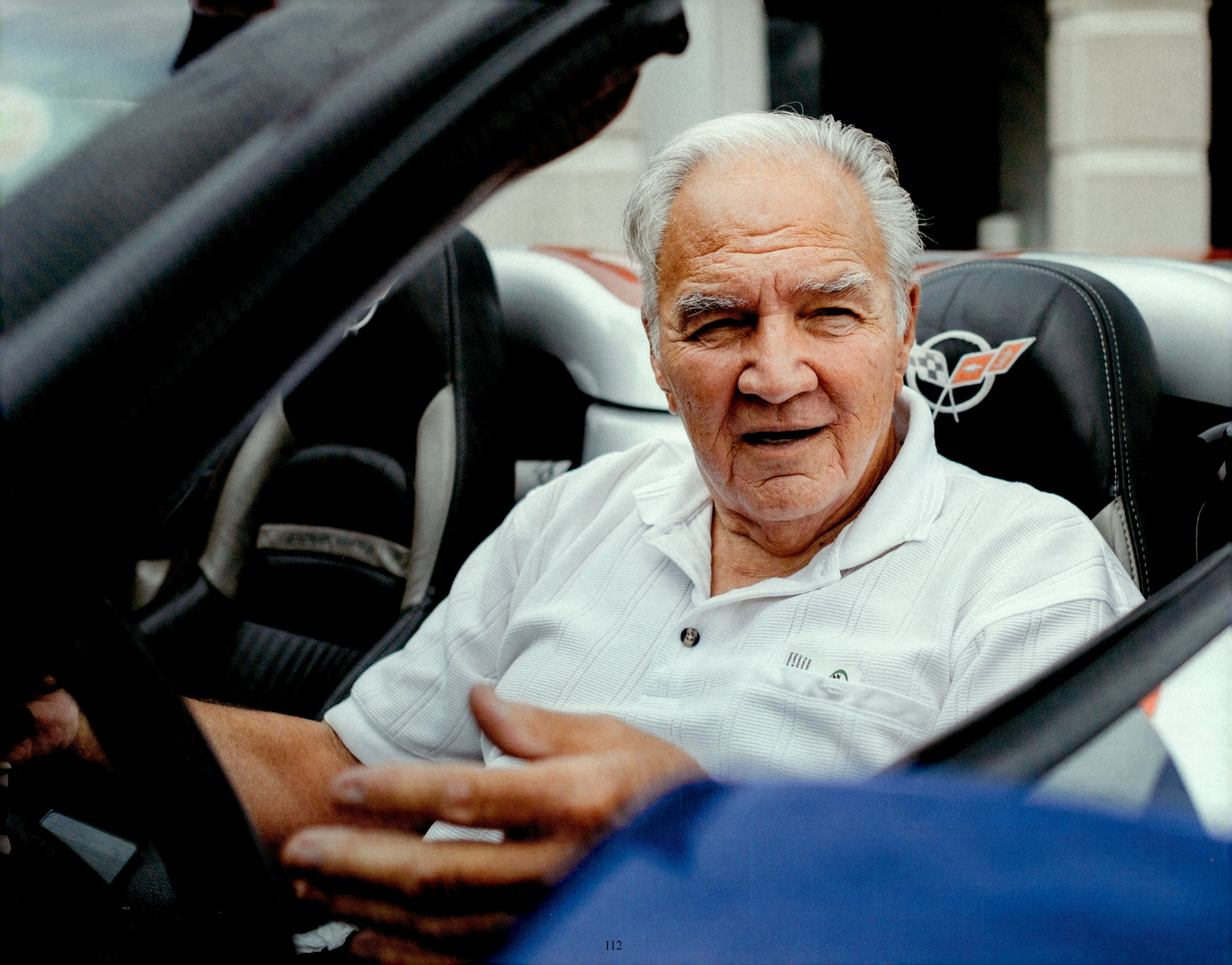

EVERYONE KNOWS THIS CORVETTE

For decades, Larry Courtney and his patriotic C5 have been an important part of the Corvette family. Everyone really knows his legendary convertible.

What's your Corvette story?
Like so many Corvette enthusiasts, I was very young the first time I saw one. I believe the first Corvette I ever sat in was a 1963 split-window coupe. A friend of mine, with whom I had grown up, had one. He was a policeman in Chicago. After he let me take it for a drive, I knew that I would also own a Corvette someday.

Time went by. Meanwhile I had a son, who was also into Corvettes. One day, he saw one parked next to a building in Chicago. The T-Tops were missing and the car was full of leaves. He was able to buy the thing for just $200. He towed it to my house, and I looked at him questioningly: "What are we going to do with that?" He replied, "I hope we can get it running." It took five or six weeks to replace all the wiring, check the hoses, and change the fluids. Then the Corvette finally started. But the car still had too many problems, including with the electrical system. The taillights didn't work properly, and we had trouble finding the right parts.

My son sold the car as a source of spare parts and made a small profit. Our next project was a '79 Corvette that was all original, black with an ivory interior. It was very worn out, and we really had to do a lot to it. The paint was starting to crack too; spiderwebs had formed everywhere. When we went to shows, we used black wax, which made the paint look great again for a few days. My son still has that Corvette.

I moved on to the next chapter of my life. In 2001, I moved to Michigan. New job, new life. I bought a 1977 Corvette, my first car with an adjustable steering wheel and comfortable seats, and the seating position was perfect for me. As part of our "Corvette Caravan," I drove it to Bowling Green, among other places. Later, however, I replaced the anemic 350-cubic-inch engine with a 300hp one.

The year 2003 brought more changes, but of a private nature. I met my future wife, Verna. A lucky coincidence, as it turned out, because she stood by me when I was fired a year later. The steel mill I worked for was taken over by a Russian company, and I was too old and too pricey for them. I came home without a job and asked Verna what we should do now. She said, "We have a little money; we have a Corvette; I think I'd like to drive it on Route 66." I've driven the 66 to Arizona and the Grand Canyon before, but never to California. The idea turned into an 8,000-mile trip. We drove from Detroit to Chicago, to L.A., and up the coast of California to Truckee. Then we went through Reno; Yellowstone National Park; Billings, Montana; and finally the northern route back home. It was a really fantastic trip. That's when I knew I was going to marry Verna. Unfortunately, about a year later my C3 was stolen and we bought our C5 convertible.

By then, I was a member of two Corvette clubs. Michigan is the perfect place to live if you're into cars. In the early spring, the garages in my neighborhood open up and all the classic cars come out. It's easy to strike up a conversation with people. There are so many car enthusiasts in the area, just great. I've always wanted to meet and talk to more different people. What's the best way to do that? You organize something yourself. I started calling different locations, like the Automotive Hall of Fame and the GM Heritage Center, and asked if it would be possible to have some people and cars meet there. The Heritage Center rejected the idea at first, as it would not be open to the public. We talked about it for a long time, and eventually they let us in. We also met the well-known collector Ken Lingenfelter. He invited us to see his collection, 150 cars. We have been visiting him regularly ever since.

In 2000, I visited the Corvette Museum for the first time, together with my son. In 2002, I signed up for the 2003 Corvette Caravan. Roc Linkov was then in charge. Roc and I got along very well and are now close friends. He gave me many valuable tips, like how to get a good Corvette meet going. In 2004, my wife and I began organizing proper events. Our charity event, Corvettes on Woodward, supports the local food bank. Over the years, we have donated more than $150,000 and tons of food. Corvette owners from the USA and Canada take part in the event every year. We have also had friends from Sweden who brought their own Corvettes, as well as participants from Austria, the Netherlands, and Brazil. We organize different shows every year. There is going be an event to celebrate the 70th anniversary of the Corvette in Michigan. Then in 2024, we will celebrate a personal anniversary. It will be exactly 20 years since we put on our first Corvette event. In 2024, we will also lead the Corvette Caravan through Michigan, Indiana, and Kentucky, something we have already done in 2014 and 2019.

Currently, our legendary American Flag Corvette has twenty-five years under its belt and 177,000 miles on the clock. We want to take part in the 2024 Caravan with 200,000 miles on the clock.

Over the years, we have met an incredible number of nice Corvette owners. We have traveled a lot to take part in events. It doesn't matter where we travel with our Corvette; we always meet people who know us or who know the car. It really is a legend.

Speaking of legends, two years ago I was at a veterans event. A helicopter flew them to the property owned by a nice gentleman. My job was to drive the veterans from one end of the property to the other in my Corvette. A guy about my size got out of the helicopter. He got in my car, and his wife asked where she should sit. One of the organizers said she could walk. Her response: "We've been married for fifty years and have never been separated." I said to her, "Just sit on his lap. As long as the door closes, it's okay with me." So she did, and we didn't stop laughing for the short distance we traveled in the Corvette. When you have something special, I think it's important to share it with others. A little bit of your time can really enrich someone's life. So let's take it for a spin.

What is your all-time favorite Corvette model?
I've driven just about every generation of Corvette. I like the look of the earlier cars, and the newer ones have incredible style and lots of power. I am very happy with my C5 convertible, a car with a real trunk. I have enough legroom, and the seats are very comfortable. The thing has 345 horsepower, and even though the Corvette has a lot of miles on it, it still goes from 0 to 100 in 5.5 seconds, and on long trips it gets 29 miles to the gallon.

◀ 1999 Corvette C5, **Dearborn**, Michigan, **USA** | September 11, 2022

TO LARRY, CORVETTE MEANS:
FAMILY, HELPING OTHERS, FUN

American spirit. Larry and Verna Courtney are known not only for their American Flag Corvette, a C5 with a whopping 170,000 miles on the odometer, but more importantly for their events, such as the Corvettes at Woodward charity event.

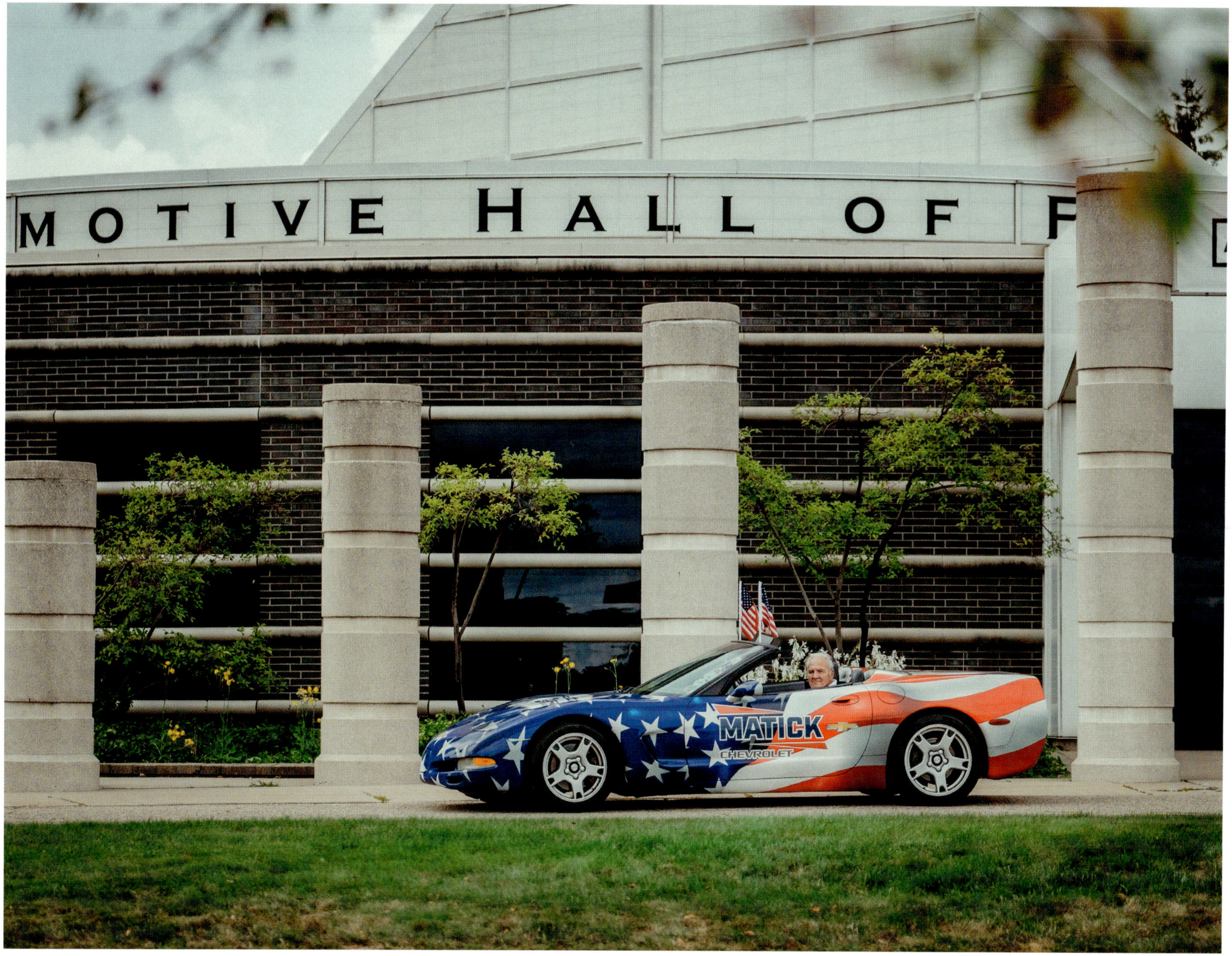
MOTIVE HALL OF F
MATICK
CHEVROLET

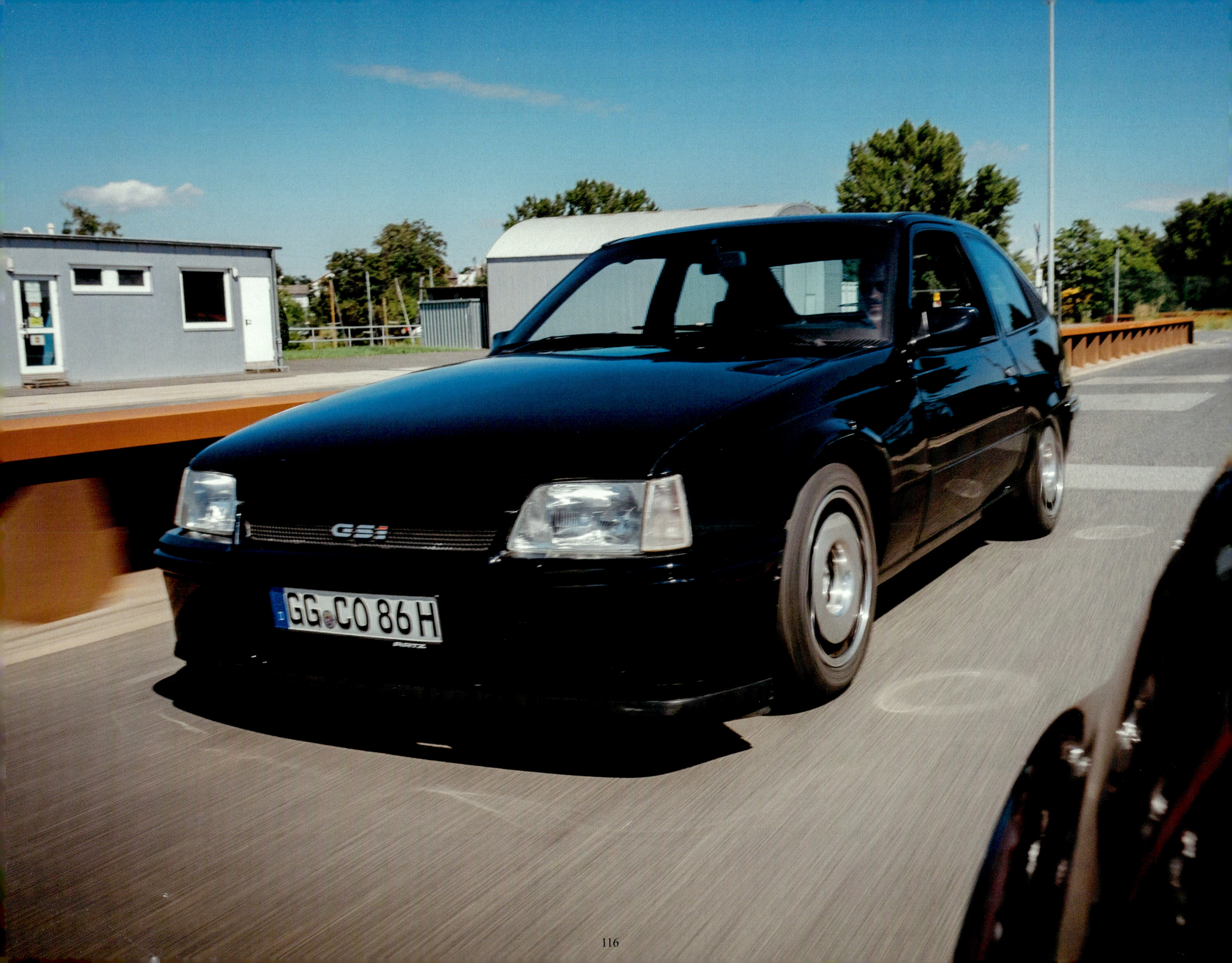
GSi
GG CO 86 H

CORVETTE MADE IN GERMANY?

For years, Jürgen Reitz was a dedicated Opel driver, until a Corvette crossed his path. And he immediately infected his wife Simone with the Corvette bug. While she now drives a C3, the man from Rüsselheim combines both worlds with his one-off Corvette.

What's your Corvette story?
Jürgen: I drove Opels for 25 years! My last car from Rüsselheim was an Omega B MV6. It was the worst car I've ever owned. After that, it was clear: "No more Opels!," and I thought about what I should buy instead. At the time, my wife was driving a Jeep Grand Cherokee. A practical car will do, I thought, and I went looking for something smaller, flatter. For a long time, I was pretty indecisive, wavering between the Porsche 928 GTS and the Corvette C5, which was fresh on the market at the time. After test-driving the Corvette, the decision was easy. I ordered a new C5.

For three years after that, it really was my standard ride. In 2001, she went away, and I ordered a new C5. From then on, I was also active in the American Corvette forum. One day I mistyped the URL and wrote ".de" instead of ".com." This led me to realize that there is also a German Corvette forum. From then on, things took their course. Since then, I am a Corvette driver, and my circle of friends has changed completely, simply due to the amount of time we spend at meetings. In the summer, we usually spend seven or eight weekends at Corvette or classic car events all over Germany and Europe.

Over time, I also acquired more and more cars. In 1987, it all started with a Triumph TR6, which I had as a pure fun car to go with my then-current Opel. Then I found out that the C5 was more fun than the TR6 under all conditions. But I absolutely wanted a vintage convertible, so in 2004 I added a yellow Corvette C3 LT-1. My third Corvette, the C5 Le Mans Commemorative Edition, was supposed to be just the interim model until the C6 came on the market. When I learned that only 46 of this edition had been made for Europe, it was clear that I would never sell it. So one car turned into another. The long hood and short rear end are the epitome of a sports car to me. And that is typical of almost all Corvette generations. The impressive thing, especially with the Corvette from the C3 to the C7, is the view over the hood with the raised fenders on the right and left.

Simone: It all started when Jürgen bought his first C5. We soon thought about getting a classic Corvette as well. After a few years, I also wanted a Corvette for myself. In the forum and at our regular tables, we heard that many women find the third generation the most beautiful, and some also drive C3s. That was the deciding factor which led to my search for such a Corvette.

We found one in the USA in 2014. It was up for auction at Mecum. Jürgen looked at the car at the auction together with a friend who knows a lot about C3s. He bid and with a little luck we won.

It's a lot of fun for me to be on the road in the Corvette. You're not in the car just to get from point A to point B, but to enjoy driving it. It's simply an experience. What I particularly like about my C3 is the two-tone paint—Metallic Dark Claret on the bottom, Metallic Claret on top, separated by a red trim line. Chevrolet wanted to demonstrate the possibilities of the new factory in Bowling Green with such paint finishes.

How did you come to the Artz Cordett?
Jürgen: In 1989, I was still a convinced Opel driver and had an Opel Kadett GSI 16 V. At that time, I read the report on the Artz Cordett in *Rally Racing* and was totally excited about the car and the concept. In 2007–2008, there was a Cordett which had been for sale for a long time at a classic car dealer in Hannover. I went there and looked at the car, test drove it, and negotiated the price. All I had to do was say yes, but then I got cold feet. With a one-off car, one might have major problems if something has to be repaired or replaced. For years, I was still upset about the fact that I had passed on the car back then. The article about the car in the *Classic Car Market* was a nasty sting in the wound.

In 2015, I became aware of an article in another sports car forum about one of the two Artz Golf 928s. The Golf had been acquired by the new owner from the collector who also owned the Cordett and a Lotus Calibra from Artz. When I saw that the collector had sold the VW, I knew that there was a chance to acquire the other cars as well. So I communicated with the new owner of the Golf and got the collector's contact information, and two weeks later I struck: both the Cordett and the Lotus Calibra came into my possession. I have never been so happy about two cars as I was about these; they were the icing on the cake.

Together with an acquaintance who also owns one of the Artz Golf 928s, we started the Facebook page Günter Artz Cars and have now united almost thirty old Artz cars and their owners in the group. Three years ago, we organized our first meeting at the Brazzeltag in Speyer, and meanwhile, the Artz fan community is quite active.

The salt in the soup of the whole car story is really the personal contacts with the people. As beautiful as the cars are, as interesting the technology is, the fun you have with other Corvette owners is enormous.

What is your all-time favorite Corvette model?
Jürgen: Purely in terms of looks, I like the C2, the C3, and the C5 best. There is a story and an emotional connection to all the cars I have here. There is simply no clear favorite.
Simone: I can give you a more definitive answer: I like the C5 the best.

◀ **1989** Artz Cordett, **Rüsselheim**, Hesse, Germany | August 14, 2021

TO JÜRGEN, CORVETTE MEANS:
FUN, JOY, FASCINATION

TO SIMONE, CORVETTE MEANS:
FUN, FUN, FUN

Perfect team. Simone and Jürgen Reitz share a passion for Corvettes. They don't care whether it comes with a C3 or an Opel body.

120

◀ **1981** Corvette C3, **Rüsselheim**, Hesse, **Germany** | August 14, 2021

V'SPERFORMANCE
25·377
MONTANA
OREGON
0116
APPORTIONED
IOWA
KANSAS
Z 260
A101
COLORADO
NEVADA
UTAH
WYOMING

THE FIRST CAR IN MY COLLECTION

Bob Funari has a unique, very special car collection. His collection began with a Corvette convertible from the last year of the C2, 1967.

What's your Corvette story?
Let me begin my story with my latest Corvette, a 2016 Corvette C7 Z06. I found the car on eBay. It was sitting on the lot of a dealer in Spartanburg, South Carolina. The dealer wanted to get rid of the car, so the price was really good. I drove the Corvette for a while here in California, and then I thought that a little more power wouldn't hurt. So I talked to some people at Callaway. In their shop, they added a 2.3-liter supercharger and a big intercooler. That increased the output from 650 to 757 hp. This definitely causes traction problems when you really step on the gas. The rear tires quickly go up in smoke. So you have to be a bit careful. The C7 has ceramic brakes, the Z07 package with a Gurney flap at the rear, and a few carbon fiber parts. Since the rebuild, the car has about 6,000 miles on the clock; so far, no problems at all. I really like the look of the C7 and am very happy to have the car in my collection. The thing goes from 0 to 60 in under three seconds and does the quarter mile in 10.5 seconds. Best of all, you don't have to spend thousands of dollars on service. You just take it to the nearest Chevy dealer, and they don't charge you a fortune.

But let's go back to the beginning of my collecting addiction. In 1983 I moved from Chicago to California but couldn't take my '78 Corvette with me. Once in the Sunshine State, however, I quickly realized that I needed a replacement for my C3. I always liked the design of the second-generation Corvette, and the one from the last model year was particularly clean and straightforward. So I had to get a C2 Corvette. In 1985, I was lucky enough to get hold of a '67 convertible. It was my first really collectible car.

The convertible came from a gentleman from Utah. He had restored the car and painted it Sunfire Yellow. It had the original 435hp Tri-Power big block under the hood, side-pipes, and the 4-speed Muncie transmission. I drove the C2 for eight or nine years. Typical of the cars in my collection, I'm always trying to take them to the next level, to optimize them. That's why I modernized the Corvette's entire drivetrain.

We have swapped the 427 cast block for a 541 aluminum block engine. Instead of three carburetors, an injection system, which is hidden under the triangular air filter, now takes care of the mixture. As a result, the engine retains the classic look of the Tri-Power power plant but has a larger radiator and delivers about 600 hp. The Corvette now also has power steering and air conditioning. The Muncie transmission gave way to a six-speed Tremec manual, and the brakes are from Wilwood. The exhaust system was also changed a bit, and it now sounds deeper and more aggressive than the original. It is still one of my favorite cars in the collection. I have made many memories with the convertible; after all, the car has been in my garage for thirty-seven years.

Of course, it's not for purists. To them, everything should look just as it did when the car rolled off the assembly line. On the other side are the customizers, for whom nothing is sacred. I count myself more in the camp of restorer-modifiers. While retaining the classic look, I try to modernize and improve the car's old technology. Driving such a car is much more fun for me, and it is also more reliable. That's exactly what I've achieved with my C2.

The story surrounding my 1963 Grand Sport is no less interesting. Zora Duntov was tired of being constantly beaten by the Cobras on the racetrack. He decided to develop what he called a lightweight race car. My car is a replica, built according to the original plans from that time. A high-tech company in South Africa produced these replicas in limited numbers.

When used on the racetrack, one of the problems with the Grand Sport was that the differential got too hot. This was remedied by a special differential cooler that kept the temperature of the oil low and thus ensured a longer service life. On my Grand Sport, the plastic body is a bit thinner than that of the original. Otherwise, it looks like the original from the outside, including the magnesium rims and everything that went with them.

At the time, I bought just the body on wheels. The car came to the USA without a drivetrain, without an engine. I had various options in mind for the car, but I finally decided on an LT-4 engine with supercharger. The 650 hp and 649.79 foot-pounds (881 Nm) of torque are easy to handle with 2,975 pounds (1,350 kilos) of vehicle weight. When you're on the road with it, all the attention is yours, if only for the sound. It's a nice tribute to the original Grand Sport, of which just five were built.

What is your all-time favorite Corvette model?
When I was in college the 1967 Corvette was just coming out. I had classmates whose fathers bought this Corvette new. Even then, I thought I would want a car like that someday. So the C2 was part of my youth, part of growing up. The look is without a doubt timeless, with a lot of character. The C2 is still my favorite.

◂ 1963 Corvette C1 Grand Sport Continuation Edition, **Los Angeles**, California, **USA** | November 9, 2021

TO BOB, CORVETTE MEANS:
PASSION, PERFORMANCE, DESIGN

Innocent lamb. Bob Funari loves classic looks combined with modern technology. Not for purists. Like his '67 convertible, beneath whose plastic bodywork there is a 541-cubic-inch aluminum block engine, fuel injection, power steering, air conditioning, and a Tremec transmission.

1967 Corvette C2, **Los Angeles**, California, **USA** ▲

▲ **1967** Corvette C2, **Los Angeles,** California, **USA**

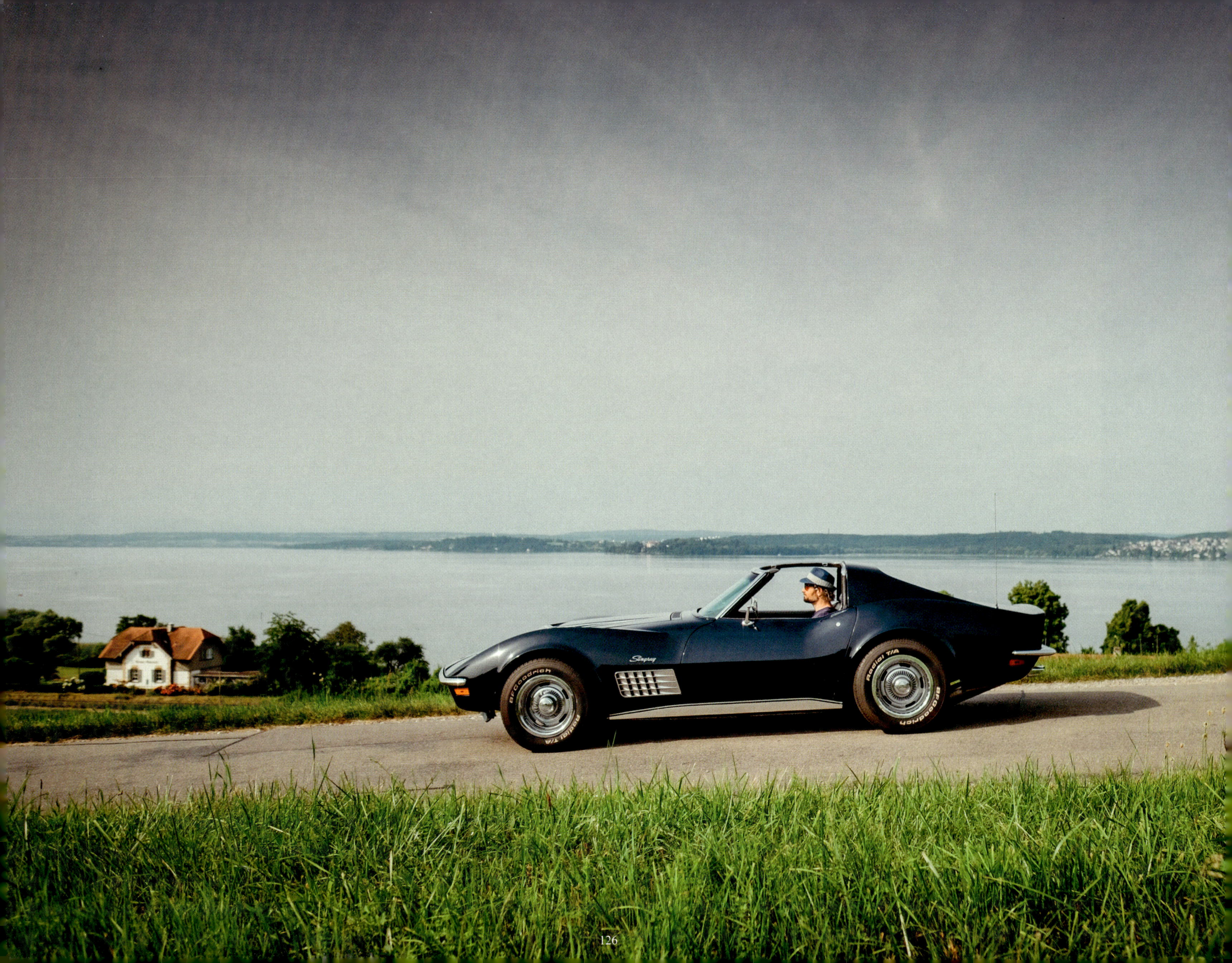
Radial T/A

TWO OWNERS, TWO COLORS

Pickup truck with three seats or a six-seat muscle car? Why did it become neither, instead a 71 LT-1 Corvette for two? Owner Ralf Elben provides the answer.

What's your Corvette story?
Before I purchased the Corvette, we spent five years abroad as a family. There I drove a '74 Land Rover. I restored it mechanically as well as the interior, but from the outside it remained as it was. Before that, I had never dared to work on cars because I thought it was too much work. Restoring a motorcycle is no small task. The complexity of a car gave me a lot of respect, although the Landy had worked out well. I then made an agreement with my wife that I would buy a classic car after returning to Germany.

In my mind, there was always something like a pickup truck. It's related to my '59 Harley Davidson Sportster that I take to vintage flat-track races. Moped on the back and off to the races, that's it. I had been looking for a long time. I wanted a Chevy pickup built between 1956 and 1958. However, there was nothing suitable for a long time, and since I have four children, the pickup seating capacity for three people was hardly ideal. Those were my first thoughts when looking for a classic. The number of seats led me to the old muscle car coupes, which are also available as six-seaters. So I looked at all kinds of cars on the net, and at some point, I stumbled across a picture of a Corvette. Until then, it was out of the question for me.

In principle, the C2 Split-Window was always *the* Corvette for me. So if it was to be a Corvette, then that one. A C3 was out of the question because of its luddite image. A '66 or '67 Corvette isn't that far away from 1971, my birth year, which of course would be a nice thing to have. So I did look at '71 models and found that the lines of the early C3 are phenomenal. The shape of the fenders, the rear end, a brutal car by design. And a groundbreaking design for the time. I began to look more closely at the early C3s.

To me it was clear that the Corvette should have a high-revving small-block, as my Sportster also has the "small" V2. After some research on the available engine options, the LT-1 caught my eye. Mechanical tappets, just like the Sportster. The classic rattle, wonderful. Then it was clear to me: it should be a 1971 LT-1. The problem with the seats was of course also an issue with the C3. It occurred to me that there is never any twosome time in a large family. A car with two seats would be perfect! With the Corvette, it would be possible for me to have special moments for two—with my wife or with one of my children.

I then discovered the Corvette by accident in the Hemmings classic car listings. 71 LT-1, one owner, 60,000 miles, original bill of sale, Protect-O-Plate. Everything was just right, including the price. I immediately contacted the seller. He sent me some pictures and offered me a video call so I could examine the car in detail. No matter what I asked or wanted to see, he answered or showed it to me immediately. The only thing I could not do was make direct contact with the owner. The owner explicitly did not want to do that, because the sale of the Corvette was an emotional burden for him. He had bought the car new in 1971, and now in his early 90s, he was parting with it because he could no longer get into the car. Otherwise, he would not have sold the C3. By the way, he originally wanted a blue Corvette. When he went to the dealership, there was a red LT-1 in the showroom, so he bought the car right away and had it repainted a little later. Blue of course. I suspect the color he used was from a Corvette from a later year.

After a short time to think about it, I got down to business. The seller organized the transport, and about two months later, my Corvette was in Europe. A forwarder then brought it from Bremen directly to me. The truck driver drove the car out of the trailer right into my yard and got the spare wheel well stuck on the ramp. The trim ring from one rim was also lost on the way, but apart from that everything was as expected.

Before I drove the car even a single foot, I removed the fuel tank to see if the build sheet was still attached to it. I wanted to know if the equipment and the color really corresponded to the seller's story. Indeed, I found what I was looking for. I removed the build sheet, wrapped it in foil, and have since had it professionally restored. I also found the correct original date codes and stickers in other areas, such as behind the door panels and under the dashboard.

When I was later on the road with the car, I noticed that every now and then the oil pressure was missing for a short time. I thought the instrument was broken and removed it, bled everything, checked and reinstalled it. The problem remained. A conversation with a friend, who has been in the classic car scene for a long time, provided the answer. "Have you ever checked the oil level?" Rookie mistake! Of course, the dipstick was dry. So I topped up the oil and the oil pressure immediately returned. Fortunately, I had oil pressure until just before and didn't drive around for two months without oil because I thought the gauge was defective. These are learning curves that you go through when you're new to a subject like this.

Of course, I would have liked to meet the previous owner and his family. Unfortunately, my attempts to contact them were met with rejection. I would simply have been interested in a few stories about the car. For example, whether he picked up his future wife on the first date with the Corvette, just stories like that. What would also be important for me is to tell him that I want to keep the car as it is; I want to retain exactly this story of the car, its history. With me it is only continued but not rewritten. The hollows in the seat, the small quirks in the body; I will not retouch all that. I am generally a rather controlled type and prefer things to run as I imagine them. Unforeseen surprises are absolutely not my thing. I deliberately expose myself to the subject of "old Corvette" because it is absolutely unreasonable to drive such a car. Just like my Harley or vintage flat-track racing. After all, you can't be sensible all the time; it probably isn't healthy either. Buying a car like that sight unseen from the US is pretty irrational. I was lucky with it, and my willingness to take risks was rewarded.

What continues to impress me is the performance of the engine at high revs. At first you think that the car wasn't really built for that, but you're absolutely wrong! You notice exactly how the engine wants to rev, and it really comes alive at 4,000 rpm. Red line at sixty-five? I haven't dared to go that far yet. I am really very happy with the vehicle.

What is your all-time favorite Corvette model?
All chrome models of the C3 Corvette.

◀ 1971 Corvette C3, **Überlingen**, Baden-Württemberg, **Germany** | June 19, 2021

TO RALF, CORVETTE MEANS:
SHAPELY, IMPRESSIVE, HIGH-REVVING

Desire. The Corvette's original owner bought it in 1971 despite the fact that it was red. His desire for a C3 with the LT-1 engine was simply too great. Blue paint was added later, which did not bother Ralf Elben, because the history of the sports car could hardly be more complete.

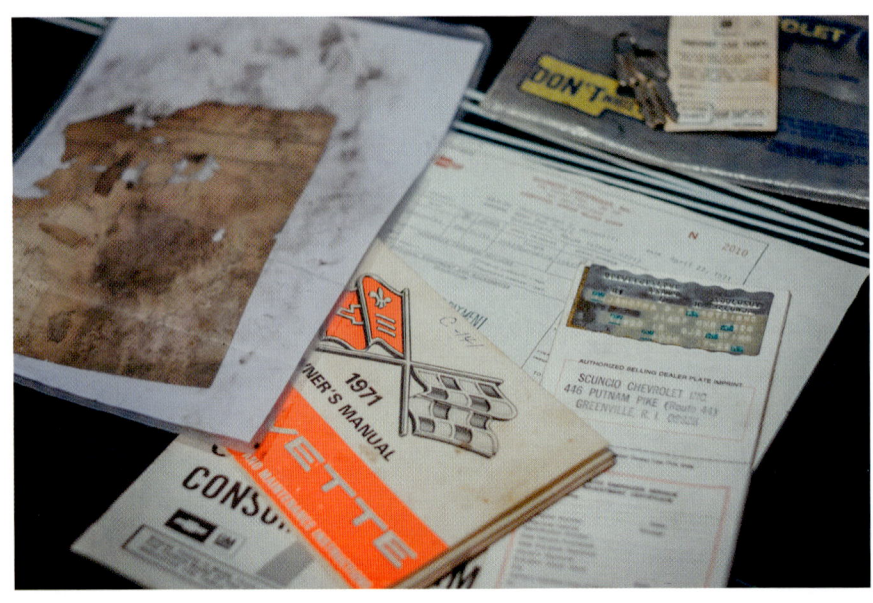

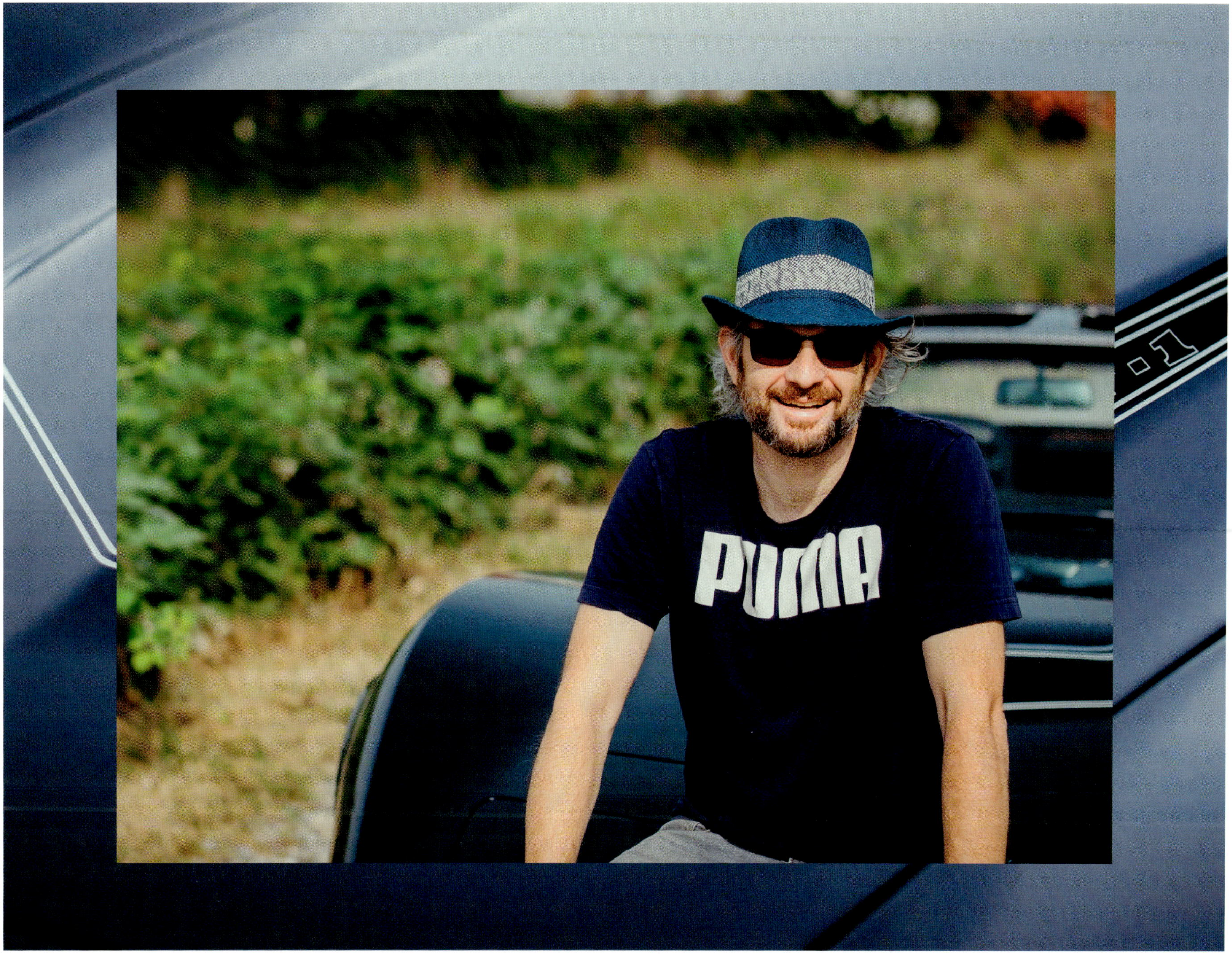
PUMA

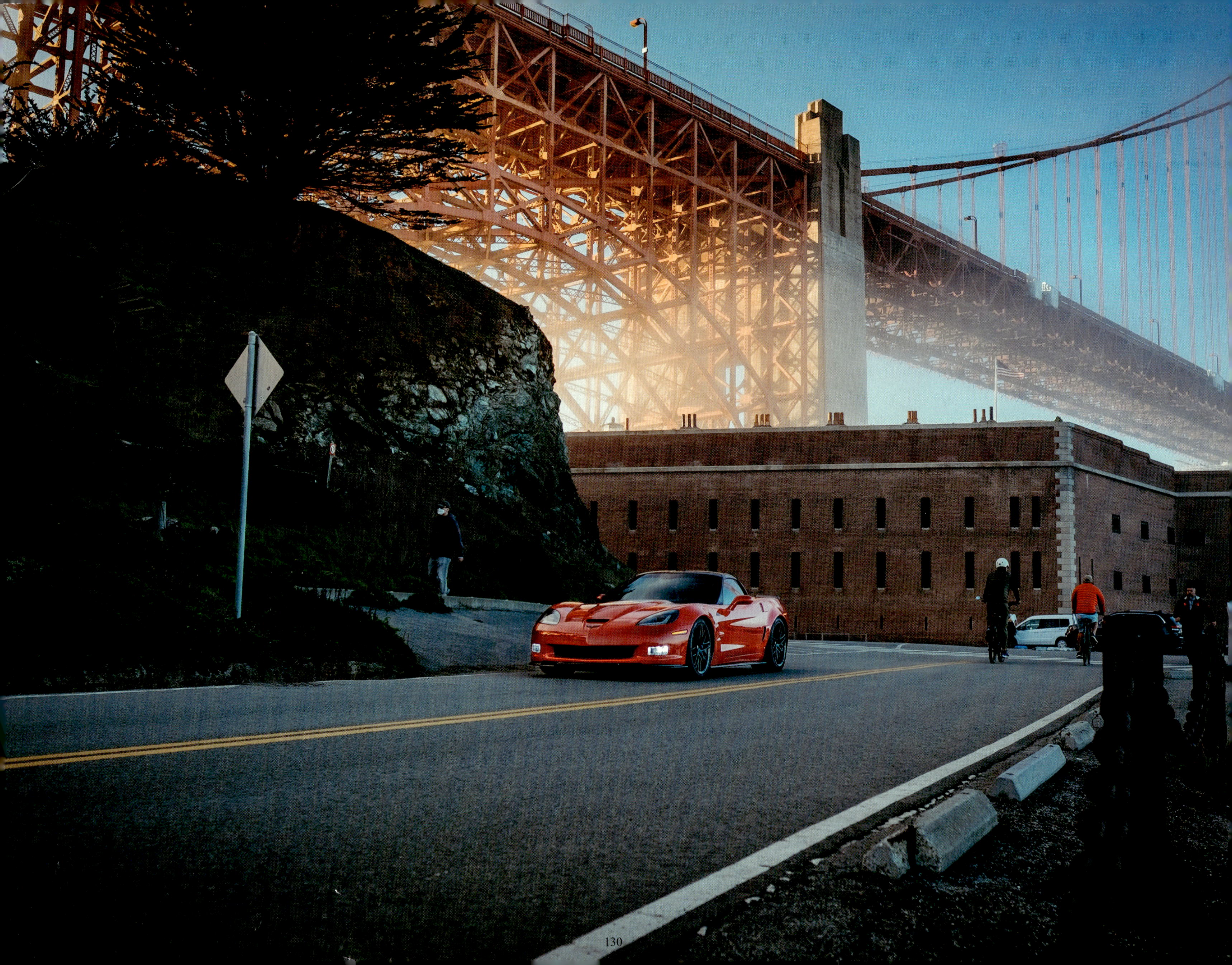

CORVETTE IN VICTORY RED

Andre Valentino Dumadaug was inspired by his father to buy a Corvette. With his Victory Red ZR1, he now owns one of 130 ultimate C6s.

What's your Corvette story?
The design and the power of the Corvette have always fascinated me. In the 1980s, my father had a black C3, and I think that encouraged me to buy a Corvette myself at some point. It is simply the ultimate American sports car. There is nothing like it. The first Corvette I had was a C7 Z06, built in 2015, but I didn't keep it long; I needed money. My wedding was coming up, and that's not a cheap pleasure. Nor should it be. But I definitely wanted another Corvette, as soon as it was again financially possible. At some point, I started looking for a C6 ZR1. In 2020, you could still get the sixth-generation Vette at fair prices, so I decided to buy one. I surfed a few used car sites and finally found a C6 that appealed to me. The car was located in Chicago and had been built in 2009. What makes it special is the fact that it is the 163rd ZR1 out of a total of 4,684 examples that rolled off the production line between 2009 and 2013. It is also one of only 130 Corvettes ordered in Victory Red in 2009. I bought the C6 sight unseen and had it shipped to me in California. A lucky purchase that I have never regretted.

I love the power and sound of the LS9 V8 engine. And of course, I love the manual transmission in my ZR1; it's so much more fun than an automatic. My C7 Z06 was also a 7-speed manual. Currently, my ZR1 is still pretty much production, except for a Corsa Extreme exhaust system with X-pipe. However, I plan on modifying the car some more. For example, I want to add a Synergy Cold-Air air intake, a Synergy Raceport, a 2.4 Upper Pulley, 1050 injectors, American Racing manifolds, and a 103 throttle body. The Corvette is already really fast, 0 to 60 in a little under 3.5 seconds, but you can never have enough power. I've been on the drag strip with the car a couple of times, but you can cover longer distances in it without any problems. With the brutal V8 and this power, I get about 240 miles on a tank of gas, which isn't bad.

You like to share your cars with the community online. When did you start your Instagram channel?
I started my channel in 2009, but it really took off with my C6 ZR1 in 2020. People just love my red Corvette, and the community is growing all the time. I constantly get comments and messages from people telling me that the C6 ZR1 is their absolute dream car.

What is your all-time favorite Corvette model?
No question, the C6 ZR1.

◀ **2009** Corvette C6, **San Francisco**, California, **USA** | November 12, 2021

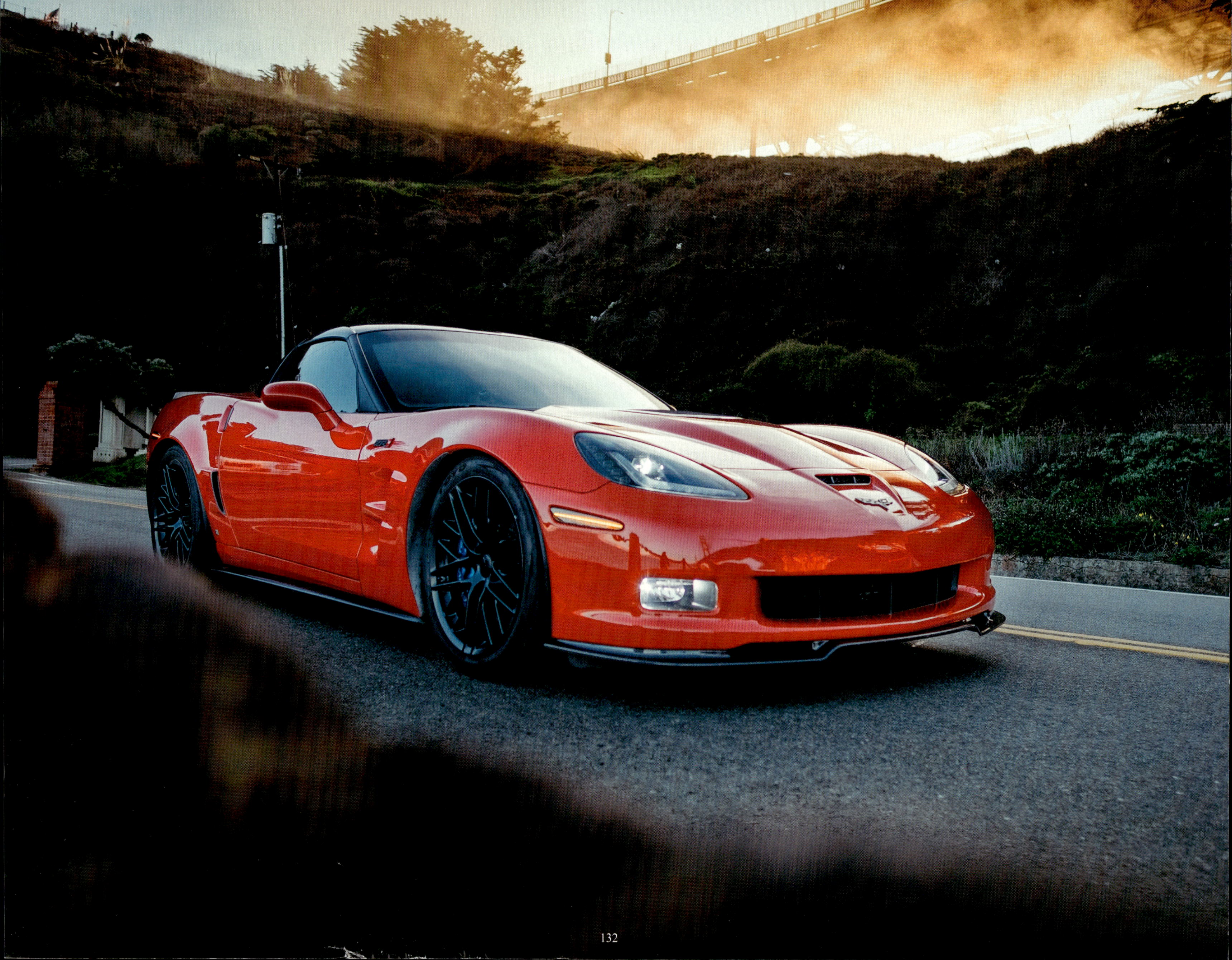

TO ANDRE, CORVETTE MEANS: LEGENDARY, TIMELESS, EXCITING

Golden hour. With the warm evening light in the background, the Victory Red of Andre Valentino Dumadaug's Corvette looks even more intense. Such lighting conditions are not a matter of course around San Francisco's most famous structure.

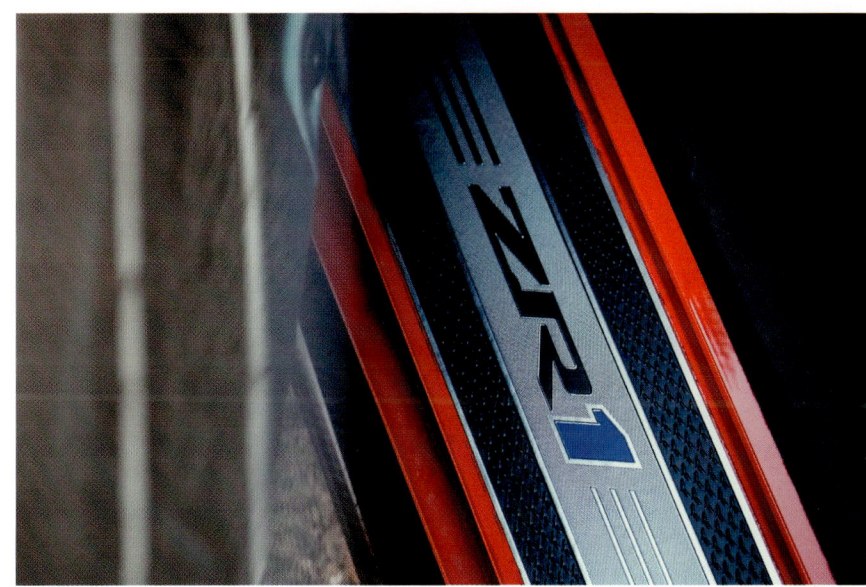

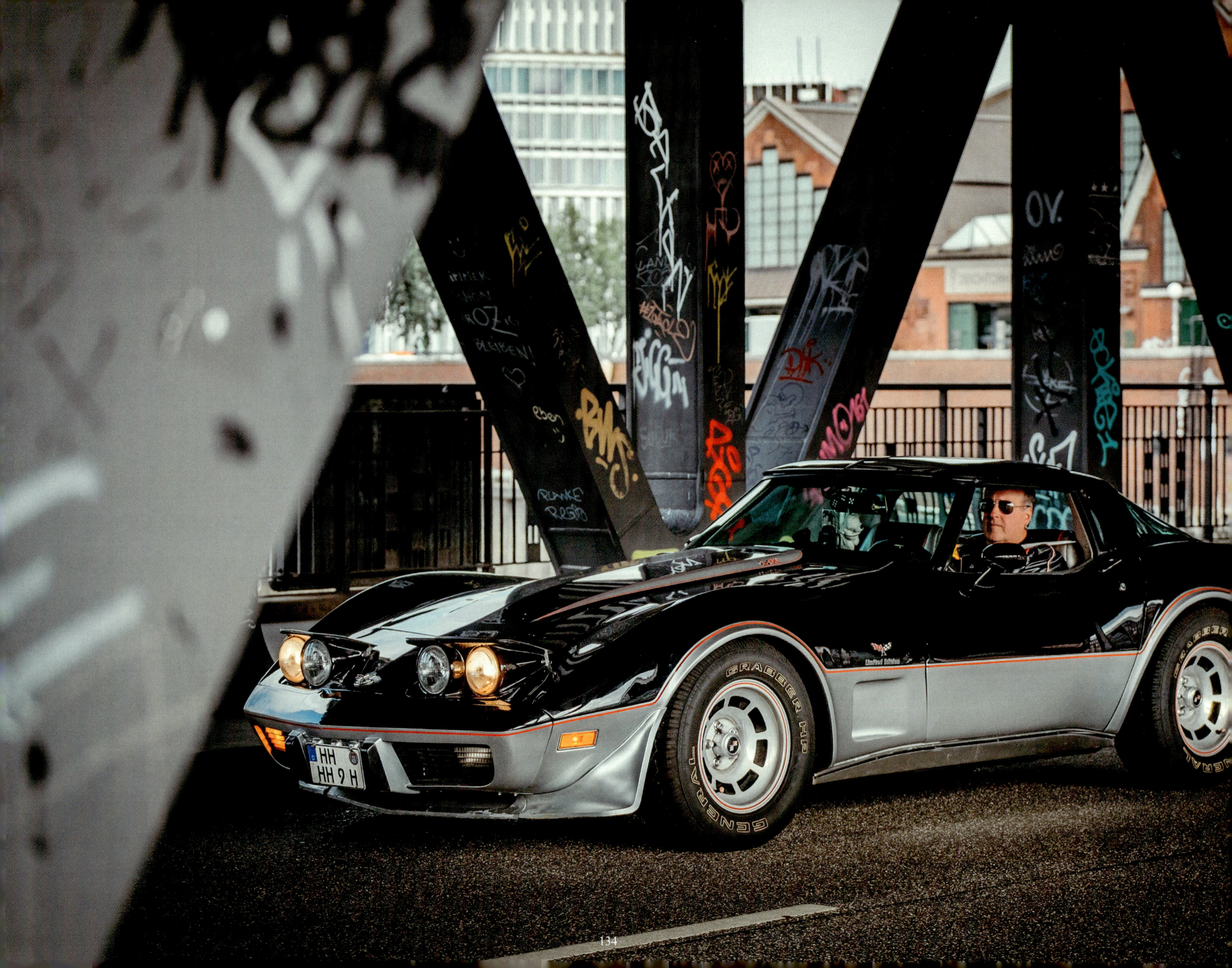
HH
HH 9 H
GRABBER HP
GENERAL

REPEATED GOOSE BUMPS MOMENTS

Rüdiger Jampert saw his first Corvette at the age of twelve. This awakened the desire to have one himself. Forty years later, he fulfilled this dream with a C3 pace car.

What's your Corvette story?
I saw a Corvette for the first time just before becoming a teenager, at the age of about 12. I was standing on the side of the road, and one rumbled past me. At first, of course, I heard the sound of the engine, and then when I saw it, my eyes got bigger and bigger. Half an hour later, I was still standing there with goose bumps and a fixed gaze. Then it was clear to me: someday I will buy a car like that.

That took more than forty years, but there are still a few other things in life that one has to do. When I had the time to deal with the subject in detail and to search for a Corvette, I first looked around here in Hamburg and the surrounding area for a C3. Unfortunately, there was a lot of junk in the area, cars that fell apart or were oily from front to back. After that, I was quite disillusioned and actually already through with the topic of a Corvette.

A little later, I struck up a conversation with one or two Corvette owners at a car meet. After forty years, I was asked for the first time if I would like to sit in a C3. Of course, I couldn't say no and was immediately infected again, just like when I was a kid. As a result, I started looking not only in Hamburg and Germany but all over Europe.

The very first Corvette I then found on the internet was my current C3. It was in the Netherlands. I saw the picture and knew—I'm going to buy it! For six weeks, there were many emails back and forth. Then it was clear that I wanted to look at the Pace Car, and I called the dealer and told him clearly that I wasn't about to drive 1,200 kilometers (745 miles) to look at another piece of junk. He said I could take the car and test drive it, and he would show me all the details I was interested in. He had nothing to hide, and the car was in really great shape. So I went with my wife to the Netherlands, and the salesman was as nice as in his emails and phone calls of the last weeks. He immediately put the key in my hand and said I should just drive off with the Corvette. No sooner said than done.

We were on the road for half an hour, but it was actually already decided when I turned the ignition key for the first time. On the test drive and otherwise, there were no nasty surprises. We negotiated briefly and sealed the deal with a handshake. There were really very few moments in my life when I had a tear in my eye, but when the deal was concluded, I had to get out of the store very quickly; it was really emotional. Forty years of waiting and then my dream car. Just as I had always imagined. No, actually even more beautiful.

I had never seen the C3 in this two-tone livery, and I didn't even know what a pace car was until then. I then researched the subject and found out that the C3 was used as a pace car at the Indianapolis 500. Of the pace car replicas (i.e., the production models), a total of 6,502 units were built. You can recognize real pace car models by the "9" in the eighth position of the thirteen-digit vehicle identification number. Standard 1978 Corvettes had a "4" there.

Every time I go into the garage, get in, and turn the key, I get goose bumps, like when I was twelve. I also think it's important to let people touch the car at meets. When a father comes to me with his son, I always like to let the little ones sit in the car. I know how it was for me back then, and I try to pass something on to the next generation. It would be too bad if such cars disappeared from the road.

What is your all-time favorite Corvette model?
Still the C3.

◀ **1978** Corvette C3, **Hamburg**, Germany | **August 5, 2021**

TO RÜDIGER, CORVETTE MEANS:
INCOMPARABLE, POWERFUL, GOOSE BUMPS

6,502. That was the number of special Pace Car models made in 1978. With their striking black and silver paint and front and rear spoilers, these vehicles are probably the best-known version of the C3.

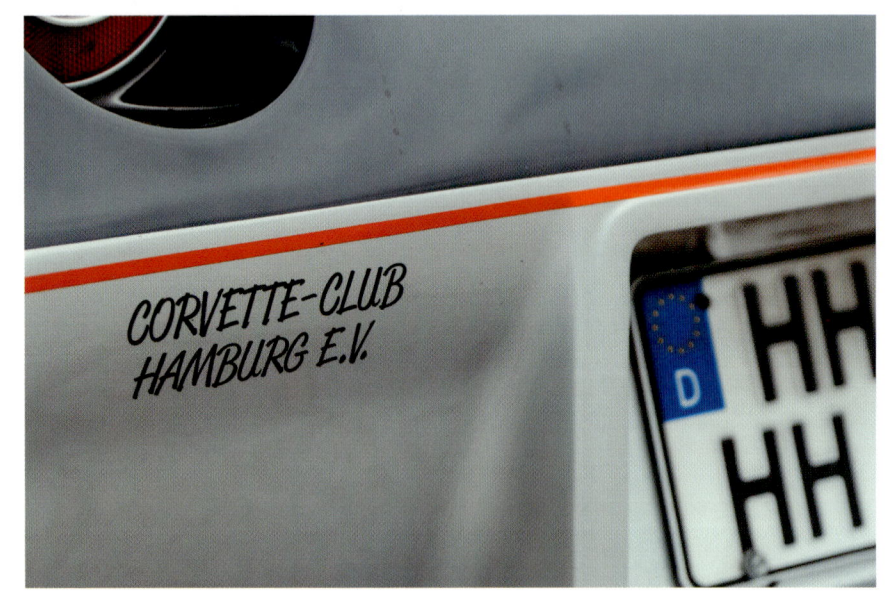

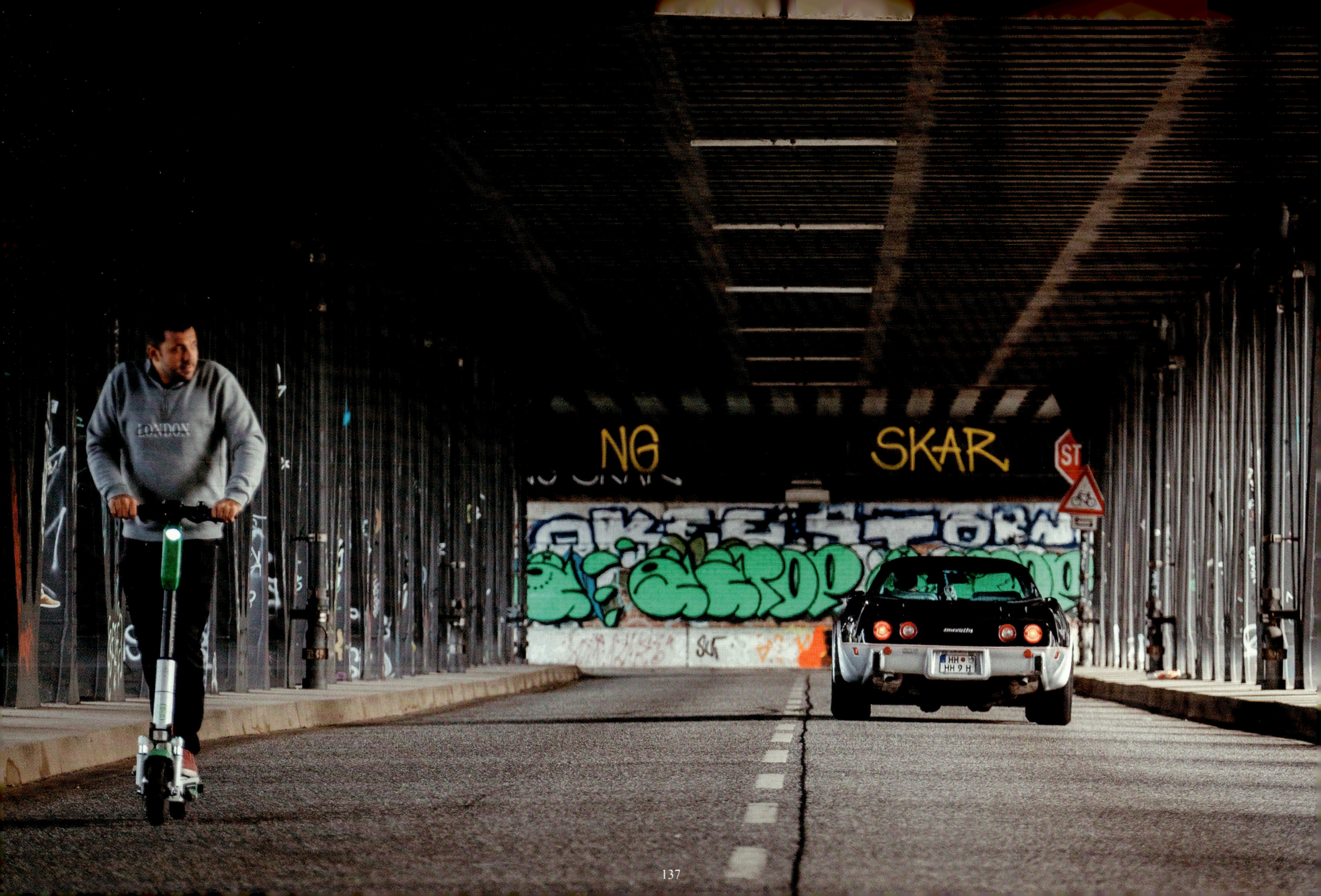
LONDON
NG
SKAR

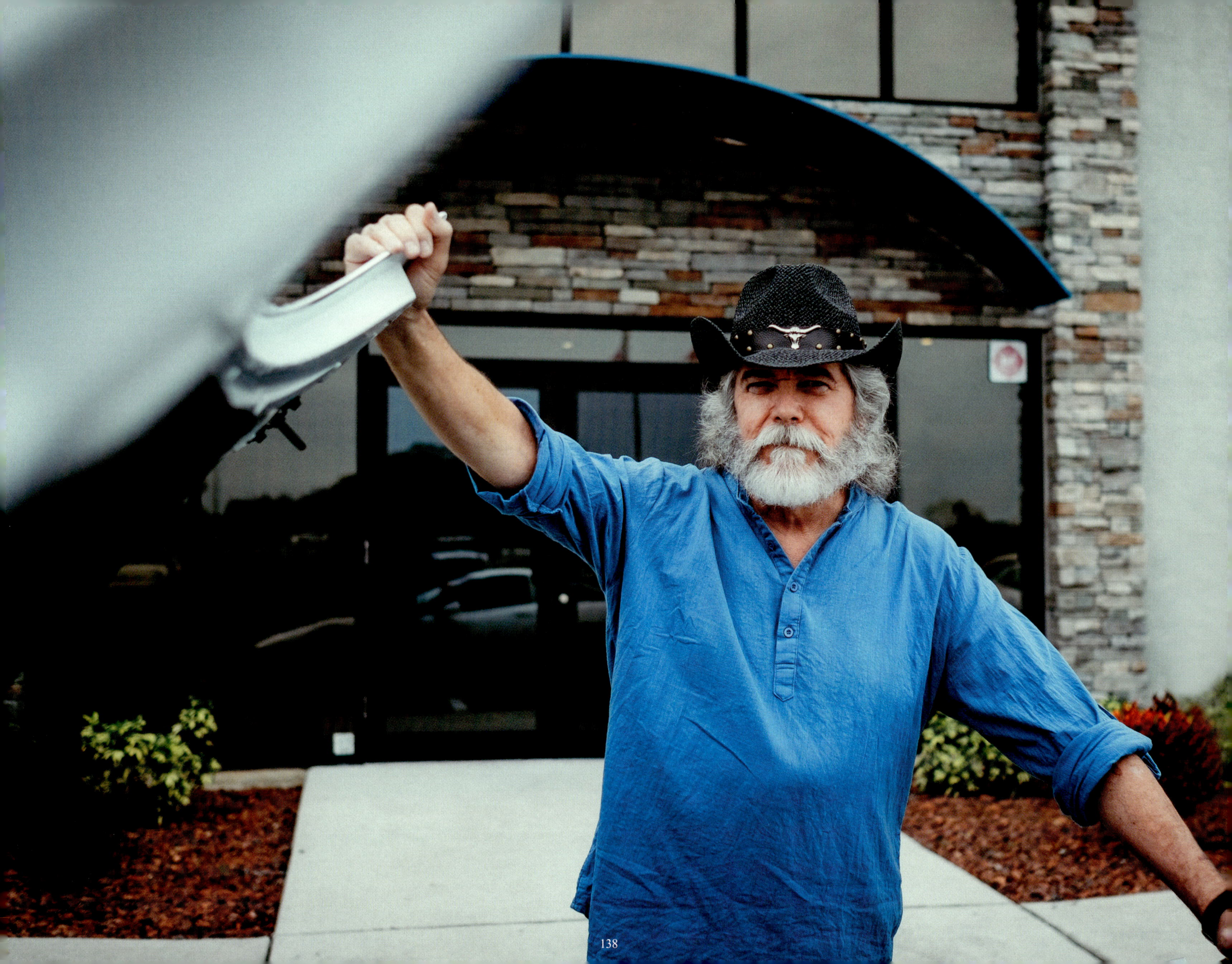

THE CORVETTE REPORTER

Scott Teeters started drawing cars at an early age. Today, he earns his living with his illustrations of Corvettes and stories about them.

What's your Corvette story?
Even as a child, I loved to paint and draw. When I was about ten years old, I became interested in cars and started sketching them. On the way home from school, I studied the different emblems and shapes, and at some point, I could tell a Chevy from a Ford or Pontiac. Those interested me the most because my older brother drove a nice '57 Chevy Bel Air. One time he had to take the car to the dealer to get something fixed. When we got there, he told me to wait for him in the showroom. There I found a '65 Stingray coupe spinning on a platform. I must have been standing in front of the car with my mouth open because a salesman came up to me and said, "You like this car? Here's a brochure for you." He wrote his name on the catalog, perhaps thinking that my father might come and buy a Corvette. I proudly took the brochure home; the car was the most beautiful thing I had ever seen.

Shortly thereafter, I found out that a local toy store sold Corvette model kits. The assembly instructions described each part, such as cylinder heads, manifolds, and carburetors. So I learned a lot about the cars. Then I discovered car magazines for myself, and one of my classmates told me, "My big brother has a Corvette, and when you buy a Corvette, you get the Corvette magazine for free!" You got a free magazine when you bought a Corvette? That just made it the coolest car in the world to me.

I read everything about the sports car I could find and also learned more about a guy named Zora Arkus-Duntov. When I was eleven or twelve, I wrote him a letter. I wanted to know more about the Corvette and asked him for technical specs. A few months later, I got a package from GM—unfortunately, not from Duntov personally. In the package was some information about the Corvette and the Chevelle. There were also some issues of *Corvette News*, and they said that they had added me to the mailing list. I got the magazine regularly, every three months, until 1974 or '75.

All I wanted was a Corvette! I finally bought one in 1973. It was a pile of junk, a '67 Big Block that had really been abused. I only had the thing about six months, but I got a taste for it. Then about a year later, a 1965 coupe showed up on my doorstep. It had a 327 V8 and was silver in color, with a big-block hood and side-pipes. I drove the car for a year and a half, then it was stolen. That was really tough because I had just overhauled the engine. The police found the Corvette two days later. The perpetrators had removed the valuable parts such as the engine, the transmission, and the side-pipes. I was broke, as I had put all my money into the engine! I sold what was left of the car and bought a 1968 Camaro. After that, the opportunity to own a Corvette didn't come along for a long time. I got married, we had a child, and I sold my motorcycles.

Nevertheless, my passion had to be satisfied somehow. I considered applying to *Vette Magazine*, the first independent magazine devoted exclusively to Corvettes. That was a pretty cool thing to do, because until then you had to make do with the occasional Corvette story in *Hot Rod Magazine* or *Road & Track*. Marty Shore was the editor, and he also put out one of my favorite magazines, *High Performance Cars*. Since I had already drawn cars for a couple of magazines, I just packed up my best work, wrote a cover letter, and sent it to Marty Shore. A week later, a guy with a thick New York accent called me: "Hi, Scott, this is Marty Shore. I got your drawings, really good. What do you have in mind." And so I started drawing for *Vette Magazine* and occasionally writing stories. That was in 1976.

The magazine was published quarterly at first, then bi-monthly, and by the mid-Eighties, every month. In 1997, I had the idea for a regular column called "The Illustrated Corvette Series." It was to tell the chronological story of the sports car, starting in 1953. The editor liked the idea, but he had no more space in the magazine. A few weeks later, he called me: "You know the guy who writes our Corvette column? He doesn't feel like doing it anymore, so we have room for your idea if you like." Of course I agreed, but soon realized what I had gotten myself into. I expected a total of fifty installments, but in the end, there were 263 stories. My column was in every issue for 23 years! I had made drawings of all the Corvettes, of every year of manufacture. It proved fortunate that I own the rights to my illustrations, because when I stopped working for the magazine, I started selling prints of my drawings. Today, I earn money with works that are thirty years old.

Around 2017, I moved to Florida and started thinking about a new Corvette of my own. I had already met my buddy John, who owned a '96 Grand Sport. I liked the 1996 Collector Edition. This special edition model was only available in silver and had the look of a ZR-1. I told John what I was looking for and he just said, "Yeah, those are great cars, but you'll probably get a better car if you find an early C5." And indeed, the fifth-generation Corvette is so much better than the C4. In my opinion, the C5 was the most revolutionary Corvette ever built up to that point. It had the LS1 aluminum engine, the transmission was in the rear for better weight distribution, and the frame was so much more torsionally rigid than its predecessor. When I started looking for a Corvette, the C7 was already on the market. Consequently, a relatively old C5 could be purchased at a reasonable price.

I found my coupe on CarGurus. It was in Fort Myers, about an hour and a half away from me. I wrote to the seller and asked how long the car had been on the net. His reply, "Since this afternoon." I showed the pictures to my wife, Karen, and told her that I had possibly found our new car. It had already been lowered slightly and had the Z06 chrome patches on it. So I drove to Fort Myers and test-drove it. The car ran good and straight; the brakes were perfect. It was a great car that was only going to cost $11,000. I went for it and got the C5. We've enjoyed the Corvette ever since. It's comfortable and great for long trips. You can drive it for eight hours and still not want to get out of the car. I'm very happy with it, and it hasn't let me down so far.

Thanks to the car, I also met a lot of great people and am now a member of the Highlands County Corvette Club. We meet once a week for breakfast. It has really surprised me how great this community is. I am also a member of the Lake Country Cruisers hot rod club. It's special to get to hang out with these cool people and see all these special cars.

What is your all-time favorite Corvette model?
The C5 is precisely the Corvette I wanted; I love this car. But I would also like to have a '65 coupe with side-pipes again. The C2 Stingray is simply a beautiful vehicle with incomparable lines.

◀ **1999** Corvette C5, **Sebring Raceway**, Florida, USA | November 18, 2021

TO SCOTT, CORVETTE MEANS:
STYLE, PERFORMANCE, SPEED

Role reversal. Normally, illustrator and journalist Scott Teeters interviews Corvette owners for the stories he writes for various digital and print publications. This time, however, the focus was on him and his white C5.

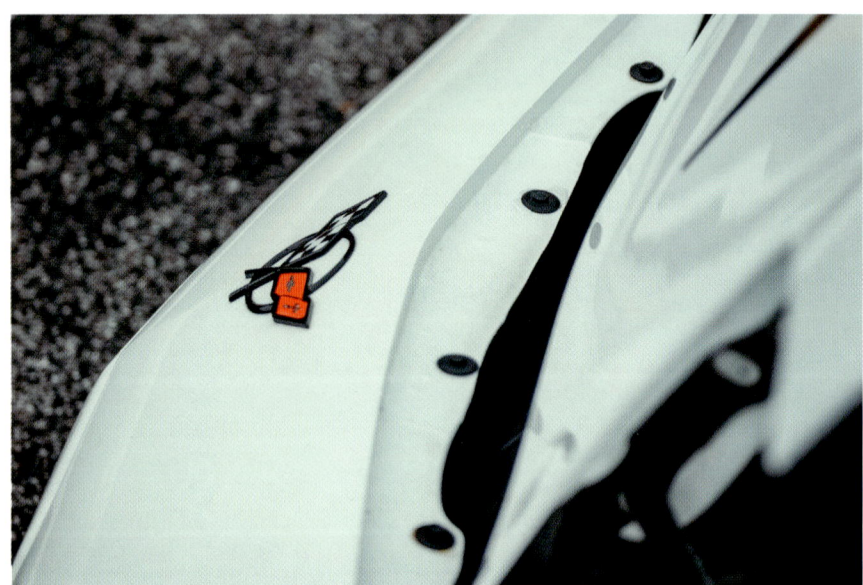

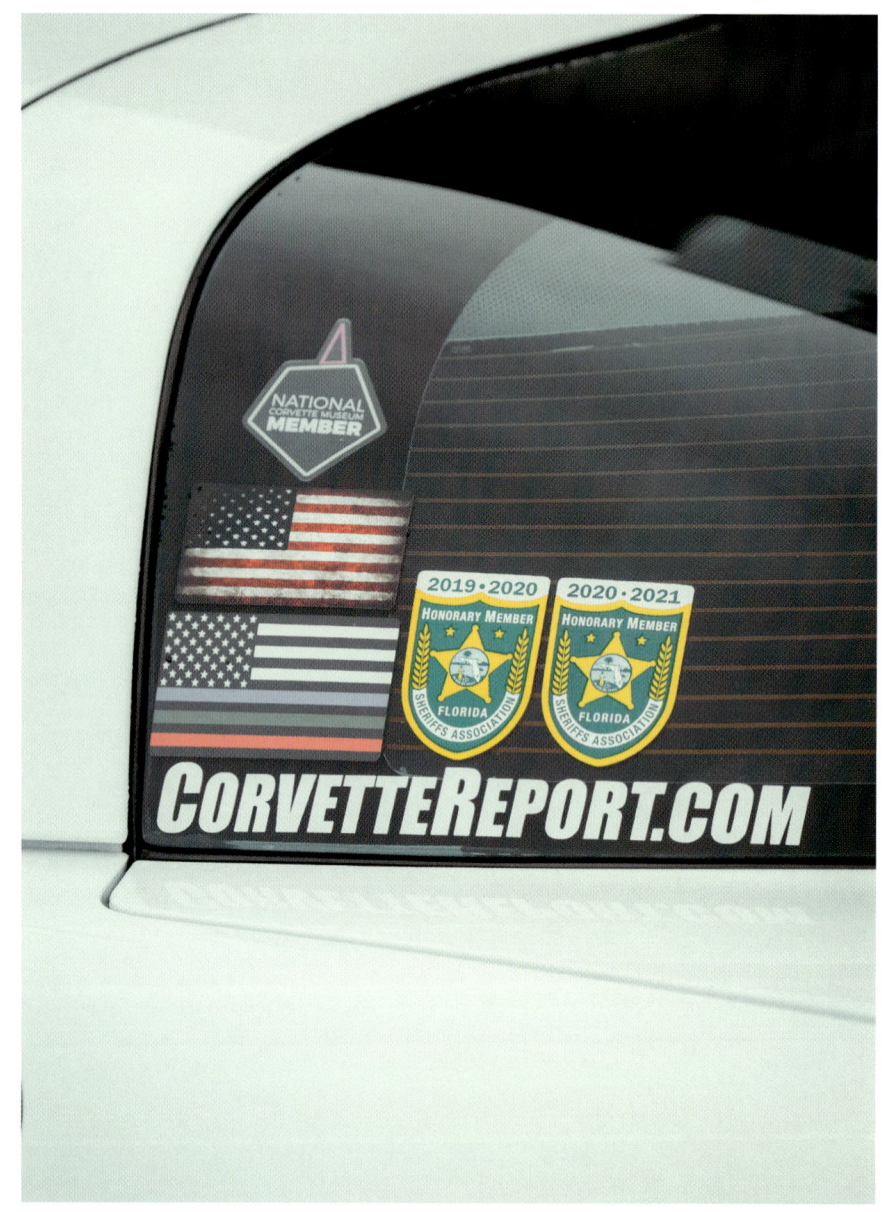

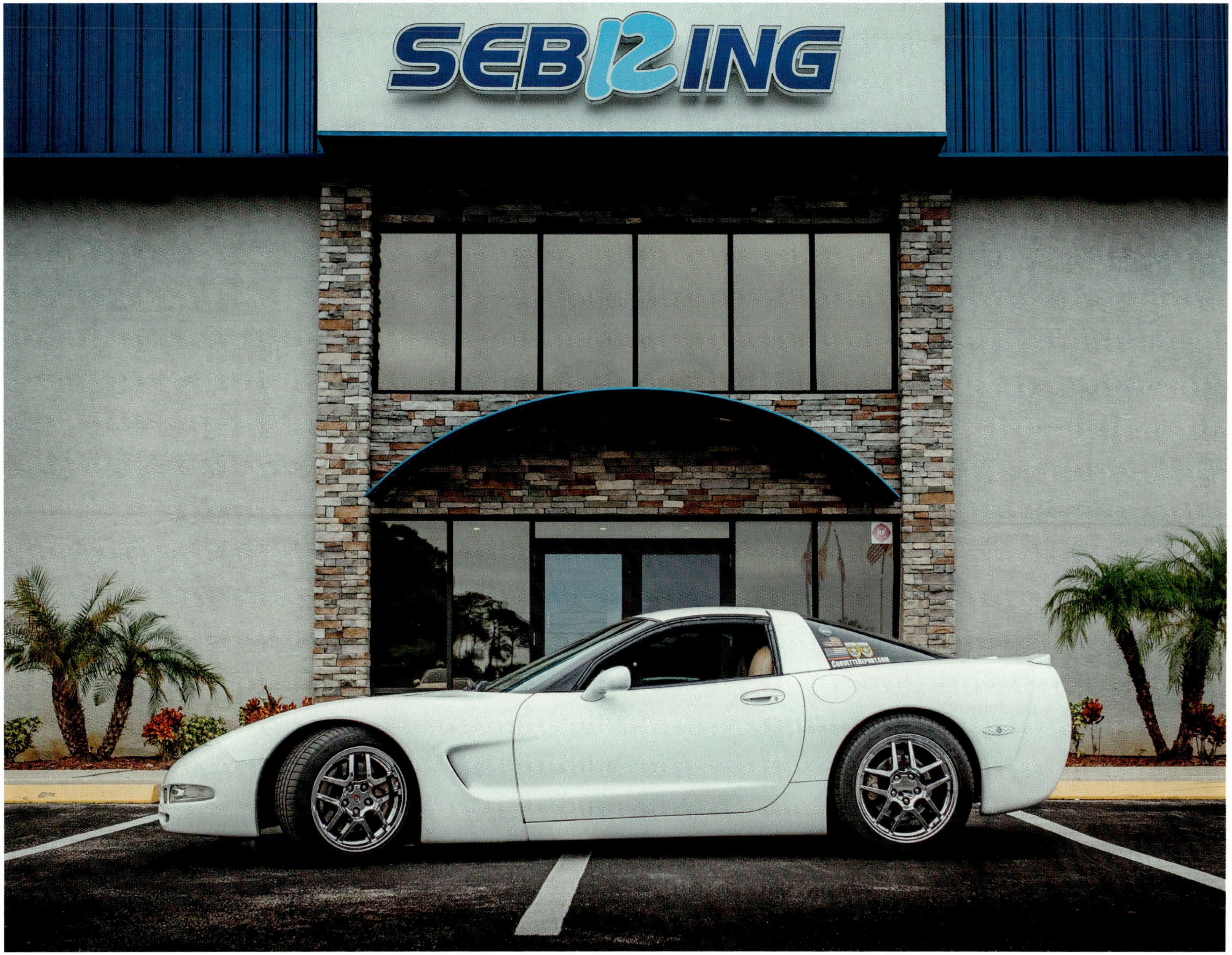
SEB12ING
CORVETTEDEPOT.COM

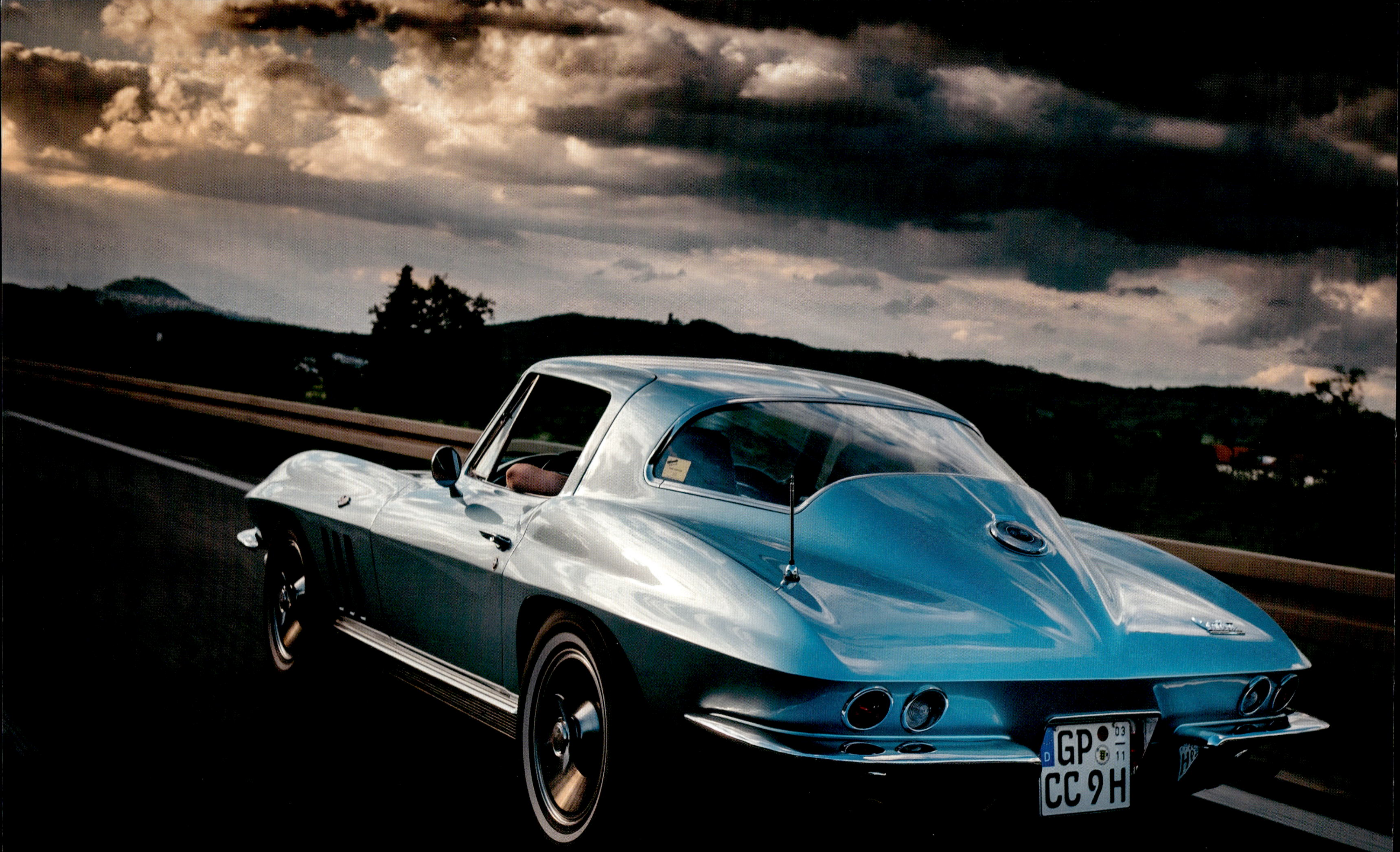
GP
CC 9H

TWO BROTHERS, ONE PASSION

Marc Wiesenberg was infected with the American car virus as a child. It was a long time, however, before the native of Swabia got his own Corvette C2.

What's your Corvette story?
When I was ten, I went to the Street Nationals in Munich for the first time with my parents and my brother. Until then, I only knew the usual American vehicles: the Mustang and the Corvette. So I took a close look at all the other cars and was blown away by the shapes, engines, and especially the sound. When I saw a '32 Ford tearing up the asphalt with its fat tires, I was done for, and I knew that I absolutely had to have a hot rod!

My brother is three years older than me, but we've always had the same interests. We're almost like twins, went to the same school, did our technician training together, work for the same company, and always thought the same cars were cool. My brother's first car was a fourth-generation Camaro with a 3.8-liter V6 engine. When I got my driver's license at 17, my brother really wanted to upgrade to a V8. I bought his car from him, and he bought a Z28 Camaro, also fourth generation. So we went to meetings together. An indescribable feeling. But I soon realized that the V6 wasn't enough for me either, so I started looking for a V8. In the Black Forest, I found a suitable vehicle, also a Camaro Z28, and my father took over the six-cylinder. So we had three Camaros and could go to meetings in convoy as a family.

Our interest in American classic cars continued to grow, and my brother again took the lead. He bought a '71 Ford Torino, which had been his favorite Autoquartett (card game) car from childhood. I still had the dream of a hot rod in my head, but I didn't want to sell my Camaro because I didn't know if hot rodding was feasible. There weren't exactly a lot of them for sale on the net. Then my father said he was going to sell his V6 Camaro, and if I found a hot rod, he would take the Z28 off my hands. Same game as last time. I'm very grateful that our parents always supported us and didn't put a stop to our craziness.

The search for the right rod took several years. Then in 2013 near Tübingen, I found exactly the hot rod that I had admired as a teenager at various meets. A '39 Ford Deluxe coupe with a 355-cubic-inch V8 and a TH700R automatic transmission, which had been converted into a street rod in Sweden in the late Eighties and was known throughout Europe. So I couldn't help myself and had to fulfill this wish. The love affair lasted seven years, until my desire for a manual transmission grew. The Corvette C2 was of course already the dream par excellence at that time, but for me, it was in a different price league. At the time, I thought such a car was only for the rich and beautiful.

So with a heavy heart, I set out to sell my Ford Deluxe coupe so that I could be happy with an American car with a manual transmission. I was looking for a compact car that would fit in my small garage, a Chevy Nova or Plymouth Barracuda. A Mustang was out of the question, too mainstream for me. And then while searching, I happened to stumble across a C2 that fit my budget. So if I could sell the rod for a good price, the dream Corvette wouldn't be completely out of reach for me after all.

In mid-2019, by which time the hot rod was already gone, I began busying myself with the subject of the Corvette more deeply. I spoke by telephone with every Corvette specialist I could find on the net, including Oliver Trieb. I asked him how much I would have to invest for a solid C2. His answer was at least €10,000 higher than I had imagined. He also observed that one would have to invest even more to eliminate all the minor imperfections. So I was back at the beginning, and "too expensive" was the bottom line. For the first time, I forced the subject of Corvettes from my mind, or at least I tried to. My focus lay on other cars, but there too I had no luck. And I could not shake my thoughts about the C2. I was left with one solution: increase my budget.

I traveled all over Germany and looked at four or five Corvettes. Each time, I took countless photos and sent them to members of the Corvette Forum to get expert feedback. None of these cars were suitable. They all had holes in the birdcage or frame and usually cracks of catastrophic dimensions. Bernd Janssen of Stingrays Vintage Corvette Parts was so nice and reached out to his private contacts for me, trying to find a Corvette that had possibly not yet been advertised.

I received a recommendation for a C2 in the Netherlands, a 1965 with complete "matching numbers" and original side-pipes. After a few telephone calls and the exchange of photographs, I made up my mind. My wife and I drove to the Netherlands over the weekend, and I had a closer look at the Corvette. When I got there, it was obvious from thirty feet away that there were serious problems. The fiberglass was poorly patched everywhere, there were raised areas and runs in the paintwork, and there was a hole in the birdcage, the metal structure surrounding the cabin. None of this could be seen in the photos I had received earlier. The other Corvette in the dealer's showroom was in a similar state. Frustrated, we immediately started on the long drive back to Germany.

On the way home, my wife told me that she was going to search the net for a C2 for me. I was familiar with all the cars on offer, but I let her try. In fact, she chanced upon a 1966 C2, a Trophy Blue Corvette near Duisburg. The advertisement was quite brief; therefore, I telephoned the owner. An hour later, I arrived. It was a small backyard garage, a yard that was for the most part just gravel, in the open a hall with a hydraulic lift, and everywhere were shipping containers, some with cars sitting on them. It had been pouring rain, and the Corvette was in front of the garage. The seller was very nice. He immediately drove the car onto the lift in the garage and said that I should examine the car at my leisure. He even let me remove the kick panels and the fairing on the A column so that I could see how things looked beneath them. Everything had so far made a good impression, except for a few oily spots on the engine. Minor details; time for a test drive! The car idled like a sack of nuts. The rpms fluctuated wildly, clouds of smoke rose from the engine compartment caused by oil dripping from the valve covers onto the manifolds, and the headlights wouldn't close. The seller stated that he would take care of all the problems. Despite the improperly adjusted engine, I was quite enthusiastic after the brief test drive. One's first experience driving a Corvette never leaves one cold.

I made the decision to buy on the spot after consulting Bernd Janssen again and describing the problems to him. The substance was the most important thing to me; the rest were minor issues that could be fixed. We therefore tried to negotiate the price in my direction, so that I would have a budget for the repairs. The tactic didn't work, for by the next day the seller had fixed all the problems. The engine ran silky smooth and no longer dripped oil. Even the headlights now opened and closed again. After lengthy negotiations and a telephone conversation with the owner, we were able to agree on a price.

Three weeks later the Corvette received a new TÜV (Technical Inspection Association) certification, and I was able to drive it from Duisburg to Swabia without problems. Since then, I have enjoyed every drive in my '66 coupe. I have fulfilled my second great dream, which I thought would always remain one.

What is your all-time favorite Corvette model?
Without doubt the 1966 Corvette C2 coupe.

◀ **1966** Corvette C2, **Geislingen an der Steige**, Baden-Württemberg, **Germany** | June 12, 2021

TO MARC, CORVETTE MEANS:
NOSTALGIA, JAMES BOND FEELING, LE MANS

Brothers in cars. The Wiesenberg siblings' passion for cars began with Camaros. While Marc realized the dream of owning a C2 Corvette after a long search, his older brother fulfilled his wish for a Ford Torino 500.

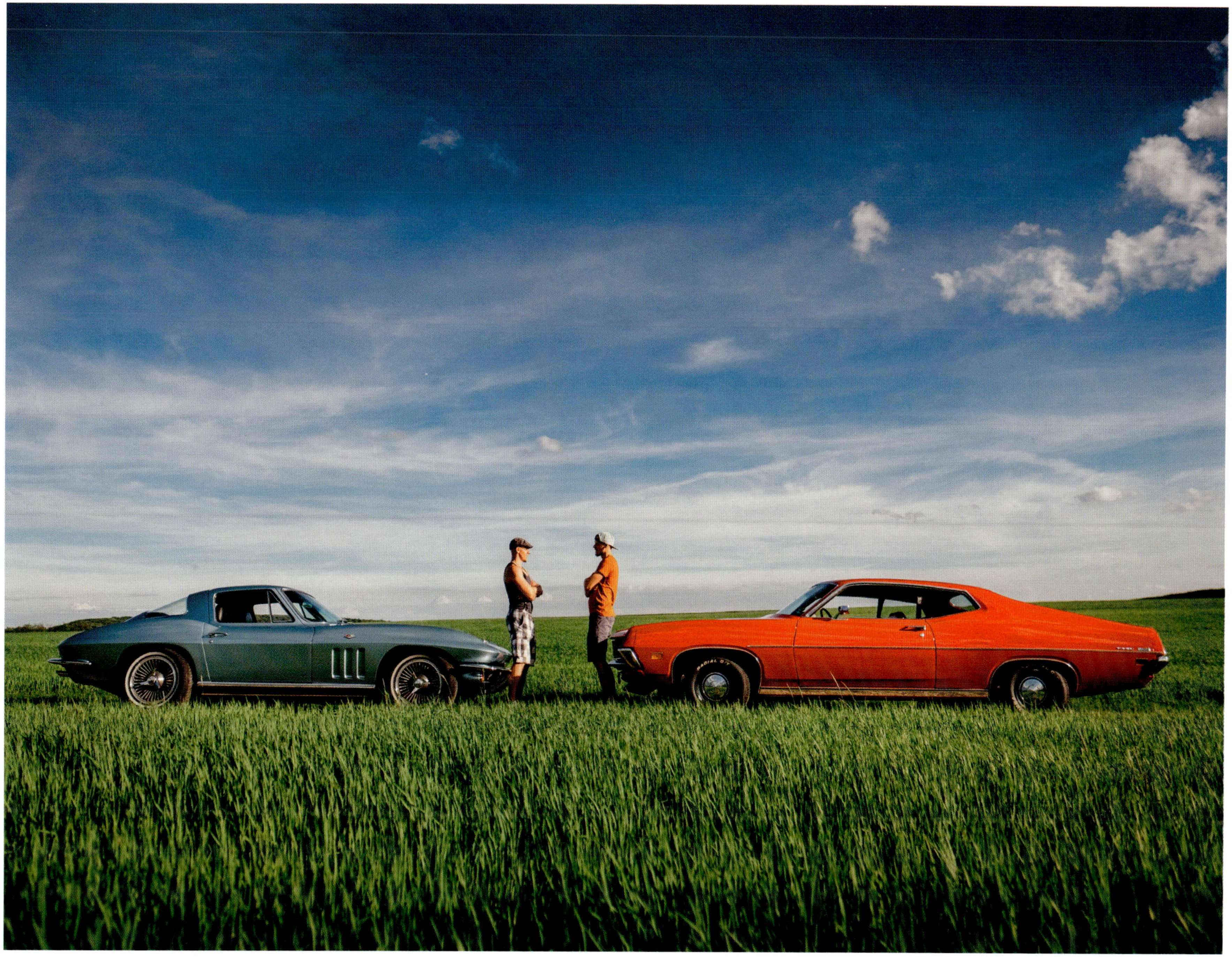

CORVETTES
NAPLES
NATIONAL COUNCIL
CORVETTES OF NAPLES
CORVETTE CLUBS, INC.

A CORVETTE FOR CHRISTMAS

Glenn Hutchinson has been president of the Corvettes of Naples club for thirty-two years. To him it's more than a club; it's a big family with more than 400 members.

What's your Corvette story?
In 1982, I bought a 1966 Corvette. I had the car for about a year, then my wife said that she would like to have her own Corvette. I found an ad for a yellow C3 in a New Orleans newspaper, and a few days later, we were on our way there to have a look at the Corvette. The car had the big 427 engine, 390 hp, servo linkage, brake booster, side-pipes, and a vinyl hardtop. Except for power windows, the C3 was pretty much fully equipped. I reserved the vehicle, paid for it the next day, and set off for home in the car. My wife got her yellow Corvette for Christmas 1983.

She drove the car to work every day, and for ten years, the Corvette was her daily drive. Once she even transported the block from an outboard motor on the passenger seat. A Corvette can certainly be a practical car! In 1994, I broke the C3 down into its individual components, removed the old paint, and repainted it. A complete frame-off restoration. Even afterward, it was to be a car that could be driven every day, not a restoration according to the strict NCRS Top Flight rules. My wife wanted to be able to go touring in the C3 with her girlfriends of the New Orleans Corvette Club without any problems. At that time, she made several trips across the USA with ten or twelve women.

I am a member of the National Council Corvette Club. Since 1986, I have taken part in NCCC shows with the C3. For 25 years, I was Concours Champion in my class. I also won three national competitions with the C3. In 1985, I established the Cajun Corvette Club in Louisiana. In 1986, we moved to Florida, and I joined Corvettes of Naples. I've been a member of the club for thirty-two years and am even the president. A long time. Corvette clubs have always been an important part of my life.

For just as long, my wife has been Membership Director, meaning she looks after everything concerning club memberships. There is always a lot to do. Incidentally, Corvettes of Naples is the third-largest club in the NCCC, and we currently have well over 400 members. Everything the club does, all the money we collect, is for charitable purposes, 100 percent. Our life is also centered around the club. We take part in something with other members almost every weekend. We all love our Corvettes; to us it is like a big family. There are so many engaging people in the group, and the cohesion in our organization is unique. Simply a great club.

We also met Manuela Feicht from Germany through the club. We call her Mandy. She is not only a member of Corvettes of Naples, she is also the president of the Bavarian Corvette Club in Germany. It is really a privilege that we got to know Mandy, visit her overseas, and be able to take part in several great tours through Europe with her. She organizes European trips for Corvette enthusiasts from the USA. There is nothing to worry about. You can just climb into your Corvette and drive away. The entire trip, including events, all the overnight stays and so on, are planned in advance. If you have an interest in cars, then you should definitely take part in a tour like this. We made our next trip with our friend in the summer of 2022.

What is your all-time favorite Corvette model?
That's difficult to say. If you're looking for a car for general use, one you can drive every day without problems, then the C8. If I had to choose just one model, then it would be the C3, especially the '69. It's my absolute favorite.

◀ **1969** Corvette C3, **Fort Myers**, Florida, USA | November 19, 2021   **2021** Corvette C8 ▶

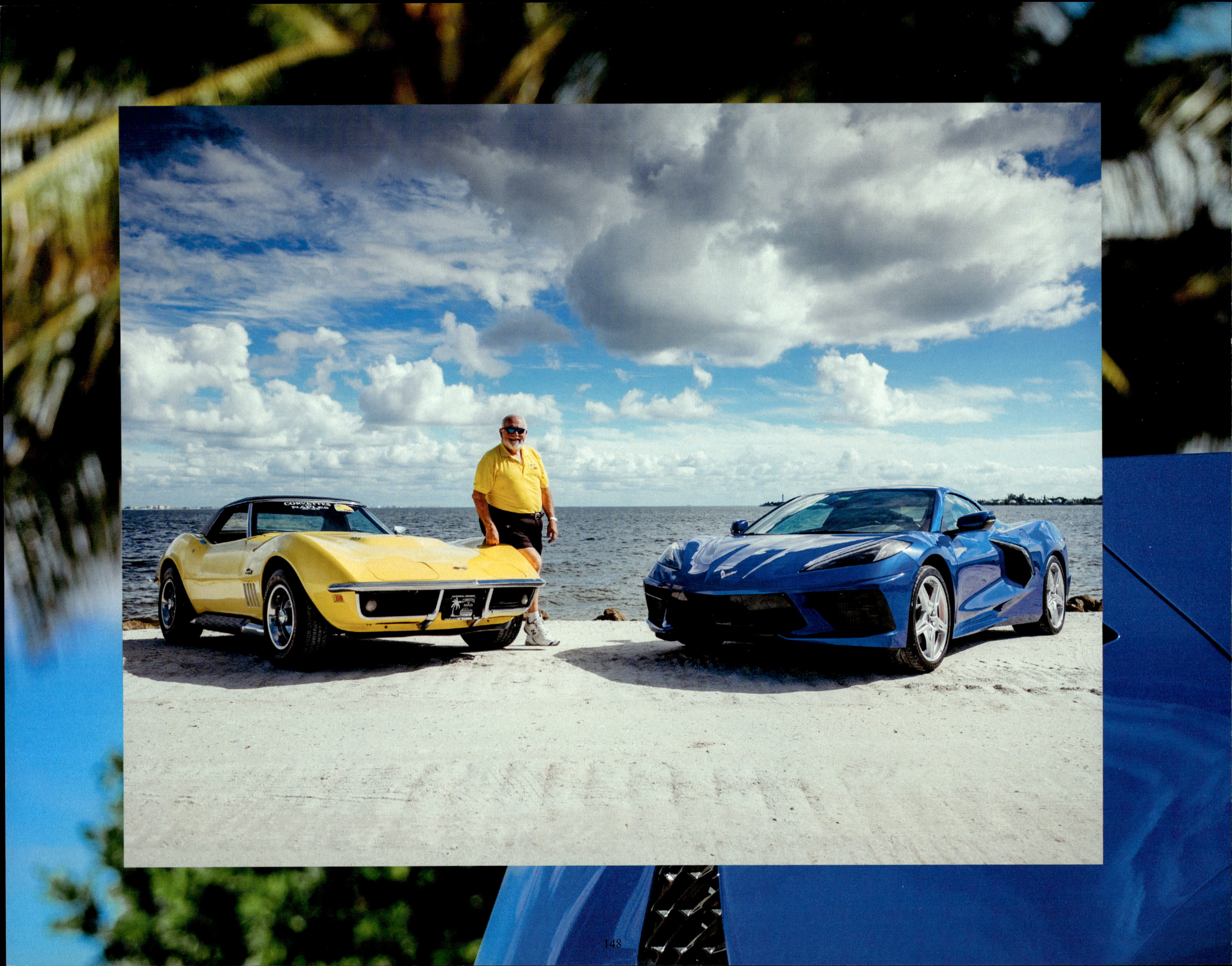

TO GLENN, CORVETTE MEANS:
IT IS MY FAMILY

Family ties. Glenn Hutchinson gave his wife this yellow C3 for Christmas in 1983. It has been in the couple's possession ever since and even served as their everyday car for a long time. Today, when they go to meetings of the Corvettes of Naples Club, they also like to take the modern C8.

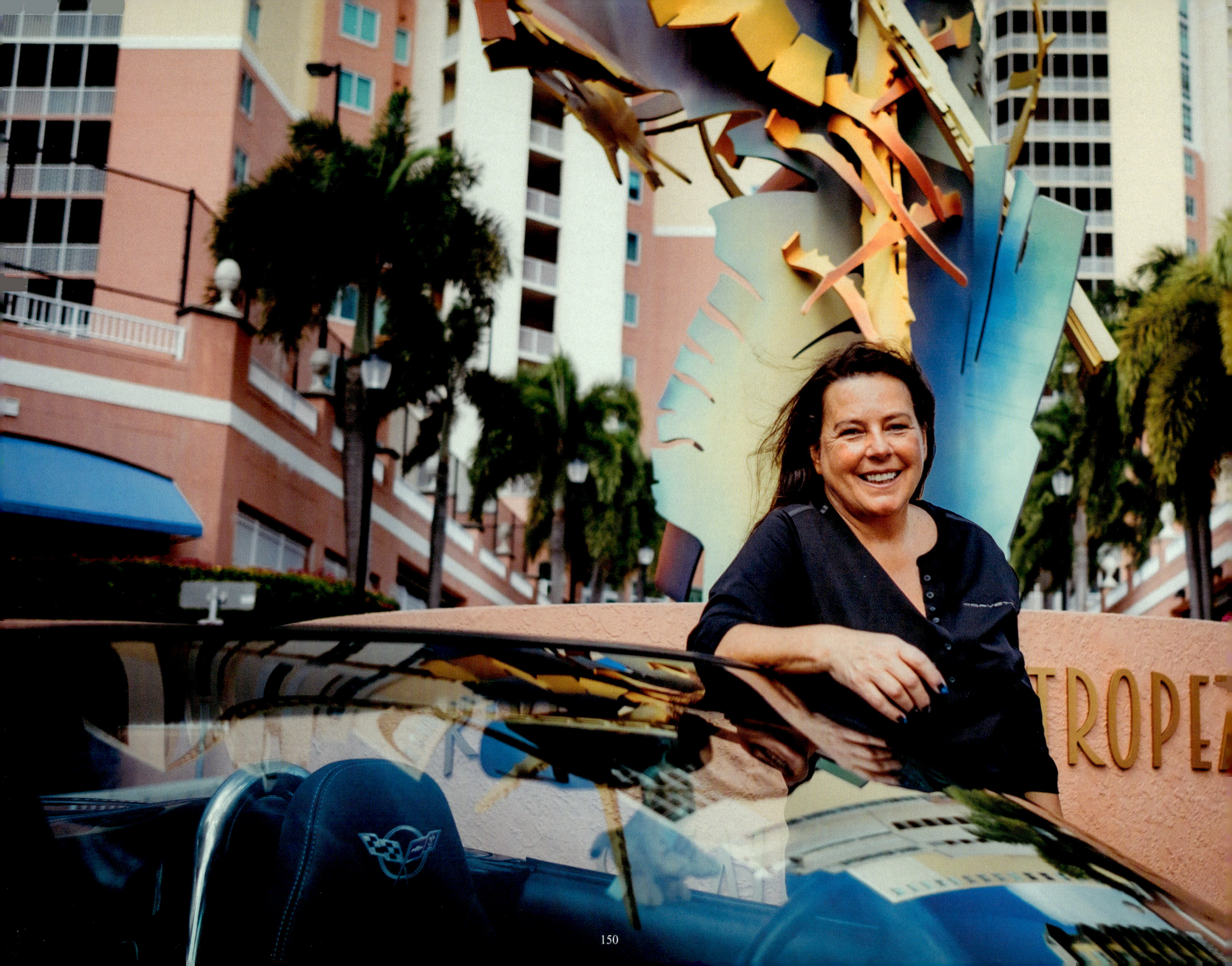

GERMAN-AMERICAN LOVE STORIES

Manuela Feichts's great love is the Corvette. As president of the Bavarian Corvette Club, she organizes trips in the American sports car through Europe for American Corvette owners.

What's your Corvette story?
I first visited the USA in 1983 to see relatives. They had a friend with a Corvette. I had never seen anything like it before—simply an awesome car. At the time, I didn't know exactly what kind of car it was, but it was clear to me that I had to have one.

Back in Munich, I began gathering information. I found out that the car that had so excited me was a Chevrolet Corvette C3. Until then, I had never heard of a Corvette! But now I was completely fascinated by the car and began looking for one. I met Mike Barretta in late 1983 or early 1984. He was then the first and only American car dealer in Munich. Unfortunately, at that time he had no Corvettes for sale, but he went looking for one. Then in 1984, we found a Corvette in Kassel, and I immediately bought it. It was a red '73 coupe, my first Corvette. Incidentally, I got along with Mike so well that he stayed with me for nine years.

The first years I had the red coupe, I actually only drove it to car races. Mike was a racing driver, and every weekend, we went to racing events somewhere. We had an entire race team with us, with mechanics, tires, tools, and everything that went with them. We went to Monza, Zolder, Zandvoort, and the Nürburgring, as well as the Hockenheim, Salzburg, and Austrian motorsport racetracks, simply everywhere. A great time! Through Mike I met Walter Hagl, one of the founders of the Bavarian Corvette Club, which then was still the Corvette Owners Club Germany. I joined the club in 1984 and have been an active member since. Once you have had the Corvette virus, you never get rid of it. For a long time, I served as the club's secretary, clerk, and treasurer, and since 2013, I have been president of the Bavarian Corvette Club. In that time, I have met many great people. I made friendships back then in the 1980s that I still maintain today. I'm still in contact with Walter Hagl, for example, the founder of the club. He still has his garage, still lives above it, but now he only works on his own cars.

Unfortunately, I was forced to sell my first Corvette. I was only in my mid-twenties at the time. But that very Corvette is now owned by our vice-president. He bought the car from Mike and by chance became a member and vice-president. I have therefore stayed in contact with my very first Corvette.

How many different Corvette generations have you owned since?
Every generation except the C2. The C2 is the only Corvette that I've never had. Actually, I've always had a C3. When I lived in Los Angeles for several months in 1986, I drove a C4 convertible. I bought it when it came on the market.

For a long time, I found the fifth generation too wide, too masculine. But then in 2011, I added a C5 in Florida. When I'm in Fort Meyers, it's my primary mode of transportation. My C6, which I ordered new in 2005, was the first C6 convertible delivered to Karl Geiger in Munich. I picked up the convertible on June 16, 2005. I drove the C6 until 2019, and in 2014, I also added the very first C7 convertible delivered to Germany. Of course, it was also from Karl Geiger. Then in 2015, the C7 convertible went to Austria when I got my blue C7 Z06 convertible. In 2016, it was joined by a yellow C3 Big Block convertible, which I had Karl Geiger get for me from a Barrett-Jackson auction. Three years later, I sold my wonderful C6 convertible due to lack of space.

In March 2020, I received one of the first C8s in the USA. I was looking forward to driving it in America, but then the coronavirus came. No one was traveling; there were no car shows. My business involving Corvette trips through Europe was also halted by the pandemic. I therefore sold my C8. It found its way from the USA to Berlin. Recently, I tried to buy it back, but the new owner read my email too late and had already disposed of the car. I am now waiting for the C8 Z06.

How long have you been organizing Corvette tours in Europe?
That began in 2015, but I had been organizing almost all of the events and tours by the Corvette Club for more than twenty years. That's how it was, and in 2015, I drove through Europe with a larger group of Americans for the first time. The participants were so enthusiastic that I thought it would be a good business idea. I always try to combine the trips with events in Europe; for example, with the *Mille Miglia* in Italy or our annual sports car meet in the Zillertal. The last two years had to be canceled because of COVID, but fortunately I am fully booked again for 2022, and I hope that the trips can go ahead. I'm looking forward to it very much!

What is your all-time favorite Corvette model?
Difficult question. In any case the C3, because that was my first Corvette, and I find it the most beautiful in terms of shape. Then the C8, no question. But I also have to say that I love my C7 Z06 very much. Actually, whatever Corvette I'm driving at the moment is my favorite model.

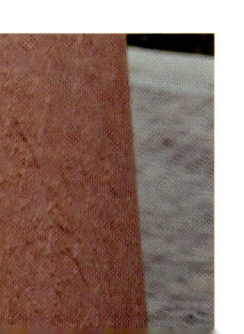

▲ **2016** Corvette C7, **Munich**, Bavaria, **Germany** | July 23, 2021

1999 Corvette C5, **Fort Myers**, Florida, **USA** | November 19, 2021 ▲

TO MANUELA, CORVETTE MEANS:
MY LOVE FOREVER

Mrs. President. The only story in the book that was photographed both in Germany and the USA is that of Manuela Feicht. She is the chairwoman of the "Corvette Club Bavaria" and drives a C7 Z06 in Munich in the summer and a C5 in Florida in the winter.

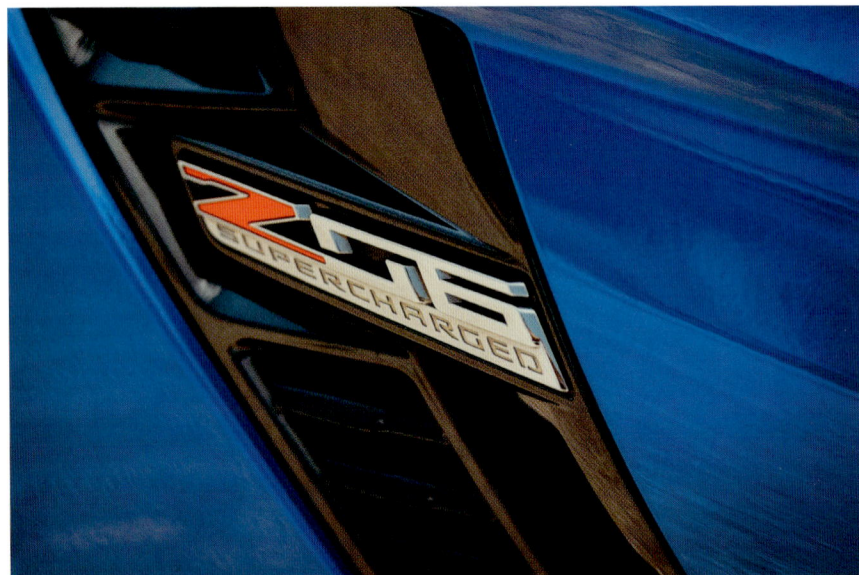

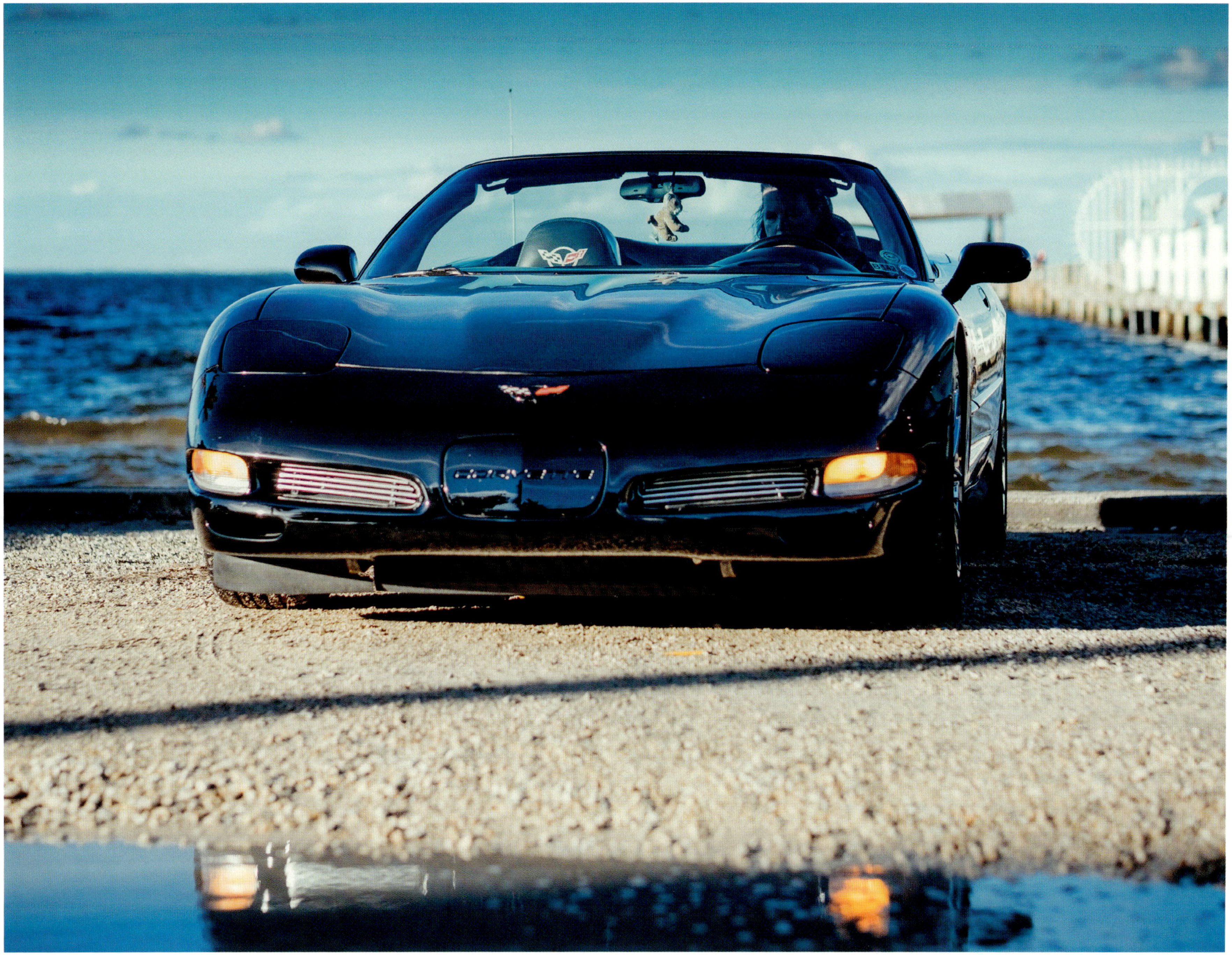

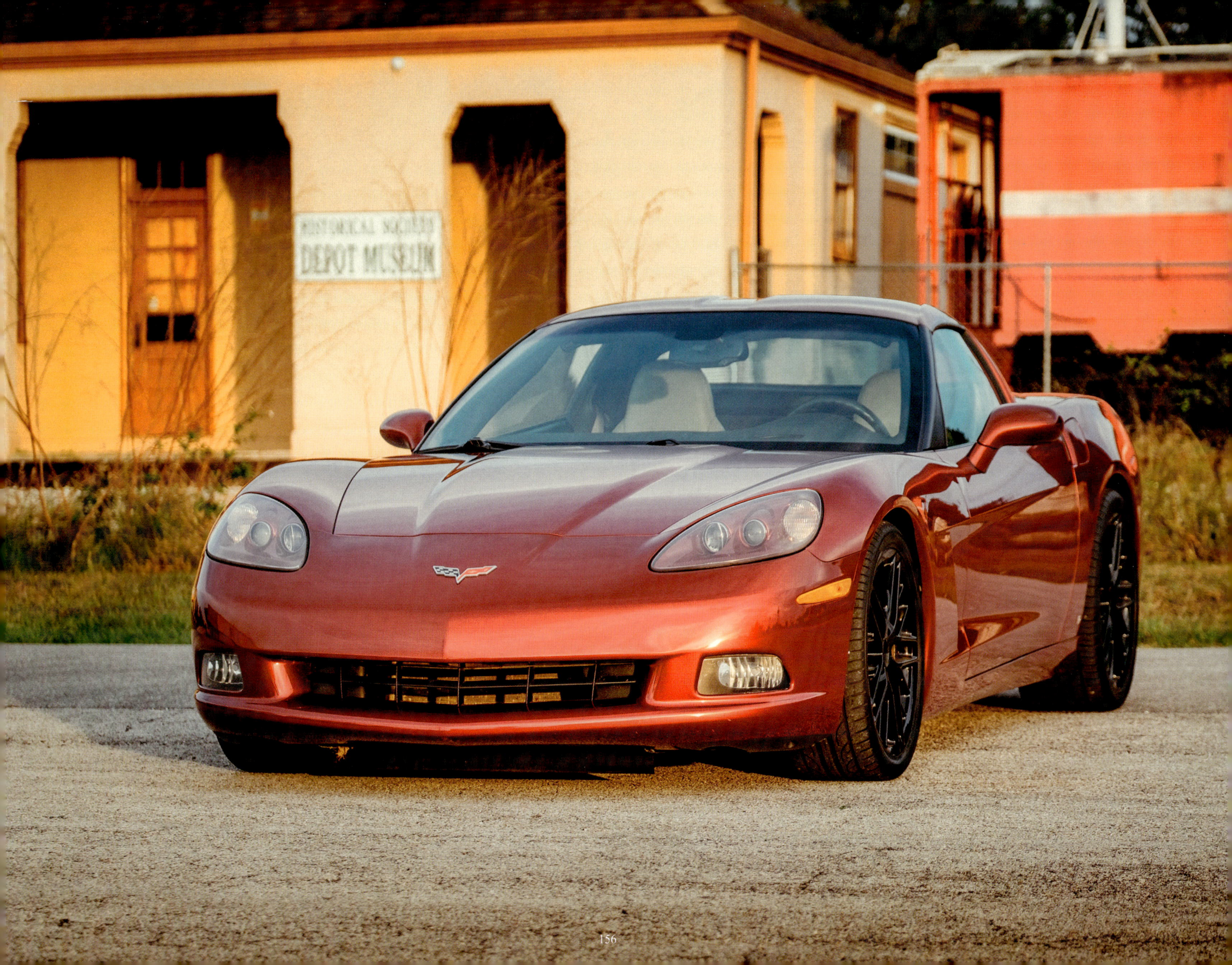
HISTORICAL SOCIETY
DEPOT MUSEUM

GUEST FROM MONTEREY IN LAKE PLACID

Jack Murphy bought his first new Corvette in 1981. He has remained true to it to the present day. In addition, he now also has a C6. And there is a C8 on his wish list.

What's your Corvette story?
I have been interested in the Corvette for twenty-five, thirty, actually forty years. I got my first new one in 1981. I also had a few older Corvettes—a '62 convertible, a 1969 Big Block C3, and one from 1977. They were all great, which is the reason I keep buying Corvettes. I also like deep red cars, of which I have two. Four are silver and one bright red. Compared to some European sports cars, the Corvette is not too expensive, and with it you get more car, more performance for your money. I am more of a leisurely through-the-country kind of driver, and I don't race my Corvettes.

I got my current 2006 C6 in 2015. It's a Z51 that had 40,000 miles on it when I got it. The Corvette had one previous owner who worked for Chevrolet. The car was therefore in excellent condition and was always parked in his garage. The car is Monterey Red, a color that could only be had for the C6 from 2006 to 2008. As I said, it had the Z51 package and the 3LT options. This means that good stuff was used in the interior. The interior color is Cashmere. Of course, it's not made of real cashmere, but at least it's made of leather. To make the C6 sound a little better, I retrofitted a Corsa exhaust system. The black rims are from a 2009 ZR1, and they look great on the car. Through the spokes you can see the large, internally ventilated brake discs. These are the only parts of the Z51 package that are clearly visible from the outside.

What is your all-time favorite Corvette model?
I would say that depends on the respective generation and how well the cars are equipped. I like the C3; the shape is just great. The Corvette I bought in 1981 is still in my garage. I like the style and design of the C3 the best, but you can't compare the handling with my newer Corvette; they're worlds apart. My C6 has great handling and looks great, and it's a perfect package. If you look at the C6 from the side, I also find it nicer than the C7 or the C8. I will definitely keep my C3 and my C6, no matter what happens. I will get a new C8 Z06, but it won't replace the other two.

◀ **2006** Corvette C6, **Lake Placid**, Florida, **USA** | November 17, 2021

157

TO JACK, CORVETTE MEANS:
A FANTASTIC DRIVING EXPERIENCE

Sharp-dressed girl. Visually, the C6, which appeared in 2005, is an evolution of the C5, but with a much sharper design. It showed the edgy direction in which the design of future generations would develop. By the way, Jack Murphy's 2006 Corvette wears 2009 ZR1 wheels.

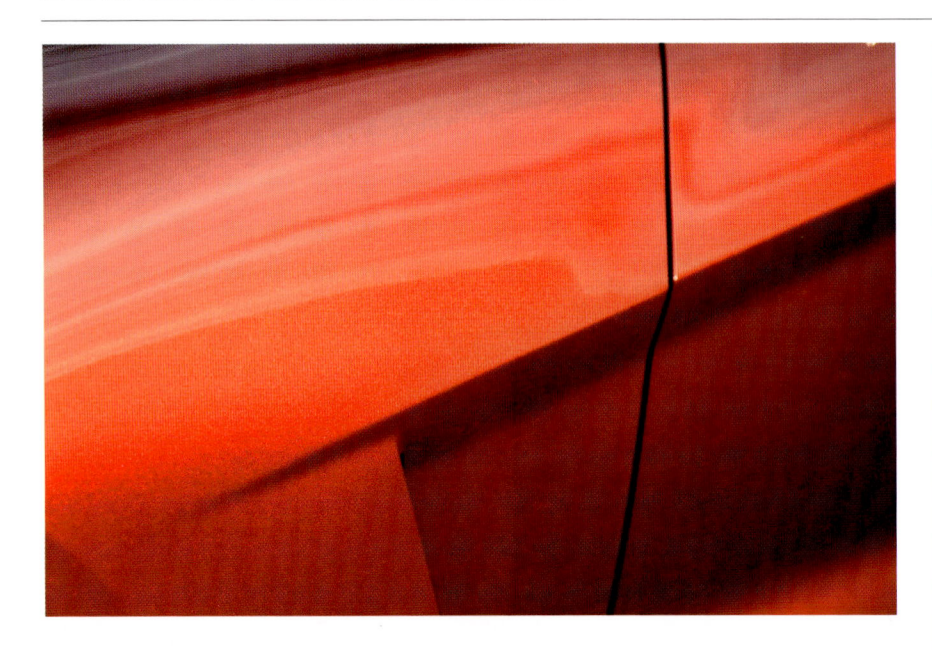

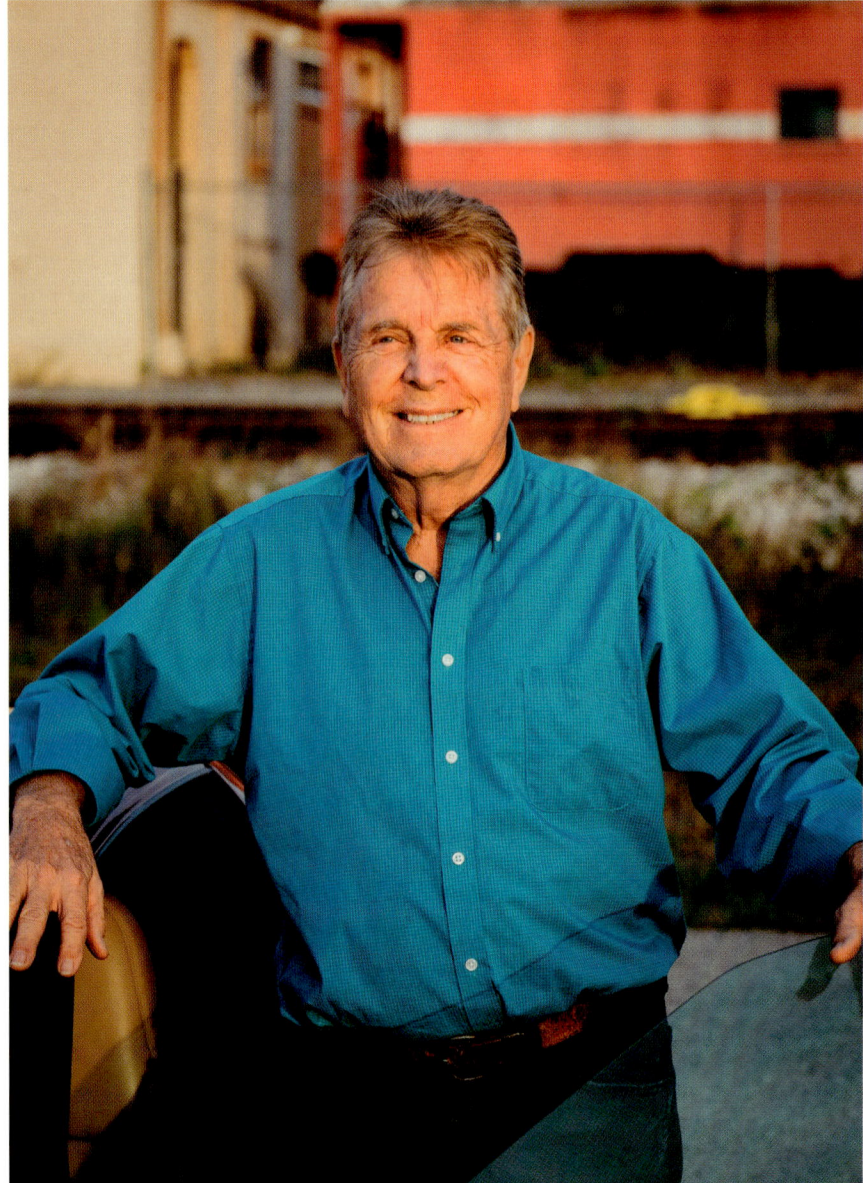

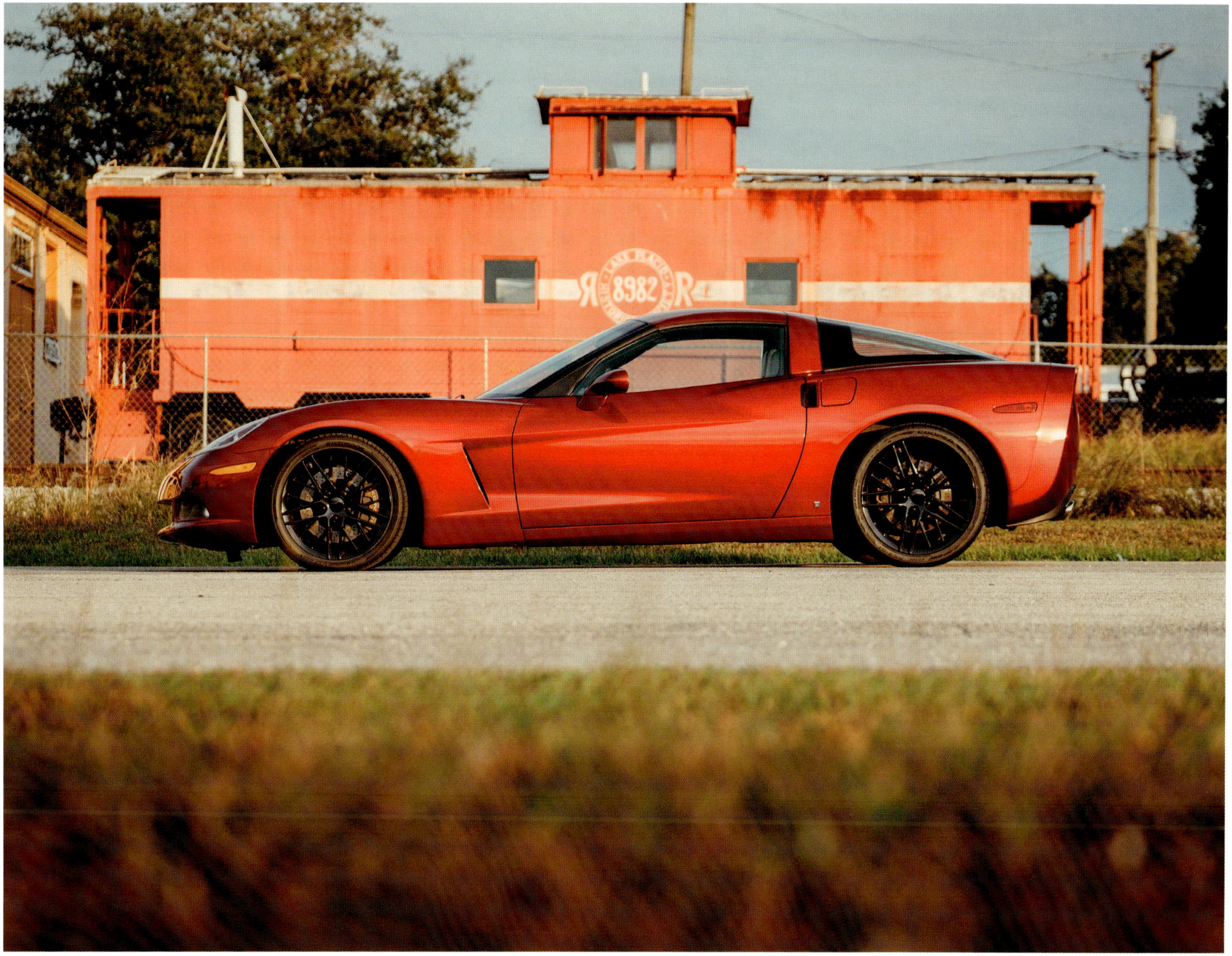
8982

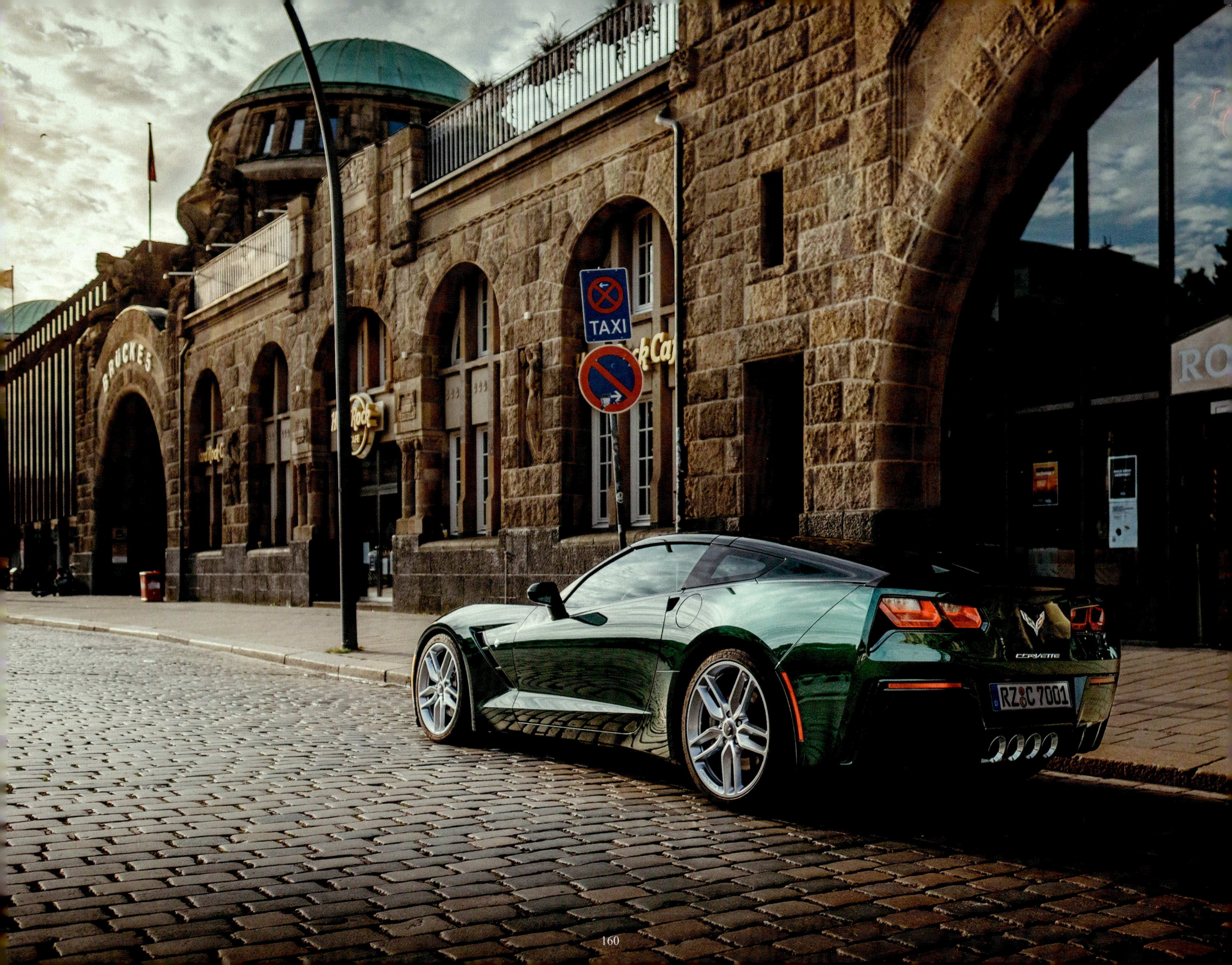
TAXI
RZ C 7001

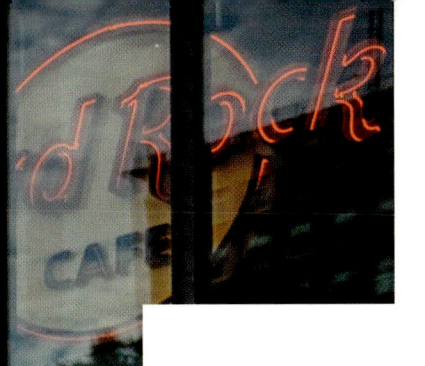

INSPIRED BY HARD ROCK

A rock legend indirectly inspired Stefan Krogmann to buy a Corvette. He was even able to personally thank his idol for the fact that, thanks to him, he now has one of the American sports cars in his garage.

What's your Corvette story?
In late 2013, I saw a tweet from an idol from my youth, Paul Stanley of the rock group KISS. He had posted a picture of himself and his C7. As a result, I became aware of this car for the first time. The Corvette itself was, of course, a household name to me, but the C7 was new. I was totally blown away by the design; the look is just impressive. I really wanted to learn more about the new Corvette and began researching.

From the Seventies and Eighties, people knew the Corvette as the iconic American sports car. But one also heard again and again about the quality deficiencies of American vehicles, so I was never interested in driving a car from the States. But the C7 was said to be a quantum leap forward in terms of technology, and so I simply took the plunge.

At the time, the C7 was brand new on the market. So I went looking and found a Corvette in the color Lime Rock Green at a small importer in the Sauerland. When I saw the car on the web, I thought that nobody would buy a green car, but out of curiosity, I went there anyway. That was definitely the right decision, because in person, I found the color combined with the design absolutely spectacular! The decision was made quickly, and on my fiftieth birthday, my wife and I put the car in our garage.

Over the years we've thought about a C3 from time to time. That's the classic Corvette par excellence, which is still reasonably affordable at the moment. But you need more technical knowledge, and if you're unlucky, the car is in the workshop eight days out of ten. That would not be for us. We prefer to enjoy the sportiness and technical amenities of our modern C7.

You personally thanked Paul Stanley for inspiring you to buy the C7?
Yes, we are not only Corvette enthusiasts but also big KISS fans. The band has been doing regular cruises in the Caribbean. There are 2,000 rock fans from all over the world on the ship. On one of these cruises, we had the opportunity to talk to Paul Stanley. We told him that it was his tweet that got us our Corvette, and that we are really grateful to him for that. It's been so much fun; we've met so many new, nice people. The Corvette community is great! The personal contacts are also a part of the Corvette driving experience for us.

What is your all-time favorite Corvette model?
Well, if all eight models were lined up here now in perfect condition, I would perhaps choose a C3. It's just the classic oldie. But in terms of driving, handling, and suitability for everyday use, the overall package, I would definitely go with the C7!

◀ 2014 Corvette C7, **Hamburg**, Germany | **August 7, 2021**

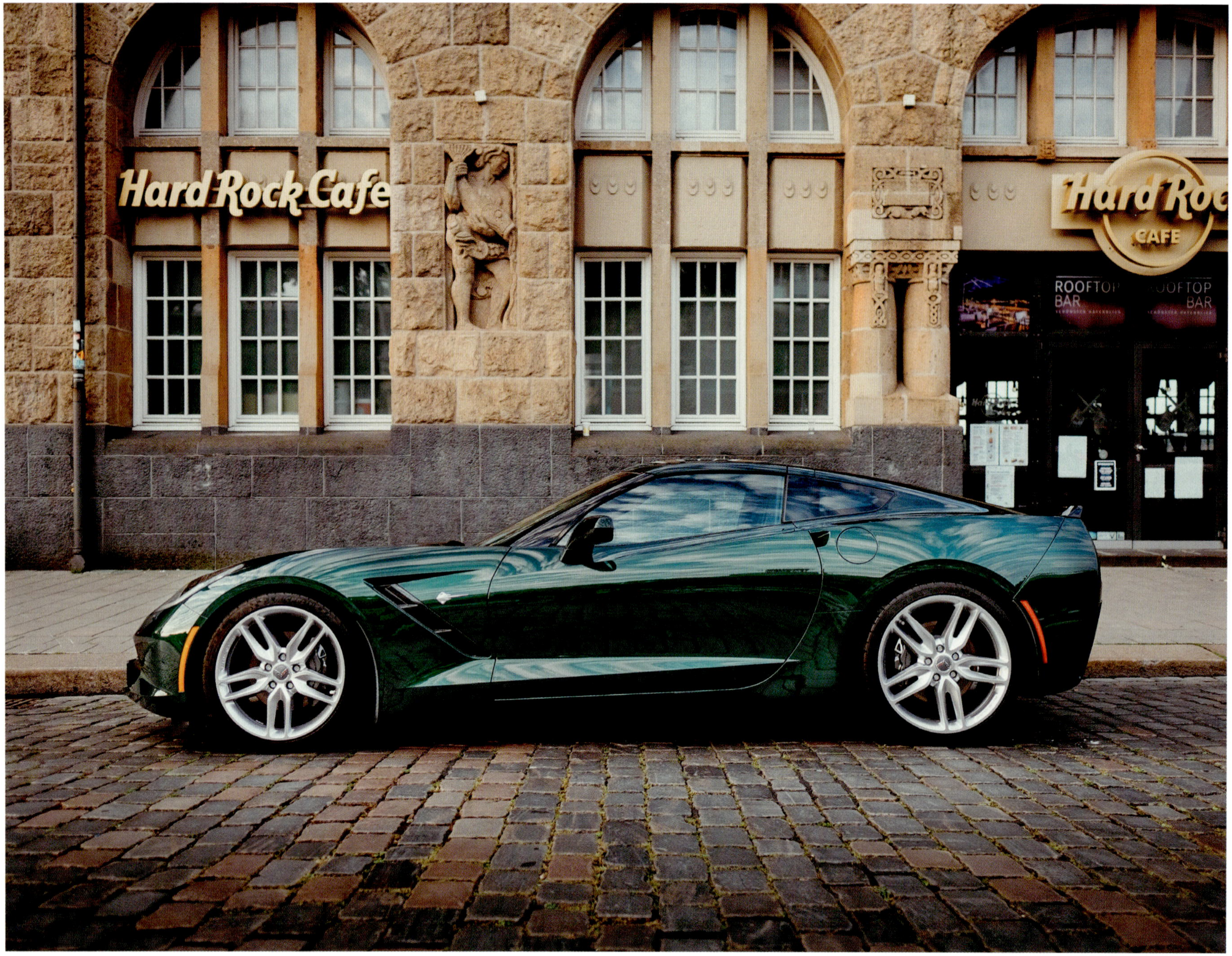
Hard Rock Cafe
Hard Roc
CAFE
ROOFTOP
BAR
ROOFTOP
BAR

TO STEFAN, CORVETTE MEANS:
LOW, WIDE, FAT, CORVETTE

I was made for loving you! Stefan Krogmann not only loves his Stingray, he's also a big fan of the rock group KISS. The band's guitarist and singer Paul Stanley had posted pictures of himself with his Corvette in a tweet, which first put the Hamburg native on the trail of the then-new C7.

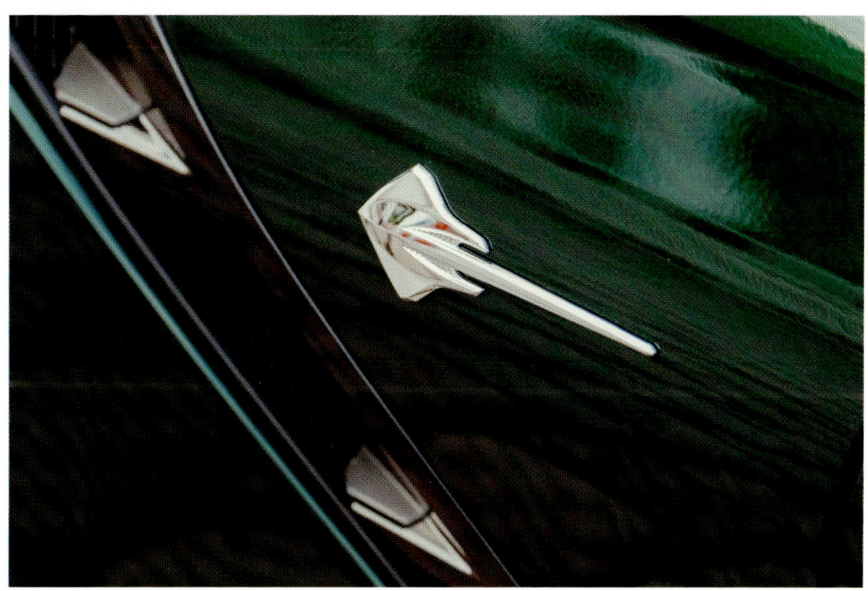

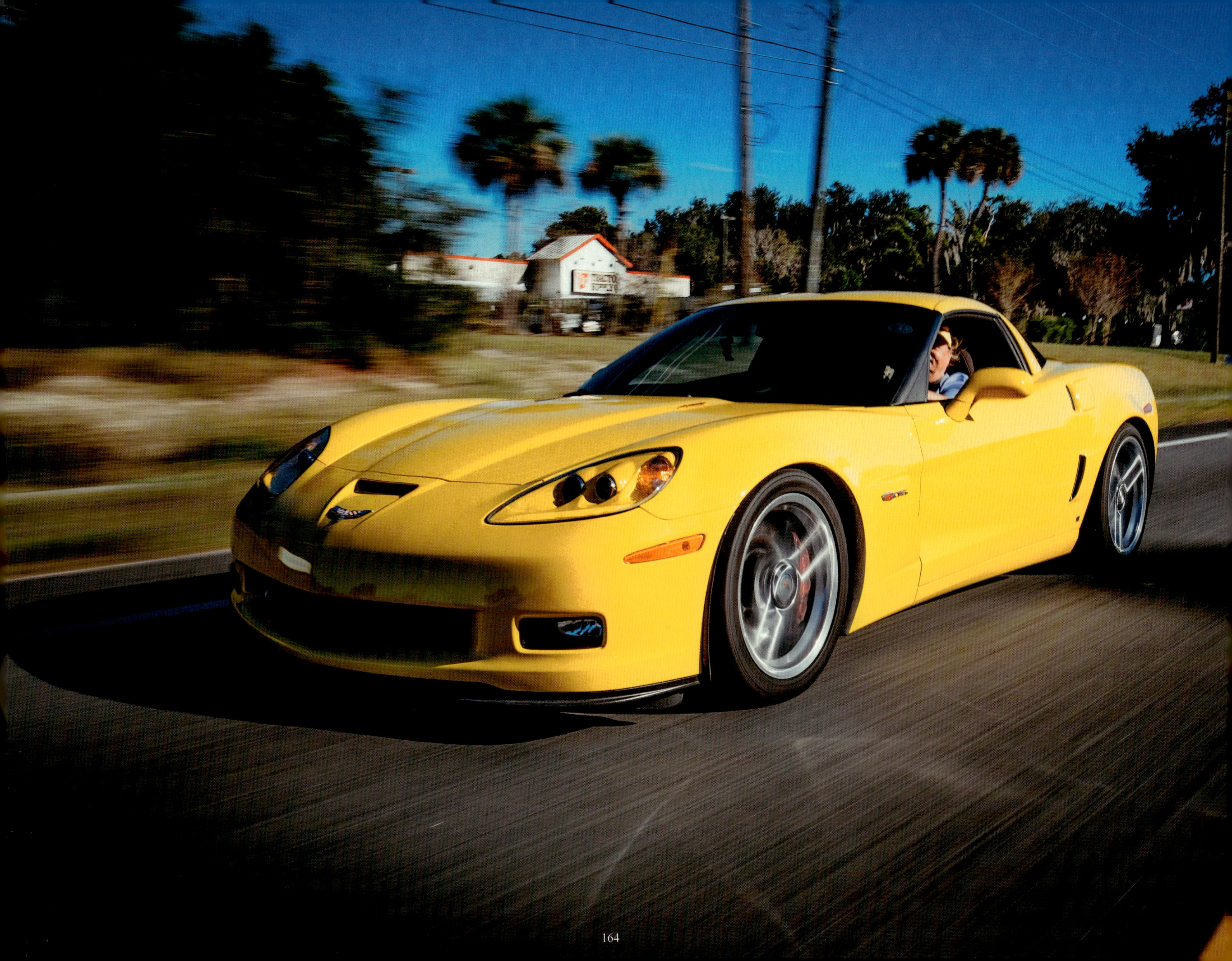

BETTER THAN A MUSTANG

During his studies, Bill Kassebaum became convinced that the Corvette is much better than a Mustang. The was the beginning of his passion for the American sports car.

What's your Corvette story?
Among other things, I have a degree in automotive engineering. My professor at the time was a former Corvette engineer and owned a 1967 Corvette. I was a big Mustang fan at the time, and I also used the Ford on the racetrack. One day, he offered me the chance to drive his Corvette and said he would like to take my Mustang for a spin. No sooner said than done. My summary: "Unbelievable; compared to the Corvette, my Mustang drives like a truck." On that day, I fell in love with the only American sports car, the Corvette. It was some time, however, before I had my first one, about four or five years after I drove my professor's car.

In 1978, the time had come. I bought my first Corvette while working for the Department of Defense in Idaho. A couple of my work colleagues owned Corvettes, and I still had a Mustang at the time. My interest was in the C3, which was the current Corvette at the time. When I visited my parents in Oregon, I found a very well-maintained 1964 C2 convertible. It was a 365hp L76 V8 with a 4-speed manual transmission. The thing cost $5,000, about half the price of a brand-new base C3. Today, the Corvette is worth a bit more. It still sits in my garage, and I'm currently in the process of restoring it. Unless there is a valid reason to get rid of it, it will stay with me for the rest of my life, that's for sure.

In 2020, I joined the Cape Kennedy Corvette Club, which gave me a taste for autocross racing. At the age of sixteen, I was already involved in go-cart racing, and I drove regularly until I was forty. Now my love of motorsports flared up again, and I was going to racetracks like Sebring, Daytona, and a couple of other local tracks here in Florida. I started looking for a C6. The reason: racing! After six months of intensive searching, I acquired a yellow 2007 C6 Z06 in 2021. I was lucky, as the car had few miles and was in tiptop condition. I found it at a dealer in Pompano Beach, that specializes in expensive boy's toys. There were some McLarens; about fifty brand-new Porsches, including some GT3 RSs; half a dozen Lamborghinis; and a few Rolls-Royces. He had purchased the C6 from a lady who lived on the west coast of Florida. Her husband had been the original owner, and in fourteen years, he driven it just 5,050 miles, mostly to car shows.

Most of the miles I have put on it are racing miles. For some years now, we've been meeting up with a Porsche club from the area and racing against each other, the Corvette vs. Porsche Challenge. Currently, the winning stars are all on the side of the German sports cars. So far. We're getting better, and it's always been very close, with only a quarter of a second difference between the best of both camps. We have some really good drivers and great Corvettes, and we'll win next time!

Every now and then, I enjoy driving the Z06 on the roads of Florida. But driving it in traffic is a big thing. It's so loud and has so much power, you can get into trouble. It's a race car, not necessarily for driving around. My '64 convertible will be my Sunday car to drive to meets. My former neighbor in Key Largo was eager to buy the car from me. He offered me a good price for it, even though the C3 barely ran and needed restoration. But I've had the car for over four decades, and I couldn't sell it. My plan is to pass the Corvette on to my son.

What is your all-time favorite Corvette model?
I have little experience with the C1, but I don't think it would be for me. The C2 is beautiful, but I also love my Z06. It's the one I enjoy the most.

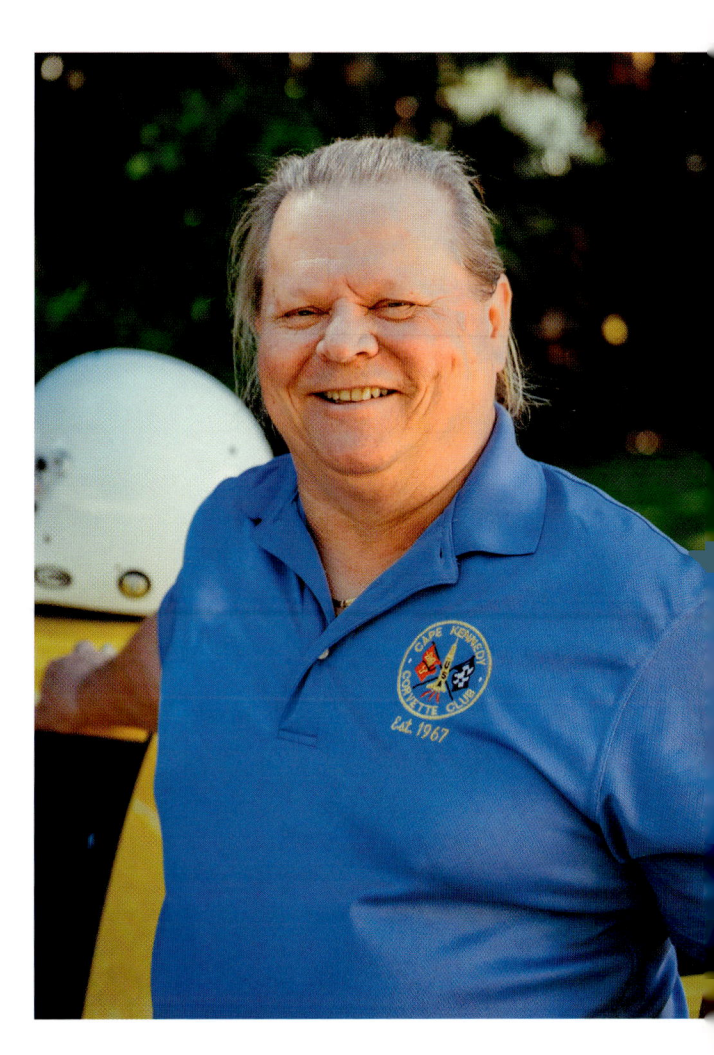

◀ **2007** Corvette C6, **Titusville**, Florida, **USA** | November 16, 2021

TO BILL, CORVETTE MEANS:
AMERICAN-MADE FUN

A contrasting program. While the restoration of the C2 is proceeding at a leisurely pace, Bill Kassebaum is taking a sportier approach with his C6. Together with club friends, he likes to take on the German sports cars from Zuffenhausen in the Corvette vs. Porsche Challenge.

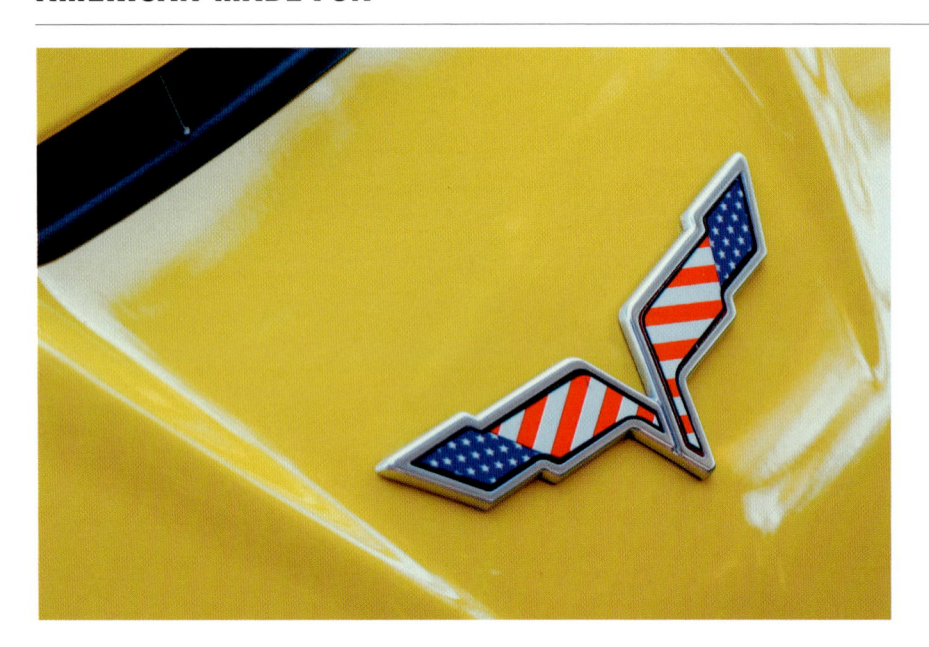

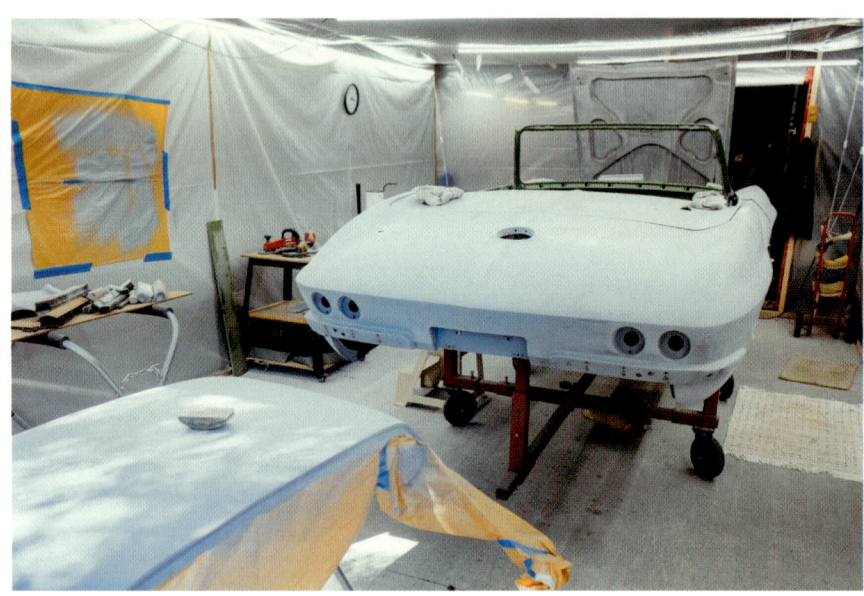

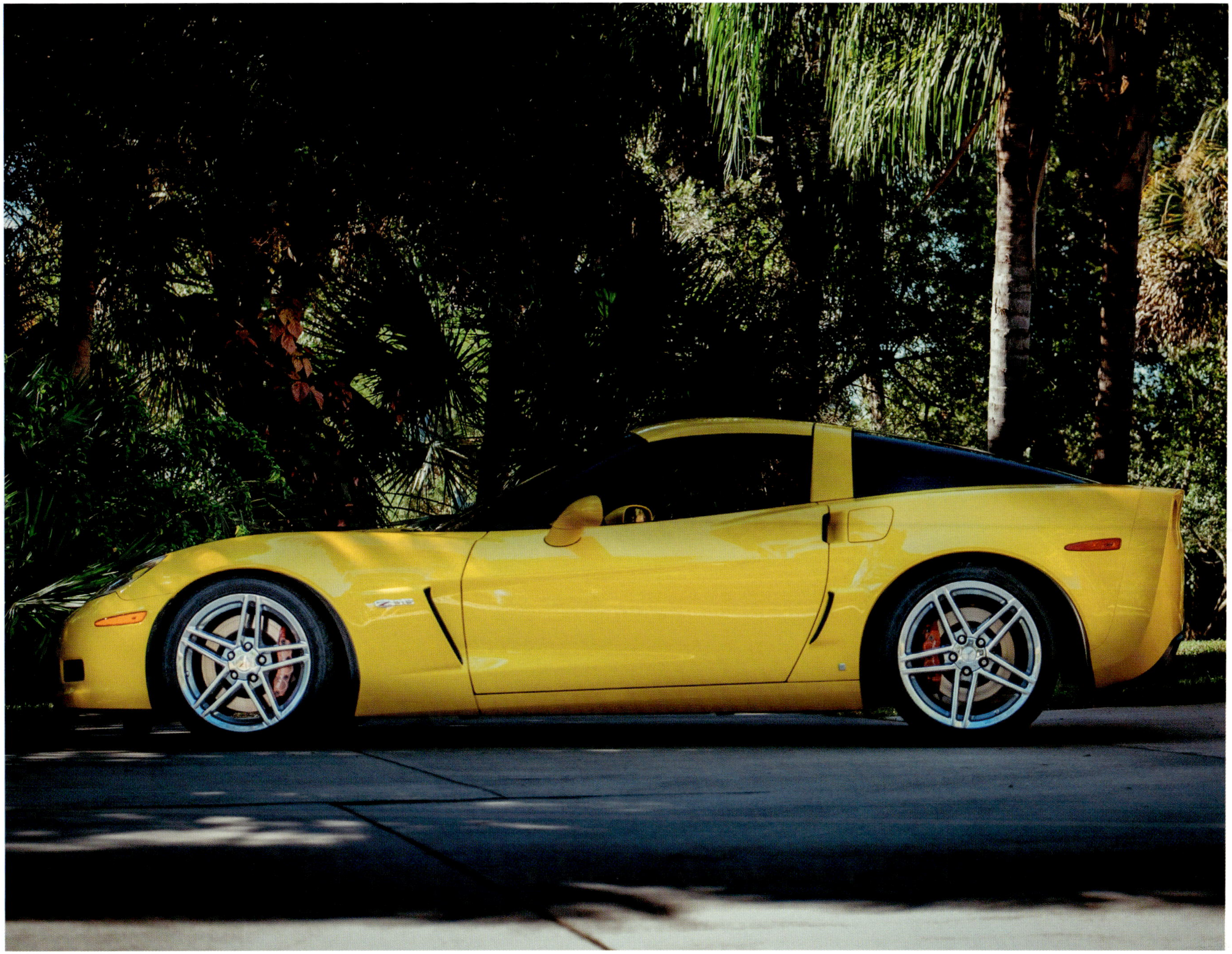

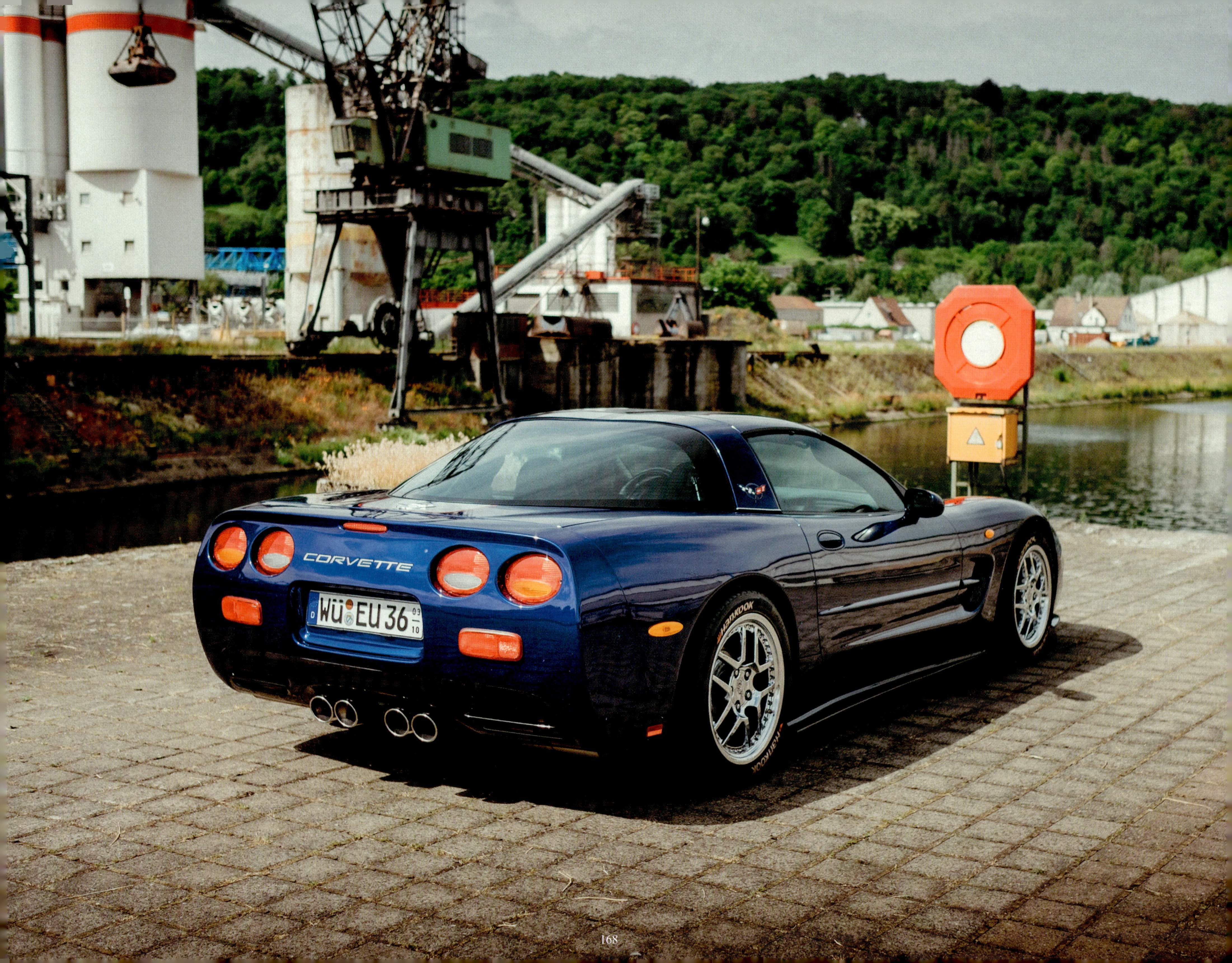
CORVETTE
WÜ EU 36
Hankook

ONE OF 46, BLUE INSTEAD OF YELLOW

Carsten Jordan is a big motorsports fan. The victories by the C5-R made him into a Corvette enthusiast. It is no coincidence that he purchased one of the 46 C5 Commemorative Editions built for Europe.

What's your Corvette story?
I came to the Corvette via motorsport. In the past, I often went to DTM races with my father. There are pictures of me standing next to a BMW with BBS rims, and I was only as tall as the tire. In 1999, my father unfortunately passed away. In the following years, I started to be interested in endurance motorsports: for example, the 24 Hours of Le Mans. At that time, Corvettes dominated their class, winning the French classic in 2001, 2002, and 2004. Only in 2003, with the blue livery, were they unfortunately not at the top of the podium. That's where my enthusiasm for the Corvette originated.

Two strokes of fate when I was in my late twenties made me aware of how quickly life can be over. And you can't take anything with you to the other side. At that time, a good friend had bought a sports car, a Nismo 370 Z. It was clear to me that now was the time to get one, too.

It was definitely going to be a sports car with retractable headlights. When I was a kid, my dad gave me a Ferrari F40 picture book, and I loved the retractable headlights on that car. Initially, I wanted a Corvette C6, but you have to look at what else is out there. I didn't really like the Porsche 944. And who wanted a Mazda RX-7 with a Wankel engine? That's when my focus fell back on the Corvette.

I then wanted a C5 Z06, and a yellow one at that, because I always liked the yellow motorsport Corvette with the black rear end. Definitely a switch. In 2016, I started looking and drove hundreds of kilometers through the republic but couldn't find a good Corvette with a manual transmission. At some point, I went to an importer to find out what it would cost me to import such a Corvette import from the States. It would have been much more expensive than I thought. With this new information, I expanded my budget for the car purchase a little.

Then I spotted a C5 on eBay, but it was blue, not yellow. I just wasn't sure if it was supposed to be that one. After a week, I decided to go and have a look at it, because after all it was a super-rare European 24 Hours of Le Mans Commemorative Edition Corvette. Only forty-six of these were made, and they were also quite different from the American versions. But then the auction was no longer active. Fortunately, I had noted down the phone number given in the listing, took a chance, and called. The Corvette was still there and was still for sale. It had simply become too taxing for the owner to deal with all the people who were not really serious about buying.

I went there, took the car directly to the TÜV (Technical Inspection Association) while on the test drive, and drove it onto the lift. From underneath, the C5 looked almost virgin with its 56,000 kilometers (34,796 miles). The current owner had had the car for fourteen years and only drove it with seasonal license plates. Without closing the deal, I went back home and gave the matter some more thought. A few days later, we renegotiated the price a little bit, and in the end, I closed the deal. I had my first Corvette!

There was still a little work to be done on the car. All the seals had to be replaced, and the seats needed new upholstery, but that was it. Technically, there were no problems. I just did some preventive maintenance, such as replacing the crankshaft damper, installing new belts, and so on. A new steering wheel and side skirts were added, and the seats were freshly upholstered and covered.

By the way, the upholstery is that of the Z06 top model with embroidered Corvette C5 logo. This is one of the features that distinguishes the European version from the American one. Both versions, of course, have the blue paint that Chevrolet used to race at Le Mans in 2003. The EU version also has the suspension (FE4), carbon-fiber hood, and red and silver stripes of the Z06 special edition. Either way, the car is really well equipped for 2004. One of the coolest features is the head-up display. It not only displays speed, but also the tachometer readout, oil pressure, temperature, and so on.

We are trying to track the forty-six European models on the forum to see if we can discover where the others are. Last week, I met with someone who has the number 1 and the number 13 cars. There are a few in France, I know of one in England, and there are several in Scandinavia. Mine is number 36 from the series. At one time, 150 of this C5 final edition were planned, but in the end, not that many were built. Marketing started in April 2003 in the run-up to the 24-hour race, but the first cars were not delivered until late 2003 or early 2004. In the meantime, many customers had already decided to buy a regular C5.

I am super happy with my Corvette. I often go touring with an acquaintance who owns a C4 and, of course, with my boyfriend, who has the 370 Z. I'm very happy with the car. It is absolutely the fulfillment of a dream for me.

What is your all-time favorite Corvette model?
For me, it is quite obviously the '63 Corvette C2 Split-Window.

◀ 2004 Corvette C5, **Würzburg**, Bavaria, **Germany** | June 20, 2021

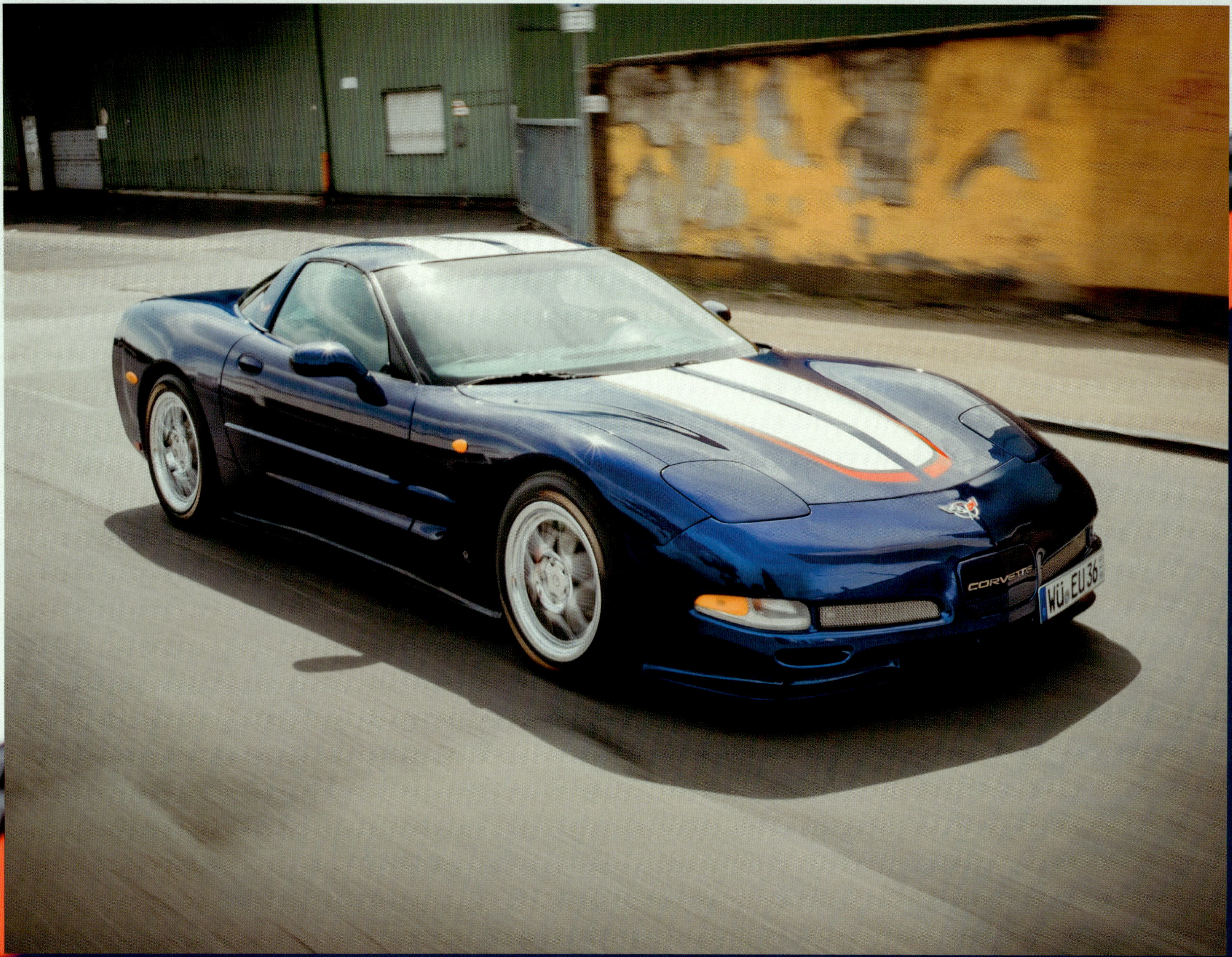
CORVETTE
WÜ EU 36

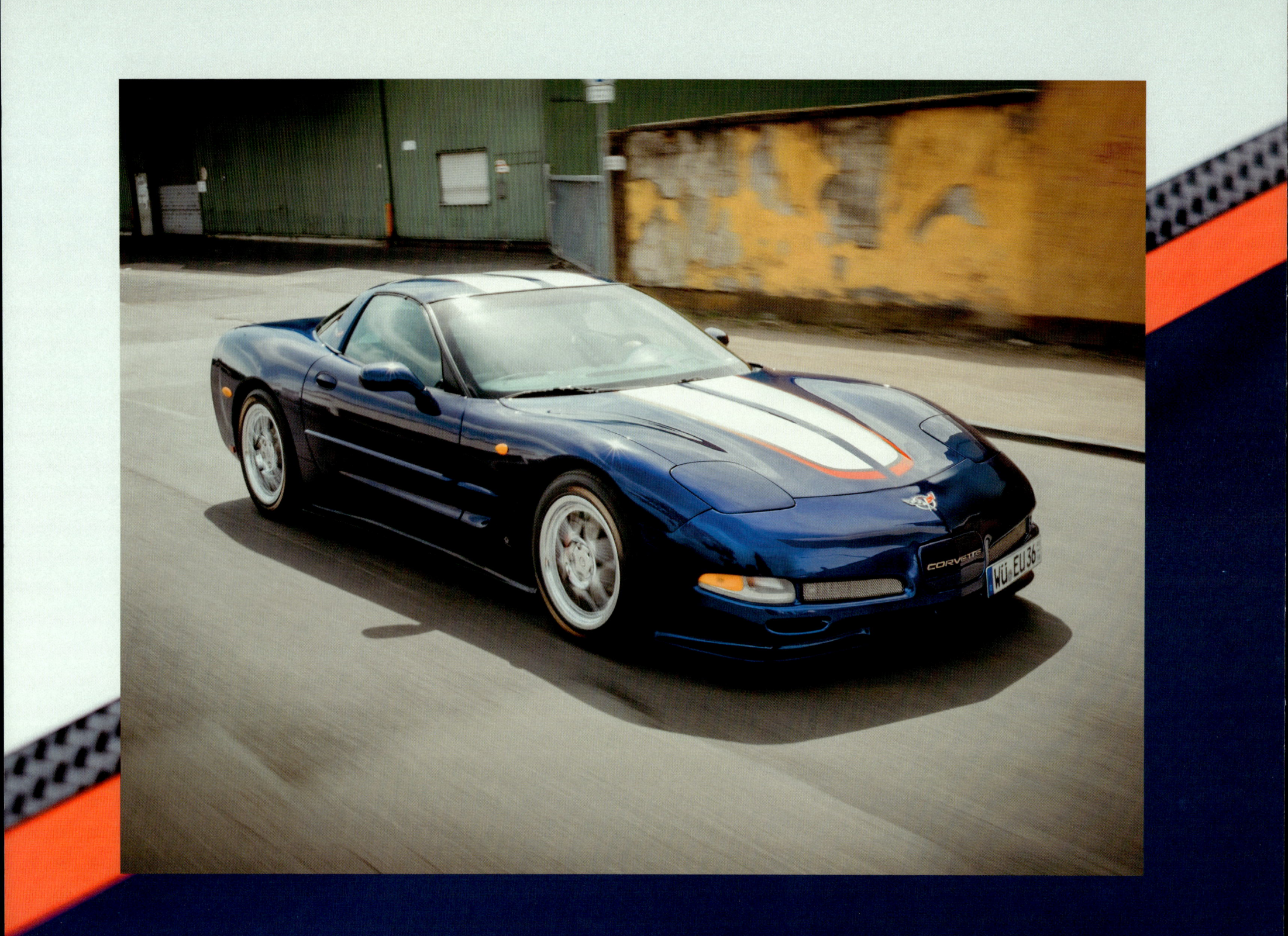

TO CARSTEN, CORVETTE MEANS:
V8 SOUND, RETRACTABLE HEADLIGHTS, SPEED

Blue Mauritius. The 24 Hours of Le Mans Commemorative Edition is the unwieldy name of this rare special model. The forty-six examples built for Europe differ from the American models in a number of features, including the carbon-fiber hood, chassis, and seats from the Z06.

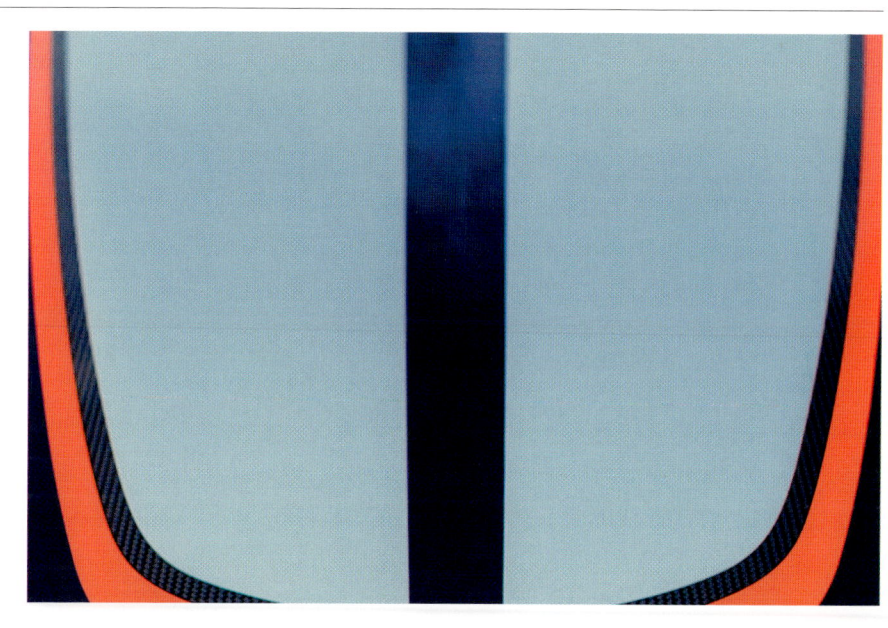

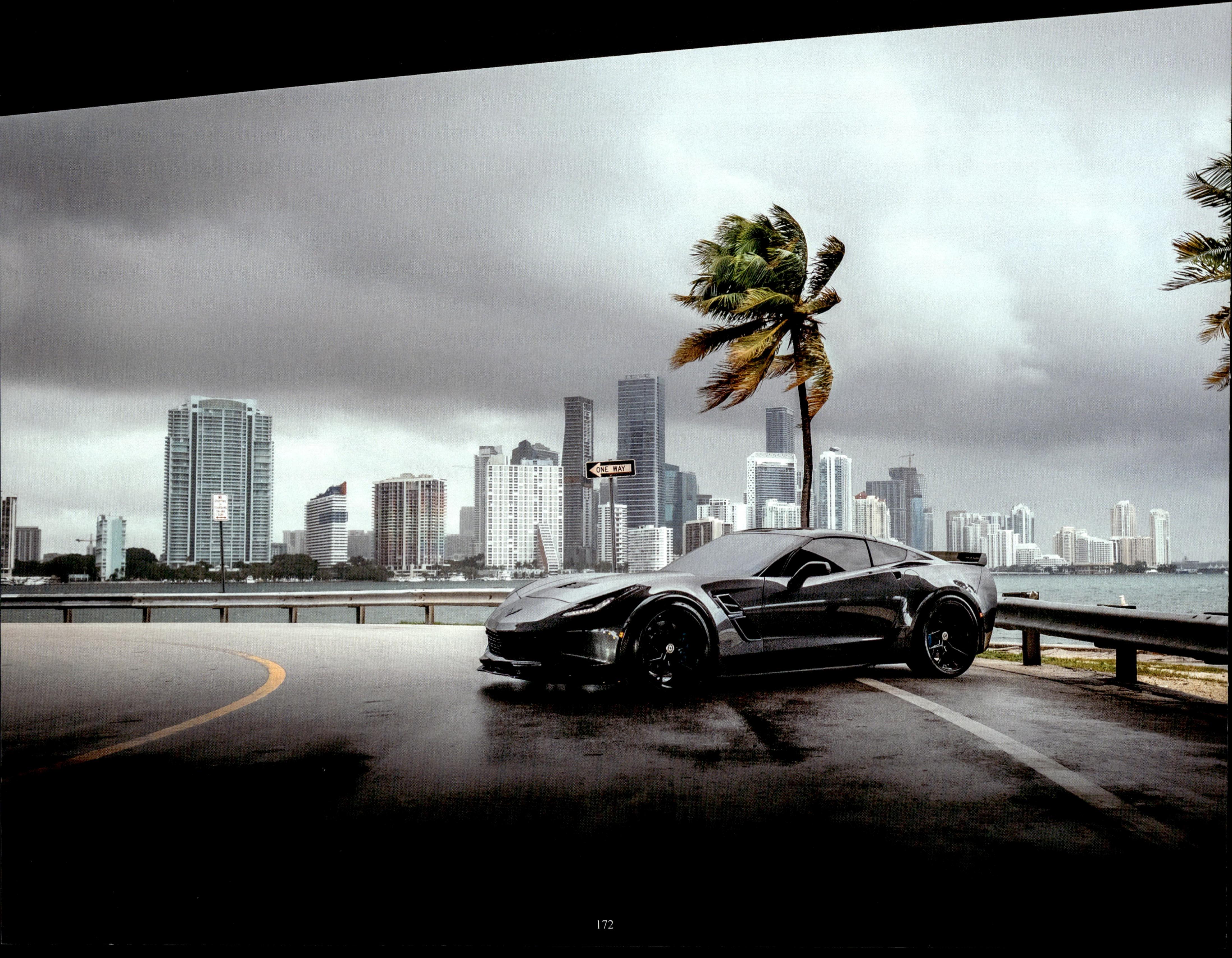
ONE WAY

THE MIAMI CORVETTE SOCIETY

Since he was a little boy, Adrian Valle dreamed of the ultimate American sports car. Now, he has started the "Miami Corvette Society" and is living his dream.

What's your Corvette story?
I came to America as a little boy, and I still remember the first time I saw a Corvette on the road. I think I was about seven years old at the time. That car captured my imagination, and I fell in love with it. When I was a little older, I bought many model Corvette cars and imagined driving them. This sports car fascinated me. My family always dreamed of living in the USA, and to me the Corvette is the American car par excellence.

As I became older, my passion for the Corvette grew, and I knew that one day I would own one. Four or five years ago, I started looking for one in earnest. I read every article about the Corvette I could find and watched lots of videos on the internet. In the process, I discovered that a C7 Collector Edition was a pretty rare car. GM only made 935 of them in 2017. This was just the Corvette for me! I wanted something special that not everyone had. So I went looking for one of these special models.

Due to the low number of units made, I found just five cars in South Florida at that time, and only one of them, in Tampa, was for sale. I concentrated my efforts on getting this Corvette, and I communicated with the owner for more than a month and a half. Of course, it was all about the price and how I would get the car to Miami. I finally booked a flight to Tampa, paid for the car, and drove it the 280 miles back to Miami. That was a very special moment for me.

After fulfilling my sports car dream, I founded the Miami Corvette Society, an Instagram fan page dedicated to everything about the American sports car. I not only enjoy owning a car like this, but also sharing it with the community. There are also a lot of people who don't know much about the Corvette and specifically about the Collector Edition. It is my pleasure to educate these people about the car and the long history of the Corvette. At every meeting, everywhere I show up with the car, I end up talking with people. The C7 Collector Edition is unique, with its color combination of metallic gray exterior and Tension Blue interior. And that's what I love about this C7. It's a piece of the finest American engineering. I'm really a big Corvette fan and always excited to see what GM will come up with next.

What is your all-time favorite Corvette model?
That's a tough question. The C7 will always be one of my favorite models; that generation was a game changer. The design compared to the C6, the Z06 with the Supercharger, just badass! And now the C8. There has never been a production Corvette with a mid-engine before! I was extremely skeptical when I read the first reports about the C8. I was never a big fan of a mid-engine Corvette; it's just a drastic change for American automotive engineering. But GM has outdone themselves with this car! With the C8, they can now compete with cars like McLaren, Porsche, Lamborghini, and Ferrari; it's incredible.

I'm still a big fan of the C7, the last Corvette with the long hood and the engine in front—definitely one of the best Corvettes ever. Now the C8 Z06 is waiting in the wings, with 600 hp from a naturally aspirated V8. Everyone in my crew is already very excited about the new top model. I'm on the waiting list for a Corvette C8 Z06. But it will be hard to sell my beloved C7.

◀ **2017** Corvette C7, **Miami**, Florida, **USA** | November 20, 2021

TO ADRIAN, CORVETTE MEANS:
INSPIRATION, PASSION, RECOGNITION

End of an era. The seventh generation of the Corvette was on the market for just six years, from 2014 to 2019. It was the last with the engine in front and rear-wheel drive. Just 784 coupes (Targas) and 151 convertibles of the Collector Edition shown here were made.

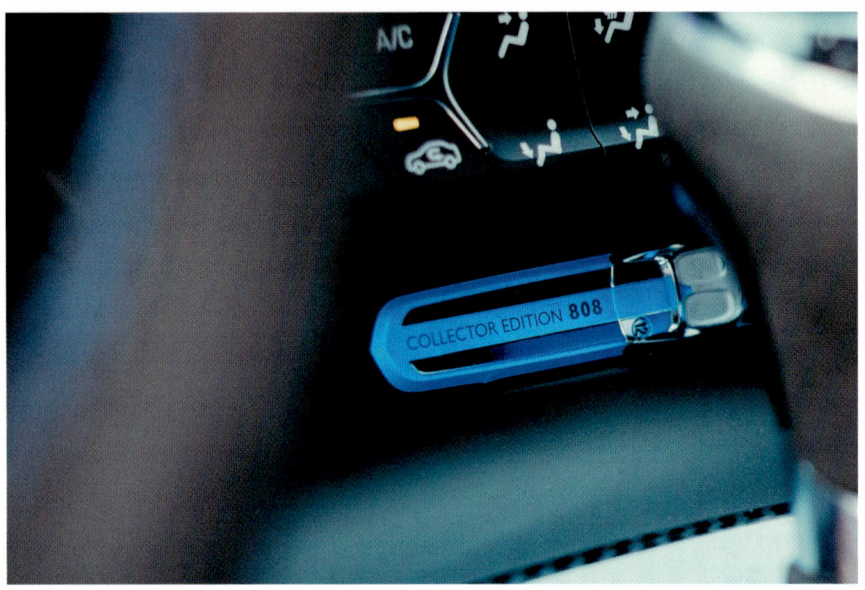

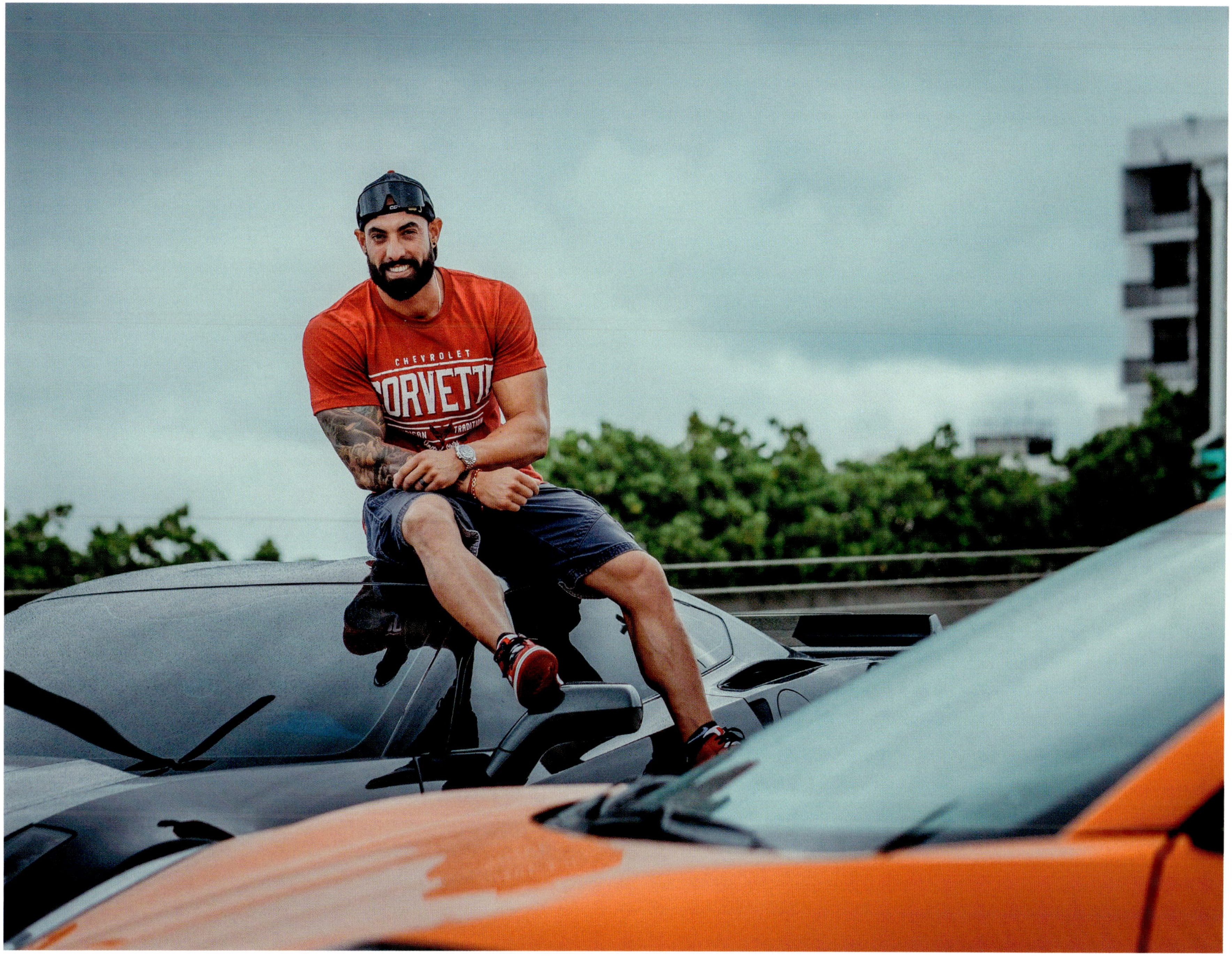
CHEVROLET
TRADITION

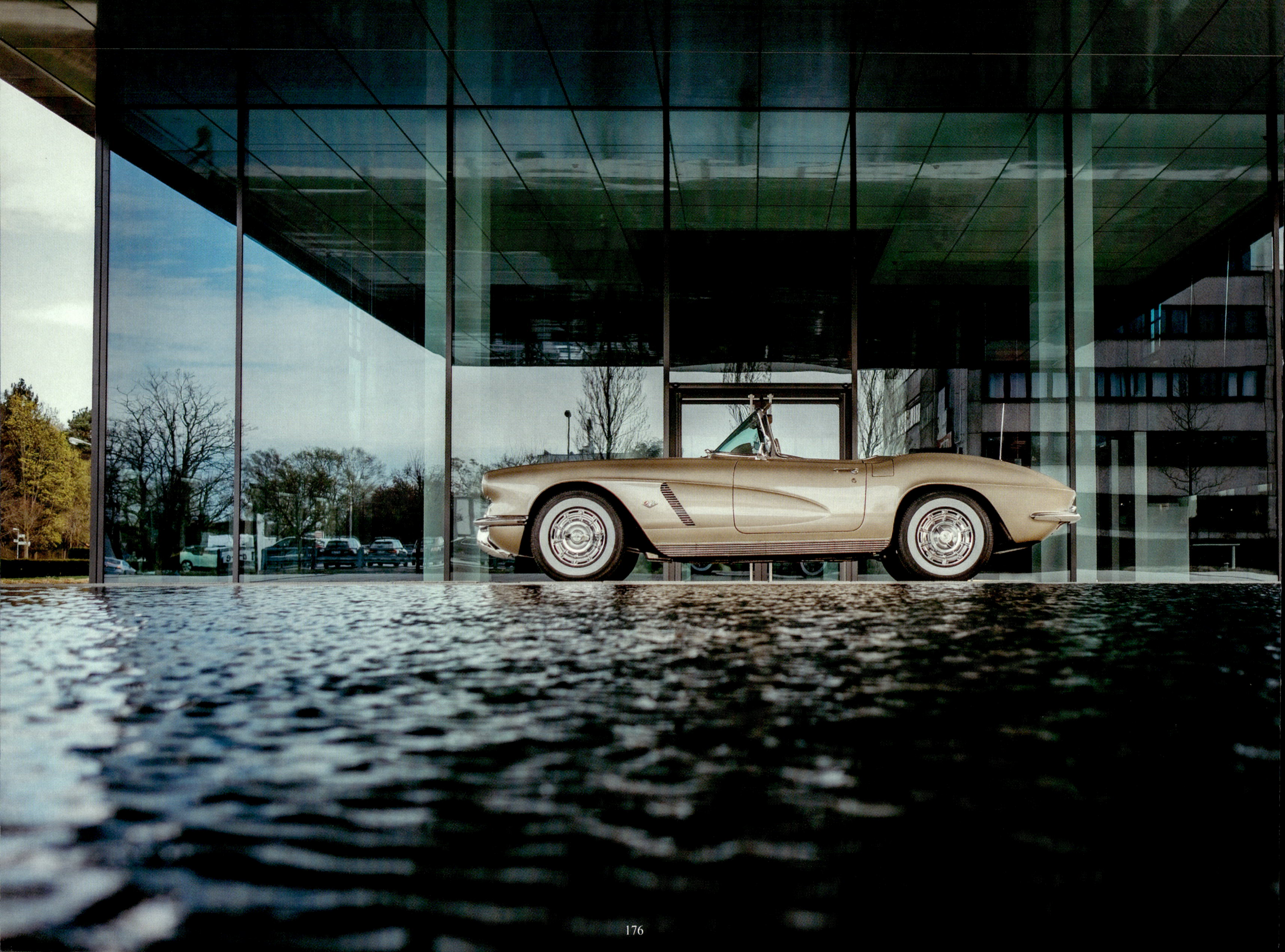

FROM A V2 TO A V8

Ingo spent seven years looking for a Ford Mustang. When he saw a C1 on a dealer's lot, he forgot about the Pony Car in seconds.

What's your Corvette story?
After a serious accident on my Harley in September 2013 and all the operations that followed, in November I went in search of an American classic car. My previous V2 was to become a V8 engine. My choice initially fell on the Ford Mustang. The Corvette was never on my radar, and I didn't know there was an automatic version of it. But every time I saw one, I said to my wife, "Look at that. Very cool car, but I'll never get in and out of that with my prosthetic leg!" A few weeks after my accident, I already had my eye on a Mustang, a '68 fastback that was sitting in Arizona. It was actually all set to go. I had organized the on-site appraisal, as well as payment, pickup, and overseas shipping. But then the dealer suddenly wanted all the money for the car up front, by flash transfer the next day. I didn't go for that. After that, I couldn't find a Mustang that met all my requirements. It just didn't "click" anymore. There is also a lot of junk on the market, and the prices keep rising.

In the course of my search, I became aware of a dealer in the Netherlands, whose website I regularly searched for new offers. On a Wednesday or Thursday in June 2020, I saw this Corvette on his website. The C1 wasn't red or black like many others before but wore elegant Fawn Beige. It also had an automatic transmission. It touched me immediately, and I picked up the phone. The next day I drove to Holland with a friend.

The Corvette had previously been registered in the Netherlands. The former owners, a couple in their eighties, had bought the car from the original owner in the States and had it completely restored in Europe in the late '90s. At that time, I had practically no technical knowledge about Chevrolet's sports cars and bought the convertible quite naively. But I was sure that I could sell a Corvette from that year, in that rare color, with an automatic transmission and documented history. There were many pictures taken during the restoration, all the registration cards and the original "Black Plates" from California as well as many other documents. It was purchased in Los Angeles in 1962 at Kenneth Chevrolet and registered to Edwin H. Tompkins Jr. in Palos Verdes Estates on February 3, 1962. It sat unused in his garage from 1981 and was not registered again until it was sold to the second owner and completely restored in 1999. It was the first time in my life that I had seen such a Corvette in person. I bought it without hesitation.

Since the dealer had many deliveries to make at the time, I did not get the C1 home until the end of October 2020. I changed all the fluids and had the brakes redone, and the German TÜV (Technical Inspection Association) acceptance and registration were organized. That took some time. In 2021, I was able to drive it properly for the first time, and a few technical problems quite quickly arose. The gearbox wouldn't shift when cold, and the engine developed an ever-growing rattle. I decided to have the engine completely overhauled. Luckily, I found someone in my area who really knew about V8 engines and Powerglide transmissions. I have driven well over 1,000 kilometers since the engine overhaul and am enjoying this great Corvette, which I certainly won't part with unless I have to.

Did you regret not buying a Mustang?
No, never. While I was at the dealership, getting in and out of the Corvette with my prosthesis, I tried it once with a '68 Mustang that was there in the showroom. I had a much harder time getting into that one because the door didn't open as far. When the top is down on the Corvette, I am able to get in and out with no problems at all. When the top is up or the hardtop is on, it becomes a bit of a challenge, but I manage it. Regardless, it was definitely the right decision. The C1 is a great car and a lot of fun to cruise in. And many people I've talked to about American cars from that era say to me, "What do you want with a Mustang? The Corvette is so much more awesome!"

What is your all-time favorite Corvette model?
Well, of course my 1962 C1! Should it suddenly burst into flames or otherwise be destroyed, I would expand my spectrum to the final years of the C1 and perhaps also to the Corvette C2. I don't care for the rear end and the very early interior of the C1 model up to 1959. But thank goodness we don't all have the same taste! I think I would buy a 1962 C1 again. I find the lines of this vintage with the more modern rear end just beautiful. However, I would not want one in red or black; I would try to find a rarer color again.

◀ **1962** Corvette C1, **Dreieich, Hesse, Germany** | April 10, 2022

TO INGO, CORVETTE MEANS:
JOIE DE VIVRE, TECHNOLOGY, DRIVING ENJOYMENT

Wishlist. In 1961, GM offered its Corvette customers seven colors, including the rarely chosen Fawn Beige that this example wears. Incidentally, it was also the last year in which it was possible to order contrasting paint colors for the side indents.

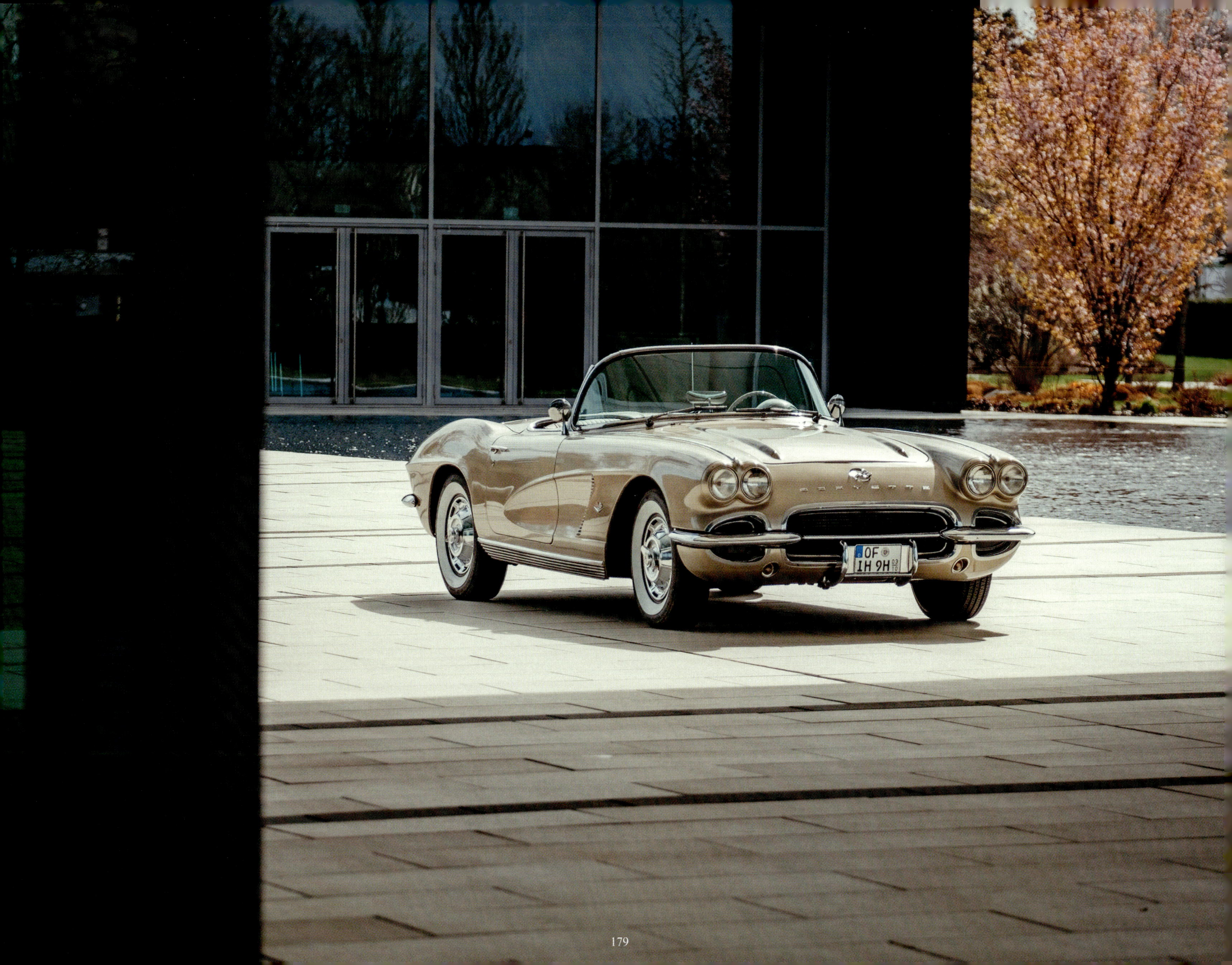
OF
IH 9H

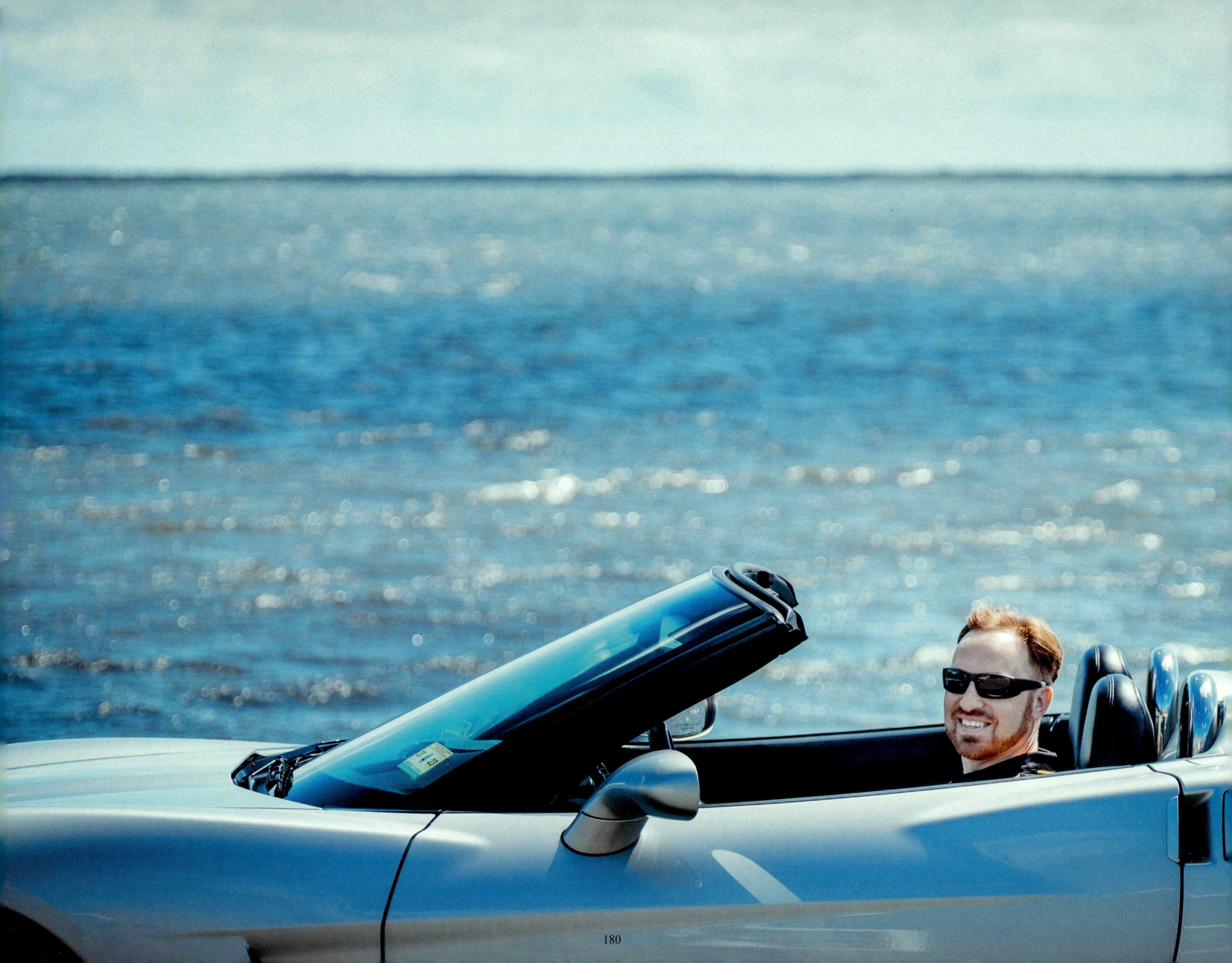

SILVER SURFER ON THE COAST

Since Steven Stachelski has owned a silver-colored C6, his friends no longer ask why he is a Corvette fan. Now he even helps them in their search for one.

What's your Corvette story?
When I was a little boy, I dreamed of owning a Corvette one day. I had Corvette magazines, catalogs, and posters all over my room back then. When my father took his car in for service, I often accompanied him to the Chevy dealer. There I would look at the latest Corvette in the showroom and dream of owning one. I was always a Chevy guy. One of my first cars was a Chevy S-10 pickup, lowered, with IROC-Z rims, NASCAR-style tires, and a mega sound system. I have also owned two Chevy Tahoes, a 1987 IROC-Z Camaro, a '72 Impala coupe, a 2010 Camaro RS, and a Mercedes SLK 300, which, as a two-seat roadster, came the closest to my dream car.

After that, I seriously looked around for a Corvette. In 2018, I finally found a silver C6. The car had had one owner and was very well maintained. It was a 2005 model that had some special features made for just one year, like the steering wheel and various electrical components. Thirteen years later, the original owner brought the Corvette back to the dealer he had bought it from to get a new C8. The C6 was, of course, checkbook maintained, had 52,000 miles on the clock, had always been kept in a garage, and was in immaculate condition. The dealer gave me a good price, and nothing stood in the way of fulfilling my dream. I love my Corvette.

Every year since I've owned my convertible, I have gone to Corvettes at Carlisle in Pennsylvania. The largest Corvette show in the USA goes on for three days. It's like Disneyland for Corvette owners. I also often go to local car meets. My wife, Marisa, and my two young sons, Carter and Gavin, join me in the everyday car. Marisa and I share a passion for cars and have passed it on to our boys. This Sunday, I will be participating in the Ocean City Boardwalk. I wanted to be there last year but didn't register in time. I've also been to a few events where GM introduced new Corvettes, like the C8 and the upcoming Z06. If there is any event that has to do with Corvettes, I try to be there. Some of the shows donate money to charity or foundations, and I like to support that.

When I was younger, many of my friends asked me what I thought was so great about the Corvette. Now we're all a little older and some of my friends are themselves looking around for a sports car made in Bowling Green. I also get asked if I can keep my eyes open for them, since I'm naturally more in the scene and often hear about cars for sale before they become public.

One of my neighbors also has a Corvette, and we often talk about our cars or meet at events. I drive my C6 as often as I can or sit in the garage and just look at the car. All my life, I wanted a Corvette, and now it's finally here. It's like a member of the family.

You're on the waiting list for a new C8. Will you sell the C6 to get it?
That's a tough decision I will have to make when the C8 arrives at the dealers. I would like to keep the C6, but if nothing changes, I will probably have to sell it to get the new C8. We will see what I decide when the time comes. If possible, I will keep both cars. Of course you can only drive one car at a time, and if I sell it the C6 will always hold a special place in my heart as my first Corvette.

What is your all-time favorite Corvette model?
I always loved the C6, the perfect car for me. To me, it is the best mixture of performance and design. Somehow, one can see every Corvette generation in it. If you ask me today what my favorite model is, I lean strongly toward the new C8. With its mid-engine and all its technical advancements, it is a big step for Corvette. I also find the styling superb. But after being at Carlisle as many times as I have, I have also fallen in love with the C2. I walked around one such car a dozen times. I simply couldn't stop looking at the car and admiring it. It simply cast a spell over me. One day, perhaps I will also imagine a C2 in my garage.

◀ 2005 Corvette C6, **Lanoka Harbor**, New Jersey, USA | September 8, 2022

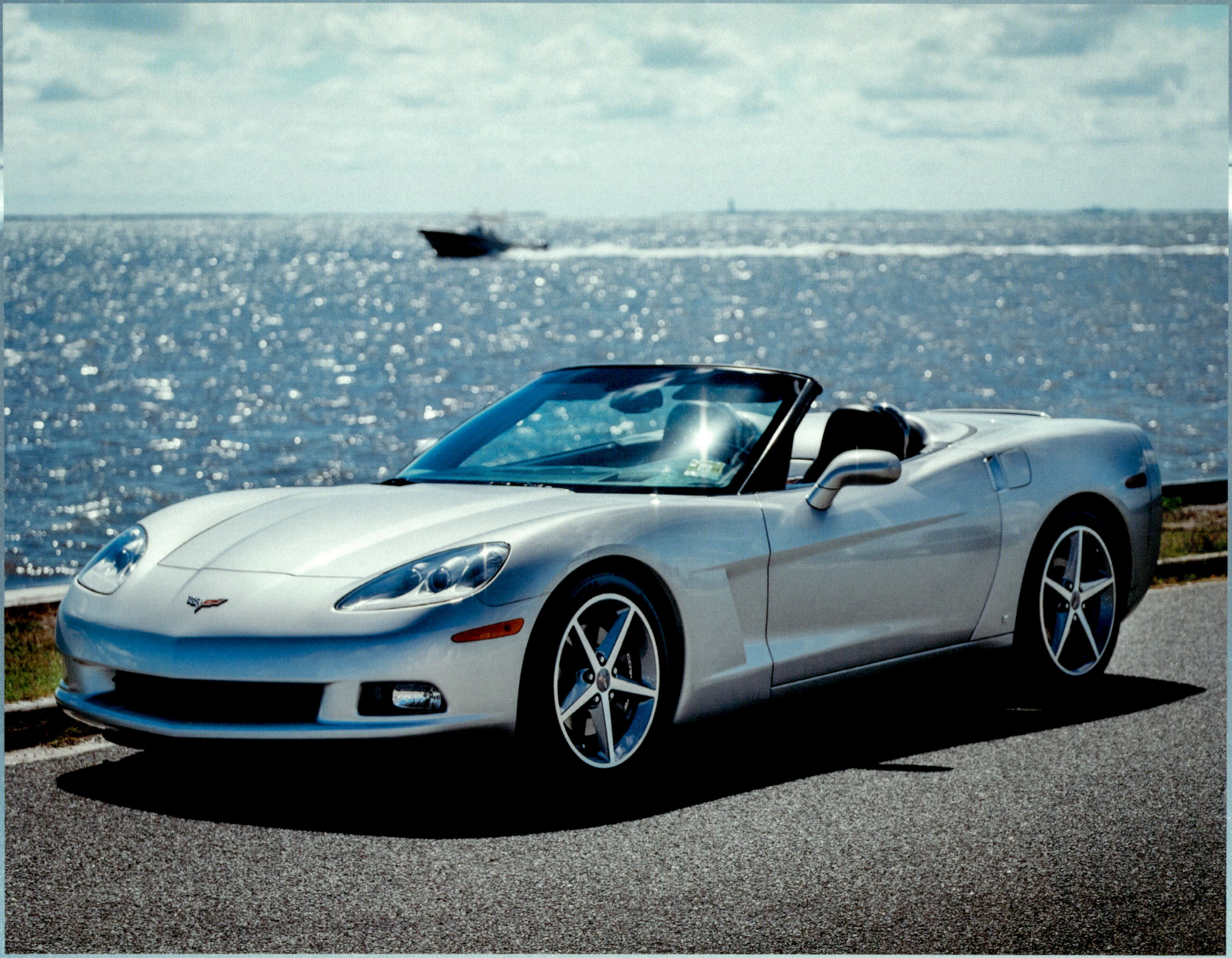

TO STEVEN, CORVETTE MEANS:
PERFORMANCE, LEGENDARY, AMERICAN

Hardcore. When he can, Steven Sachelski takes part in every event that has to do with Corvette, be it the launch of the new C8 or the legendary Corvettes at Carlisle. Along for the ride, of course, is his C6 convertible, which he acquired from the original owner.

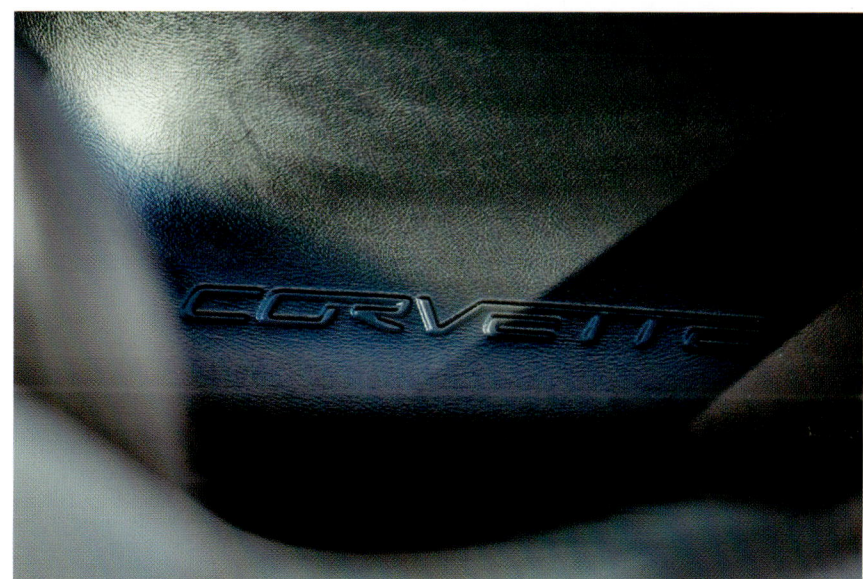

Originals
AMERICAN
FASTBACK
Grandprix
USA
DAYTONA SPEEDWAY
Team

BLACK EXTERIOR, RED INTERIOR

Black exterior, red interior. From the factory of course. To Uwe Gramlich, not only was the year of his Corvette important, but also its combination of colors.

What's your Corvette story?
I was born in the Eifel Region, just 20 kilometers from Nuremberg, in 1958. My enthusiasm for everything that moves on two to four wheels is part of my Eifel DNA. I have gasoline in my blood, or in modern German, I am a "gas head."

When I was a child, the US Air Force had bases at Bitburg and Spangdahlem. And the coolest thing for me to see as a ten-year-old on Saturday afternoons in these sleepy little towns was the American GIs with their mirrored Ray Ban aviator's glasses, their left arms hanging casually out the windows of their C3s as they cruised through our small town. The deep growl of the V8 engines, usually from side-pipes, was by itself impressive and gave me the goose bump feeling, which I still get when I turn the ignition key of a Corvette and its V8 begins rumbling. It was then that this "I must have one when I grow up" feeling fixed itself deep inside me.

At the age of 18, due to my lack of the required cash and my desire to move as fast as I could, I bought a Honda CB 750 K2. The Corvette was still in the back of my mind, but at that time it was not quite at the top of my "must have" list. My life went on. I performed my national military service in the Bundeswehr, then I signed up and underwent officer training. I studied economics at the Bundeswehr University in Munich, became a career officer, and spent the last 20 years as the head of a procurement department with NATO in Luxembourg. I took part in various foreign deployments, including two years in Bosnia-Herzegovina, then in Kosovo, and later in Afghanistan as well.

In 2008, I was diagnosed with tonsillar carcinoma, followed by the "whole nine yards": surgery, chemotherapy, radiation, rehabilitation, then hearing loss in both ears. At the time, my oncologist said to me, "You have two options: Carry on as before, and then the next thing will be a heart attack or stroke. Or stop and enjoy life." I decided on the latter.

After leaving the military, I first purchased a '73 Honda CB 750 Four and then a '75 Kawasaki Z 900. Meanwhile, I got my '85 Suzuki GSX-R 750, which I had bought new as a reward for the completion of my studies and which for the past 15 years had been sitting idle in my garage, running again. I realized that the time had come to finally turn my long-held wish for a Corvette into reality.

From the beginning, it was clear that it had to be a '58 C1, with special "matching numbers." The year of the car had to be the same as the year of my birth. I especially liked the double headlights, the washboard on the hood, and the chrome strips on the trunk lid. I had very precise requirements for my Corvette: it had to have an engine more powerful than the basic 230hp one, it had to have a manual transmission, and it had to be painted black and silver with a red interior. That is an unbelievably elegant color combination. I reserved personal plates with the desired number "GOH-C 1958" and repeatedly blocked it again after expiry of the ninety-day reservation period.

On the internet, I found the C1 buying guide by Cord Brügge, printed it out, and almost learned it by heart. At that time, I had no contact with the German-speaking Corvette scene, and in fact, I didn't even know that there was one. But I did have an acquaintance in Alabama, a retired colonel from the US Army, who had been involved with the Corvette his whole life and whose "stable" contained no fewer than sixteen examples of the American sports car. I spent hours talking with him by telephone and learned as much as I could about the model.

I spent two and a half years searching for the car I wanted until, in July 2013, on eBay I discovered a '58 that met my specifications. The Corvette was in Fort Wayne, Indiana. From the very first telephone call, I got along extremely well with the seller, Pete Keelan, a retired US Air Force pilot. We agreed that I would have the car inspected by Road Ready Inspections. It inspected vehicles using an approximately 160-point checklist, including from below with the vehicle on a lift. A roughly ten-mile-long test drive was also part of the inspection, as was a photo documentation consisting of 50 pictures. After receiving the inspection report on Thursday, Pete and I agreed on a price. I sent $1,000 as a down payment, whereupon Pete ended the eBay auction. I flew to the USA on Saturday to have a look at the Corvette. Pete invited me to stay with him until I took possession of the C1.

When I arrived in my rental car and we had said hello, he suggested that I park the car behind the house. Then he pressed a car key into my hand and said that I could drive that car while I was his guest. It turned out to be the key to a 2006 Ford GT. That alone made my trip to the USA worthwhile! Pete had a huge building housing about a hundred classic cars, and on its roof in big white letters were the fitting words "Toy Store." The C1 was exactly what I had imagined. We completed the purchase the same day and organized the pickup for the following Wednesday. Seeing his collection, spending three days with him, and driving the GT 40 was simply cool! He even took the time to show me part of his businesses. The money transfer was completed by the following Thursday, the title was signed over to me, and I was present when the C1 was loaded up and transported away, which of course I documented photographically. This would later prove to be a stroke of luck.

The car arrived in Germany the day before my 55th birthday. When the 20-foot container was opened, I almost began to cry. During loading, someone had walked around on the red upholstery and the carpet with oily shoes, the body was damaged on the lower right front, and the paint on the hood had been scratched in several places in the area of the grille. What a sad sight! Fortunately, the transport insurance took care of the damage very quickly, probably because of the detailed photo coverage I had. In any case, I had gotten my '58 C1 and was able to register it with the personal plate number I had reserved.

From the beginning, the C1 exercised an unbelievable fascination on me. The Corvette's steering wheel must somehow have become contaminated by a virus, for after a time, I sensed that the Corvette grew lonely when left alone in the garage. I needed a second one! The year 1958 was an outstanding one for the first Corvette generation. Which model did I immediately like from the second-generation C2? The 1963 Split-Window, of course. The specification sheet for the C2 I wanted was soon completed, apart from the approximate year, then copy and paste: '63 coupe, black exterior, red interior, 4-speed transmission with more powerful engine, and with as many original parts as possible. Of course, I immediately reserved the corresponding personal plate number: GOH-C 1963.

◀ **1958** Corvette C1, **1963** Corvette C2, **Bendorf**, Rhineland-Pfalz, **Germany** | June 12, 2022

A year and a half later, in mid-December 2016, as it were as a Christmas gift, a matching Split-Window appeared on eBay. It was listed by CoolCars in Columbia Station, Ohio. My friend from Alabama knew Bob Dombrowski, the seller, and had already completed several car deals with him satisfactorily. My friend characterized Bob as one of the few serious sellers whom one could trust, which subsequently proved to be true. I agreed with Bob on a price and sent him a down payment of $1,500, whereupon he ended the eBay auction. In early January, I flew to see him. I examined the C2 the day I arrived, and it was immediately clear that this '63 was going to be the one! A beautiful Split-Window with completely original interior, the original L76 340hp engine, and a T-10 Borg Warner 4-speed transmission. My second Corvette in the configuration I had wanted and imagined. I was once again able to register the car with the personal plate number I had reserved. A small but, to me, important detail.

My next Corvette is already in the pipeline: a 1991 Corvette C4 ZR-1, also black and red, and of course, with the reserved plate number GOH-C 1991. One can and should dream: I would like to round out my small collection with a '68 or '69 C3 T-Top Coupe in the same color combination. We will see if I can make that happen. No such vehicle has been offered on any of the known sales platforms or auctions during the last three years.

But back to the German Corvette scene. As I said before, I knew nothing at all about it, which changed after my purchase of the C1 and my participation in various classic car events. I was surprised how quickly one met very interesting people there. Conversations developed quickly because of our shared passion. Most of the Corvette drivers I know have kept both feet on the ground, and I find the community very sympathetic. As a Corvette owner, the absolute highlight for me was the invitation by *Auto Bild Classic* to take part in a four-generation Corvette comparison test at Parchim airfield near Schwerin in August 2020, which would be featured in an article in the November issue of the magazine. While the C2 was trailered to Parchim, my son Kevin and I drove the 385 miles there and back in my C1, one day each way. An unforgettable father-son experience. Although I drive about 3,000 miles annually in the C1, I had never before covered so long a distance in one go.

The icing on the cake was that there were absolutely no problems. The fascinating thing was that the Corvette ran quieter and smoother with each passing mile. And on the A7 south of Kassel, which is six lanes wide, one got the feeling of driving on an interstate in the USA.

I have been a member of the Central European Chapter of the National Corvette Restorers Society (NCRS) since its founding in 2019, and since 2021 I have been secretary in its management board. There I have found like-minded people, who tick like I do and for whom striving for originality of a Corvette is the most important thing. The exchanges between us are often characterized by nerdy details, which is always a lot of fun for me.

What is your all-time favorite Corvette model?
The 1958 C1 was and remains my favorite.

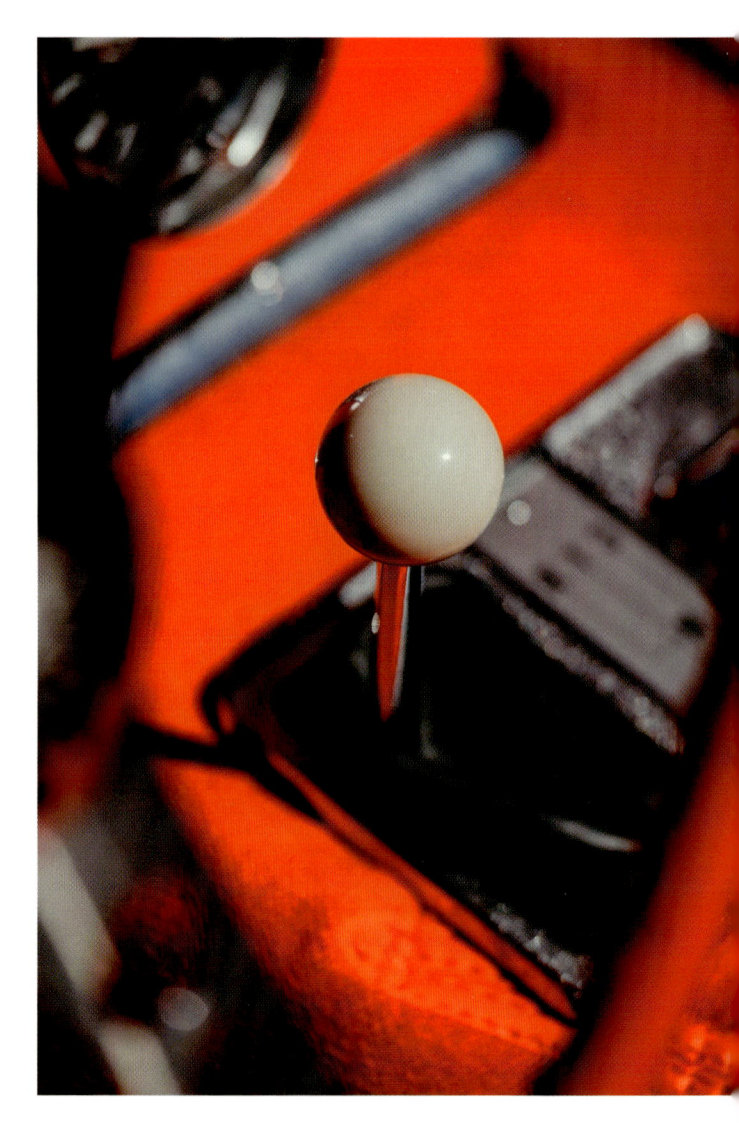

One year only. In 1958, the Corvette got two trim strips on the trunk lid, which disappeared again in 1959. Everyone knows that the '63 C2 with its split rear window is unique.

TO UWE, CORVETTE MEANS:
JOIE DE VIVRE, ADRENALINE, FRIENDSHIP

Black is beautiful. Uwe Gramlich buys any Corvette as long as it has a black exterior and a red interior—from the factory, not repainted. By the way, the name of the color on the '63 coupe is the same as on the '58 convertible: Tuxedo Black.

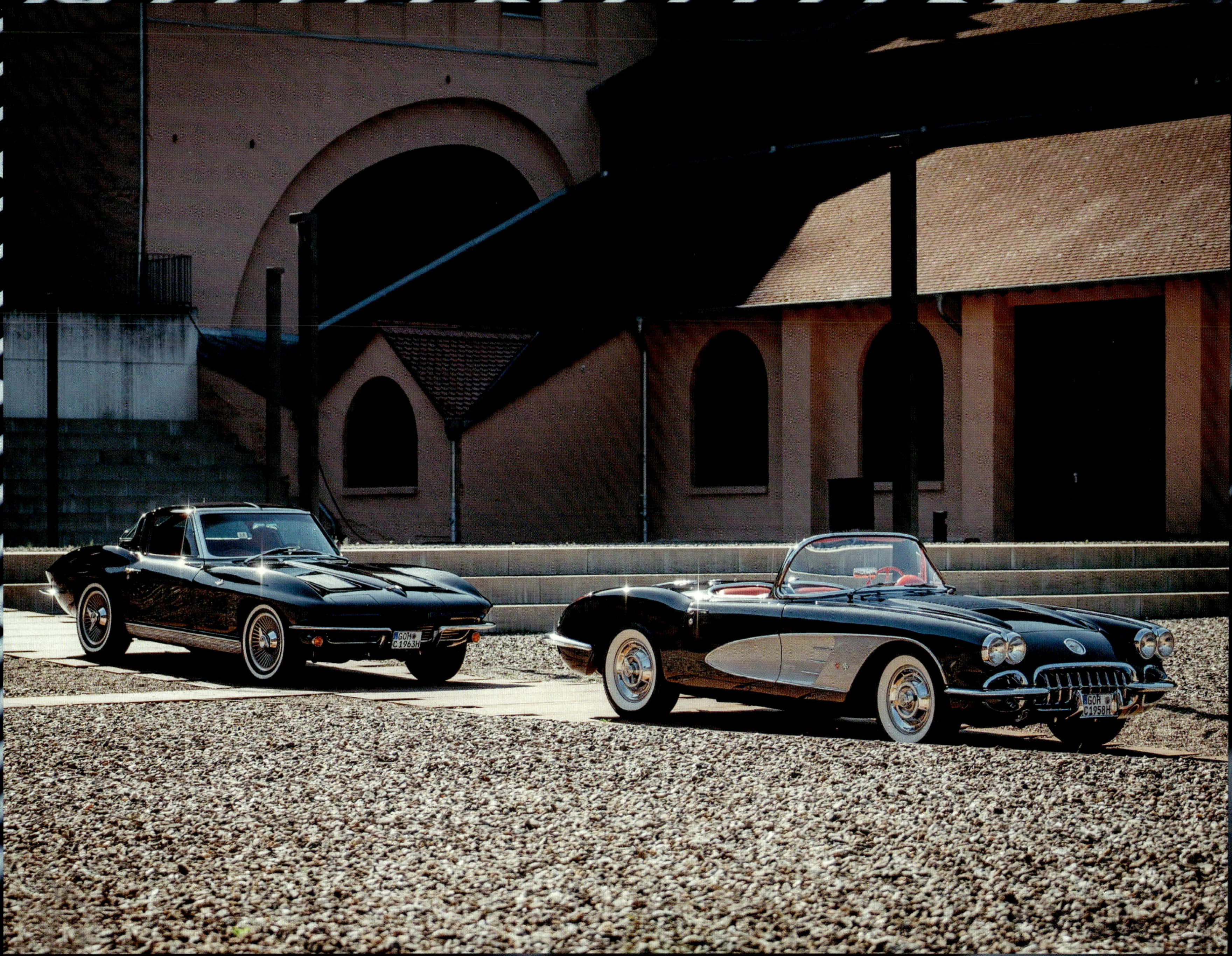
GOH C1963H
GOH C1958H

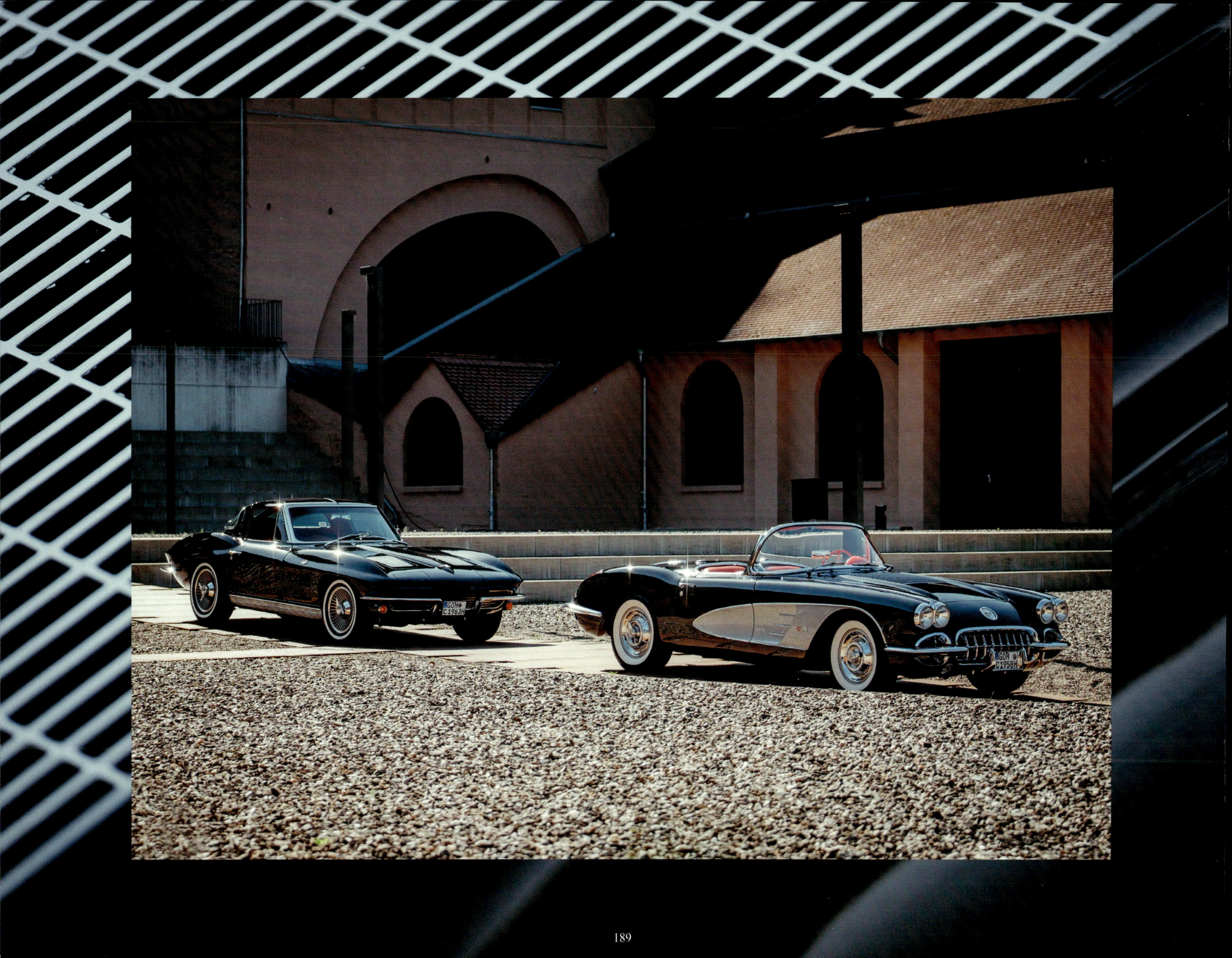

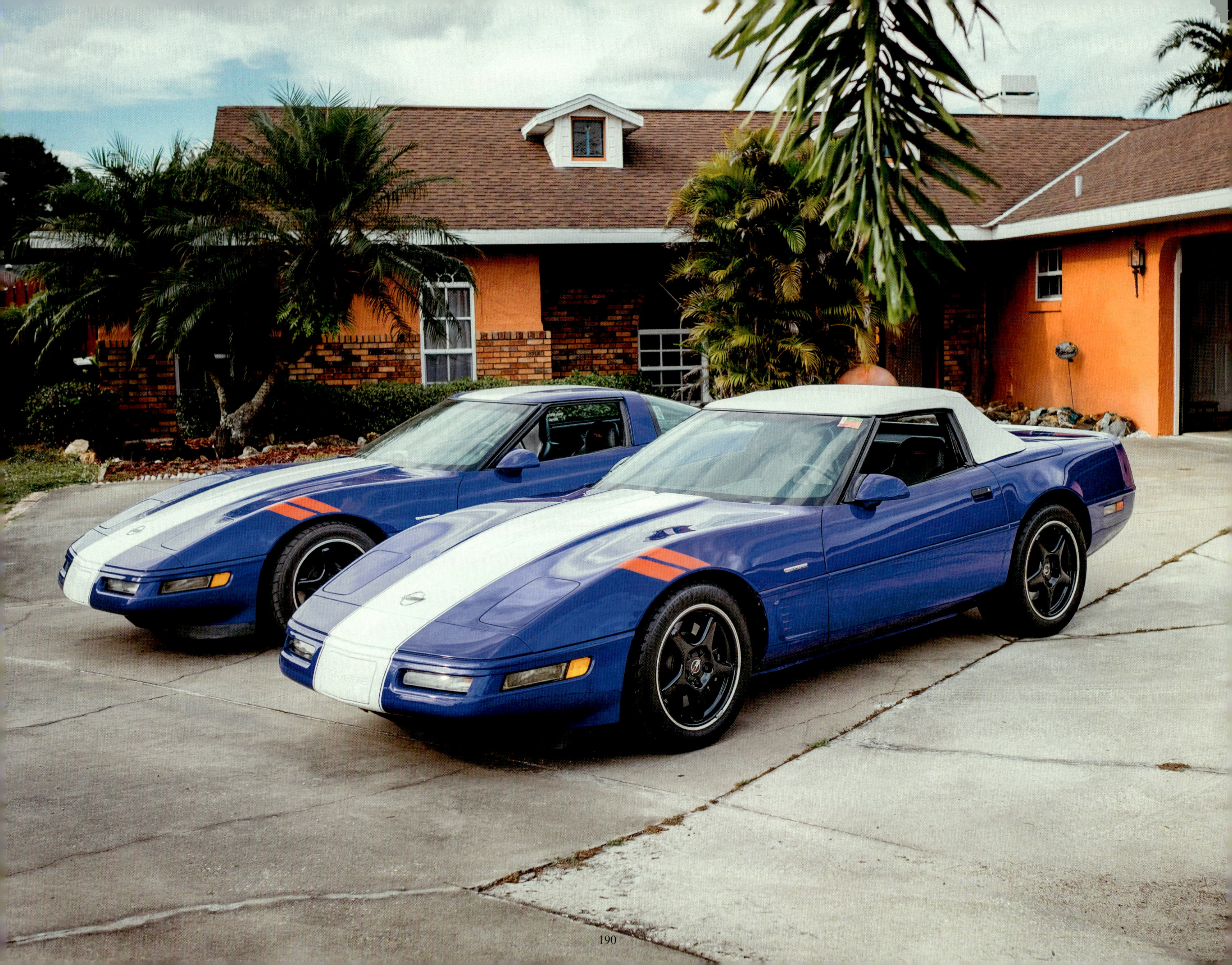

THE GRAND SPORT CONVERTIBLE

John Meyerhoff immersed himself in the Corvette world from an early age. Years later, when he bought a Grand Sport convertible, he had no idea that this special model would be one of 1,000.

What's your Corvette story?
My Corvette story began fifty years ago. I was then a young naval officer and had a '64 Plymouth convertible with a big block V8 and a four-speed manual transmission. Another officer was transferred to my ship in Panama, and he had a '63 Corvette Stingray. I was very impressed by his C2, and it awakened in me the desire to have one too. I therefore sold my beloved big block and ordered a 1966 Corvette with the big 427 engine. It was also a convertible, in Mosport Green. That's how it all started, and it never stopped. I wish I had never sold that car. I searched for it for more than ten years but never found it. Meanwhile I had a small car collection, and my wife was known in Florida as the "Queen of Corvette."

How I came to have my Grand Sport is another great story. Among my cars was a 2001 C5 convertible in Magnetic Red. It was tuned to about 450 hp and ran like a C5 Z06. I drove that car a lot and had lots of fun with it, and I also joined a Corvette club. At some point, I decided I also needed a Corvette that I could drive every day to take some of the load off my red C5.

I went looking for another Corvette and came upon the Grand Sport. I knew nothing about this special model; I only knew that it looked great. A fellow from Montgomery, Alabama, was selling the car. We communicated and quickly made all the arrangements. I sent him a down payment of $500, and he was supposed to hold the car for me until I had time to come and get it. As he didn't let me know if my check had arrived, I called him ten days later. "You were supposed to let me know if you received the check!" His response: "My wife walked out of the garage one day, looked at the Corvette, and said that we shouldn't sell it." Understandable, but I still wanted my check back.

After this bizarre experience, I resumed looking. Another Grand Sport finally turned up in Saginaw, Michigan. At the time, I was living near Buffalo, New York. A friend and I flew to Saginaw, and I looked at the Corvette. I took cash with me just in case. That proved to be a good idea, because the convertible was like new and had just 200 miles on the odometer. As before, however, I really had no idea what I was buying. The "Grand Sport" on it didn't tell me much. I thought it was just another variant of the Corvette. Not until one or two years after I sold it did I stumble across the Grand Sport Registry and learned how few of them had been made. Altogether just 1,000 Grand Sports were built and just 190 were made as convertibles. It became clear to me that this car would not decrease in value like a normal C4. The NCRS assessed my convertible as Top Flight. It was therefore almost a perfect car, which even had the original tires. Naturally, one cannot take it on long tours, but it is good enough for local meets and events.

What is your all-time favorite Corvette model?
I can answer that question easily. I say to everyone: if you want a Corvette and it will be the only one you will ever get, buy a C5. They are low-maintenance cars with which you can drive across the USA, and they are roomy and comfortable. And you can easily improve the performance, as I did with my C5. I am probably a typical Corvette guy; I just like fast cars.

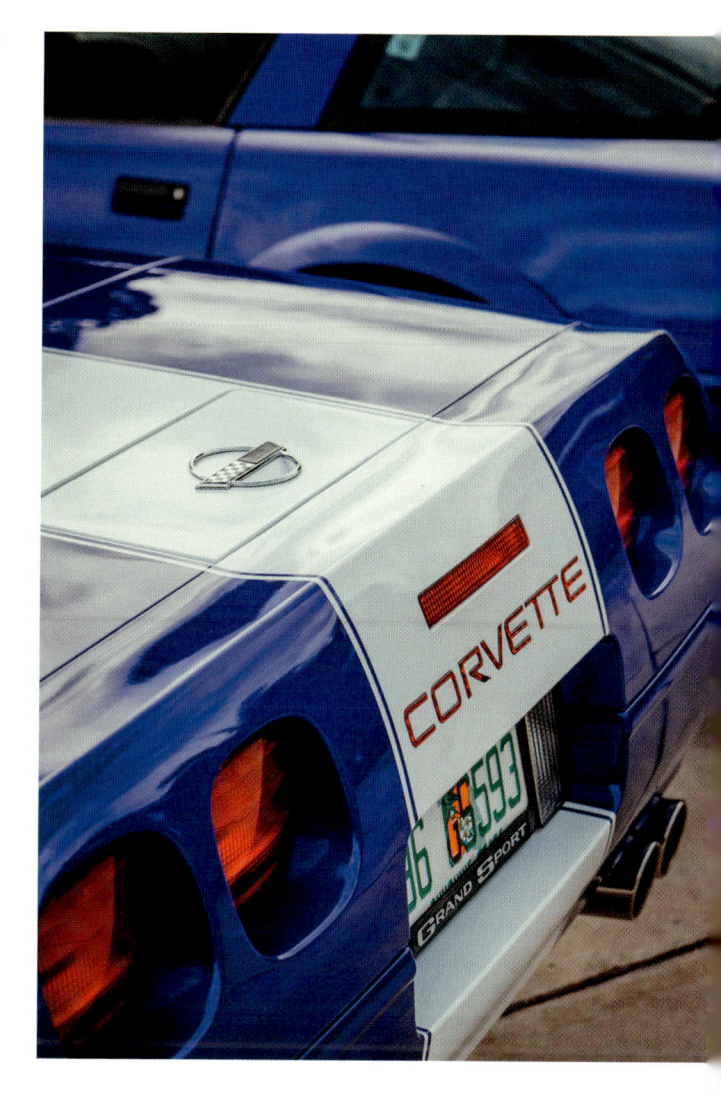

◀ **1996** Corvette C4, **Lake Placid**, Florida, **USA** | November 17, 2021

TO JOHN, CORVETTE MEANS:
IT IS A LIFESTYLE

Fraternal twins. The meeting of John and Ron with their rare Corvettes happened by chance, something that doesn't happen every day, even in the USA. A total of 1,000 Corvette Grand Sports were produced in 1996.

TO RON, CORVETTE MEANS:
IT'S MINE

193

THE GRAND SPORT COUPE

The children had left home, and he had overcome his health problems. Time for Ron Ellerman to think of himself. Time for a Corvette of his own.

What's your Corvette story?
My Corvette story began in 1996. By then, one of my children had already finished high school; the second was just about to graduate. I had paid the college fees, and I was financially independent. I thought it would be a good time for a Corvette. At that time, I had a small business and could buy vehicles through the company. I was thus planning to buy a new company car when I unexpectedly developed health problems. Several operations followed, all of which went well, but for the next twenty years, my health was not the best.

But back to the car purchase. I was in the showroom of a Chevy dealership, intending to look for a new company car, when I saw this Grand Sport Corvette. The model was then brand new and had come onto the market about six weeks earlier. After I had settled everything with the salesman concerning the company car, I asked him in passing what the Corvette would cost. He said that the car was not for sale, as the owner of the dealership wanted to keep the limited special model for himself. I nevertheless spoke to the owner about the Corvette, and to my surprise we came to an agreement. I therefore went away with two cars that day. Because of my health problems, at the time I thought that they would probably be the last new cars in my lifetime and that I should therefore get what I really wanted. And I wanted a Corvette.

My Dad was still alive when I bought the Corvette. He knew that I had just bought a new car. When he saw that I had bought the Corvette too, he said, "You shouldn't have bought that; look what you did. You bought a car that only holds two people." I asked him if he wanted to drive it, but he just said, "No, I'm not driving that damned thing!" I eventually got him in the driver's seat. I told him to take off in first gear, then put it in second and step on the gas. He immediately had a big smile on his face. He never looked back: he was hooked. That's a great memory.

I kept the Corvette in the garage for many, many years. I was living in a colder climate at that time, and I didn't drive the car that much. By then I couldn't work anymore. I sold my assets and moved down to Florida. I shipped the Corvette down. It had just 10,000 miles on it when it got there; now it has 20,000. I have been here eight years and I drive quite a lot. When I moved here, I wasn't into the car culture and tried to sell the car. But once I discovered what the car culture was in this part of the world, it gave me a little more motivation to keep the Grand Sport. And I am very happy that I still have it. I've enjoyed it ever since. It has been part of the family, and now my children look forward to driving it one day. That's my story. I had my own business, I worked very hard, I paid my way, and it was time to get something for myself.

The car culture here is just amazing. I didn't realize how many people have Corvettes, hotrods, or very special classic cars. Being part of this group just enhances your hobby. There's a guy in our auto club who's owned more than 250 Corvettes. I've known him for four years, and he probably had fifteen Corvettes in that time. That's the kind of folks you get to meet, and they are just great people. And our group is still growing.

What is your all-time favorite Corvette model?
I used to think that the newest is always the best. Over the years, I have followed the development of the new Corvette generations, and today I find that my Grand Sport looks cooler than many of the newer models. It drives and feels like a new car, and I am still happy with my C4.

1996 Corvette C4, **Lake Placid**, Florida, USA | November 17, 2021▶

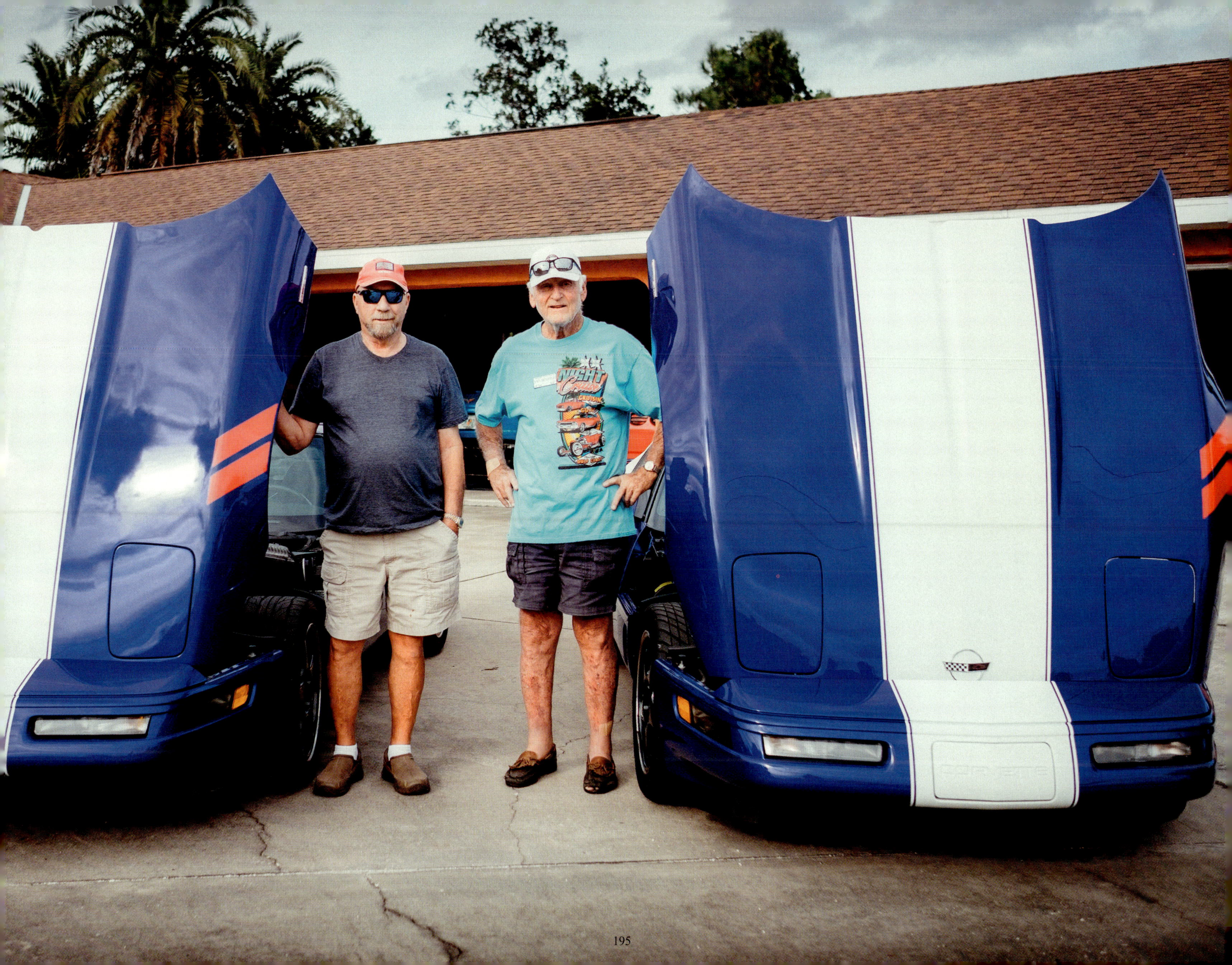

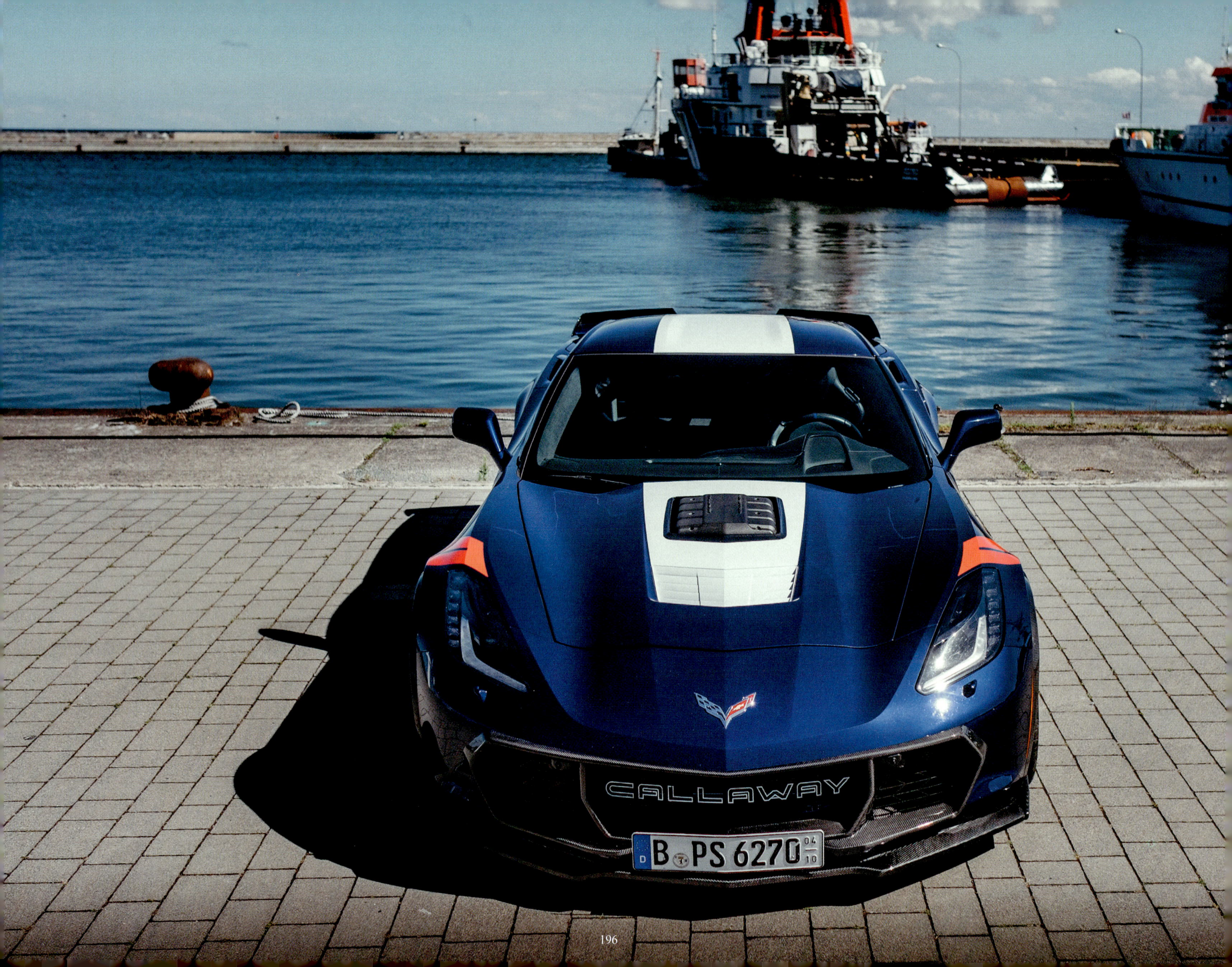
CALLAWAY
B PS 6270

CALLAWAY PREMIERE IN BERLIN

His first American car was a Camaro Z28. Peter Schierz now owns a special Callaway C7 and a C4 ZR-1. Are they the beginning of a collection?

What's your Corvette story?
I have liked American cars since I was eighteen. I remember being in Hansa Park here in Lübeck. After our visit, we headed home on the country road. I had just gotten my driver's license and was behind the wheel of my old Opel D Kadett. We passed a car dealership and saw a black C3 sitting on the lot. I immediately turned around to have a closer look at the sports car. Since that day, I have liked American cars, especially the Corvette.

I began saving up for one. And it had to be a C3! Unfortunately, my plan came to nothing. It was too expensive. I did, however, have enough money for a 1987 Camaro Z28, which I bought when I was nineteen or twenty. I had saved up 20,000 deutsche marks. The Camaro was in Hamburg and cost 19,900 deutsche marks. I cleaned out my account, drove into the Hanseatic city, and bought the coupe. That was the real beginning. I began working on cars myself, repairing and optimizing them. Around 1994 or '95, I had no other choice up here in northern Germany. There were no dealers or garages in the area that were familiar with the car. Not a chance. One had to understand how such a car worked and know where one could find help and knowledge.

I had the Camaro for ten years, then I was forced to sell it because I was unemployed. Having to sell it made me extremely unhappy. I was then thirty years old. Until five years ago, I did not have another American car, but I regularly bought magazines like *Chrome and Flames*, went to meets, and the whole time yearned for American cars. With a house, business, and family, for a long time I had no time for the hobby.

Then when the children had left home, by chance I discovered the *Autohaus* Kramm in Berlin through a newspaper advertisement. It was right around the corner from me. Why not drive there and see what they had on the lot? As my wife and I walked through the lot, I said to her, "Look, there are two Callaways. How did they get here?" I was astonished to see two of these Corvettes here in Berlin. It was a most unusual sight. I had never seen a Callaway, even at the meets I had attended. Of course, I went to the salesman and asked him directly where they had come from. He then told me, somewhat reluctantly, that they had received a license from Callaway USA to convert and sell the vehicles here in Europe. At the time, Kramm sponsored the Callaway Competition racing sport team at the GT Masters, and it was probably because of that that they wanted Callaway's permission to produce the car.

The Kramm technicians had flown to the USA and at the Callaway facility learned how to properly convert the Corvette. This began with the cutouts in the hood over the supercharger right up to the cooling system. Kramm planned to officially open the Callaway workshop in Berlin in October 2017. But it was now only early April. I told the good man that I wanted to purchase one of the two Callaway Corvettes on the lot. He replied that he could not yet sell the car with all the modifications, as the whole project was not supposed to officially begin until autumn. I replied that he could do that if he really wanted to. It went back and forth like this for a while. In the end, the salesman came around, but I had to keep everything to myself and could not let myself be seen with the car. It made no difference to me. I even signed a corresponding confidentiality agreement. The main thing was that I got this crazy car.

We finally agreed that they would complete the Corvette and I would get it at the end of July. There were still a few problems with registering the conversion. They wanted to register the car in such a way that it would receive an independent registration, which would allow you to register the Corvette anywhere in Europe with the data sheet. As promised, I finally got my Corvette at the end of July, months before they officially became available. And in October, I was supposed to take the Corvette to the last GT Masters race, where they would officially hand over the car. Unfortunately, neither happened. The weather and my schedule unfortunately threw a wrench in the works for me.

Instead, that same month I naturally went to the opening of Kramm's Callaway garage in Berlin. There they had a large board with photos and descriptions of the first customer conversions, and of course my Corvette was also depicted there. At some point, my wife quite brazenly asked if we could take the board home with us after the event. It now hangs in my office. Very cool.

That is how I came to own my first Corvette. I always wanted one, but I had to wait until I was older to be able to fulfill my dream. Unfortunately, I still have too little time to be able to drive the Corvette regularly. I am pretty busy with my construction company, and I am privately converting my parents' home on the island of Rügen. I am doing it completely on my own, which takes time. But from the beginning of July to the middle or end of August, I am trying to only do with my wife what gives us joy. We are also going to go to a car meet or to the Elbe Sandstone Mountains in Saxony. We have a property there that we have to look in on, and we happily combine that with a brief vacation and a trip in the Corvette.

How did you come to have a C4 ZR-1?
I bought it last year in April. In the 1990s, I thought the C4 was a really good car, especially the ZR-1. Of course, then they were prohibitively expensive. I would have had to mortgage everything I had to afford a C4. Many say that the C4 is the ugliest Corvette ever made. In my opinion, it is one of the most timeless of Corvettes. I sometimes sit on a chair in front of my Corvette and look at it. The thing simply looks good. Metallic Dark Polo Green is, however, a rather grandiose color for a C4.

I bought the 1990 Corvette, because it was right around the corner in Berlin and because I wanted a car I could work on myself, which I still like to do. And there really is a lot one can do oneself on the fourth generation. It is a completely underappreciated car. One must remember that it is thirty years old and that the ZR-1 version reaches a top speed of 290 kph (180 mph). That is not normal, however. If my C4 was completely overhauled, then I might try to reach 290 kph.

The two owners saved every receipt and every document concerning the car since 1991. No matter what was installed or modified, what part was ordered, where which repair was carried out, simply everything. You can go back to 1991 and still find service invoices from Geiger in Munich.

Back then, I had nowhere to park the Corvette inside. For a time, I parked it at my door. Now we are in the process of building a garage complex. The goal is to have a building that can accommodate a lift and the cars. When it is finished, I will probably add to the two Corvettes.

What is your all-time favorite Corvette model?
I think the C4 ZR-1. I simply see it as a timeless design, and you have absolutely no problem keeping up with modern cars.

◄ **2017** Corvette C7, **Sassnitz**, Mecklenburg–Western Pomerania, **Germany** | June 12, 2022

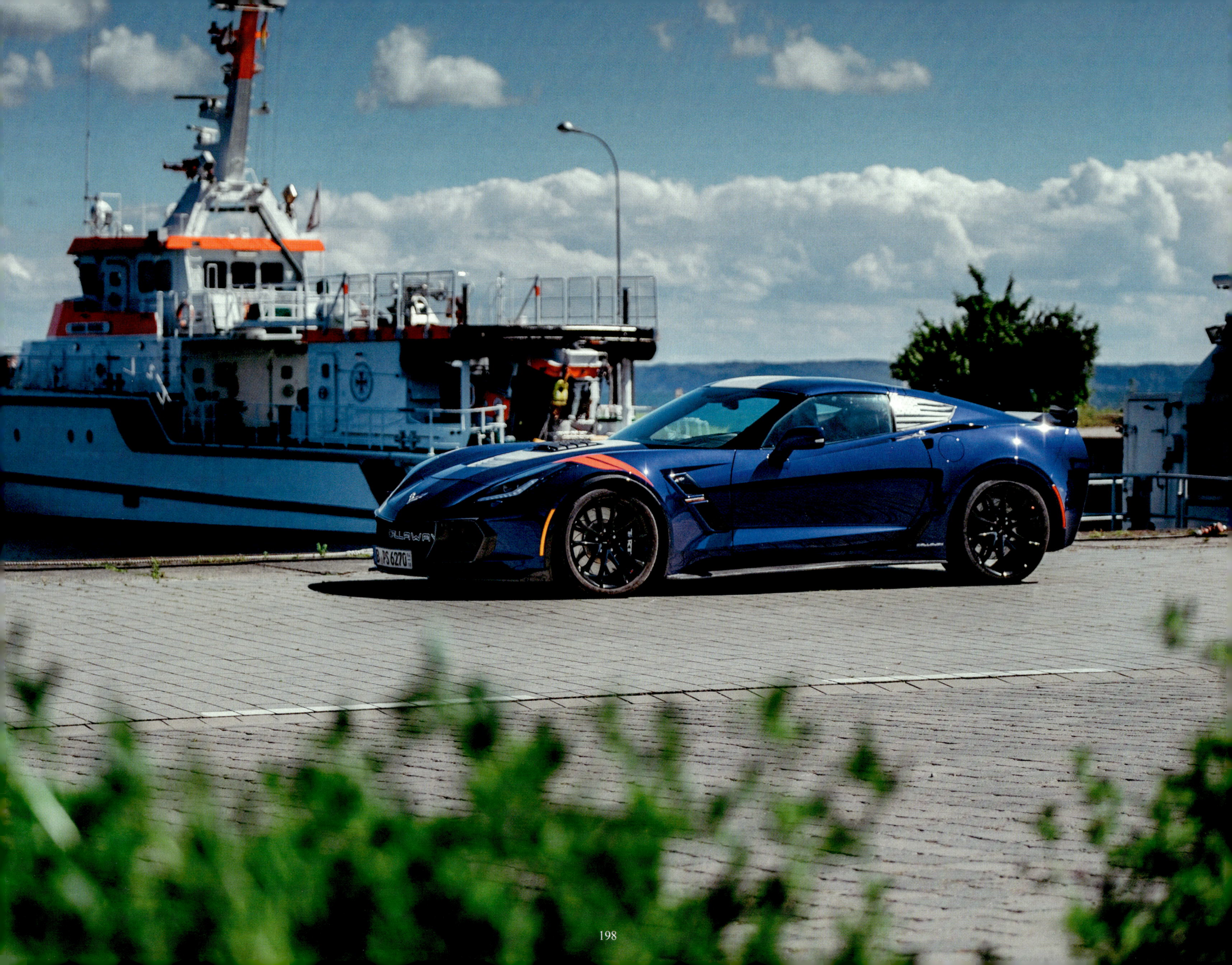

TO PETER, CORVETTE MEANS:
FUN, RELAXATION, HOBBY

Powerful vehicles. In addition to his Callaway Corvette, which is force-fed by means of three intercoolers and a supercharger developed by the Californians themselves, Peter Schierz also owns a C4 ZR-1, then the most powerful Corvette, with the legendary LT5 DOHC engine.

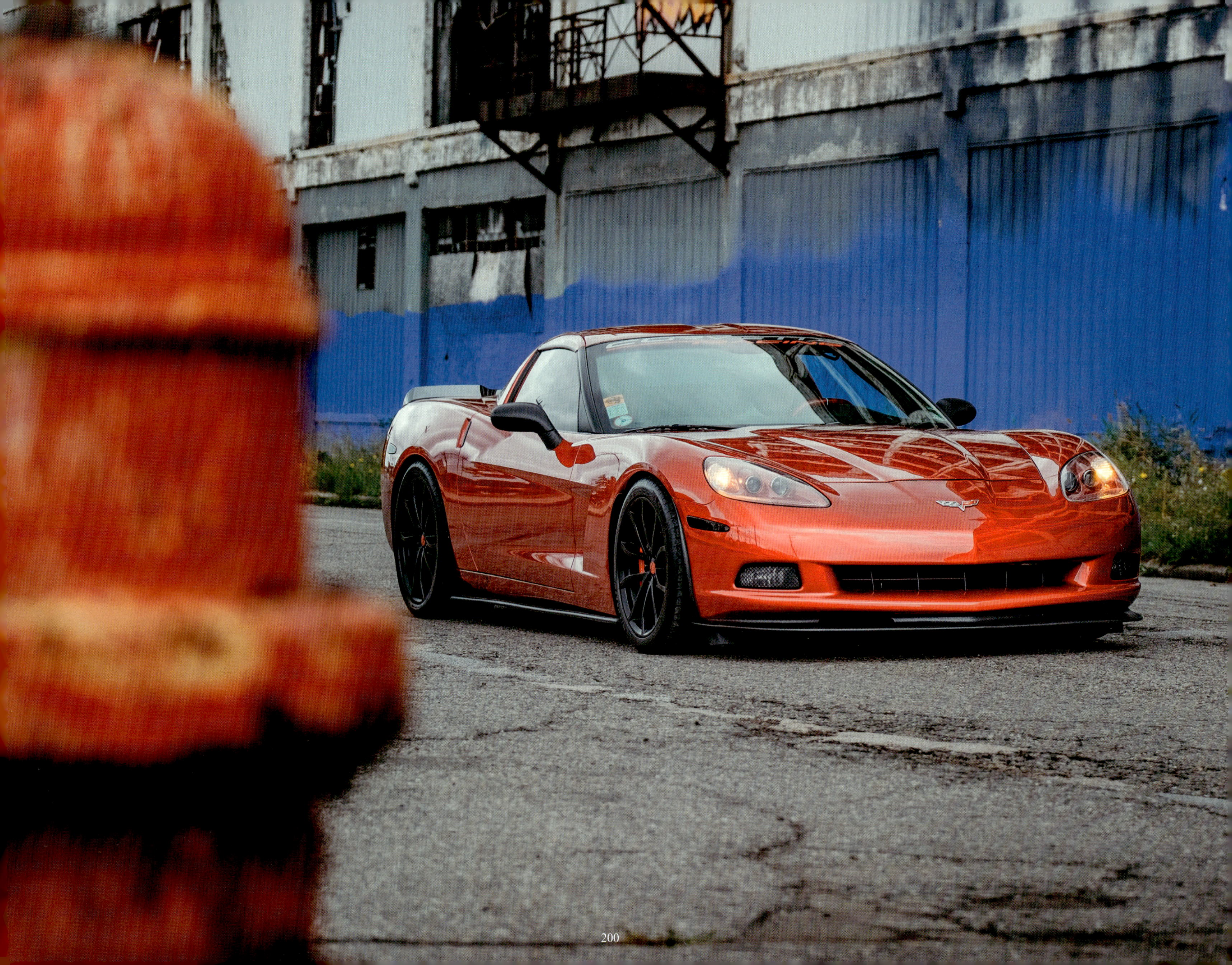

MAY I INTRODUCE: SOPHIE

Kurt Pierce bought his red C6 from one of his customers. His wife named the Corvette, and his neighbor, a C6 owner himself, inspired him to carry out some modifications to make it his own.

What's your Corvette story?
A Corvette was never really on my list of cars. I have always liked cars. I had a twenty-year-old 2000 Mercedes CLK 320 that I bought from a customer of mine. She was an eighty-year-old woman who had bought it new. I had always wanted a Benz. I loved the car, and with some hard work I got it looking like new and had no interest in selling it. Then in walked another friend and customer who had a Corvette that I had admired for years. It was his pride and joy.

A few years later, he told me he was moving to Florida. I asked him what his plans for the Vette were. Of course, he said he was taking it with him. I tried to convince him he was too old to drive the car 1,700 miles to Florida. He and I went back and forth for a few weeks about him selling me his beautiful 2005 Magnet Red II Corvette.

One bright sunny day in late June, Michael T. walked up to my desk and tossed the keys to me. "Let's go for a ride," he said. I knew at that moment that she was going to be mine. That evening, I showed Ann the photos, and the next weekend, the Fourth of July, Sophie was parked in our garage. That was three years ago.

In Michigan, Sophie spent the first winter in our garage. All winter long, day after day packages arrived for the transformation from bone stock to what she is now. It all started with an exhaust.

The biggest transformation happened this past winter. Racing engine builder K-Tech had her for a few weeks, building a fire-breathing monster. I have loved car racing since I was a young boy. It's never too late to try something new, so I started building her into a car that could be driven on the street but also taken to the track. Suspension and brake upgrades were next, and we have been to five different tracks and made more than a few road trips. The car attracts attention wherever we go. One day while sitting in the living room, Ann started talking about Sophie as if she were a person. I asked if a new neighbor had moved in. The answer was no, Sophie had been here for some time. My reply was to invite her for a visit. My wife told me that Sophie could not make it up the stairs. I was confused. Then Ann explained to me that Sophie was my Corvette, and that is the story of how Sophie got her name. This year when I renewed the plate, I got one with SoFee on it, as Sophie was not available.

On the track last year, the transmission temperature reached 320 degrees C (608°F), which is quite warm. At the next event, it reached 362 degrees C (682°F), and I decided to get off the track and let it cool down. I drove the car the rest of the year with no issues. At the first track event of the next season, it became obvious that something was wrong with the transmission. Fortunately, the gentleman who had built the engine for me was at the same event. After a long discussion with him, he concluded that I had cooked the tranny the previous year when it had overheated. A month later, a high-performance racing transmission was installed.

I give a lot of thanks and credit to my neighbor and friend Tim for all he has done to help me make Sophie mine. He enjoyed spending my money on the modifications.

What is your all-time favorite Corvette model?
I have to say the C2. When I was a kid, the guy a few houses down had a light blue C2 convertible. I do remember him racing up and down the street, occasionally with a police car in hot pursuit. The body lines of that car are like the lines of a beautiful woman. It gets your blood flowing. I always wanted a car with a vertically mounted radio. That's so cool.

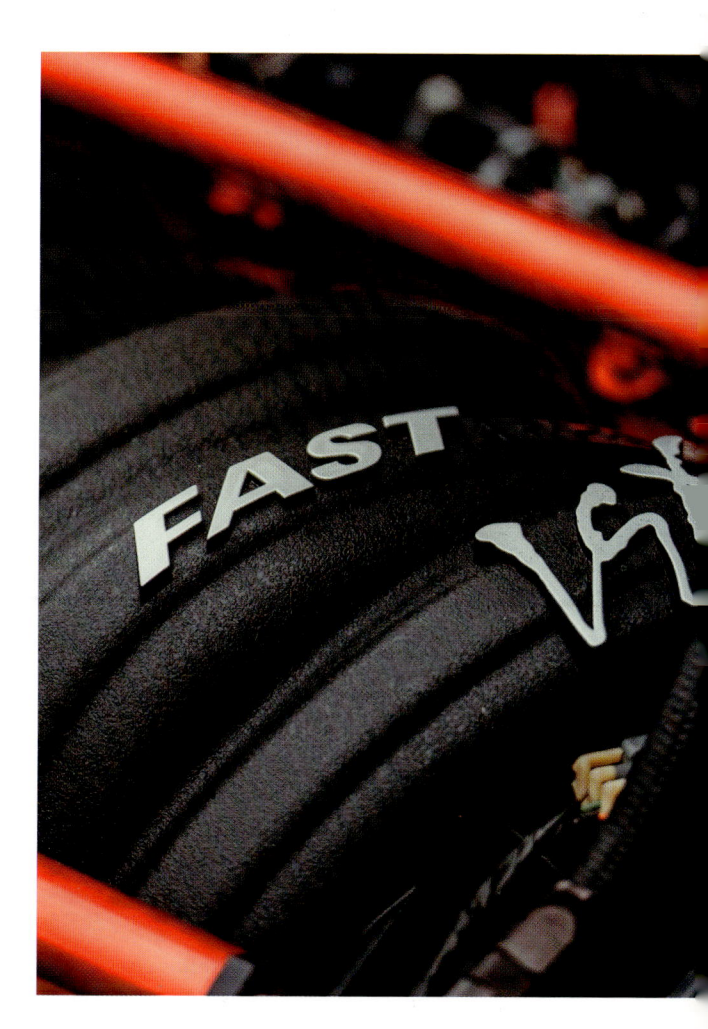

◀ **2005** Corvette C6, **Detroit,** Michigan **USA** | November 17, 2021

TO KURT, CORVETTE MEANS:
FREEDOM AND THE OPEN ROAD

Racetrack brother. You can tell by looking at Kurt Pierce's Corvette that it wasn't modified for fun. The man from Michigan loves to drive it on the racetrack. The name of the C6 can be seen on the license plate: "SoFee."

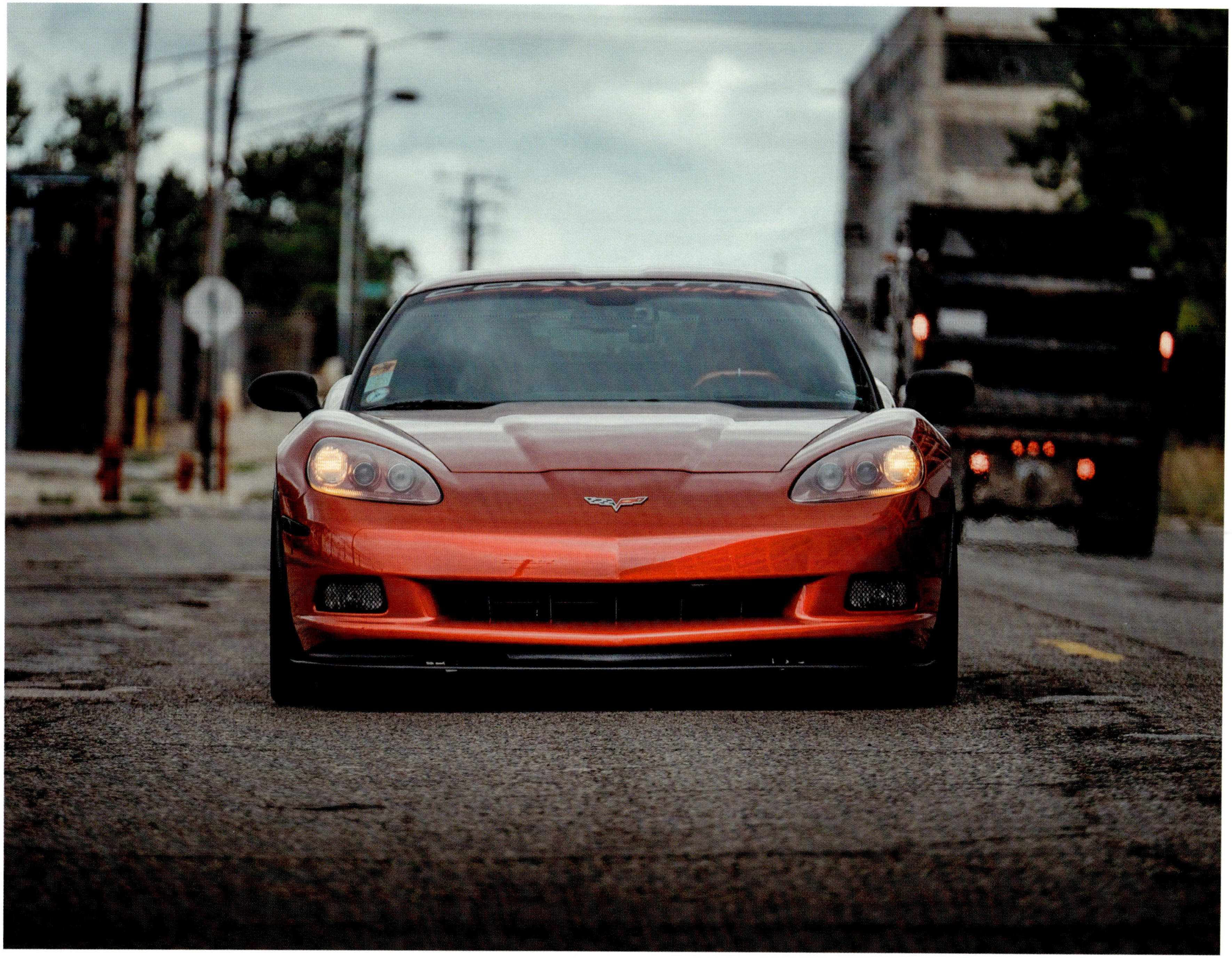

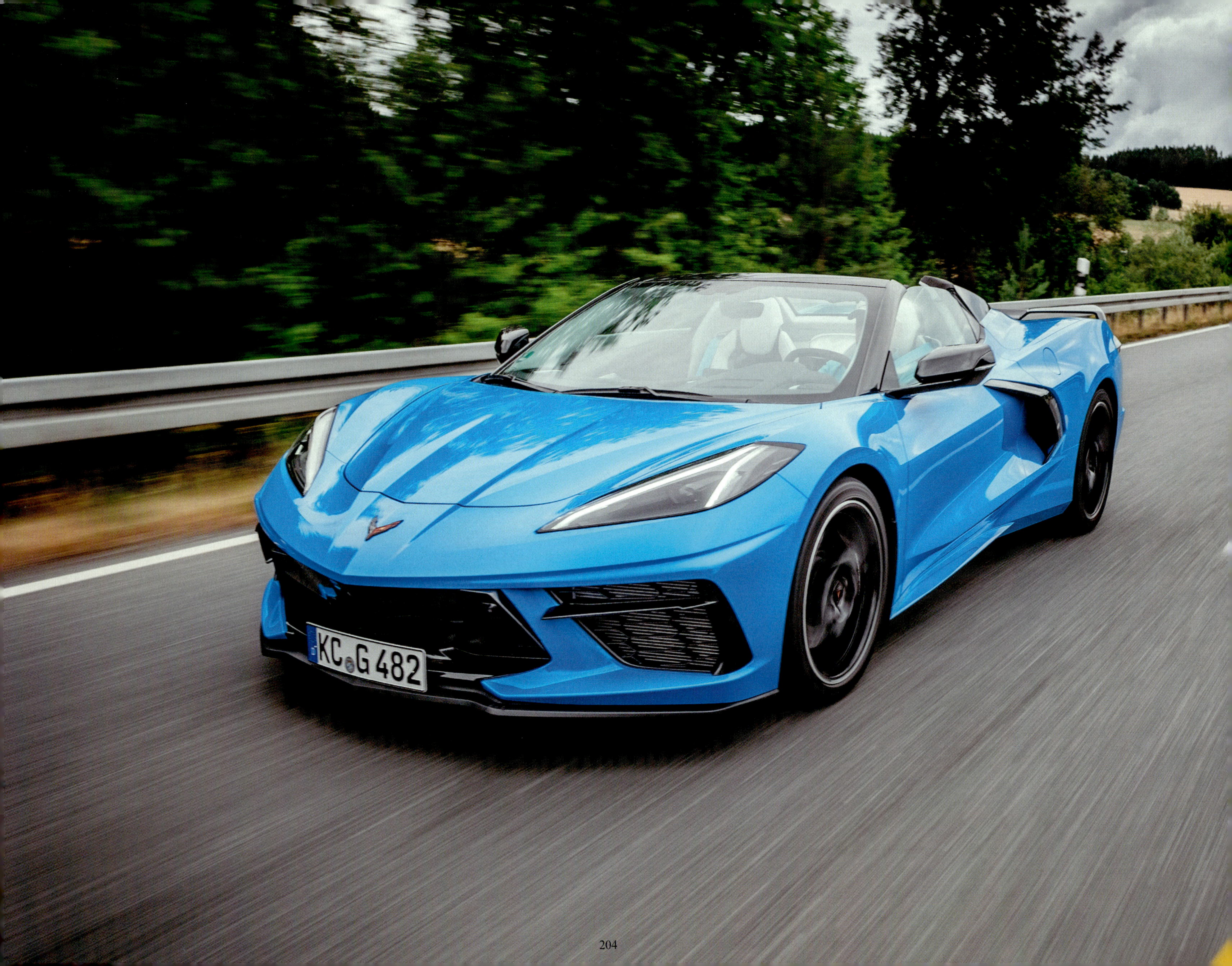
KC G 482

THANKS TO THE CORVETTE COMMUNITY

Is there anything more beautiful than a father-son team with the same passion for automobiles? Certainly not to Ludwig and Jens Gleichmann. That is why they have not limited themselves to just one Corvette.

What's your Corvette story?
Jens: There are many beautiful cars. Whether Porsche, Ferrari, or Lamborghini, they all have their own character, their own sound, and are simply beautiful to look at. I don't like making direct comparisons between such vehicles. But now when one compares the car communities to one another, one quickly discovers major differences. Before we bought a sports car, we often went to the different brands' meets and events. Then an acquaintance, himself the owner of a Corvette, invited us to an event in Suhl, one of the largest and best-known Corvette meets in Europe.

There we discovered a very different scene. The people were very open, told one everything about their cars, gave tips, offered contacts. There, everything was very friendly and warmhearted—the opposite of what we knew of other communities. That was one of the first positive experiences that took us in the direction of the Corvette. We found the community—and of course, the cars, too—exciting.

As a result, in late 2012, my father and I decided on a Corvette C6 Z06 and bought the car. Then the whole thing got going, and we made more and more contacts with people from Luxembourg, Switzerland, Austria, and France. We had come into contact with so many great people at the meets and not just at the event in Suhl.

In the beginning, we always took turns driving the C6. At some point, I thought, wouldn't it be nice if each of us could drive his own Corvette. And so our motor pool slowly began to grow.
Ludwig: Of course, our wives wanted to go with us, so we had no other choice but to buy a second Corvette. It was a C4 ZR-1 that I found in Spain.

We again attended the meet in Suhl in 2015, and a dealer was offering test drives in a Corvette C7. We were immediately impressed by it and began negotiating directly with the dealer. We could trade in our C4 without any problems. That's exactly what we did, and today we are the proud owners of a yellow C7. Now we have a coupe and a convertible. All that's missing is a classic Corvette.

On the birthday of "Dr. Strange," one of those we met on the Corvette forum, we looked at some of his cars in Bavaria. He had to sell several of his treasures because he was slowly running out of space. That was most convenient for us. One of them was a Corvette C3, which is now in our garage. And that's how the community led us to this dream car.
Jens: We put some work into the C3 in order to make it ready for everyday use. Power steering, brake booster, and so on. There were a few things to optimize so that we would be able to drive long distances without breaking down straightaway.
Ludwig: Then they unveiled the C8, what a beautiful car. We immediately thought about buying one. I gave myself a C8 as a birthday present and ordered one in 2020.
Jens: That was the first Corvette that we really configured ourselves. All the others had already been built. We couldn't afford to order them new or, in some cases, bought cars already on the dealer's lot.
Ludwig: Now I drive the C8, my wife drives the yellow C7, and Jens drives his C6. Only the C3 isn't driven as much. The new C8 is unlike all the others when it comes to handling characteristics, although we were already very satisfied with our C7. Our next, longer tour with the new car is already planned, to Graz in Austria.

It's not unusual for you to make longer tours in your Corvettes, is it?
Jens: No, but my father takes part in them much more often than I do, as my job keeps me quite busy.
Ludwig: We now have an excellent group with whom we regularly go on tours. We mainly met at the meets in Suhl. We make spring tours, travel to meets, organize drives at the end of the season. Most of our longer tours are to Italy or France. One member of our group is actually already planning the next tour. We are always on the road and as a group have a wonderful time. My wife, Petra, is our navigator. That allows me to enjoy the drive without having to worry about the route.

What is your all-time favorite Corvette model?
Ludwig: I haven't been able to test the C8 long enough, as it has less than 2,000 kilometers on it. Consequently, at present I would still say the C7. We will see how it looks in a few months.

Jens: The C6 is really ideal for normal use, also for our tours. If I now look at all the Corvette generations, the C2 Stingray Split-Window is a very beautiful car that would be a great addition to our collection.

Rest in Peace
In loving memory of our Petra. Heaven now has another guardian angel, who accompanies us on our travels and watches over us.

◀ **2020** Corvette C8, **Redwitz an der Rodach,** Bavaria, Germany | July 9, 2022

TO LUDWIG, CORVETTE MEANS:
V8 SOUND, COMMUNITY, LONG-DISTANCE CAPABILITY

TO JENS, CORVETTE MEANS:
V8 RUMBLE, AMERICAN CAR FEELING, ACCELERATION

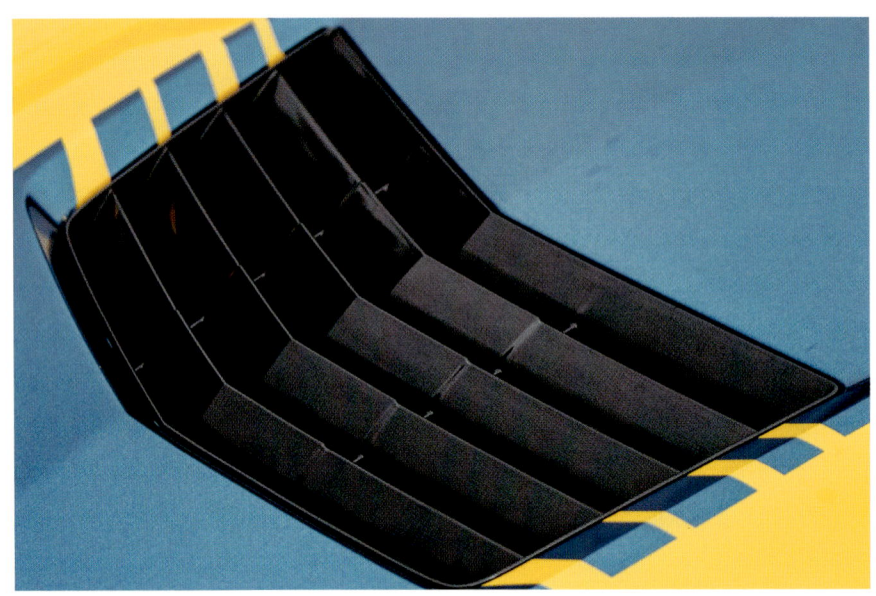

Father and son. To the Gleichmann family, Corvettes are simply a part of life. Whether with the C6, C7, or C8 in everyday life or in the classic C3 on weekends, they can't do without a sports car.

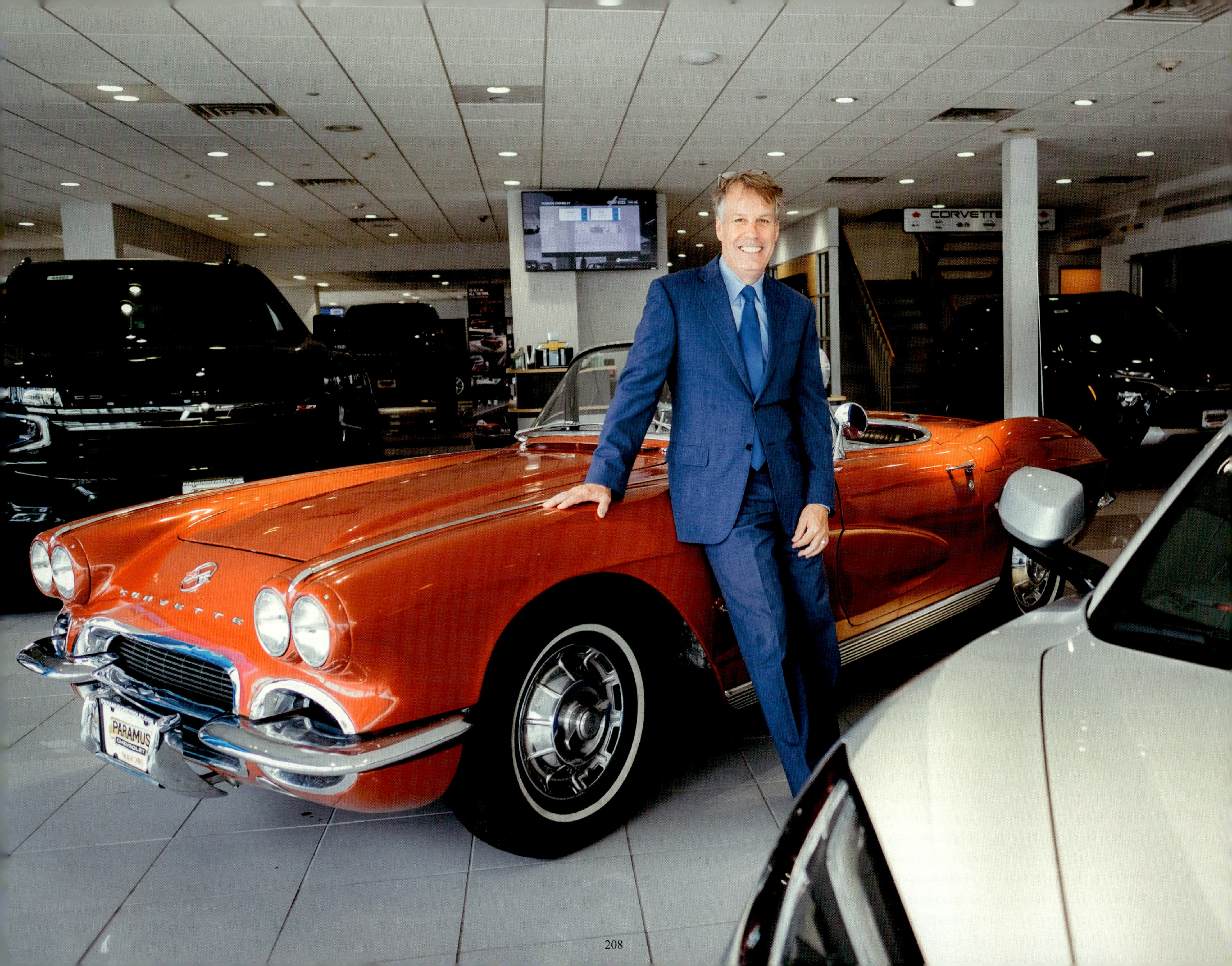
CORVETTE
PARAMUS
CHEVROLET

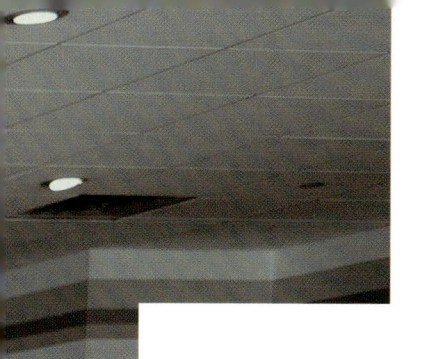

WELCOME TO PARAMUS CHEVROLET

Bill Grunner grew up in a car dealership. Now he is working at a GM dealership with a lot of history, just like his classic red Corvette C1.

What's your Corvette story?
I've been around cars my whole life, and Corvette has been the American sports car since I was a kid. I grew up in a car dealership and ended up owning a bunch of them, then getting out of the dealerships and getting into consulting and advertising. At one point I had the opportunity to come and work for this dealership in Paramus. It was the number one Corvette dealership in the world back in the days of the C1 and C2 Corvettes. That's why we have a separate Corvette showroom with a lot of history. I always knew as a kid that this is the place to come and look at Corvettes.

So when I came to work here, I had to have a Chevrolet. I couldn't have another brand of car. I was able to get a Corvette C7 at that time so that I could drive what I sold. And then of course the C8 came out. Everybody had been watching it for years. I had my name on the list for two years, just like all my customers. When I got my C8, I really wanted to go back and start looking at older cars to work on with my two sons. We started out with an old MG as a platform on which to teach my sons a little bit about simple mechanics. Then I decided that I wanted to get into Corvettes, and I wanted to start at the beginning.

I looked at what was available and just kept poking around, trying to find a car. They were either too wrecked, or too far away to look at, or too nice. I wanted something I could work on with my sons and have some fun. I was online constantly looking for cars, and one day a red C1 appeared on Facebook Marketplace. I thought, "This is a nice-looking car." It was an interesting color and the right year. I was looking for a 1962. And it was a 327, an engine I knew from my youth, when I helped out older boys who had C2s with 327 engines. Then there was this car on Facebook. I put my glasses on and scrolled through the pictures. The car looked a little scruffy. There was stuff in the trunk and all over the place. It really looked like a barn find. But I looked more closely and found that it was right down the street from me.

It was located at a garage that is literally at the bottom of my hill, perhaps a mile and a half from my house. I immediately went on Facebook Messenger and asked, "When can I look at the car? Is nine o'clock okay?" And so, I drove down on my way to work and took a look at the car. We talked about all kinds of things, including the price. I took it out for a drive, and it was a mess. The guy who was selling the car was a mechanic, and one of his former customers had moved to Pennsylvania and then passed away. He was the car's second owner. His daughter asked the mechanic if he could sell the car for her. So it ended up back in New Jersey. It wouldn't shift; it wouldn't turn right; it was just a mess. So I said, "Okay, I'll take it." That was about a year ago.

What is your all-time favorite Corvette model?
I think the C2. That is the car I grew up around in the Seventies. Back then, it would have been an older car that younger kids could get and work on. They couldn't afford to buy a one new and instead bought ones that were five, six, or seven years old. I think the C2 has the best lines of any Corvette, and it introduced disc brakes and some other innovations. These days I am looking for a C2 to add to my collection, or I might get rid of the C1. I am looking for a particular car, a '65 or '66 convertible, Nassau Blue with a white interior, 327 V8 with four-speed transmission.

◄ **1962** Corvette C1, **2020** Corvette C8, **Paramus**, New Jersey, USA | September 7, 2022

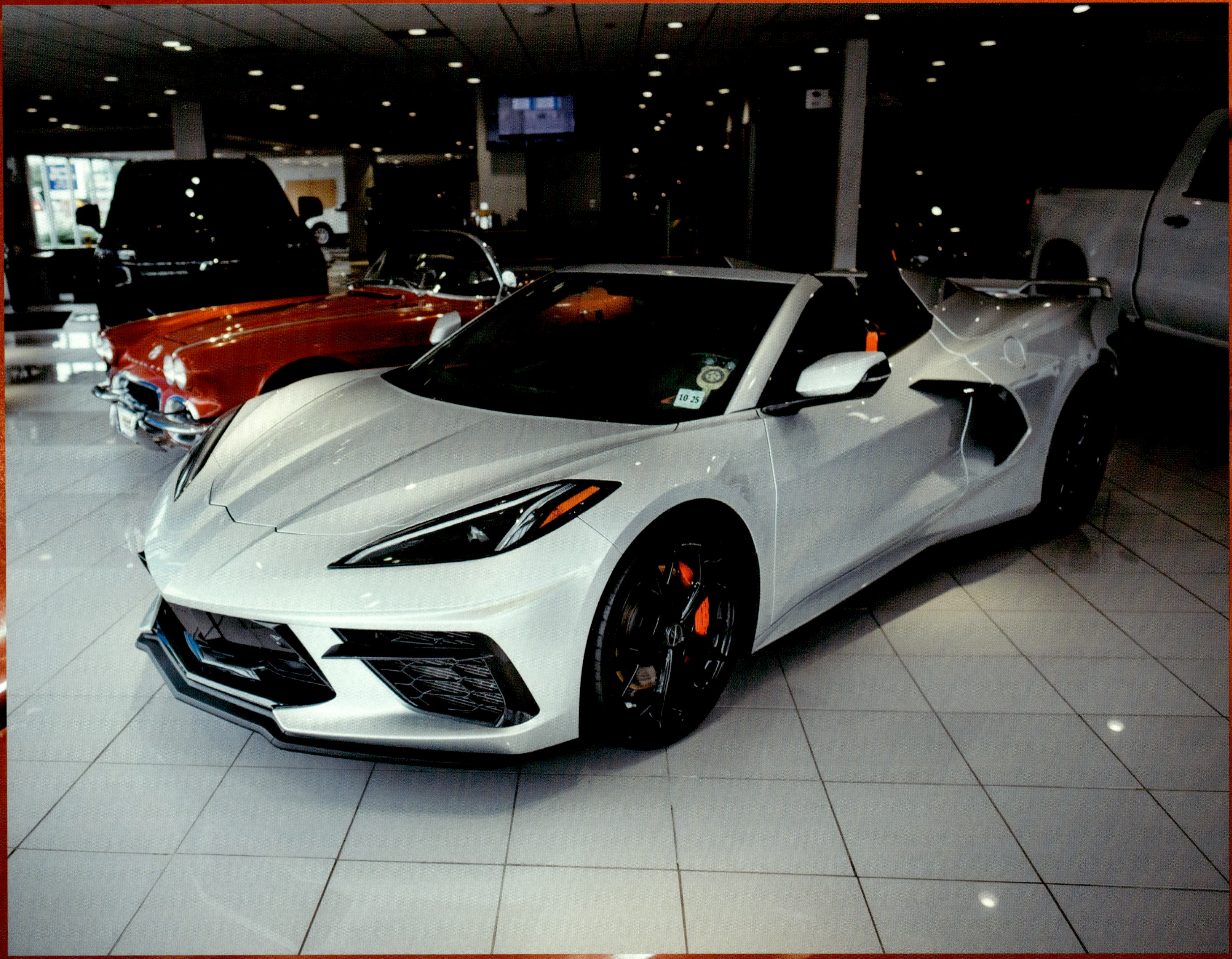

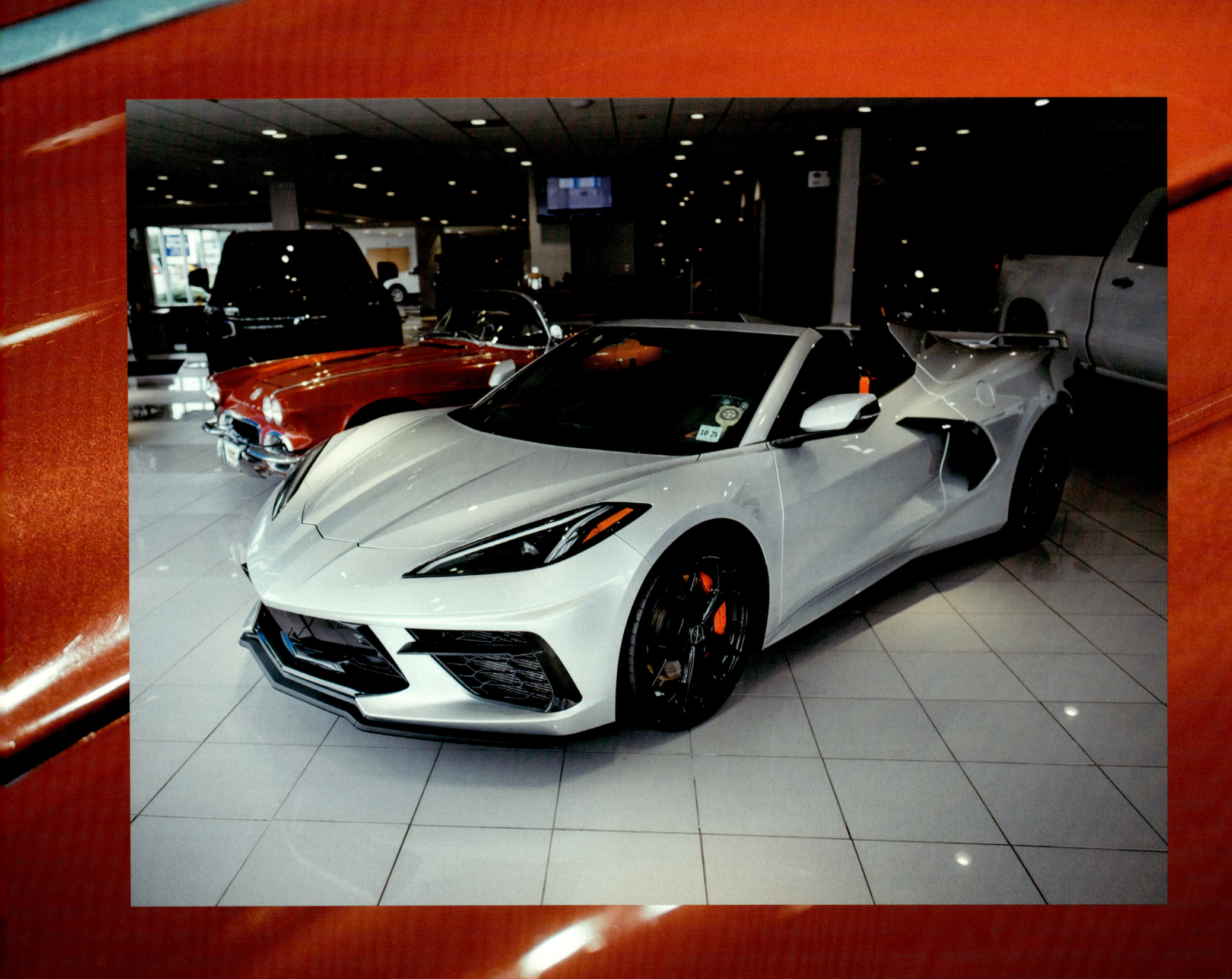

TO BILL, CORVETTE MEANS:
DESIGN, SIMPLICITY, CULTURE

Sense of tradition. Bill Brunner practically grew up in a car dealership, and today, he runs Paramus Chevrolet, which used to be the largest Corvette dealership in the USA. In the showroom, of course, are his C1 and a new C8.

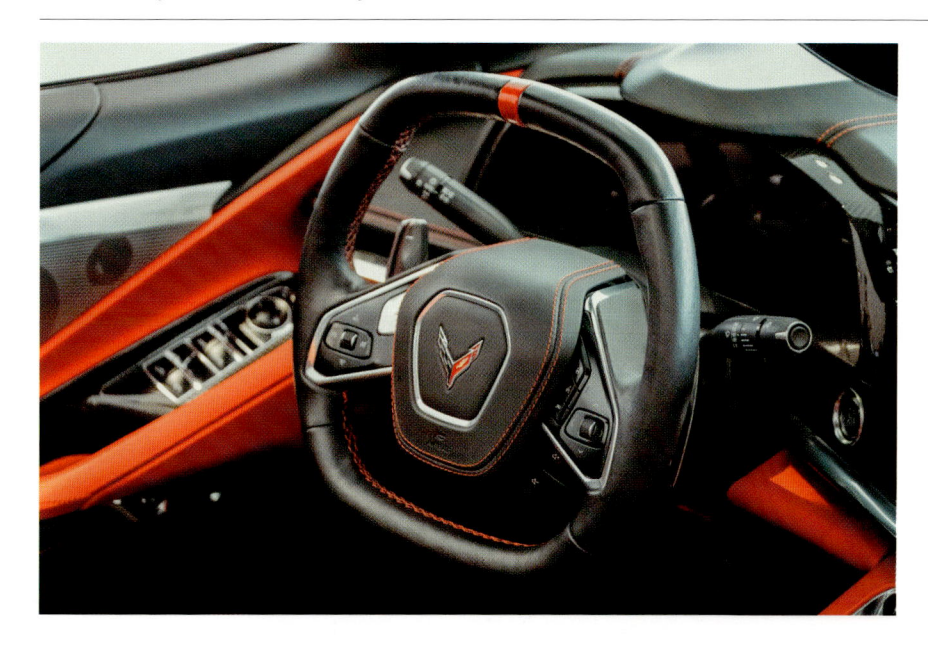

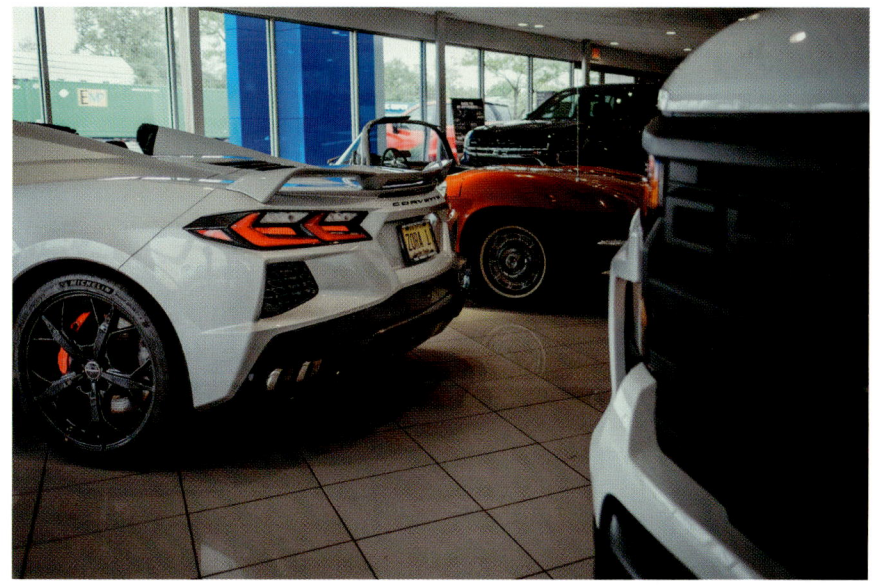

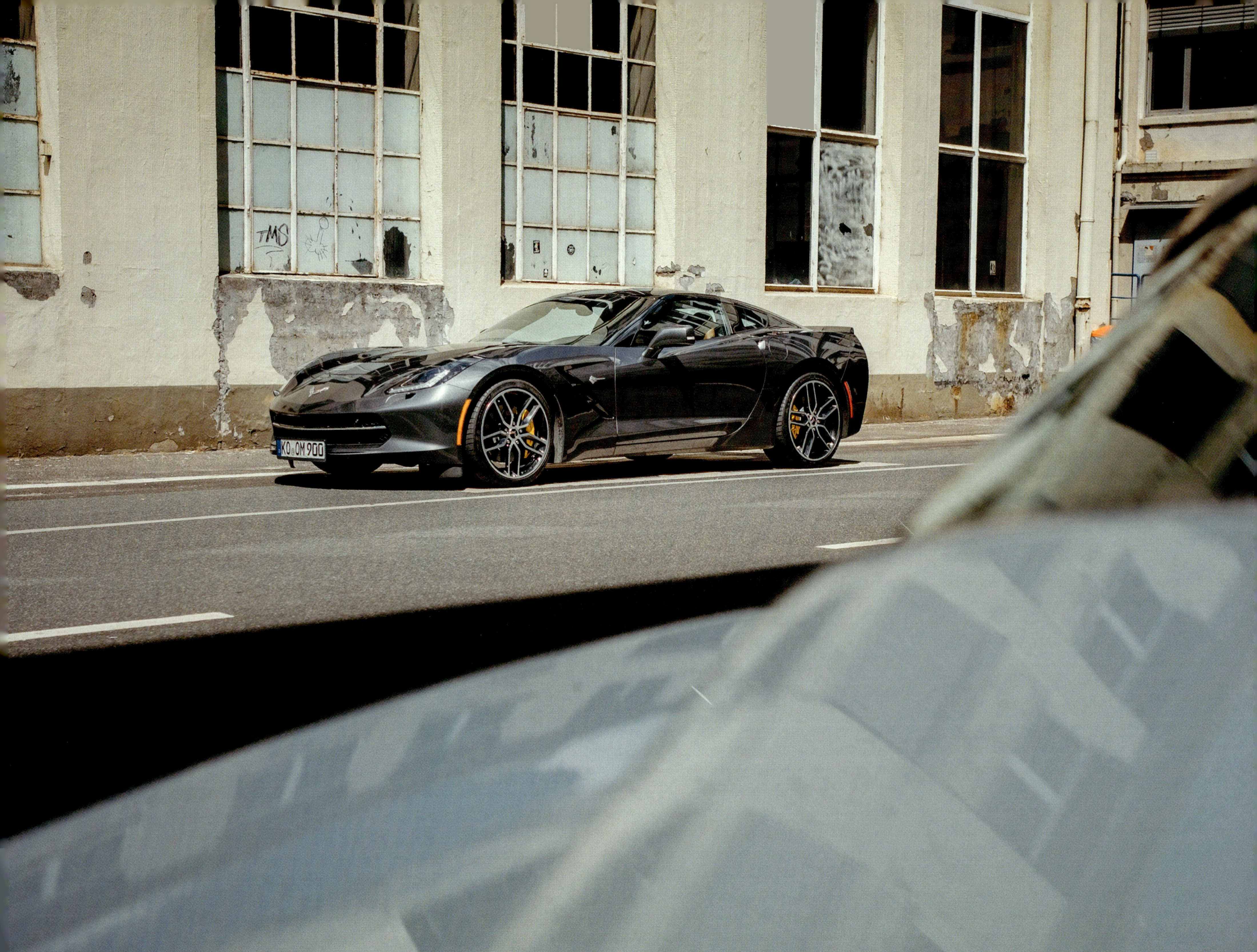
KO OM 900

A CORVETTE FOR EVERYDAY

Prof. Oliver Mohrs enjoys driving his Corvette C7 daily and, with his C2, has fulfilled a great childhood dream.

What's your Corvette story?
My predilection for American automobiles probably began because my father always dreamed of a Harley Davidson and Route 66. Some people of my generation regarded American cars as unreliable, but the television series of the 1980s helped make them popular. In my youth, there were two series that had a lasting impact on my taste in cars. One was the series *Spenser for Hire*, which featured private detective Spenser, who drove a dark green '66 Mustang Fastback. And there was the series *Stingray*, whose main character drove a black '65 Corvette Stingray coupe. In both series, of course, there were many street scenes with American cars, which enhanced my infatuation for American vehicles, especially from the Sixties.

At some point in 1995, while I was studying medicine, my father called. One of his friends had seen a black C3 at a gas station near my hometown of Coblenz. And as chance would have it, there was a "for sale" sign on it. Even better, the price was reasonable. We set off and found a broken-down C3, but when the owner turned the ignition key, I was hooked. Against all reason, I bought the Corvette with my savings and invested the money from my student job in spare parts. At some point, however, I was forced to admit that the C3 was becoming a waste of money. I was forced to sell it and, for the first time, left the subject of Corvettes behind me. My enthusiasm for the brand remained, however.

After completing my studies, promotion, and specialist examinations, in 2008 I was in the process of writing my postdoctoral thesis. When I was finished and just a few days away from my appointment, I treated myself to a break. At last, I once again began rummaging about the internet for a Corvette. I quickly discovered a white '66 C2 Stingray coupe that was offered at a very favorable price and was described as a solid, good, and honest car for the conditions at that time. The thought immediately entered my mind that I could have the car repainted black to make it look more like the car from the Stingray series. Anyway, I bought this Corvette and after some time decided that a white C2 coupe showed off the car's shapes and lines much better than a black one. Later I did have the car repainted, but I stayed with white: a very good decision as it turns out.

Over the years, I also bought a 1995 C4 ZR-1 in Dark Red and a 1967 C2 in Marlboro Maroon. It is a convertible in perfect condition, equipped with the breathtaking L71 engine and side-pipes. The previous owner restored it meticulously to NCRS standard. Several years later, my C2 was awarded an NCRS Top Flight Award by the Central European NCRS Chapter, as was my ZR-1. I had meanwhile joined the National Corvette Restorers Society (NCRS) and am even a founding member of the society's Central European Chapter. We organize exciting meets, events, and so-called judging events, at which one can learn a great deal about the originality of vintage Corvettes.

I have since passed my L71 Stingray and my ZR-1 on to good hands, as I am more driver than collector. There is, however, one more Corvette on my wish list: a '61 or '62 C1. While that model is not the most loved among collectors, I love it because of the combination of the classic C1 front end and the new C2 rear. And as a convertible, the model has a trunk with enough space for longer outings. The C1 presents just one problem for me: my body length. I have already spoken to a garage about it, and there are several concepts that will allow even me to sit in the C1. This tampering with originality would prevent me from receiving an NCRS award for this Corvette, but it would be a Corvette tailored to my needs—a very individualized treatment for my Corvette virus, as it were. I am already looking forward to this next chapter.

The trend toward new electric vehicles has been obvious for some time. Therefore, for several years, I have known that I don't have much time left for my dream of happily driving a V8 as my everyday car. When the Corvette C7 came on the market, it happened to me again. I got one in 2017, and since then, I have been driving it daily. It now has 200,000 kilometers on the clock. For me, the C7 Stingray Targa is the perfect combination of driving enjoyment, general utility, and design.

What is your all-time favorite Corvette model?
That is a difficult question. My absolute favorite model is the C2, but you just can't always drive them as your everyday car. The C7 would be my favorite as an everyday car. This Stingray also has many of the features of a C2.

◀ **2017** Corvette C7, **1966** Corvette, C2 **Rüsselsheim**, Hessen, Germany | June 11, 2022

TO OLIVER, CORVETTE MEANS:
PASSION, RELAXATION, SPECIAL

Sacred ground. The shoot with Oliver Mohrs took place in Rüsselsheim on the grounds of the former Opel plant. This was once the European headquarters of General Motors, to which the brand with the lightning bolt belonged for more than eighty years.

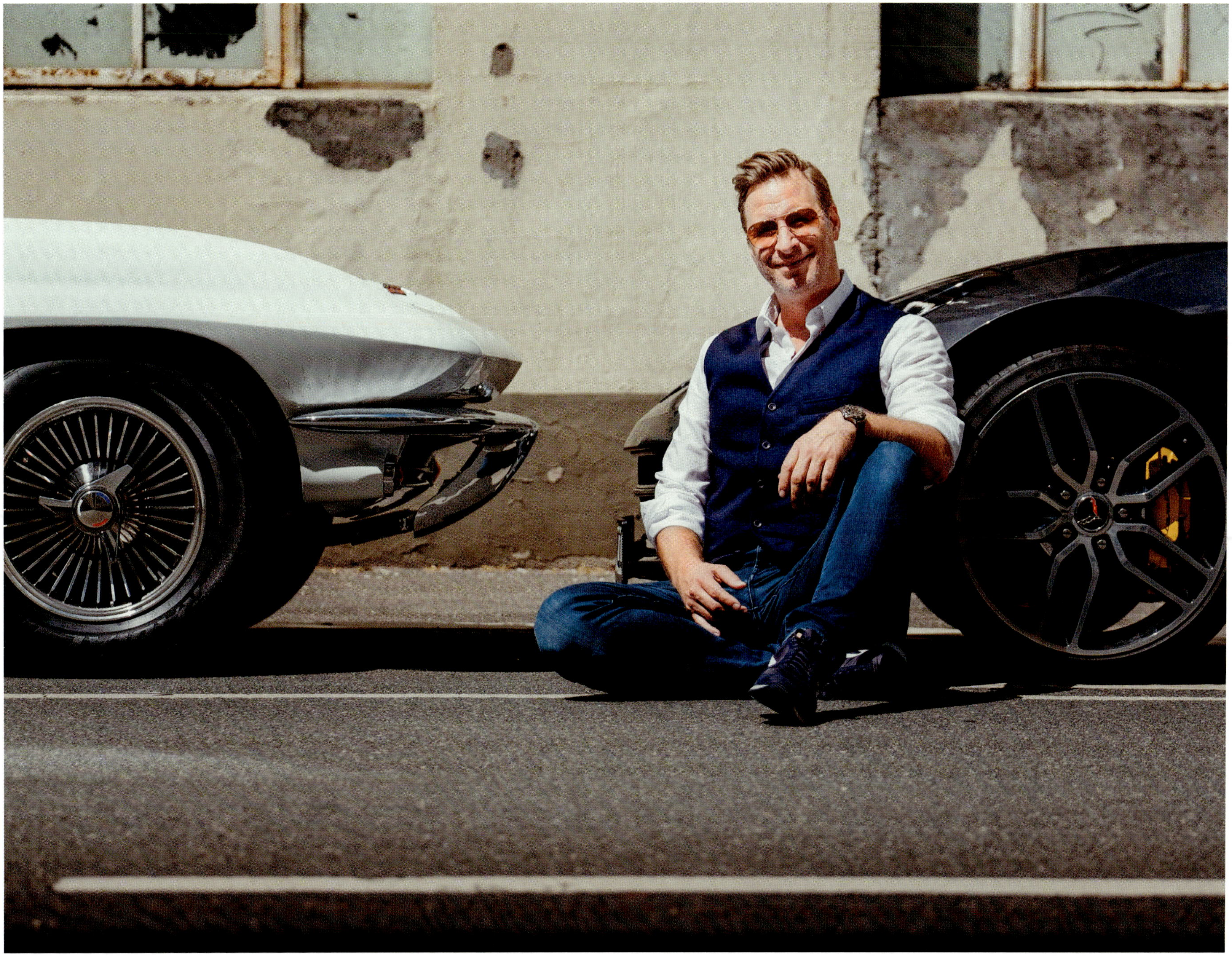

216

THE RED VETERAN VETTE

When John Carson met his future wife for the first time in the Sixties, she owned a 1965 Corvette. Some years later, when he returned from serving in Vietnam, he bought his own Corvette, which he still owns today.

What's your Corvette story?
When I met my wife, she was just graduating from high school. Her grandfather asked her what she wanted for graduation. "I can pay for your first two years of college, or I can get you a car." Julie, being 18 years old, answered, "I want a car!" He asked her what kind of car she wanted, and Julie responded, "I want a Corvette." Normal cars back then cost $2,000 or $2,500. Corvettes cost between $4,500 and $5,000. Her grandfather Harry Hausman was a little surprised and said, "I can pay for part of the Corvette, but you will have to contribute your share." So Julie got a job at a law firm as a legal secretary. She really wanted that car. She got a '65 C2 coupe in Nassau Blue.

We had been dating for more than four months, and I knew nothing about her car. She intentionally always parked it a few blocks away. I think she didn't want me to go out with her just because of the car. We were married eighteen months later, but not because of the Corvette.

We were living in Iowa. The Indy 500 was coming up, and we wanted to see it. It was six or seven hours to Indianapolis. The day we left, I had to work a long shift. I came home and jumped in the shower, and Julie picked me up in her Corvette. We headed down Interstate 80 toward the Indianapolis Motor Speedway. The radio was playing, and the air blew through the open windows. At some point, I fell asleep. Then I remember her shaking me and saying, "Hey, wake up! We have a problem!" I opened my eyes, and all I saw was blue and red lights. There were at least a dozen police cars in front of and behind us. I glanced at the tachometer: 5,000 rpm in fourth gear. I asked her, "How fast were you going?" She replied, "No idea. I had loud music on and was just driving."

She pulled over to the right, and a policeman got out of his car and came up to us. "Driver's license and registration, please." Julie was a little pissed off and replied, "What for?" The policeman said, "Ma'am, show me your documents right now, or I'm going to arrest you!" She gave them to him, and he said, "Wait here a minute. My colleague, who has been behind you since Iowa City, will be here shortly." The state trooper pulled up behind us, his car smoking. He came over, and from his face we could tell that he was in a bad mood. "Young lady, do you know how fast you were going? I was doing 135 miles an hour and couldn't keep up. Where are you going?" She answered, "To the Indy 500." The officer looked into her eyes and said sharply, "You're planning to watch the race and not take part?"

Julie simply hadn't realized how fast she was driving. With her arm out the window, the wind in her hair, and the music from the radio, she drifted off into thought. Her license was suspended for a month; that was the maximum penalty. The $200 fine was almost more bearable. There was even a story about the incident in the newspaper. "Women drivers aren't what they used to be! A woman was stopped while racing down Interstate 80 in her new Corvette at 140 miles per hour." We still have the article somewhere. She got her driving style from her German ancestors. She still drives fast in her Mercedes CLK.

On November 10, 1966, fifty-five years ago today, I joined the Marine Corps. After basic training, in 1967 I was transferred to Jacksonville, Florida. We packed up the Corvette and set off on the 1,100-mile drive to the Southeast. We lived in Florida for seven months. In August 1967, I was transferred to the base at El Toro in California. The drive across the entire country took four days. The Corvette had no air conditioning, and it was August. At two in the morning, we reached Needles, California, and the thermometer was still showing over 104 degrees.

Then I received orders to go to Vietnam. Julie's mother flew in from Iowa so she wouldn't be alone. About two weeks after my departure, my young wife decided to drive to see her family in Iowa. She took the Corvette with my mother-in-law in the passenger seat, luggage on her lap. They drove the 1,900 miles back to Iowa that way. When I came back from Vietnam, we drove back to California in the C2. After five years, the Corvette already had 50,000 miles on the odometer. At that point, it was obvious that we needed a car with air conditioning. As by then we were members of the Corvette Club of Southern California, the second-oldest Corvette club in the world, we wanted another Corvette and found my C3. It was Riverside Gold, with the small block V8 and air conditioning. We gave them the C2 in trade and bought the '69 C3. For many years, it was our everyday car. On weekends, we took part in events and rallies held by the club.

When I was discharged from the military, I began working for the sheriff's office here in Orange County. At the time, there were 10,000 applicants for four open positions. They were difficult times economically, and there were few job openings. Going back to Iowa was also not an option, as the situation there was even worse. I took continuation training in law enforcement, which in the past had been very unusual. The sheriff's office was very impressed that I had taken further training on my own initiative. My time in the military was, of course, also an advantage. I was sworn in shortly after Christmas 1971, and I stayed there for thirty-one years. Except for my last ten years, I drove to work in my Corvette every day.

When I retired, I had some money put away and restored the C3. That was 2002. I had the Corvette repainted Fire Mist Red. After 350,000 miles I replaced the engine and installed a 5-speed transmission and a fuel injection system. I also added a larger radiator and a new climate control system.

When did you install the fender flares?
The rims came on the car in 1973, but the wheels and tires were wider than those of the production model and rubbed the fenders. I subsequently had to have the car repainted and decided to add the flares. They have been on the C3 since 1975. I still like taking the car to shows; for example, to a local event on Veterans Day.

When my grandson Austin was younger, he would come by and help me get the car ready for shows and clean it. He knew the car inside and out. My oldest would like to have the car when I am no longer able to get in and out of it or when I leave this life. Personally, I would still like to have a new C8. We'll see.

What is your all-time favorite Corvette model?
The '62 C1 with the double headlights and the rear end that looks like the one on a C2. To me, it is the most beautiful Corvette ever built. The C2 is also very beautiful, as of course is the C3 with the chrome bumpers. The new C8 is an absolute masterpiece.

◀ **1969 Corvette C3, Marine Corps Air Station El Toro**, California, USA | November 10, 2021

TO JOHN, CORVETTE MEANS:
LIFE, FREEDOM, HAPPINESS

Veterans Day. Before John Carson went to Vietnam, he was stationed at the El Toro base in California. At the time, his wife was driving a C2. For the shoot, he returned to his former station in his C3, which he acquired after returning from the war.

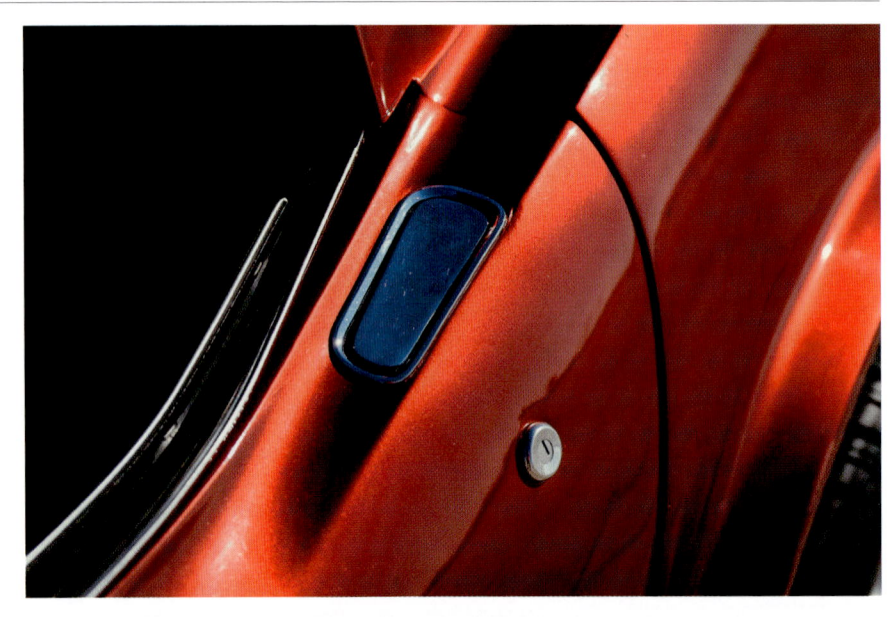

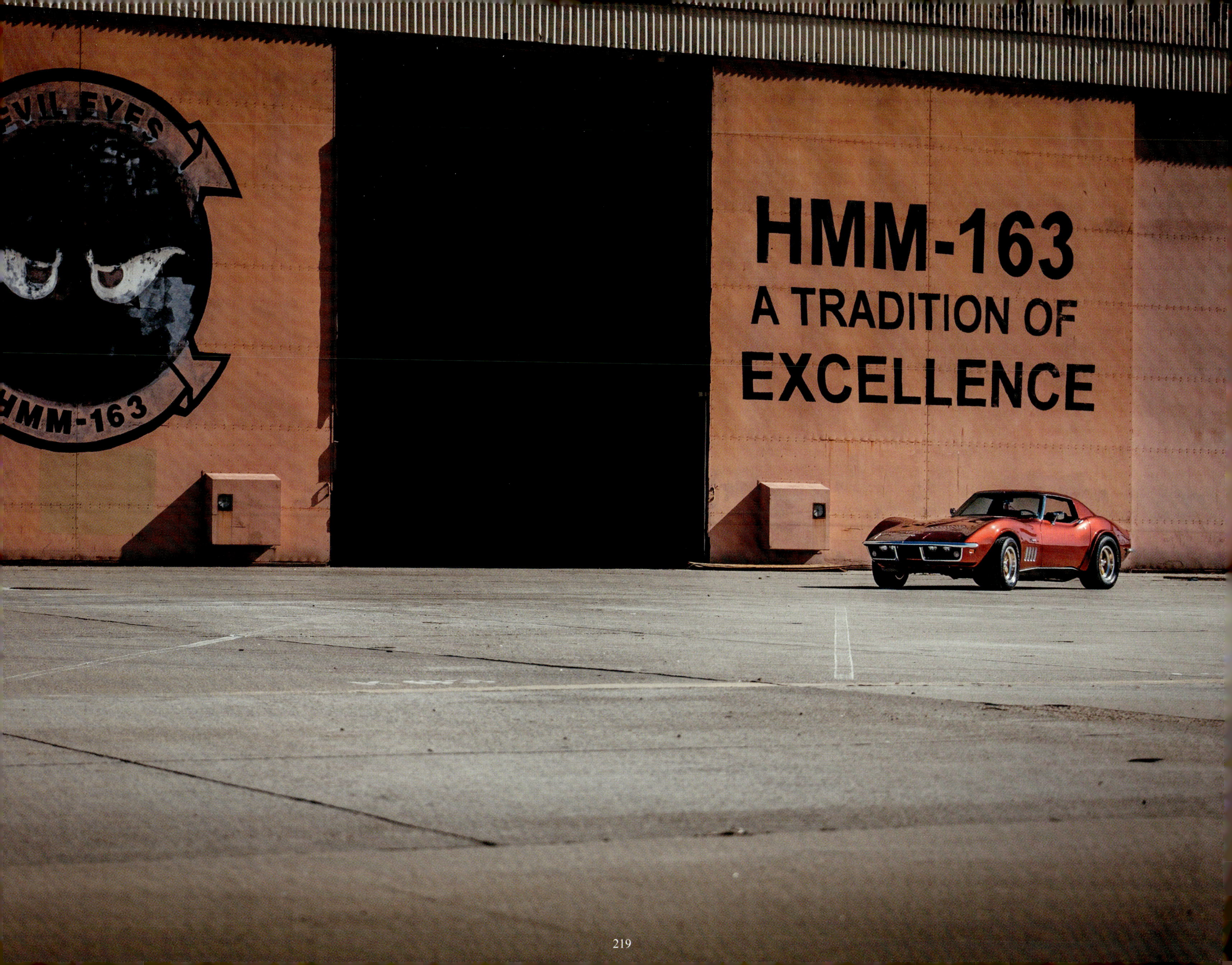
EVIL EYES
HMM-163
HMM-163
A TRADITION OF
EXCELLENCE

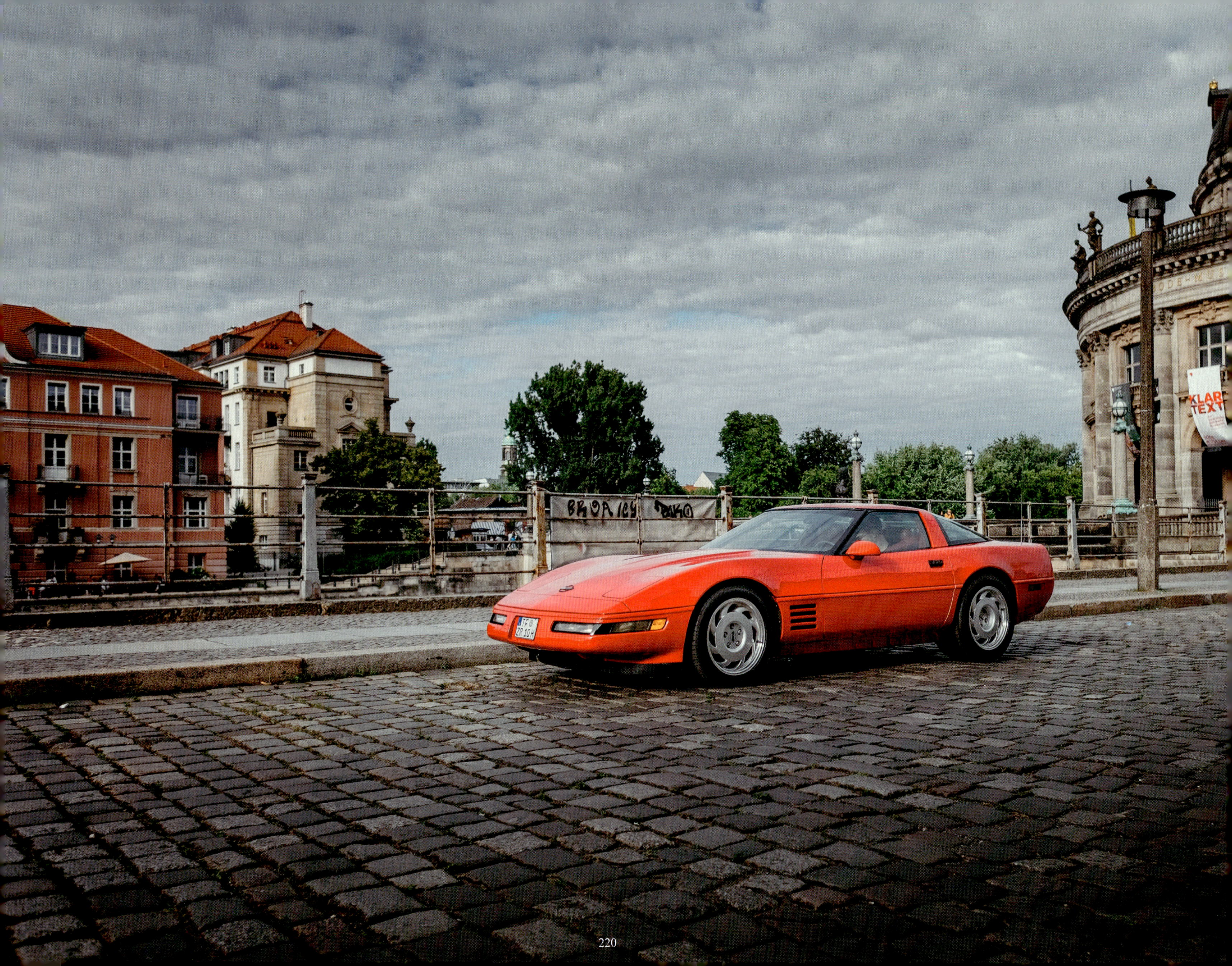
KLAR
TEXT

A CHILDHOOD DREAM, A COLOR

Thomas Benke had to learn the hard way. Before he could enjoy his ZR-1, he brought a Camaro, a piece of junk he had never seen, from the USA to Germany.

What's your Corvette story?
The beginning of my Corvette story goes back awhile. When I was a child, back in the days of the German Democratic Republic, Matchbox cars were the most valuable currency one could have. We traded them amongst ourselves like crazy. The Corvette was really the best that one could get as a model car. I had several of them, including a blue Corvette C4 Grand Sport with the red and white stripes. This was my first contact with the American sports car icon.

Sometime in the early 2000s, when I was in my early twenties, a buddy and I decided that we would get an old American V8. It was clear to us that we had to do this someday. But we were then young and poor, and at the time the dream was completely unrealistic. It would be another twenty years before I was no longer so young or so poor. Then the question arose: What should I get?

I looked and looked, and now and then I asked people if they knew of any cars that were for sale. I really wasn't sure what I wanted, as I was looking at different cars without ever choosing one in particular. One night, I was back in front of my computer looking at old American cars. At that time, I had a broker in the USA who repeatedly suggested cars to me. But mostly there was nothing—until he presented a '67 Chevrolet Camaro to me. It looked really smart in its silver-gray paint. Very well, that was the one. No sooner said than done.

After I ordered the Camaro, I spoke by telephone with several garages that specialized in American classic cars. The first ones I called immediately backed out due to lack of interest. Finally, I found one in Leipzig. The Saxons were the first ones to take the time to speak with me by phone, and I could tell that they shared my enthusiasm. I therefore had the Chevy sent to the fair city on the Elster. The boys called me as soon as the car arrived, and the first thing they said to me was "You'd better sit down." The thing was an absolute piece of junk; it was all messed up. Their recommendation was clear: "Sell it the way it is!" And I was really lucky. I was able to sell the Camaro with no great financial loss. The car was literally snapped up, even though I had identified all its shortcomings. Crazy.

After that experience, I still wanted to get an American car, but inside I said goodbye to the '60s and '70s. The market was simply too hot for me. Cars from that period were becoming more and more expensive. Then on the net I stumbled upon an IROC-Z Camaro, which at the time could be had quite cheaply. There were super cars for little money. I then began looking harder at the late '80s and early '90s and in the process discovered the Corvette C4. It was obvious that it was much cooler than the Camaro! The ZR-1 in particular piqued my interest. The best thing, however, was that the C4 definitely fit my budget.

I went looking for a C4 and narrowed down the search to three cars, once again all in the US. As a result of my experience with the Camaro, I knew a few people, and I found someone who could inspect the cars for me in the US. I had him look at a red ZR-1 that I liked. My contact sent me pictures and told me that he thought the car was in top shape. The C4 had just two previous owners and a known history. The color combination was also perfect: red exterior, red interior. I had pounced and once again bought a car sight unseen. This time, however, I had someone on the spot, which calmed me.

Before the Corvette came to Germany, I also had it sent to Marc Haibeck in Chicago. He is one of the ZR-1 gurus in the States. There the C4 was checked out from top to bottom, and everything that needed fixing was fixed. In March 2022, a little over a year after the purchase, I was able to pick up the C4 at my garage in Leipzig with fresh inspection and registration. I am completely happy with the car. It's a cool car, takes off like a rocket, has power without end, and is really fun to drive.

What is your all-time favorite Corvette model?
Either a '69 or '70 C3 LT-1, and my C4 ZR-1.

◀ 1991 Corvette C4, **Berlin**, Germany | July 6, 2022

POLITIK IST DIE FORTSETZUNG DES
MIT ANDEREN

TO THOMAS, CORVETTE MEANS:
CRUISING, SPORTS CAR, BEAUTIFUL LINES

Technology standard bearer. When the ZR-1 was unveiled in 1990, the fan community was amazed. The aluminum V8 developed by Lotus had overhead camshafts, four valves per cylinder, and a top speed of 290 kph (180 mph).

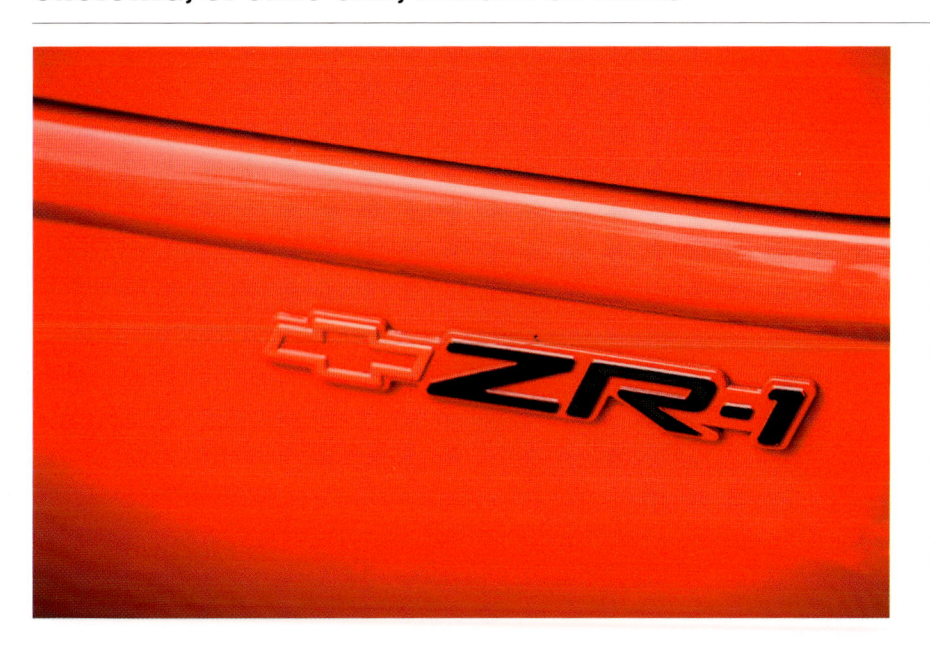

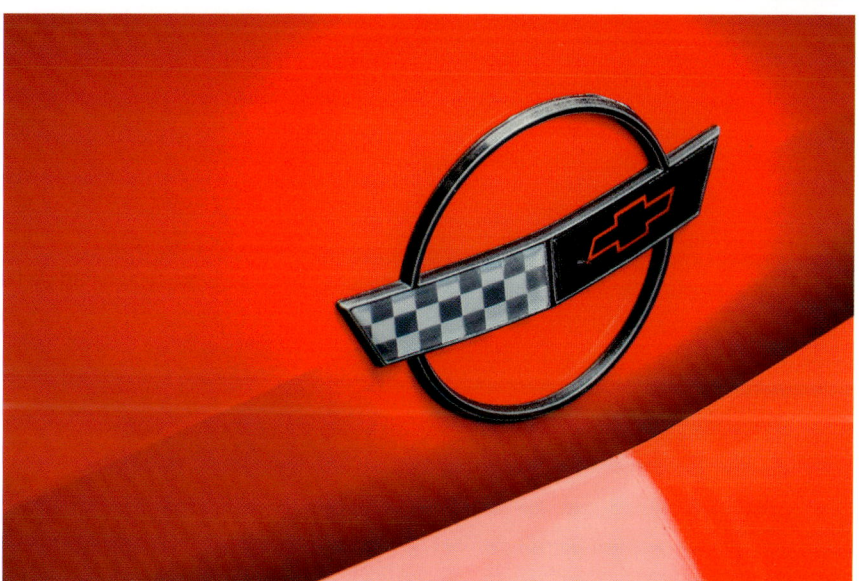

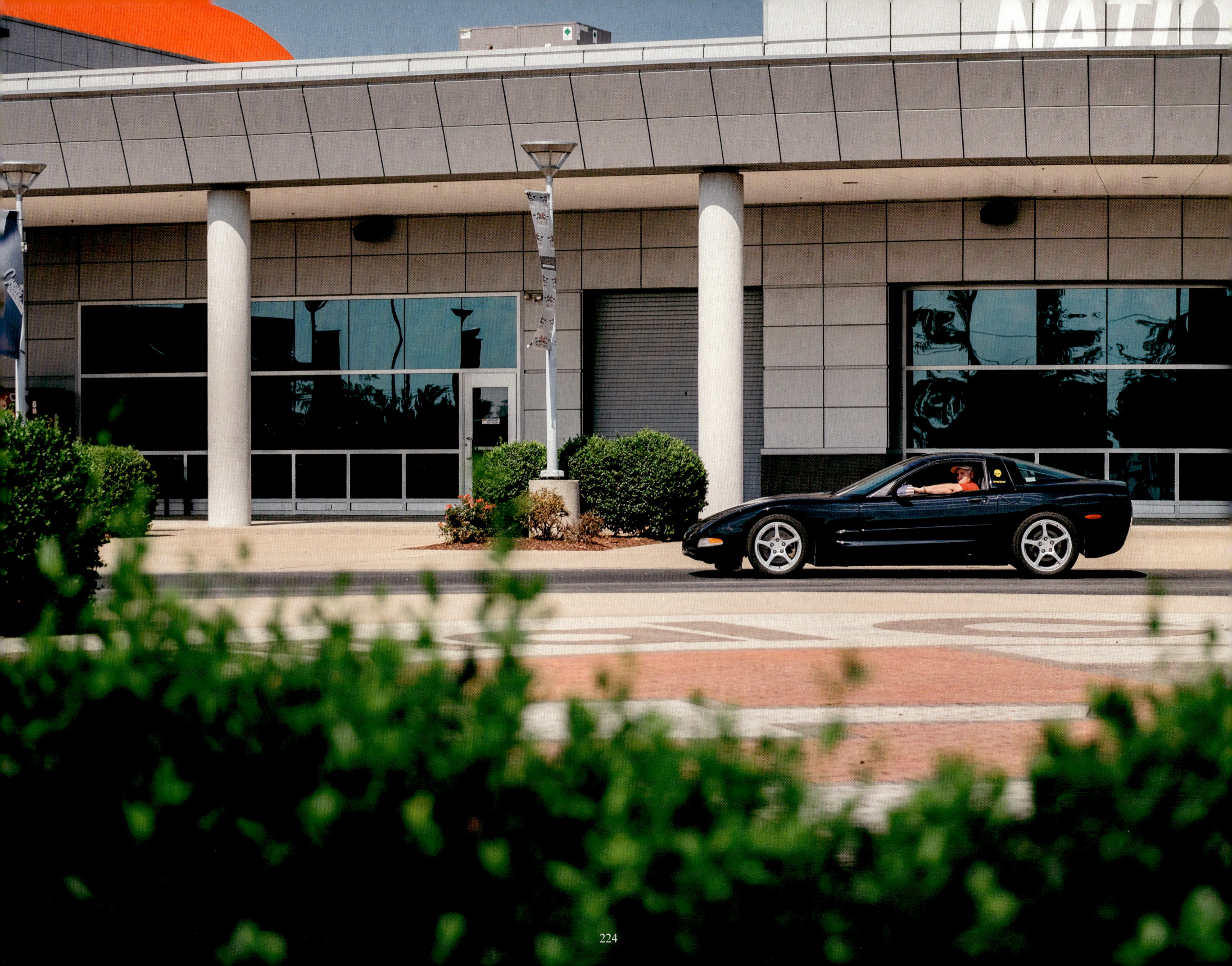
NATIO

BAND OF CORVETTE BROTHERS—PART I

Roger Holt bought his first Corvette as a young man back in the Seventies. He still owns his 1965 C2 which has a touch of Duntov about it.

What's your Corvette story?
That goes back a long time. When I was 14 or 15 years old, my neighbor across the street had a '62 Corvette. And I just admired that car. In fact, he was the only neighbor with a driveway to put the car in. My brother Donald had a little plastic model of the '59 Corvette. At the time, I wished that we could enlarge the car as if by magic. Those are my first Corvette memories.

A few years later, my brother and I went looking for a real Corvette; the days of toys were over. That was 1968. My brother, just turned 18, was unable to find a car he could afford. So we looked for a used Corvette and found a 1958 C1. He still has that car. It has since been repainted three times, the last time in the original color. His Corvette was the first one I ever drove in, both as a passenger and behind the wheel. It was also in that car that I learned how to shift a manual transmission. Not everyone can do that nowadays.

In 1973, Donald bought a new C3, but it was from the 1972 model year. The brand-new 1973 Corvette had just come on the market. His was still on the dealer's lot, but it had lots of extras. My brother thus had two Corvettes, while I had none. I also wanted a '72, but my bank wouldn't give me any credit. So for the first time, I buried my dream of owning a Corvette of my own.

One day my parents were buying some furniture, and on the way back, they spotted a C2 at a used car dealer around the corner. Actually, I had given up on the idea of a Corvette, but I looked at the car anyway. The price was good. On that day in 1973, I bought myself my own Corvette, a 1965. I still have that car. And the table my parents bought that day is still in my living room. At the time, I never thought that the Corvette and I would grow old together. After all, the C2 was nothing special. It didn't have many extras and came with the standard 300hp engine and a two-speed automatic transmission.

About eight years later, I got the Corvette I always wanted: a 1972 C3. I thus had two Corvettes and my brother had two. In 1986, I looked around for a C4. A friend found one. We went and looked at it together and bought it. Two years later, he decided to sell the car to me. Now I had three Corvettes! In 1989, that became too many for me, and I sold the C3.

Then in the autumn of 1999, I added a C5. I was at a Chevy dealer to look at used Corvettes, then a brand-new black Corvette in the showroom caught my eye . . . and once again, I had three Corvettes. The C5 was the last one I have added to date. Even after twenty-one years, the car still excites me. Perhaps I will buy a new Corvette someday, but I don't know if I will give up the C5 for it.

In 1982, I was at a car show in Connecticut, and there I met Zora Arkus Duntov, the father of the Corvette. Personally. He signed my '65's owner's manual. Meeting a legend like him was some experience. Of course, the manual is still in the glove compartment of my C2.

What is your all-time favorite Corvette model?
I find the C2 the most exciting. A '65 with knock-off rims, side-pipes, four-speed manual transmission, and fuel injection is simply a true sports car.

◀ **2005** Corvette C5, **Bowling Green**, Kentucky, **USA** | September 18, 2022

TO ROGER, CORVETTE MEANS:
AMERICAN, STATUS, FUN

Legend of Zora. In 1982, Roger Holt met the father of the Corvette, Zora Arkus-Duntov. On the spur of the moment, he got out the owner's manual of his '65 C2 and had the legendary engineer sign it—with a personal dedication, of course.

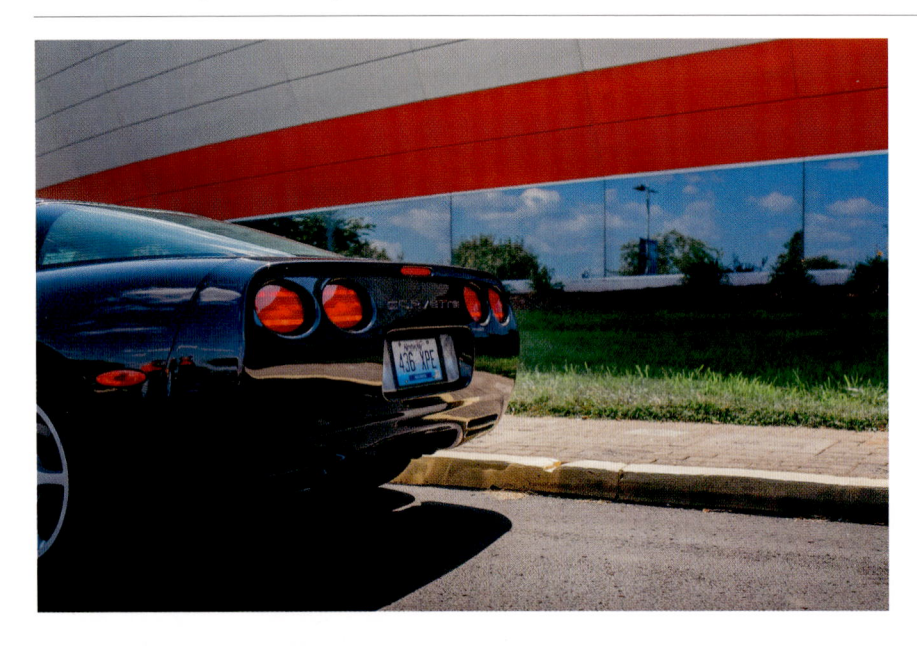

▲ **2005** Corvette C5, **Bowling Green**, Kentucky, USA

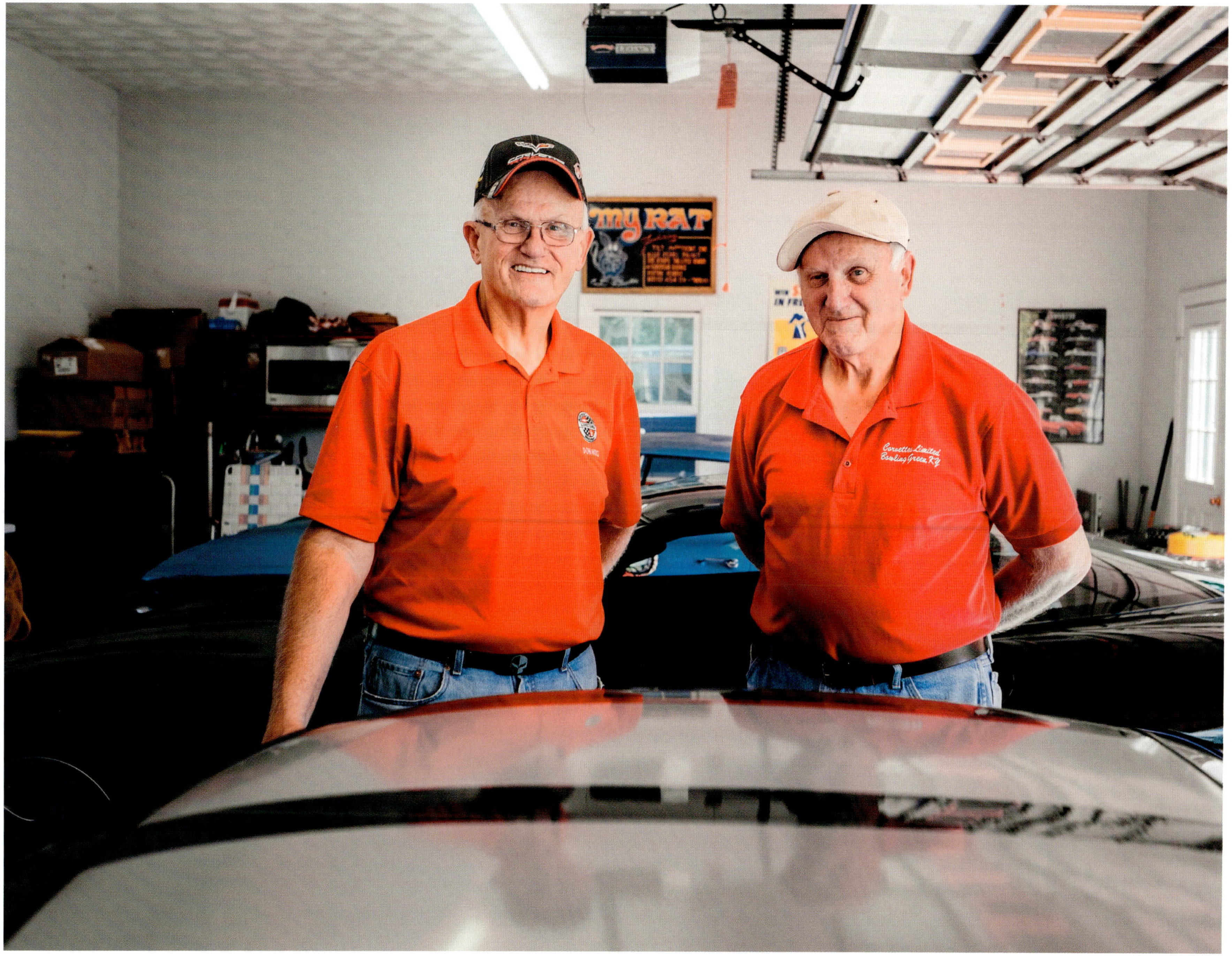
MY RAT
Corvettes Limited
Bowling Green, KY

BAND OF CORVETTE BROTHERS—PART II

One of the reasons why Donald Holt came back from Vietnam wasn't a girl, but his 1958 Corvette.

What's your Corvette story?
I don't know exactly when the Corvette thing started. I know there was someone living across the street from us who had one before we were even in high school. The guy sold it, got another one, and so on. And I always liked them; it was the one car I could identify on the street when one was driving by. And I remember building models of them when we were kids. I had this one model; it was a '59, not a '58, but it looked the same. And I used to think that it would be nice if I could make that toy bigger somehow and sit in that car.

At the gas station I worked at as a young adult, I worked with three other guys who all had Corvettes. I always wanted one, too, but they were just too expensive. A new one at that time was probably about $4,000. So I was thinking about getting an old one, and I started looking for a Corvette. We were living in Massachusetts at that time, and I looked at one in Boston. It was on Easter Sunday, and it was 1958 Corvette. The car was blue, and I took a ride in it. I really liked it. The seller wanted $1,000 for it, and that was just too much for me, so I passed on that one.

Then I found a 1960 Corvette that needed a new interior and a little bit more work. The owner wanted $1,200 for that one. My mother had gone with me to look at it, and she could tell that I was disappointed when we got home. She said, "If you really want that Corvette, I will loan you the extra money for it." So I made a phone call, and the guy had just sold the car. But as it turned out fortune was still with me because then I found the Corvette I still own today.

It's a 1958 Corvette and I bought it in 1968. On May 4 in 1968, I looked at the car. It was $800, my mom loaned me $50, and I came up with $750 of my own money. At first, I thought I had made a mistake buying that car, but I just started driving it, and every year, more people offered more money for it. I remember we had a yard sale in front of the house, and I put a price tag on the car. It must have been around 1969 or 1970, and the price I put on it was $2,500. If anyone had wanted to buy it for that price back then, I would have sold the car. But everybody said it was way too much money. Okay, I'll keep it then. And it stayed.

I was in the army, and I was being sent to Vietnam. Before I left, I put the car in the backyard. My mother said, "Why don't you just sell it and get rid of it." But I told her that the Corvette was one of the reasons I would be back. So I put it in the backyard and left it there. When I came home a year later, I took it out and started using it again. Then I finally decided to get it painted, and I ended up painting it white.

Probably about five years later, I wanted to paint it again. The white paint wasn't a great paint job, so we stripped it all off again. We never stripped it the first time, and when we removed some of the chrome, we found under it looked like primer. But that was charcoal, the original color. We painted the Corvette in that original color. Mine is the only C1 in charcoal around; you don't see it that much. It was a rare color back in the Fifties.

I have really enjoyed this car every year I've owned it. When we were up in Massachusetts, of course with the winter and everything, I actually used to have snow tires on the car and drove it in the winter, too. When it turned twenty-five, which would have been January 1, 1983, it officially became an antique car. It was snowing that day; the top was down, but we drove it anyway. We took it out to the highway and drove it in the snow. I just had to do that on its anniversary.

I have so many tales like that about the car. When I start thinking back, I remember all the stories I have collected over the past fifty-four years. Once we moved down to Bowling Green, it got even more used because you don't get any snow here like we did in Massachusetts. With all the other Corvettes around here, I like driving it now because you don't see the C1 anymore. The ones you do see are cars in a museum or show cars that had been taken out on a trailer. Mine is still a driver; I think there is still some '58 dirt under the car.

It's just been a great car, and I am so glad I owned it, and it just started me on everything else. After that one, I bought a brand-new '72, and I drove that one for twenty-five or twenty-six years. A few years later, I found my C5 Z06. That's been the team since 2004. The Corvettes have just been my and Roger's life since 1968.

What is your all-time favorite Corvette model?
I think I would have to decide how I'm going to use the car. If it was something I wanted to drive all the time, I would go with the new C8. But if I just want one to do car shows or take out on a nice day, I would have to go with the C1. My C1 has managed to stay around the longest for some reason. I will never sell that car; I wouldn't be happy with a fistful of cash while watching it pull out of the driveway. That's just not gonna happen. Some day when I am done with it, the Corvette Museum will get it.

1958 Corvette C1, **Bowling Green**, Kentucky, USA | September 18, 2022 ▶

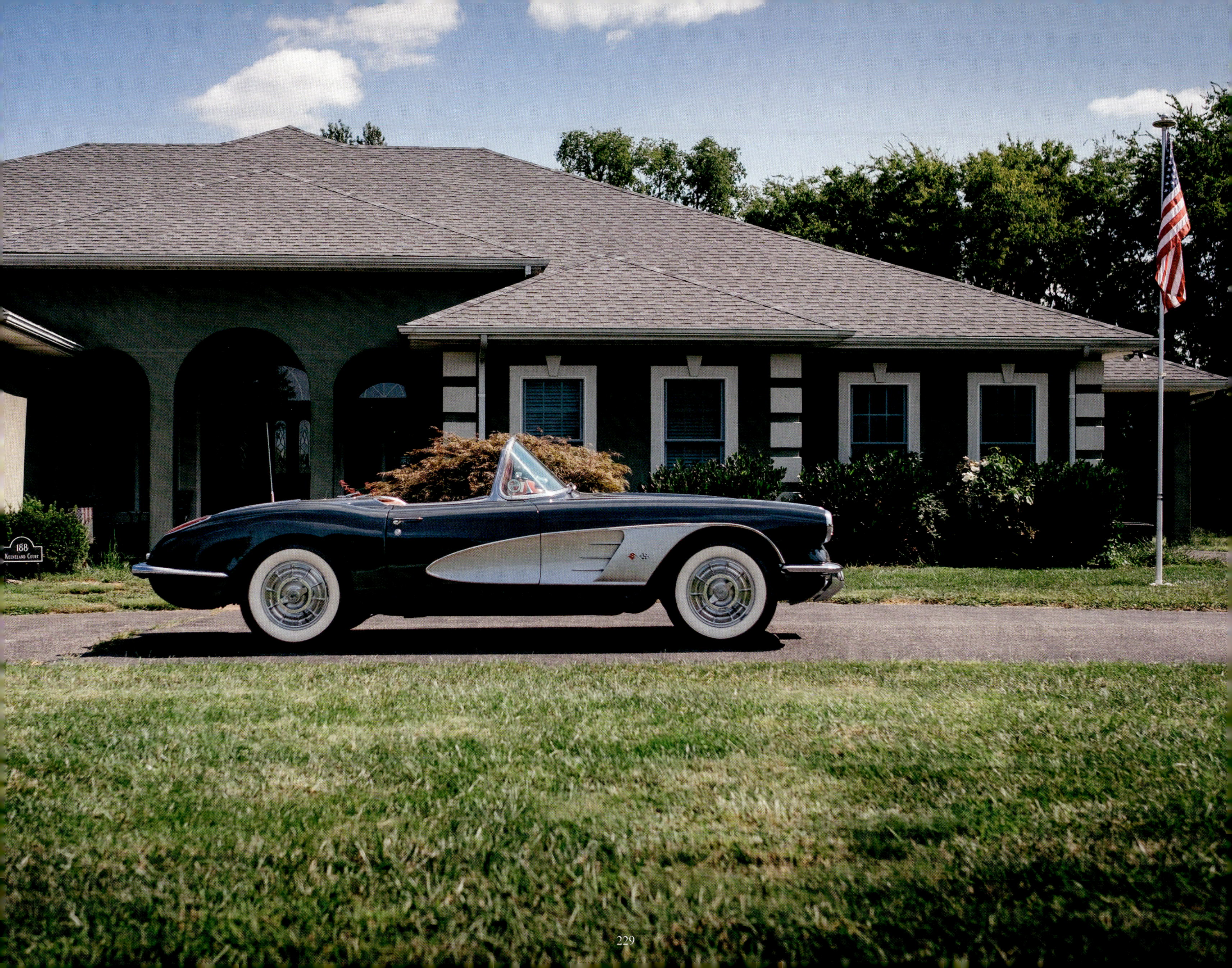
188
Keeneland Court

230

TO DONALD, CORVETTE MEANS:
FRIENDSHIP, ENGINEERING, THRILLS

Initial spark. Donald Holt assembled a plastic model kit of a 1958 C1 as a child. This miniature not only fired his and his brother's imagination, it also sparked their passion for Corvettes. Guarded like a treasure, the little car has survived to this day.

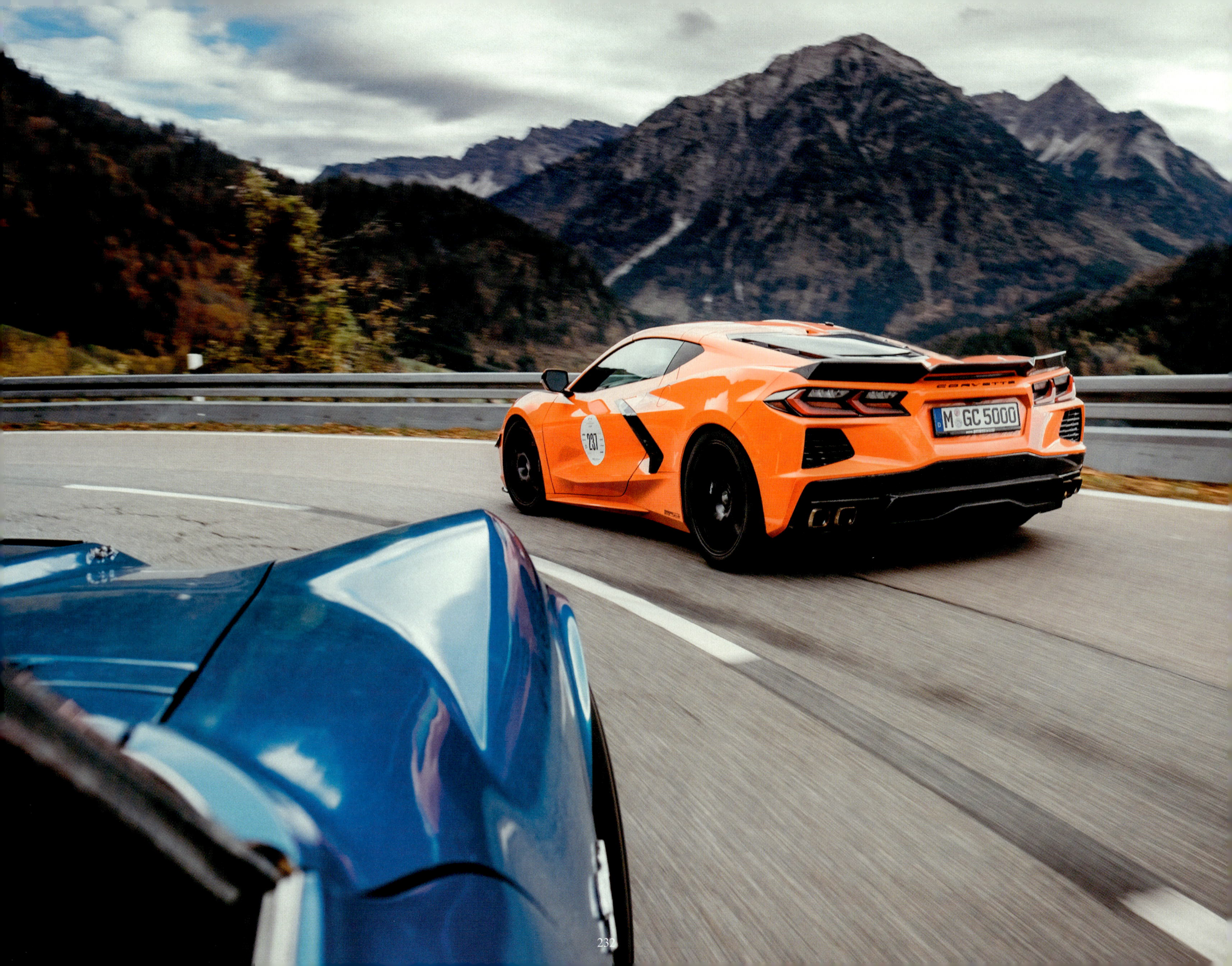
231
M GC 5000

BOSS OF BIG BLOCKS

Karl Geiger and Corvette. They simply go together in Germany. Everyone is familiar with his legendary conversions from the 1980s, and even today they attract attention—his white C2, for example.

What's your Corvette story?
Actually, I liked working on Mercedes, but in particular Daimler V8s: 3.5 liters, 6.3 liters; that was my world. The Mercedes were actually fast right off the factory floor, but despite this, I saw potential for modification. Therefore, they kept me very busy. At some point, it must have been 1981, I bought a disassembled Corvette in a crate. It was a 1971 C3 coupe with chrome bumpers and a manual transmission. Also in the crate was the engine, a four-bolt block. At that time, I knew nothing about American cars. It finally turned out that it was an LT-1 engine, the most powerful of all the small blocks. In the space of about a year, I assembled the Corvette from its individual parts. The car was impressive, with a terrific performance, and it was capable of more than 260 kph (160 mph). It had a new camshaft installed, but the suspension was a catastrophe. I always want to improve my cars and am never satisfied with stock. That was the beginning of my passion for Corvettes, from which my own business developed.

In 1984, I got my hands on one of the first C4s. As a teenager, I had a picture of a Ferrari 612 BBI König Special hanging on the wall and thought about one day building such a beautiful car. The C4 was simply the ideal vehicle for such a conversion. We were very successful with the design and conversions for the C4, and it was a big hit. We sold thirty or forty modified Corvettes the first year. The American car theme naturally continued, and people came to us because of Camaros or pickup trucks. At some point, I had left the days of Mercedes and Italian sports cars behind me and concentrated solely on American cars. All of this happened very quickly.

One could modify the American V8 engines better and more quickly. They were more simply designed, with their central camshafts. We installed better cylinder heads; raised the compression a little; added Edelbrock intake manifolds with Holly carburetors, exhaust manifolds, and Hooker side-pipes—that was it. That's simply how crazy cars became after that. You could install just as much in a Mercedes, but on a Corvette, this could be achieved with comparatively simple means.

You've had the white C2 monster for twenty-seven years. How did you come by this Corvette, and what changes have you made to it?
I in fact bought the car twenty-seven years ago; that's true. At that time, it had a flip front, but it was terribly ugly, painted matte black, and had a small block V8 under the hood, a 300hp Goodwrench engine, a very simple machine. I then began tinkering with the car; for example, I installed an LT-5 ZR-1 engine. With that the Corvette was actually finished, but I wanted to put a big block in it, so out came the LT-5. After that we optimized the axles, changed the leaf springs. I also tackled the body, and at the time, a friend from Giesheim gave me a hand. He worked carbon fiber into the hood and finally painted the Corvette.

It was a lengthy process. After my muse left me, the thing sat around in the garage for a year. After twenty-three years of tinkering, modifying, and optimizing, I drove it for the first time at the Rossfeld race. Before that it hadn't moved a foot; I really just worked on it.

Thus, the white C2 became what it is today, but we aren't finished yet. As you can see, the spindle on the rear axle is torn off. It was the last new but original part still to be found on the Corvette. Not sturdy enough for 663.8 foot-pounds of torque and just under 800 horsepower. The Michelin Cup tires and the rims from a C6 ZR-1 simply provide too much traction. I have, however, been quite brutal in driving the car, making one burnout after another, and marking various racetracks with the rear tires. Now she has said goodbye to that, thank God, while warming up the tires and not on the Joch Pass in Switzerland. We have now spontaneously decided to install a new suspension in the Corvette, one better able to handle its performance. And we want to fit it with a roll cage, which will also improve the body's torsion resistance.

What is your all-time favorite Corvette model?
To me the C1 is a classic old-timer for cruising. The C3 is not necessarily my favorite model. A big-block with chrome bumpers is nice, but I don't really sit well in it. Sure, I like the C4, of which we have built many Geiger models. Then I'll skip everything up to the C7. The ZR-1 is a very cool car, I just recently sold our last one. With our C7 Z06, called Emma, we set a record on the Nordschleife. It's the fastest Corvette and the fastest American car on the circuit. In principle, the C2 is my favorite among the classics and the C8 among the modern versions, especially if the Z06 comes with the 680hp naturally aspirated engine.

◀ **2021** Corvette C8, **Bad Hindelang,** Bavaria, **Germany** | October 15, 2022

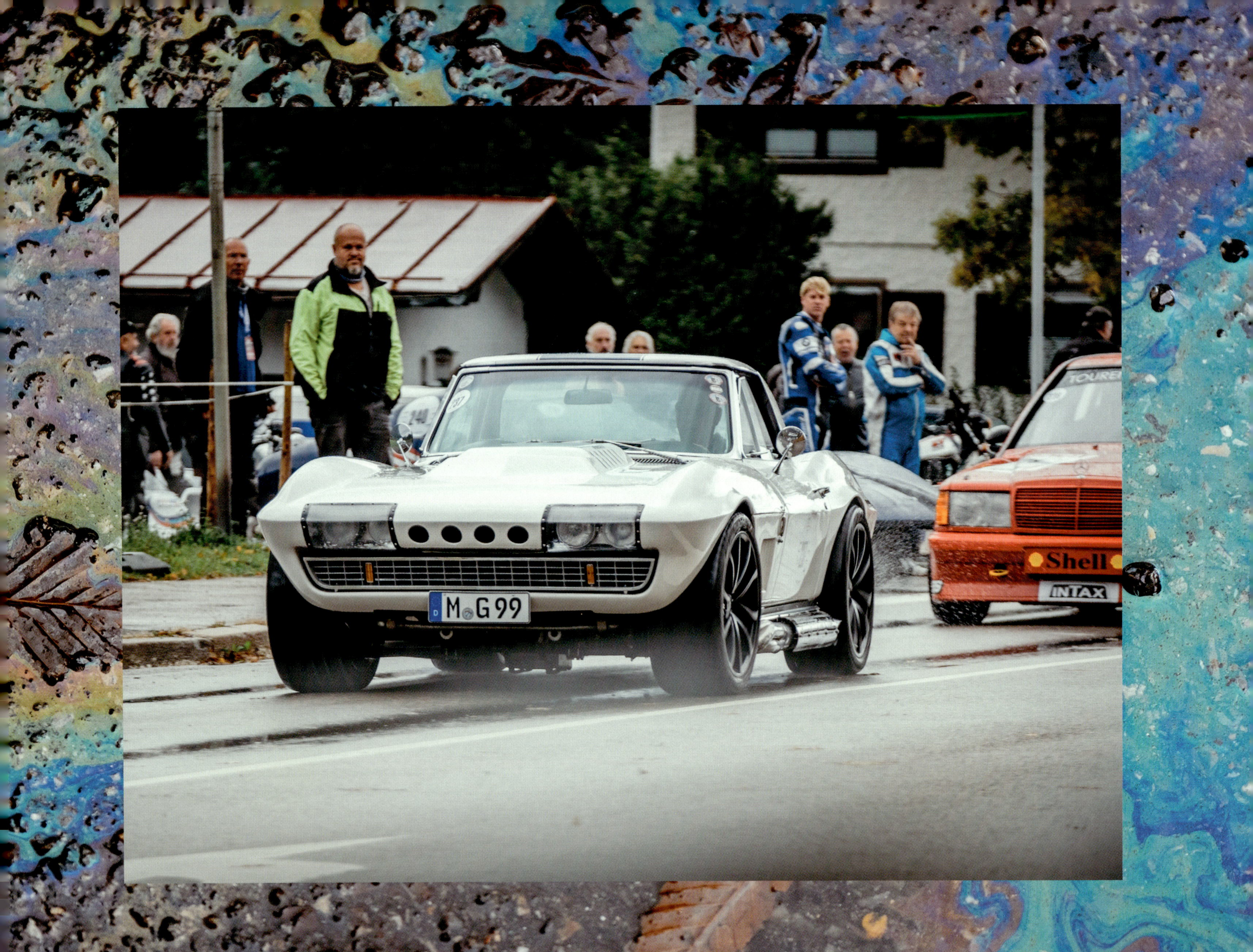
M G 99
Shell
INTAX

TO KARL, CORVETTE MEANS:
DISPLACEMENT, TORQUE, HORSEPOWER

Tired monster. At the Jochpass Oldtimer Memorial, a quick-release axle on Karl Geiger's white C2 gave up the ghost. The original part was simply not up to the enormous power of 800 hp and 900 Nm of torque.

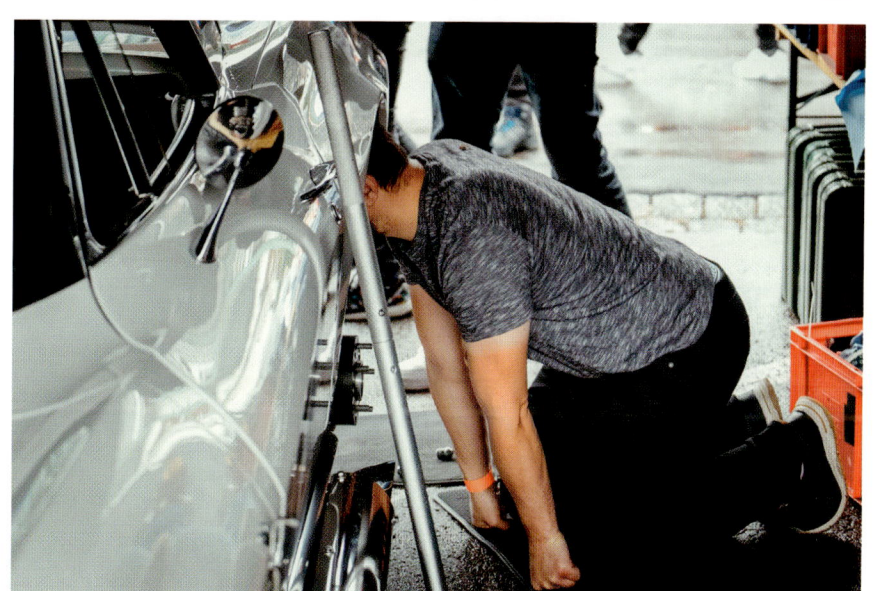

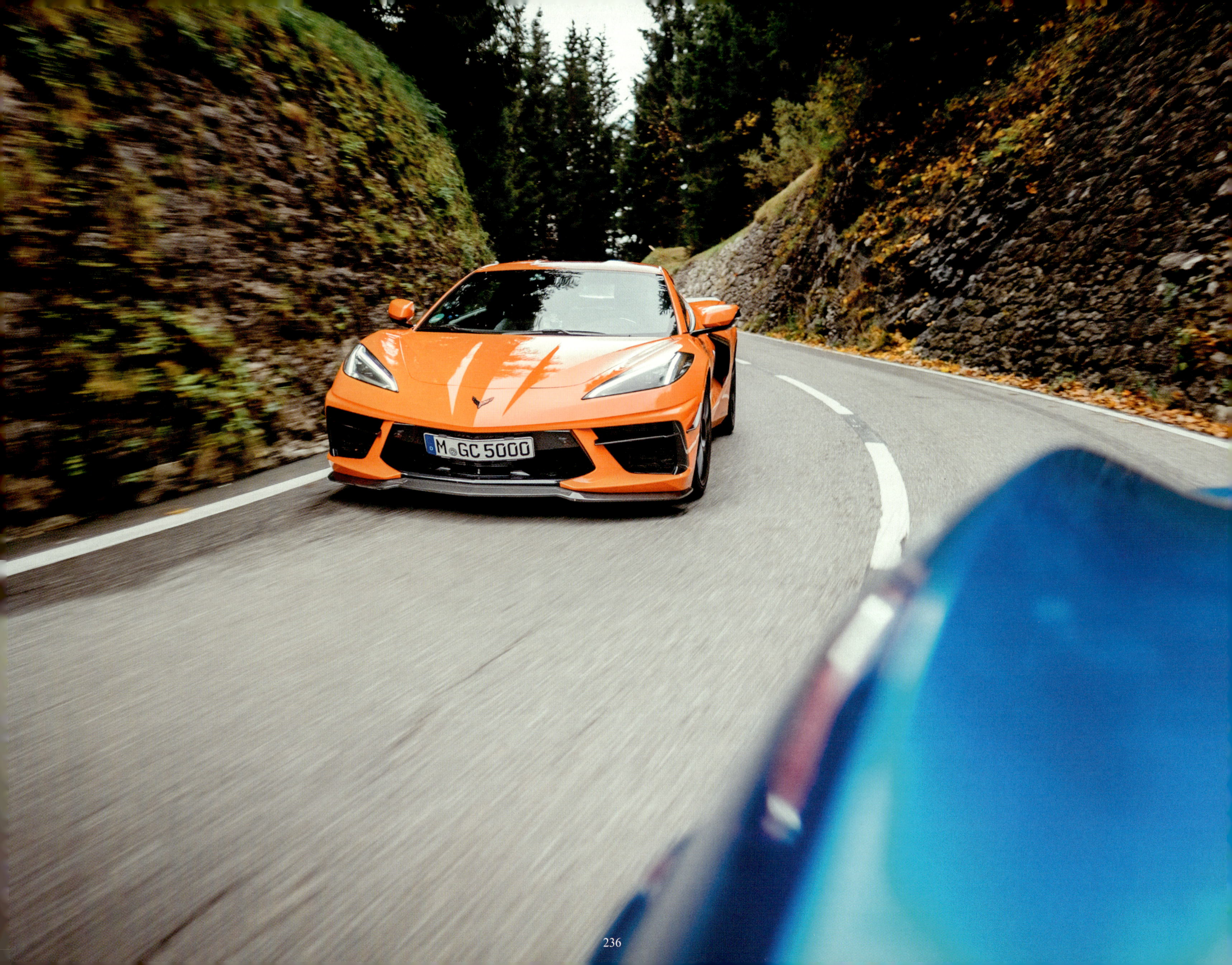
M GC 5000

Cars and coffee. Despite his fame, Karl Geiger has remained an approachable person. He always finds time for a hot drink and interesting gasoline-related conversations.

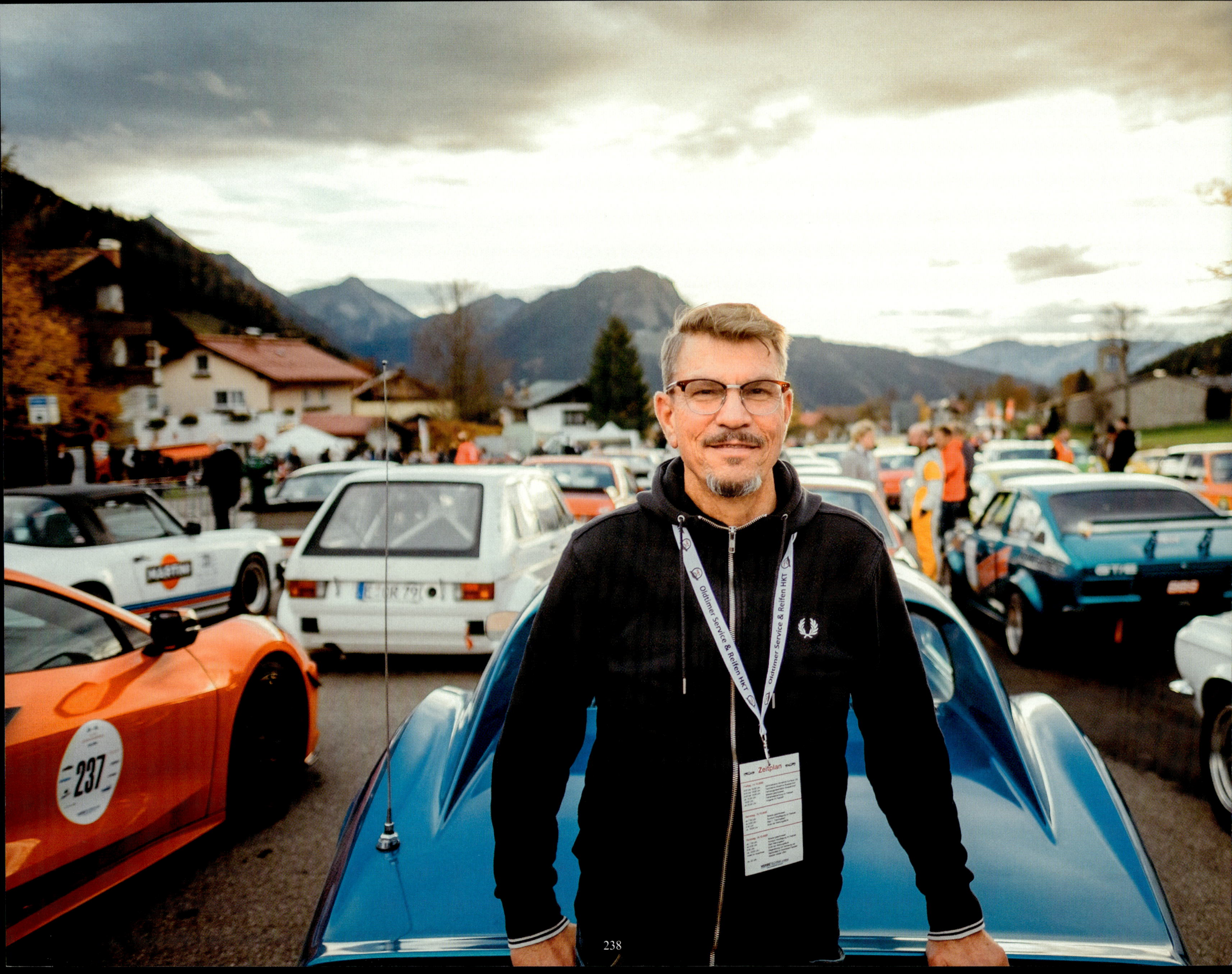
Oldtimer Service & Reifen HKT
Zeitplan
MARTINI
237

MORE THAN JUST A JOB

Thomas Pfromm and Karl Geiger have more than just a professional connection. The two are now also on the road a lot in their private lives and share a passion for motorsport and the Corvette.

What's your Corvette story?
For a long time, I worked for an auto maker. In 2012, a former superior, who by then was working for Chevrolet Germany, asked me if I would like to work for Chevrolet. At that time, they were looking for someone for Bavaria. Chevrolet was still selling Korean-made vehicles in Germany, but its range also included the Camaro and Corvette. There were more than 300 Chevrolet dealers in Germany, of which less than half—100—also sold the Camaro. There were only twenty dealers, however, that were also licensed to sell the Corvette. Of course, Geiger Performance Cars was one of these.

And so, I moved to General Motors in 2012. Previously I had had a soft spot for the Corvette, but as a result of marketing the C6 and later the C7 and C8, I became more deeply involved with the history of the flagship American sports car. Its history is truly fascinating. It has been produced continuously since 1953 and thus has a longer history than the Porsche 911 and, even in its early years, had features that were not seen in Europe until much later. Unbelievable! In fact, it is as a result of my job with GM that I became a Corvette fan.

The story of how I got my '69 is also very interesting. It was again time to visit Karl Geiger and sell him a few cars, which at that time meant the C7. I arrived in his underground garage and saw a blue C3 sitting there. I was immediately excited! "Okay, Karl. That's exactly the car I want. I definitely want a C3, I definitely want chrome bumpers, and Le Mans Blue is fantastic." All that plus a big block engine and fully equipped. What more could one want? Karl just said, "I'm not selling you any car." And why? "Because then you'll be nagging me constantly if something needs to be done. You'll always be here!" I had to spend three weeks getting on his nerves before he finally sold me the car. The C3 has been in my garage for three years now. It still wears its faded original paint, just as it did when Karl imported it. It has no great history, but it is a real survivor on which just about everything is original. And that's how it's going to stay.

How did you meet Karl Geiger?
When I began with GM, I was, as I said, responsible for Bavaria, and so I was introduced to Mr. Karl Geiger. Until then, I had never heard of him, and at our first meetings, Karl was also quite reserved. He probably thought that I was just another upstart who had come waltzing in, just another typical sales representative.

It took quite awhile for us to warm up to each other. Over the years, I initially established a good business relationship with him. Karl had of course always been a successful seller of Corvettes and Camaros, but I convinced him that the other Chevies also had good potential for him. He became one of the most successful sellers of these cars in my area. As a business developer, it's all about getting the best possible results for both parties—the manufacturer and the partner. I think this is how I earned his respect on the professional side, and our connection became closer.

Then we discovered that we also shared similar private interests—we loved motorsport. I had been racing motorcycles for a long time, he cars, and even away from the racetrack, we had shared hobbies. It was important that we both clearly separated the private and the professional. We could have different opinions when it came to business and even argue, but when that happened, Karl didn't let it affect him as a private person. We could still go out to eat and have a beer together.

GM, together with Karl, shot a follow-up to his television series in the USA for DMAX. I went with him on the trip, and we were together in Detroit, in Bowling Green, and at Pratt Miller. We visited the production line, the Heritage Center, the Performance Center, and the Corvette Museum, and we were able to see how the C8R racing Corvette came to be. That was class.

Do you often go to classic car rallies?
The first time was in 2018, when I went to the Rossfeld mountain race. I hadn't bought the car to leave it parked in the garage; I wanted to drive it. There were 38,000 miles on the odometer when I bought the C3; today it's 48,000 miles. 10,000 miles is not an excessive number of miles, but I add several thousand every year.

And how often in fact must you badger Karl because something needs to be done to your C3?
Actually, not often. But the basic thing is that you have to take care of such a vehicle. For example, we replaced the brake master cylinder and overhauled the chassis. So there was always something that came up that we had to see to. I got on his nerves more than once. But I like being around him; Karl's workshop team is just great, and he has super people.

What is your all-time favorite Corvette model?
One could now say the C2 Split-Window, that would be my absolute dream car, or the C2 generally. In addition to my C3, an upgrade to a newer model would also be exciting; for example, a C4 ZR-1, which, when it appeared in *Auto Motor und Sport* in the late '80s, made the 928 and the Testarossa look old. Definitely also a dream car. Or a C6 Z06 with the LS7 engine. But it really doesn't matter which generation one drives. For their time, they were all super-emotional, innovative cars with outstanding design.

One of my dealers in Hockenheim also sells Fords and has a Shelby Mustang GT350. We went for a drive, and at that time, I still had my C3. I therefore got to drive this super-expensive and rare Shelby Mustang and my only thought was: What's this? No comparison with my Corvette!

Just think, my '69 Big Block has 390 horsepower and even after fifty years still runs properly. And that's with brake booster, power steering, electric power windows, retractable headlights, hidden windshield wipers, T-top, and air conditioning. Fifty years ago, the Porsche 911 didn't even have proper heating yet!

◀ 1969 Corvette C3, **Bad Hindelang**, Bavaria, **Germany** | October 15, 2022

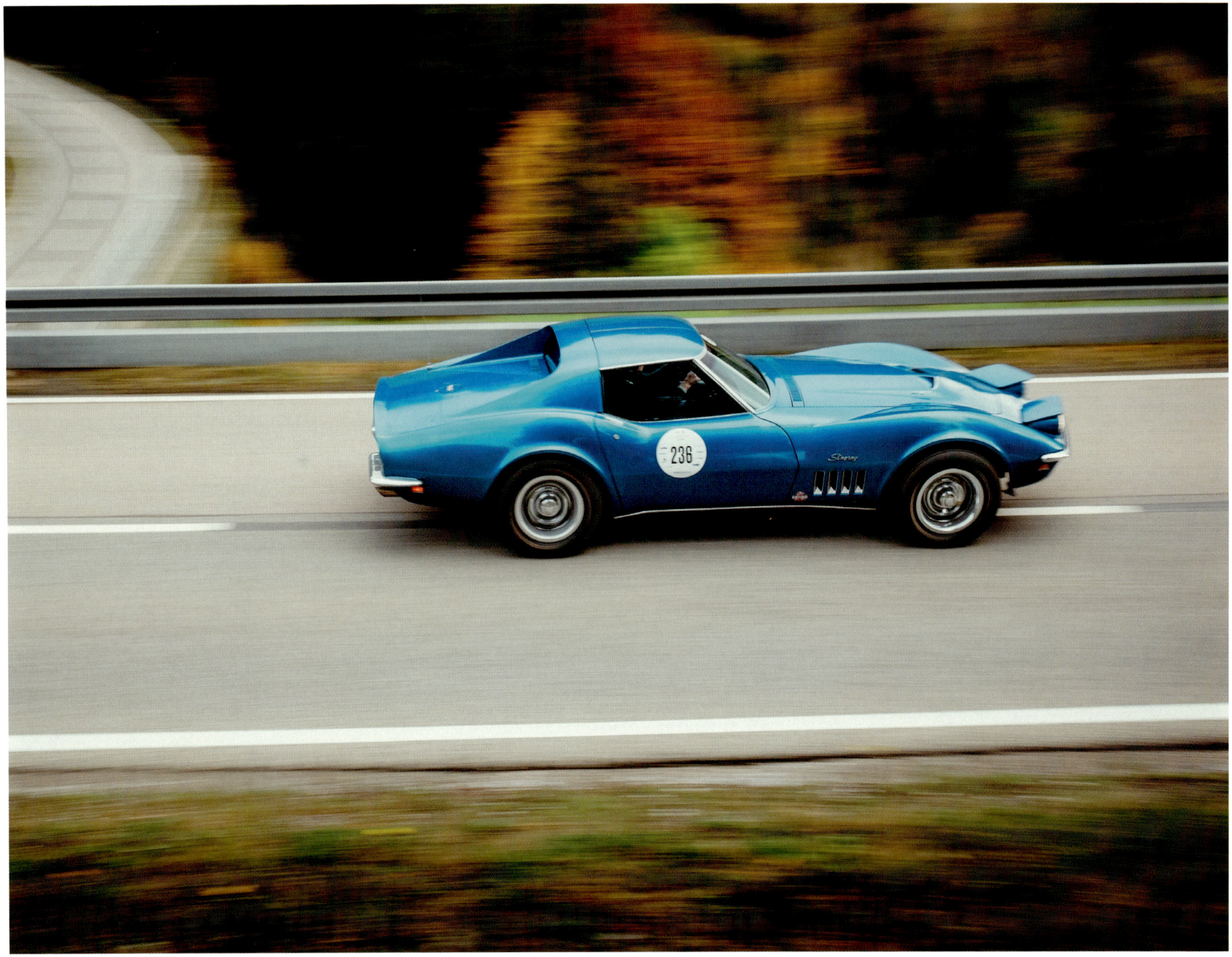
236

TO THOMAS, CORVETTE MEANS:
HISTORY, DAILY BREAD, DRIVING ENJOYMENT

Turning his profession into a hobby. Thomas Pfromm only became a die-hard Corvette fan when he moved to his current employer, General Motors. He discovered the blue C3 while visiting a customer in Munich, in the offices of Karl Geiger, of course.

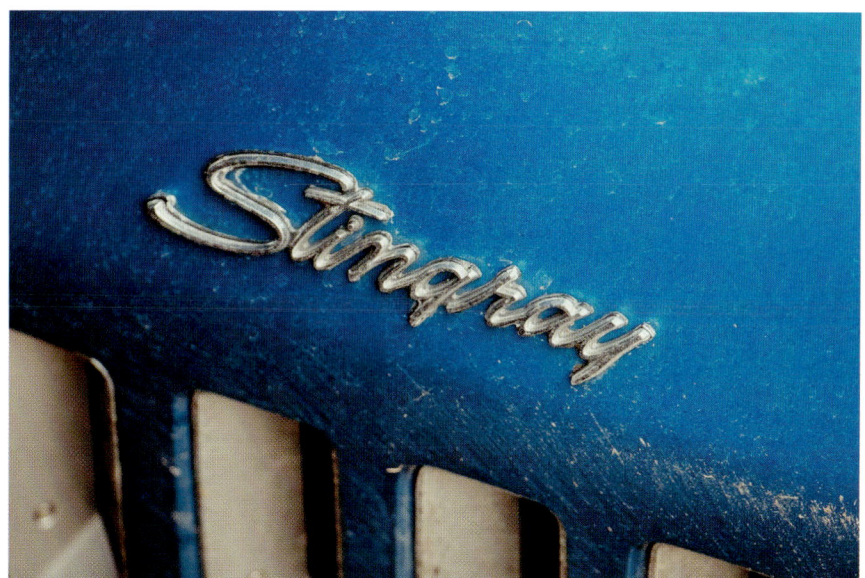

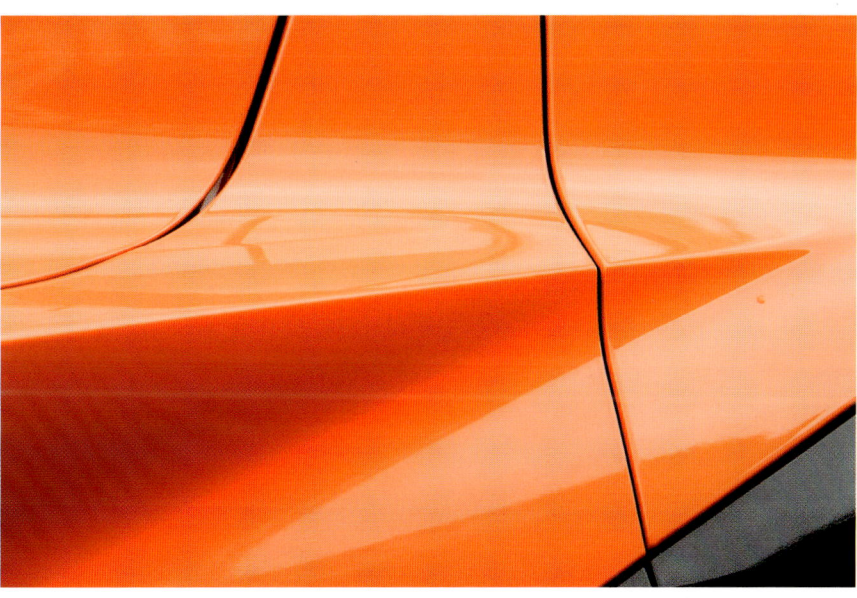

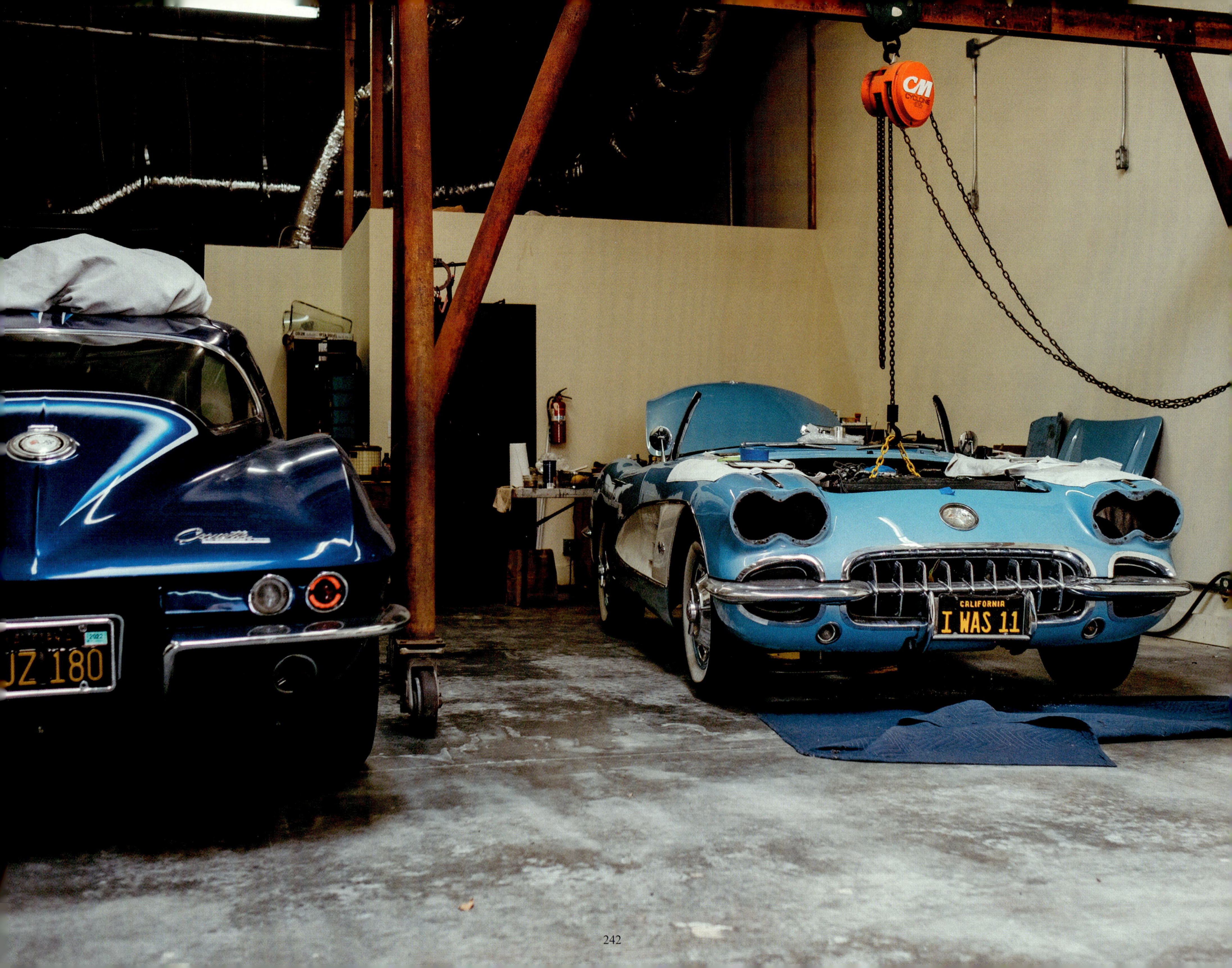
CM
CYCLONE
CALIFORNIA
I WAS 11
JZ 180

THE GUY WITH THE CORVETTE

Rick Kurshner bought his 1960 Corvette back in the Eighties, and it's been his daily driver ever since. Just a perfect California car.

What's your Corvette story?
I always loved Corvettes. Back in the day, and I am talking about the early Sixties, it was a big event when the new cars came out every year. It happened in September usually, at the start of the new school year. GM and Ford would unveil their new cars. Chevrolet would unveil their cars on the television show *Bonanza* on Sunday nights. Every commercial break would be a different model from the GM lineup, and the Corvette was always the last one. When I was very young, I begged my parents to let me stay up long enough to watch these commercials. I just always remembered the Corvette, especially the 1963. That split window was just a shocking change.

I never had a Corvette, but I had a couple of friends who were having Corvettes restored for them in Maine. I was back visiting them, and we went to the shop that was restoring cars, and my C1 was there. It was down to the raw fiberglass; the body was off the frame; the car was in a million pieces. It was being restored for somebody.

When I came back to California and I told my wife about what I wanted to do, she said, "You can buy that car. But it's going to be your car. It's not going to sit in the garage; it's going to take the place of your everyday car." I said, "That's fine." Because it was going to be frame-off restored, I presumed everything was going to be like a new car.

So I called the shop and said, "The next time you get a project, let me know because I might be interested in buying." And he replied, "You know, that '60 Corvette that I had there; the guy would like to get out of it. So if you want a project, that's available . . ." He said it would cost me $10,000 to buy the project. This was thirty years ago. So $10,000 to buy the car, and he was guessing another $10,000 to $12,000 to finish it. And I thought $22,000. Even if it´s $25,000, it's got to be worth that kind of money. So I sent him a check for 10 grand and then gradually send him more money over the next, maybe up to a year, and he would work on it when the money came in. Sometime later we were at about maybe $28,000, and it still wasn't done. So the 22 to 25 had become 28, and it still wasn't finished. I called him up and said, "This can't go on. We either have to settle on a number or you've got to take me out of it." We agreed on a number, and he finally finished the car and shipped it to me.

It was such a big thrill; it came by truck, and it´s been my everyday car ever since—for more than thirty years. My son was born in 1985, so I probably got the car in 1986 or 1987, because I remember I was driving him to nursery school in it.

When I first got it, maybe a month or two after, there was a little Corvette show that I went to. I had never shown a car before, so when I took the car down and pulled into my spot, I didn't know the protocols of car shows; that you are supposed to take the mats out and stuff. The judging was based on lots of things. Everything was supposed to be clean, and I only brought a small rag with me. I pulled into my spot right next to a guy with a '59 Corvette. He was on his hands and knees with a toothbrush, scraping the dirt off his tires. I came home and told my wife about that and just said to her, "If you ever see me doing that, kill me."

But I ended up coming in second at that car show without having done much work on the car. So it kind of got me. I thought, "This isn't so bad; I could get some trophies." Over the years, I would take it to shows, but it could never compete with the trailer queens. Whenever there was a show where you had to open your hood, I had no chance because I drove the car and never detailed the engine. But if there was a "show and shine" category? Man, I had so many trophies. There was just nothing like a 1960 Corvette that looked brand new in the Eighties. For a while, I was showing it a lot, and then I stopped. It just took up too much of my time.

But it's just so beautiful, and it gets so much attention. Sometimes, I drive my wife's car, and I wonder why people aren't looking at me. And she just hates the attention we get when we drive in the Corvette. People keep asking me about the car, what the license plate means (it reads "I WAS 11," my age in 1960), [they] want me to honk the horn, and all that stuff. To me, that's a part of driving a car like that; people really love the car. I have been to shows where there've been really high-end Ferraris or Maseratis, and people would say, "I'd take this car over that one." It's American, and it's just so beautiful. I can't get over how beautiful it still is after all these years. Even the way it looks right now, undressed.

We also used to take a picture with my son and the Corvette on the first day of school each year. And so, I have all these pictures, and the only thing that stays the same is the car. We all age, but the car stays the same. It's a part of the family. And I think someday it's going to be his car. And you know my grandson was just born, and I think maybe it will be his too. Who knows? The car has become a part of my identity; on the street where I live, I am now known as "the guy with the Corvette."

What is your all-time favorite Corvette model?
It is really between my 1960 Corvette and the 1963 split window C2. It's partially because I remember when they changed to the C2 in '63, and it was just such a drastic change! From '53 to '62, it was basically the same body style. Of course, there were a few changes over the years, but when the '63 C2 came out, it was just like a rocket ship.

◀ **1960** Corvette C1, **Ventura**, California, **USA** | November 11, 2021

TO RICK, CORVETTE MEANS:
AMERICAN, STYLE, HISTORY

There's always something. A few days before the photo session, the windshield of Rick Kurshner's C1 was damaged. When he and a friend started to replace the glass, other defects came to light that they were able to repair at the same time.

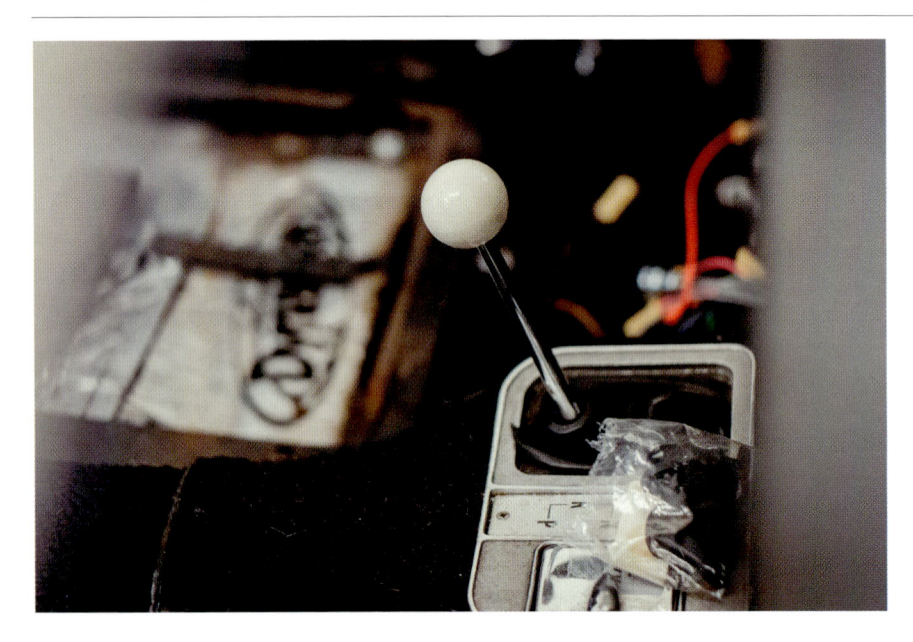

245

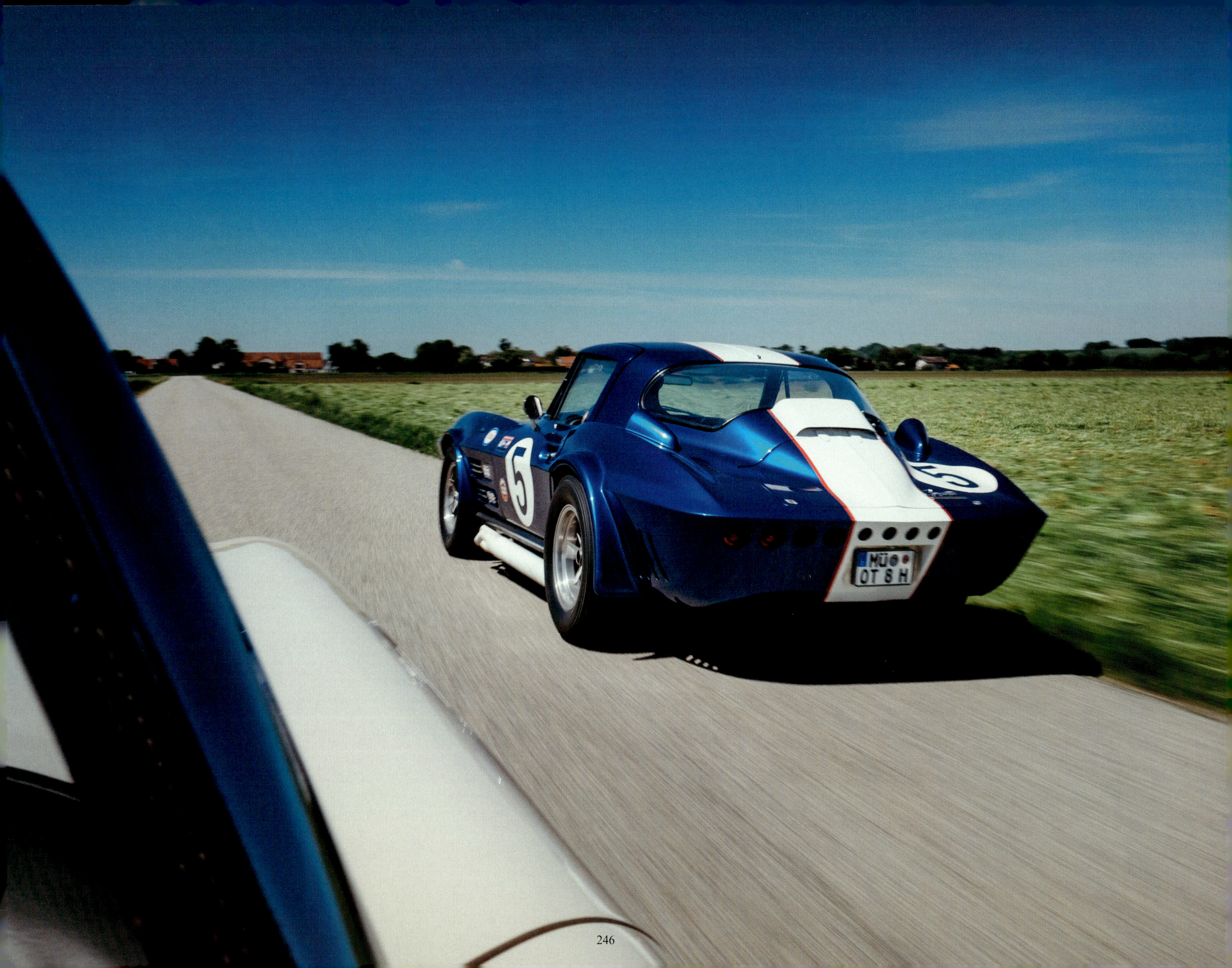
5
MÜ
OT 8 H

UNCOMPROMISING CORVETTE

Oliver Trieb lives the Corvette ideal 100 percent. His collection includes some unique and extremely rare vehicles. Among them are two Corvette C2 Grand Sport replicas.

What's your Corvette story?

My parents were always collectors, even classic flea market goers. My mother collected dolls, my father old cameras, records, and such things. I began collecting model cars as a child. At the toy store in our town, Bburago die-cast models, which were the absolute best available, cost 25 or 30 marks. One day in the store, I discovered a 1/20th-scale plastic model kit of a '67 Corvette convertible by Revell. It cost a fantastic 200 marks. I thought they were crazy, but despite that, I took a close look at the car. I was completely taken by its shape, its hood, the entire car. Even if the kit was out of my reach.

We children of course also frequently played Auto Quartett (a card game), and there, too, the American cars were always from another world. The standard cars had displacements of 1.5, 1.7, or 1.8 liters, some even 3 liters. And then along came an American car with a displacement of 7 liters. Bam! It was the same with the engine power. 60 hp, 80 hp, and the American car with 430 hp! Sensational!

When I became an adult, my father-in-law had a Camaro with a 220hp small block engine. His was the first American car I ever drove in. That was a very special experience for me. The sound, the performance, simply a brutal car. From then on, I couldn't let go of this theme, and I knew that I also had to have such a car.

In 2010, after wife, child, house, and garden were on the credit side, it was time for me to add an American V8. Without knowing the first thing about a Corvette, I bought a C2 convertible. I went for a drive with the owner, and he told me that it was a "no matching numbers" car and so forth and so on. I had no idea what he was talking about and just thought, great, the car runs and looks cool! And bang, I had my first Corvette.

I am the type that goes to extremes in everything I do, privately and professionally. That meant that I couldn't stop at one Corvette, and so over the years, I acquired more and more American sports cars. As a collector, I of course always wanted to have a C2 Grand Sport. An original was out of the question, and if I was going to buy a replica, it would have to be as close to the original as possible—no modern technology, no modern engine, no modern transmission, and stuff like that. At first, I thought about having a Grand Sport built. I had a garage prepare an estimate, and we were soon over €300,000, and that didn't include proper plans or patterns. We would therefore have sunk a huge amount of money into the project without ending up with a perfect vehicle. My dream died for the first time. Then I found a Grand Sport in the US. At the time, there were several Grand Sport replicas being offered, but I was attracted to one in particular. I looked at numerous pictures, and everything looked very authentic to me. Even the interior looked original. It was the one.

In my lifetime, I have bought more than thirty cars without seeing them in person, simply based on a gut feeling. That's how it was with the Grand Sport. When the coupe arrived in Germany, I was fortunately not disappointed. I liked it very much! I then tried to obtain more information about the car and by chance came upon a press report in which the builder of the Corvette spoke about it. He had in fact gone to see all the owners of Grand Sports and had measured the cars in detail. He subsequently built everything as well as he could. In part, he had used primitive means, but after removing the paint from the simple welded frame, we found that the Corvette was nevertheless extremely authentic. He really wanted to build a true Grand Sport, a number 6. The feeling I had had before the purchase was confirmed.

We have made a few technical improvements so that the car could also be driven really fast. We removed the body and refined the frame and suspension. We are also going to further optimize the engine bay in the direction of originality, and there is still a little work left to do. I want everything to be authentic, but not a 1:1 copy. For that, we have bought another Grand Sport, which we are specifically reworking with that goal in mind.

The covers for the headlights are still on the list. They are made of very thin plexiglas and unfortunately broke. Finding replacements is difficult. By way of a Norwegian who is a total Grand Sport fan, I came into contact with a woman in the US. She has the original shape of the covers and makes them to order. But it's not that easy with the Americans. She preferred payment in cash, and she had never shipped outside the country. We are constantly in contact with the woman and hope that one day we will finally get the covers.

I would like to drive this Grand Sport and feel the same thing as the maniacs who used to beat it around the racetracks. We have achieved precisely that. The C2 is drivable and nevertheless a brute. It really has plenty of get up and go; 500 hp is easily available at the rear wheels. A lightweight racing machine.

I also found my "heavy," a modified 66 C2 convertible, in the US. There was only a photo of the Corvette, shot from what looked like 400 yards away, plus the cryptic text: "Selling Corvette without engine." The previous owner had once had a 469 turbo engine in it, and the thing was supposedly able to cover the quarter mile in less than ten seconds. I found that exciting and wrote to him. We communicated regularly for more than three months and talked about the car. The Corvette's frame was in perfect condition, and he wanted to install a new 540 V8, an engine on which everything was the finest, a pure racing machine. He then quarreled with the engine maker, as there was probably a lot of money involved, and he made the decision to sell the car. If I were to buy the half car with all the parts and bring it to Germany and then install an engine, it was going to be really expensive. I therefore suggested that he complete the Corvette for me. That is what he did. He regularly sent me photos and videos of the car's current state, and it was really a dream to complete this car.

After the C2 had arrived here in Germany, I sent him photos of the things I had done to the car. Now when I step on the gas, the entire car coils. The thing has 8.9 liters of displacement, 775 hp, and 737 lb./ft. of torque on the test stand. And all that in a C2. Looking at the car, there is no indication of this power. It is an absolute sleeper. One can perhaps recognize it from the 540 badge on the side. They made it for me, and I mounted it on the Corvette in place of the 427 badge. It also bears a special NCRC sticker. That stands for "Not correctly restored Corvette."

Currently on my wish list is a 1953 Corvette in Pennant Blue. There are not many of those. I just love unusual colors on a Corvette. As you can see, I don't have a single red one.

What is your all-time favorite Corvette model?

There's one keeper for me: my 1966 C2 with the 540 engine. This is absolutely my favorite Corvette. When you start the engine, it's scary, it's so cool. It's just the way I imagine my perfect Corvette, even though it's not a "matching numbers" car. I don't care about that at all.

◀ **1965** Corvette C2, **Mühldorf am Inn**, Bavaria, **Germany** | May 15, 2022

TO OLIVER, CORVETTE MEANS:
EVERYTHING

Sport badge. With this Grand Sport replica, Oliver Trieb doesn't want to create a 1:1 copy, but an authentic Corvette that's not too bad to drive and in which he gets a sense of how Dick Thompson or Roger Penske felt behind the wheel of the GS in 1963.

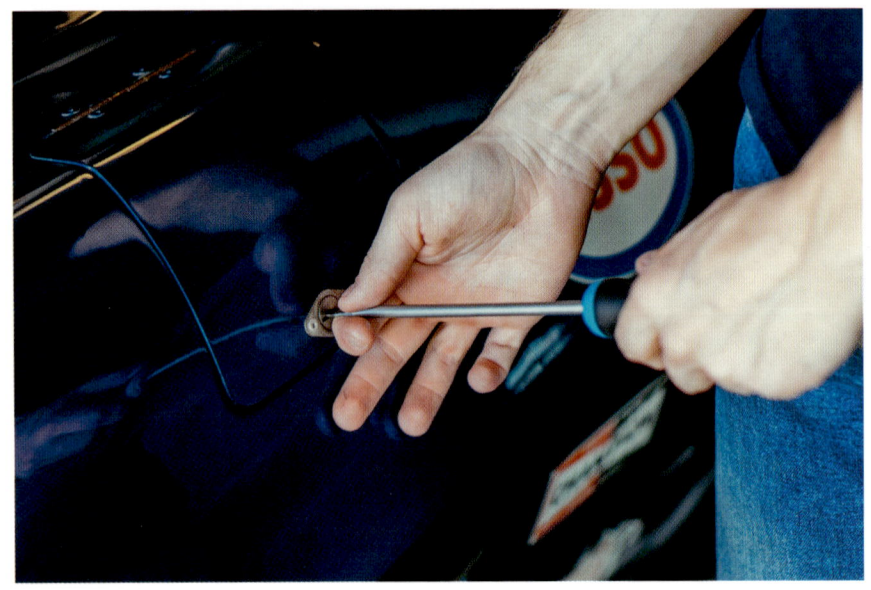

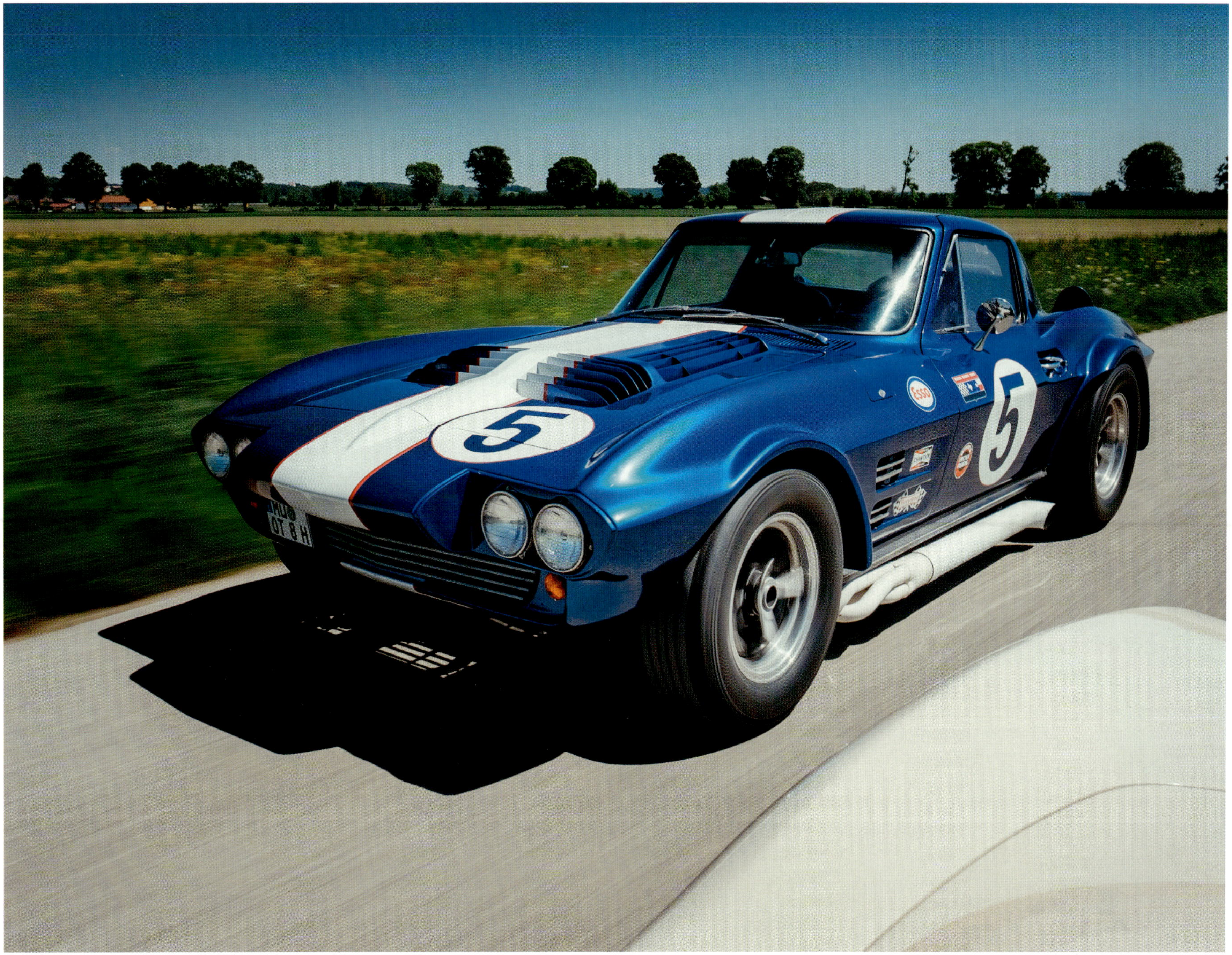
5
Esso

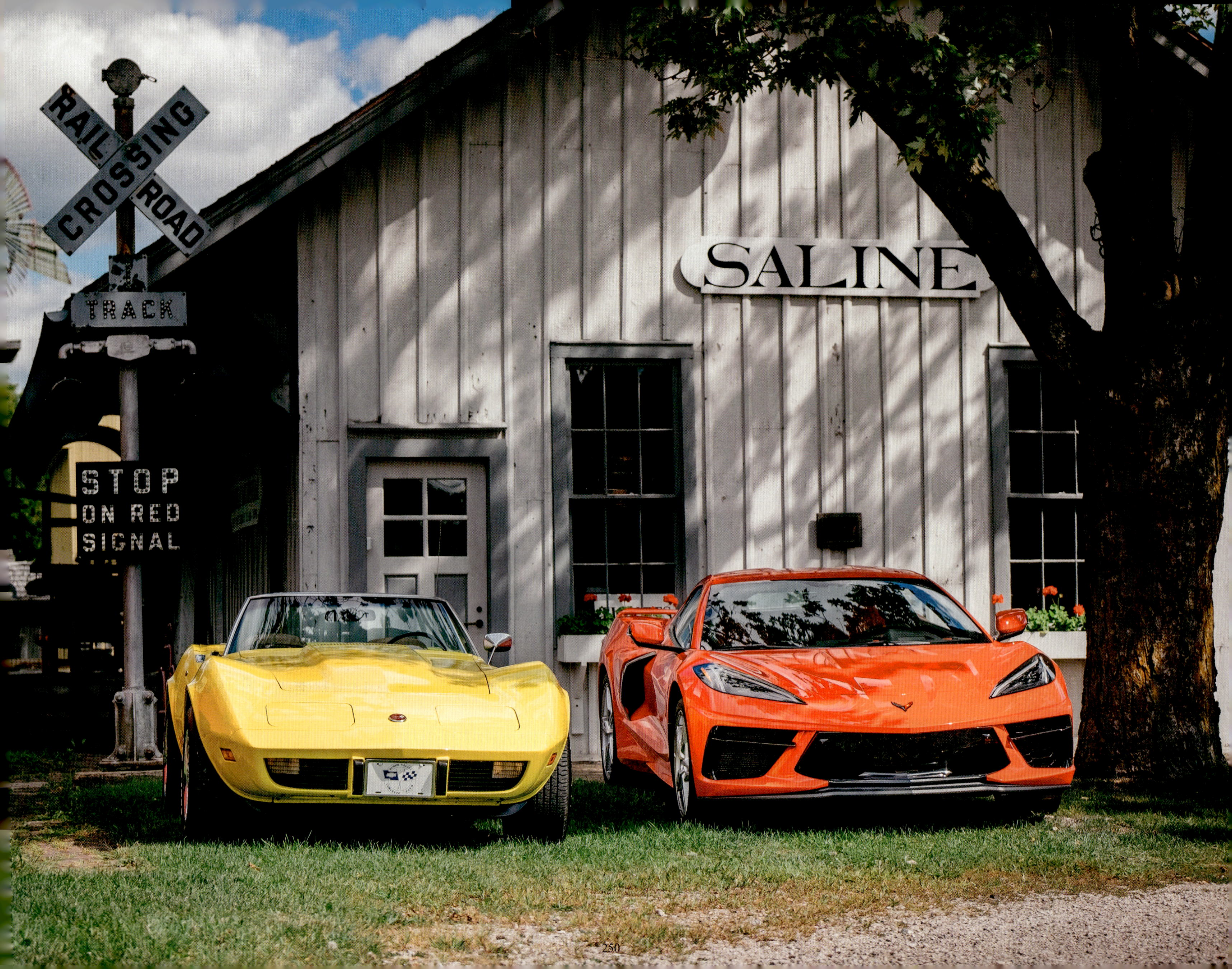
RAIL ROAD
CROSSING
1
TRACK
STOP
ON RED
SIGNAL
SALINE

PEGASUS AND THE GOD OF FIRE

Richard Dafforn bought his first Corvette at 25. He still has the yellow C3. At 70, it was time for something more comfortable. Since then, there has also been a C8 in his garage.

What's your Corvette story?
The first Corvette I ever sat in was a '63 C2 convertible. That was at the Indiana State Fair, held every year in Indianapolis. I was thirteen at the time and was there with my mother. "You know, if you save your money, perhaps one day you'll have a Corvette too," she said to me. I thought I would never be able to afford a special car like that. The C3 came on the market several years later, and I fell in love with it on the spot. The body style, its proportions, magnificent. I told my girlfriend that I wanted her permission to buy a Corvette after our wedding, which we were already planning. At that point in time, I couldn't have afforded the insurance for the C3. If one was under twenty-five, one had to expect to put down about a third of the car's value. In 1975, that was a lot of money.

When I finally went to the dealer and ordered the Corvette I wanted, I was twenty-four. I got the car in April 1975, shortly before my twenty-fifth birthday. That also settled the matter of the expensive insurance. The first tour in the Corvette took us to the legendary Route 66. We drove the Sixty Six all the way west and back again. That was back in the day when one could still drive all of Route 66. On the way back, we stopped at the Bonneville Salt Flats and visited Yellowstone National Park and Mount Rushmore. We were gone three weeks, and it was one of our best trips ever. I remember driving through the Mojave Desert. It was over 100 degrees, and the C3 had no air conditioning system. We also couldn't open the roof, because the place for the cover was taken up by our luggage. Man, was it hot! The transmission tunnel radiated so much heat that my leg became all red. It felt like I had first-degree burns.

By the way, our yellow C3 was called Pegasus. My wife, Kay, had the urge to name all our cars. There was never any question of selling the Corvette. We kept it even when our children were small. When our children had left home and I retired, we had to remain socially active. We therefore joined two clubs, one of them the Huron Valley Corvette Club. The club frequently held interesting events and longer outings. But I was sometimes reluctant to go on the long tours in a 45-year-old vehicle. After all that time, I thought perhaps we had earned ourselves a second Corvette. We decided to buy a brand-new C8.

When I saw what GM brought to the market, I could scarcely believe it. A mid-engine car for under $60,000! I had never thought that I would ever be able to afford a car like that. We ordered a C8 with everything we wanted and had to wait fifteen months for it. We were finally able to pick it up from the dealer in December 2020. In September 2021, we drove the Tail of the Dragon, an eleven-mile-long mountain road through the Appalachians, with the HVCC. In the C8, that was absolutely unbelievable. At that time, Kaye dubbed the C8 Vulcan, after the Roman god of fire.

The Huron Valley Corvette Club is simply super. There is something planned every week. We had a member who sold his Corvette and got a Porsche. He asked us if he could remain a member, just because of the people and the activities. He was allowed to stay and has since gotten another Corvette.

A year ago, we were on the Michigan International Speedway with the HVCC and our C8. There we were really able to show what the C8 could do. We had an instructor who set the speed that we could not exceed. But now and then, we let ourselves drop back a little and then step on the gas. I got to around 130 mph in the C8, and it felt great.

What is your all-time favorite Corvette model?
After all the years with the C3, it's still fun to drive. I enjoy shifting the four gears manually. You can't compare the C8 with its modern technology. What we considered a high-performance sports car in the Seventies is laughable nowadays. I mean, my C8 goes from 0 to 60 in 2.8 seconds, which is unbelievable. I would say that the C8 is my favorite, but I love them both.

◀ **1975** Corvette C3, **2020** Corvette C8, **Saline**, Michigan, USA | September 13, 2022

TO RICHARD, CORVETTE MEANS:
OPTICS, PERFORMANCE, HISTORY

Legendary creatures. Pegasus and Vulcan are the names of the two Corvettes. Kaye Dafforn loves to give their vehicles names. Together with her husband, Richard, she drives the red C8 on challenging mountain roads such as the Dragon's Tail.

253

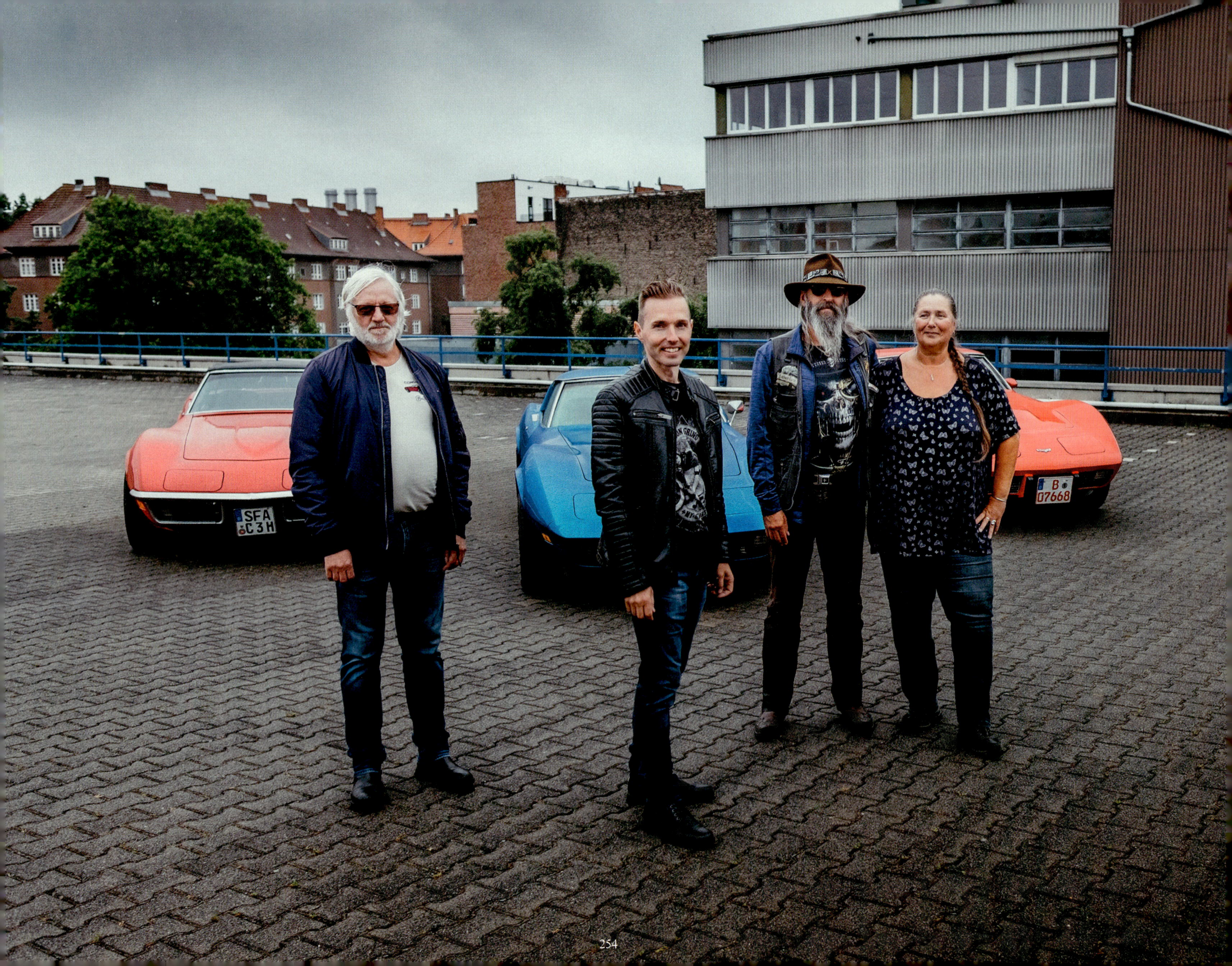
SFA C3H
B 07668

THREE TIMES CORVETTE C3

Their passion for the Corvette became a longtime friendship and a small and exclusive C3 club. Its members: Helmut Ost, Silvio Hoppe, and Harald Weinhardt.

What's your Corvette story?
Harald: For me, it began in childhood. An elementary school friend had the Corvette by Corgi Toys with removable roof halves and so on. At the time, I found this completely fascinating. This model in fact provided the initial spark. Somehow, I always kept the car in the back of my mind and never forgot it, but not in my wildest dreams did I think that I would one day own one.

I have had several normal cars in my life, although they weren't really that normal. They were always somewhat beyond the normal taste. A Volvo 244, for example. At some point, I began driving different American cars. And after having had several American cars, we in fact began looking for a Corvette. We found one and considered it, but in the end didn't find it satisfactory. Instead, we bought an old Mercedes. One year later, I wanted a classic Ford Mustang. And again, the same game. We went to look at a Pony and came home with a Corvette. That must have been nine years ago.

The C3 was at a Porsche dealership here in Berlin. We looked at the Corvette, and it was soon clear that it would be our new car. Incidentally, Lina Van de Mars is one of the car's previous owners and was seen with it in the magazine *Dream Cars*. In reality, it was easy to trace the burnouts mentioned in the article, in the form of rubber marks in the wheel wells.

Silvio: My love for the Corvette began in a very similar way. When we were small, my cousin had a model of a Corvette C3 that I really liked. As a child, I of course also spent a lot of time watching the usual TV series and recreated scenes with toy cars, whether it was *Riptide* with the C1 or the *A Team* with the C4.

It must have been 1990, and the family was on vacation in Switzerland. It was there that I saw my first C3 in real life. My mother had just taken my picture standing between two Corvettes. At the time, it was my absolute dream photo, and I knew that at some point I would own one of those American sports cars.

But some years passed before that happened. By then I was married and frequently got on my wife's nerves with my desire for a Corvette. At some point, she said, "All right." And that "All right" in 2015 was the starting shot in my search for a Corvette.

It didn't take long. I drove from Berlin to Nuremberg to look at a C3. Fortunately, it was as described, and I drove back to Berlin to take care of the financing. A few days later, I collected the Corvette with a trailer. Already on the way back, I noticed how positively the people reacted to the car. Children photographed the C3 on the trailer; that was really cool. When I got home, I had my picture taken with the C3, in the same pose as when I was a small boy. Twenty-five years stood between my first encounter with a C3 and the day one sat in my own garage.

Helmut: For years, I drove normal bread-and-butter cars and actually had no interest in the Corvette until one day when the TV series *Stingray* was playing on the tube. The sound, the lines, simply a cool car. The Corvette had cast a spell over me. I began in a small way by building models, and I now have about 150 model cars.

I often told my work colleagues and some clients that I needed a Corvette. One day, a client came to me and said, "I was just in Hamburg, and a Honda dealer has a Corvette for sale." They had put the car in the showroom as an attention-getter. Then the car dealership began undergoing renovations. The Corvette was in the way, and therefore it had to go. And I was in the right place at the right time. That was twenty-five years ago, which is how long I've had my C3. I spent the first five years restoring the Corvette. Except for the paint, I've done all the work myself.

When I moved to Berlin, the Corvette initially remained in Walsrode. I often returned to my former home on the weekends, and if the weather in Berlin was fine, it was usually raining there. At some point, therefore, I took the Corvette with me to Berlin. One sunny weekend I drove to Paaren im Glien to an American car meet and simply parked next to the two C3s owned by Harald and Silvio. We have been traveling together ever since.

Silvio: Harald and I met one another precisely two years earlier at the same meet. At the time, I showed him pictures of the Corvette I wanted to buy and asked for his opinion.

Harald: We spoke for a long time and finally exchanged contact information. Weeks later, Silvio called me and said that he had bought the Corvette. As he lived just a few minutes away, we soon met at my place to look over his new acquisition. From that day on, we frequently drove to meets together. A few years later, Helmut joined us. He became the third member of our group. We have been traveling together regularly now for five years. My wife, Sonja, is also always with me, whether at tinkering sessions, meets, or outings. Strictly speaking, there are four of us.

Silvio: Amusing fun fact: our three C3s are each three years apart—1971, 1974, and 1977.

What is your all-time favorite Corvette model?
Helmut: The '66 C2 coupe is at the top of my list. But then I ended up getting a C3, which I've never regretted.
Silvio: No question, the C3.
Harald: I agree, definitely the C3.

◄ **1971** Corvette C3, **1974** Corvette C3, **1977** Corvette C3, **Berlin**, Germany | **July 7, 2022**

TO HELMUT, CORVETTE MEANS:
SIMPLY AWESOME

TO SILVIO, CORVETTE MEANS:
FREEDOM, NO LIMITS, FUN

TO HARALD, CORVETTE MEANS:
FUN WITHOUT END

All good things come in threes. The three Corvette C3s owned by Helmut Ost, Silvio Hoppe, and Harald Weinhardt were all built three years apart. All three were made at the St. Louis plant, before Corvette production moved to Bowling Green until 1981.

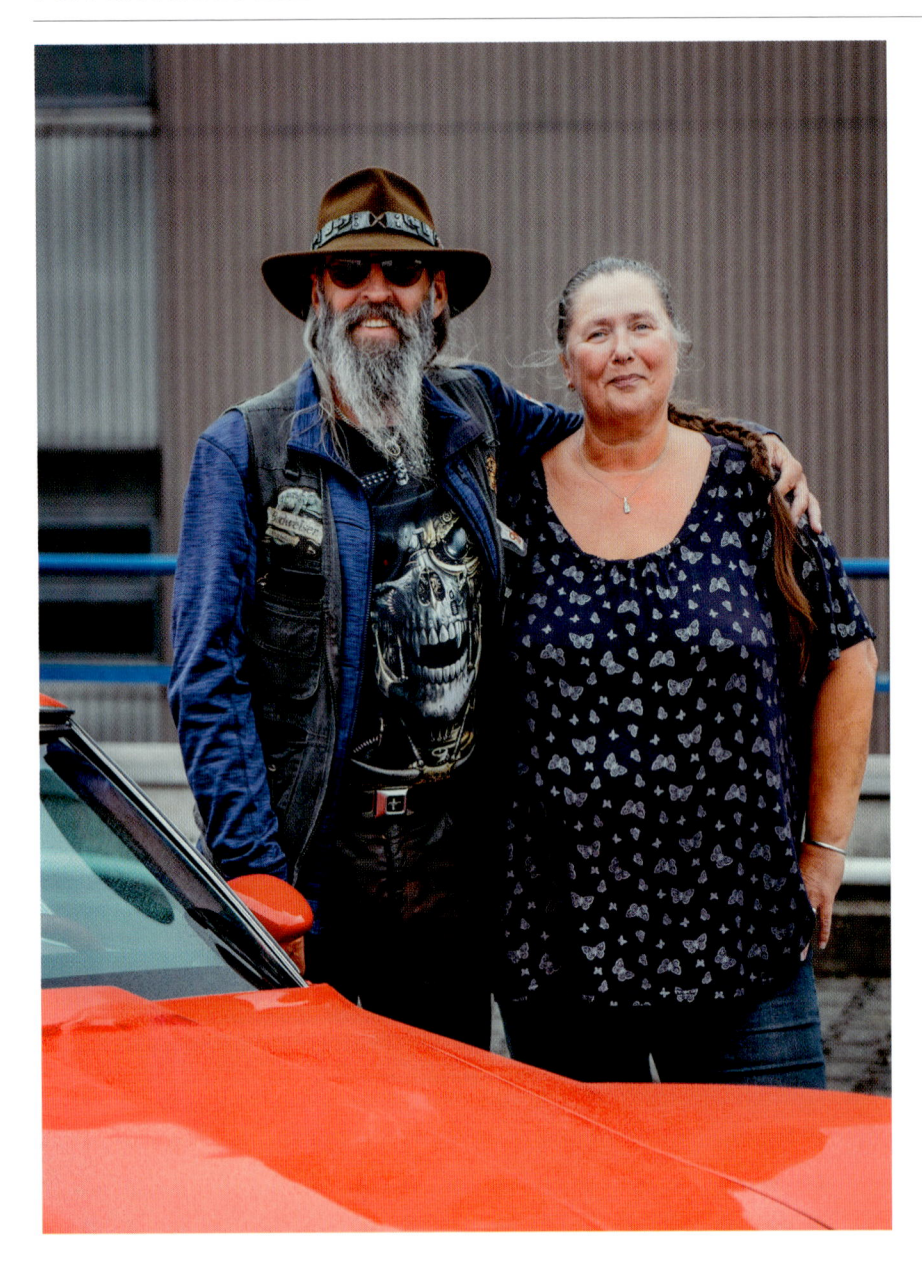

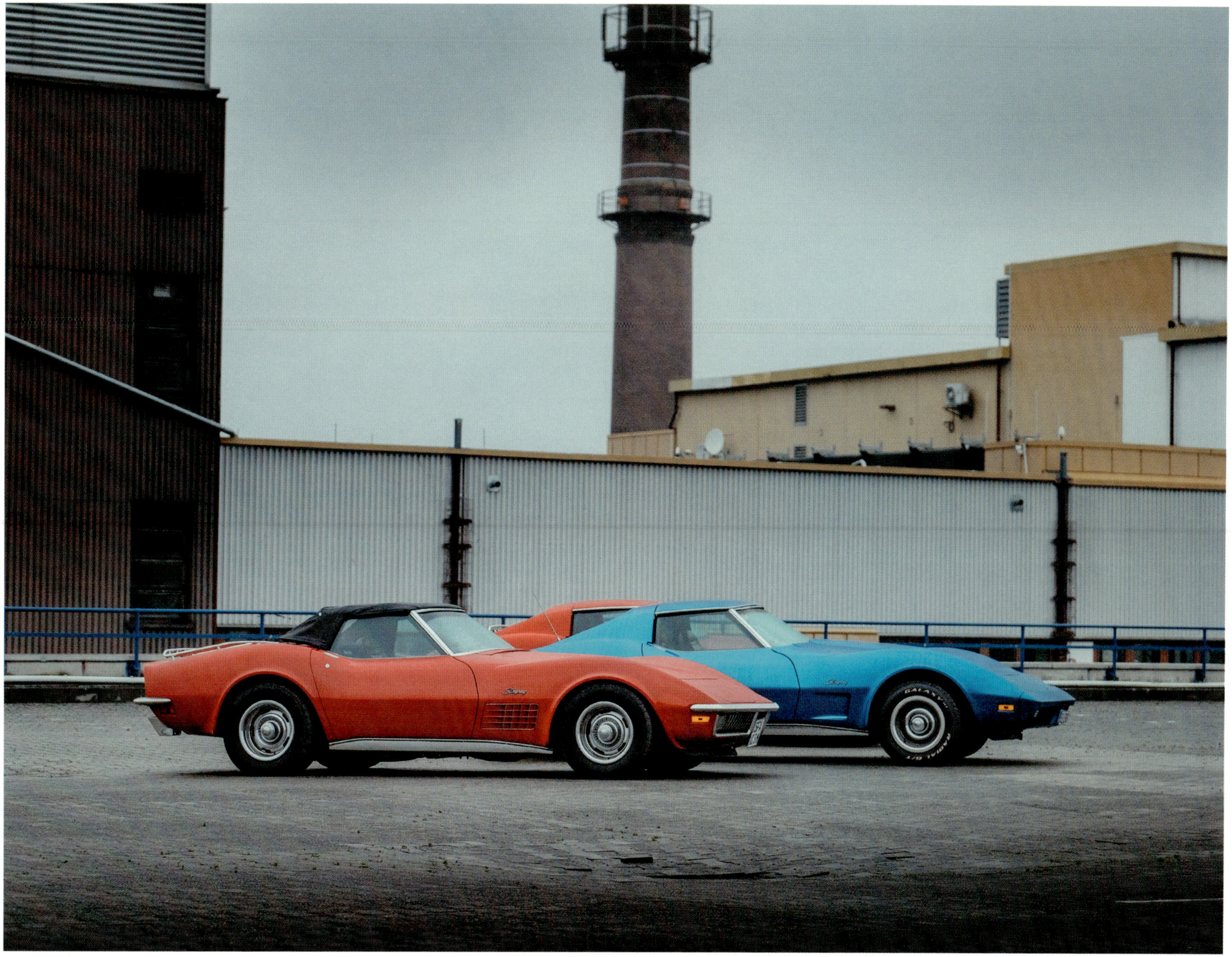

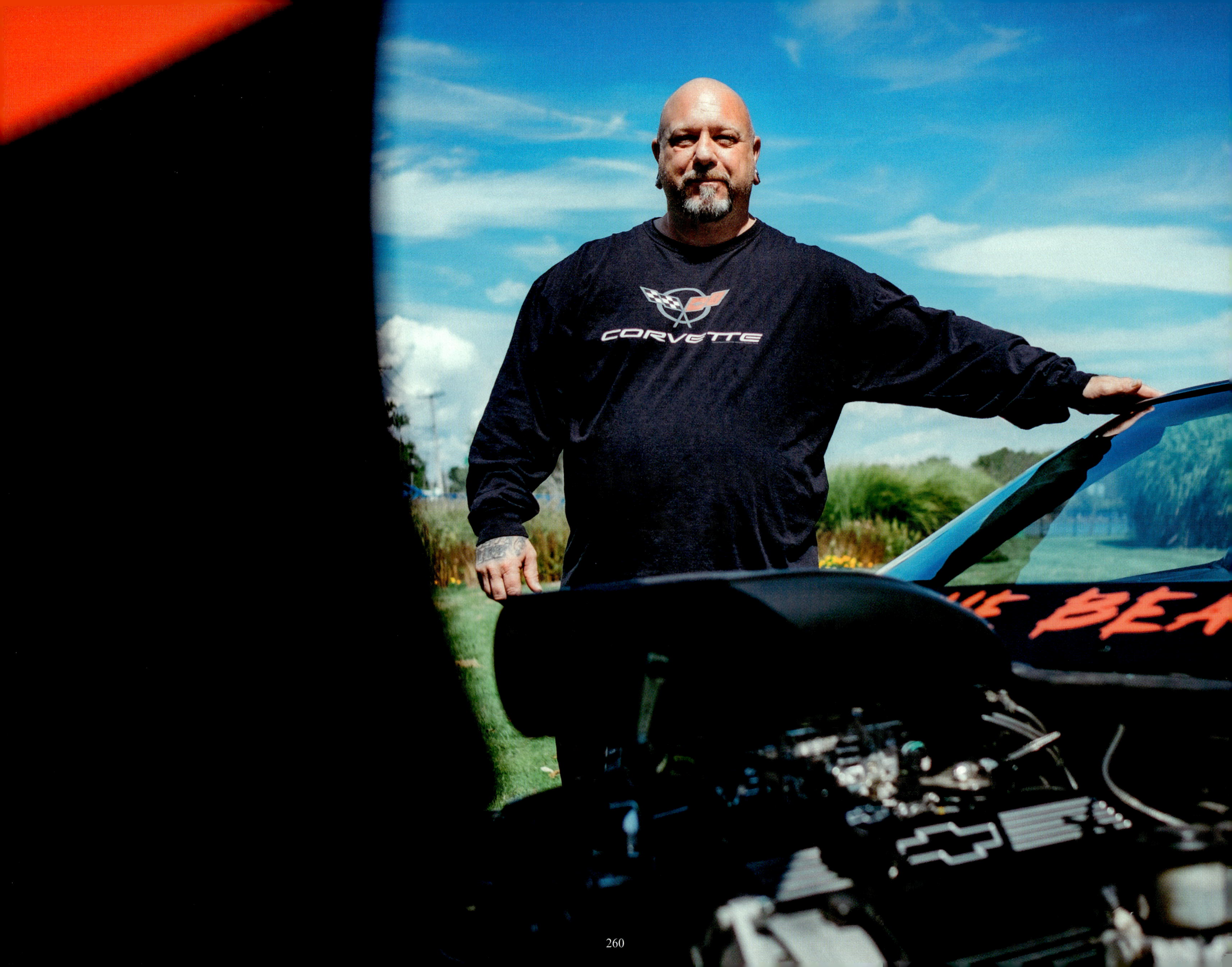
CORVETTE

THE BEAST

The Corvette wasn't Bryon M. Perez's first choice when he was looking for a car. But now, everyone knows him and his black C4, the Beast.

What's your Corvette story?
My wife of twenty-six years looked at me one day and said, "The kids are grown, and they are out of the house; you always took care of us; you always worked really hard. Now I think it's time for you to get something you really want. I know it's a car, and don't go crazy with the price, but if you can find something cheap enough, that you can work on and that will give you a hobby, something that I know you have wanted for so long, now is the time to go ahead and do it." So I began looking around for a cool car on Facebook Marketplace, and I found a Corvette. I wasn't looking for a Corvette, but the price was very good!

I went out and looked at it with my wife a couple of times. I even took my mechanic buddies Ryan and John to have a look at it. We drove it three times, made sure that everything was working properly. I literally looked at that car six times before I bought it. If you are not a Corvette owner and if you don't know what to look for, you can get yourself into a real money pit.

I bought the car, and we had some problems with the engine when I first got it. It drove fine at low rpms, but if I increased power, it would spark knock like crazy. My buddy did a full tuneup—new plugs and wires, checking all the sensors out. He thought that everything was okay, but it still had engine issues. At that point I had three choices: just drive it and enjoy, sell it, or rebuild the engine from scratch. I decided to rebuild the engine.

I wasn't really looking for a Corvette; I was more interested in a classic muscle car like a Chevelle, a Nova, something like that. But it just kind of fell into my lap, and the price allowed me to put some extra money into the car. And if wasn't for my two best friends, Ryan Palmer and John Mierzejewski, I never would have bought it. Not even two months after I bought the car, it was in John's shop, and we were already working on the engine. Everything you see now on the car was done in just one year.

We did quite a lot to it. Originally it had a 240-horsepower, tune port Chevy engine. Now it has a 355 with full roller conversion, trick flow, aluminum heads, Edelbrock air gap intake, comp cams, Big Mother Thumper cam; then we went from fuel injection back to old-school Holly 600 Double Pumper power, along with Hedman Long Tube Headers and 3.73 rear gears. It was built to deliver around 450 horsepower. Of course, with that kind of power, we also had to change the transmission. Ryan had the extra transmission at his shop. He told me, if I could buy the transmission controller for it, he would give me that transmission for free. Switching from a 700R4 to a 4L60E made such a big difference; now it has instant power.

My friends helped me so much with the car, giving me many parts for free as well as a lot of their time. I am really grateful, and thanks to Ryan and John, along with my wife, Shenna Perez, my dream became a reality.

After we finished the car, I was driving it every day. Even if I didn't drive it to work, I'd come home, get it out of the garage, go cruise for an hour, and then put it back in my garage. It was like my decompression therapy, like a vacation. If I had a bad day at work, I could just jump in the car and clear my mind. Never in my life have I had a car like this, a car that gets the attention it deserves. It doesn't matter if I stop at a light, a parking lot, or a gas station.

Wherever I go, somebody is always asking me something about my car. It definitely wasn't my first choice for a car, but now it is my car. And people know the Beast when they see the scoop sticking out of the hood along with the Beast graphic that I had installed on the lower part of the windshield.

What is your all-time favorite Corvette model?
I really like the C1, just because of the rareness of it. If you were to ask me which one I would pick for working on it or to modify it for the cool-factor? I would go with a C5 or a C6. I like the looks of them, and I like the center exhaust system.

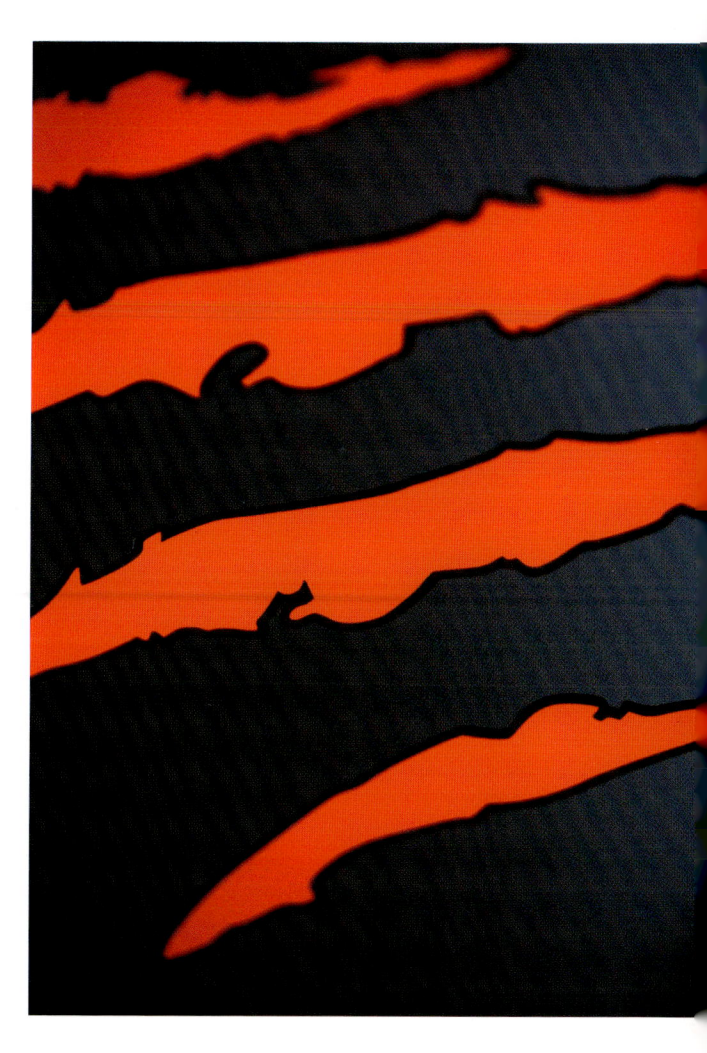

◂ **1985** Corvette C4, **Toledo**, Ohio, **USA** | September 10, 2022

TO BRYON, CORVETTE MEANS:
FREEDOM, POWER, HANDLING

The Beast. Bryon M. Perez couldn't care less what others think of his 450hp C4. "Fuck-It-Edition" is written on the dashboard, and there is an air scoop peering out of the hood. The message for purists couldn't be clearer.

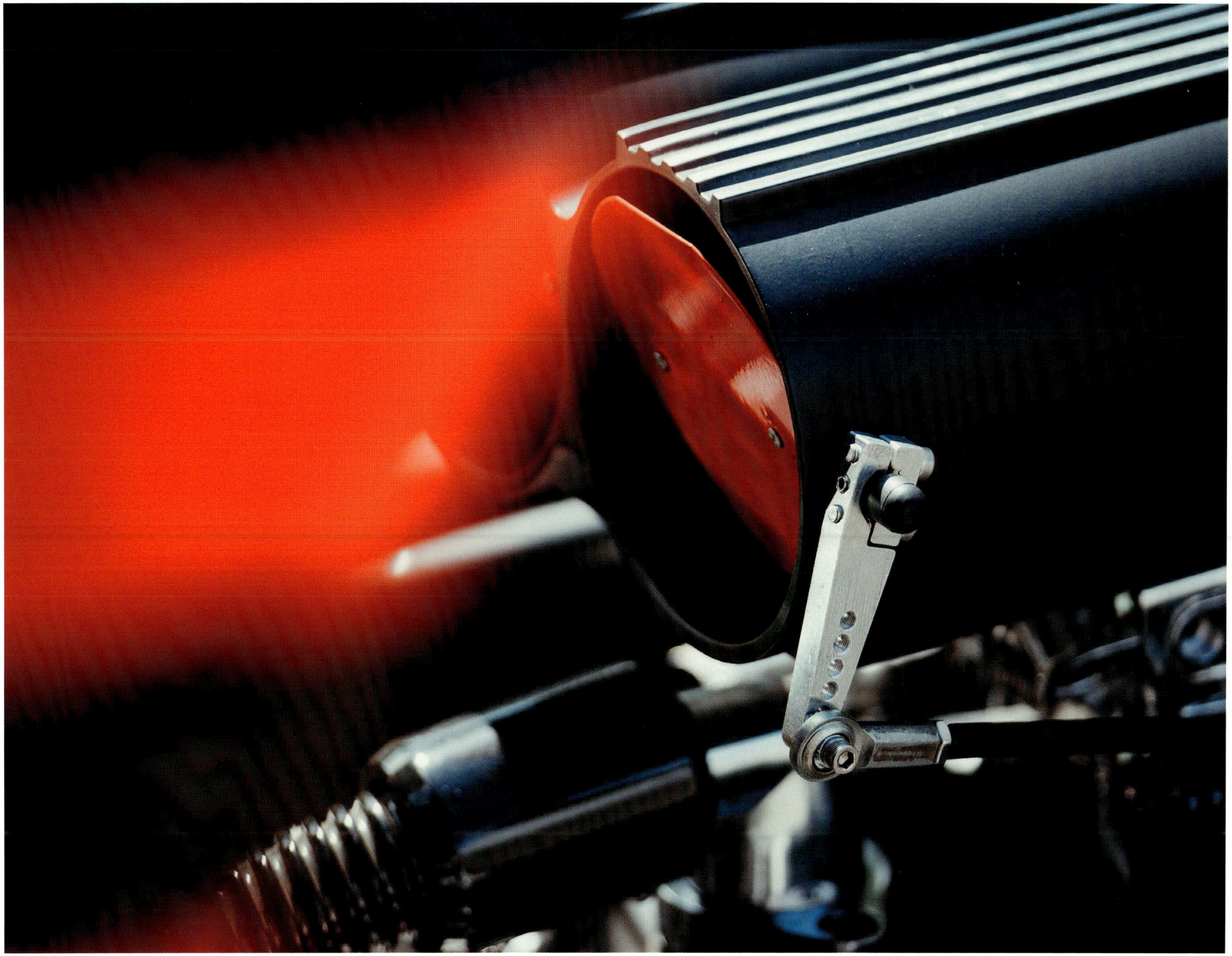

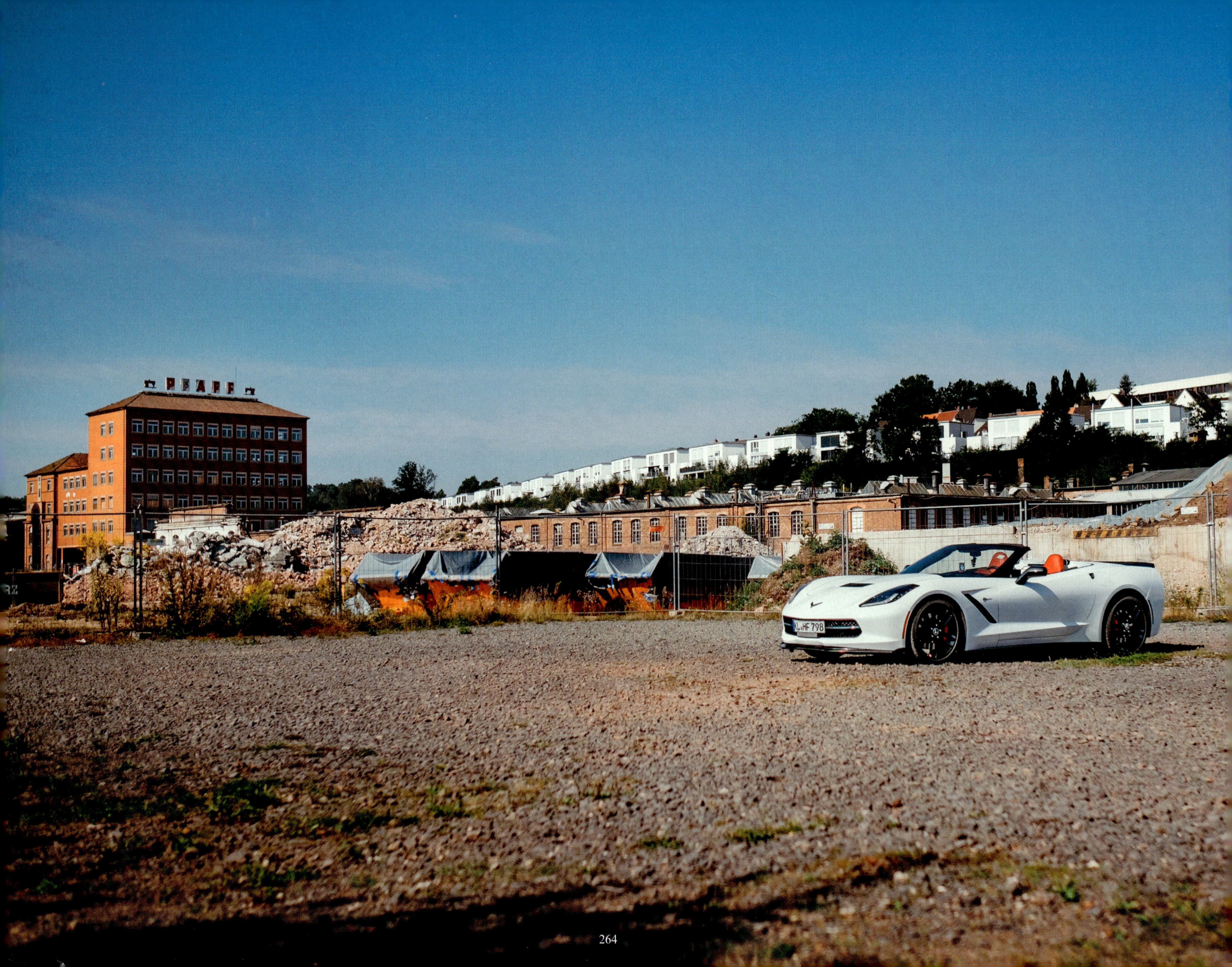
PFAFF

A CORVETTE IN K-TOWN

Eddie Menzies has driven many cars. With the C7, the American discovered his love for the Corvette. He now enjoys driving it on German roads.

What's your Corvette story?
The Corvette was never actually my thing. I had driven every type of car I could, but not the fiberglass sports car. For a long time, I was rather skeptical about the Corvette when it came to the quality of the interior. When I saw the C7 for the first time, I was surprised by the interior's high quality, especially compared to the older models. That was a clear improvement. I liked the curves but, at the same time, also the clean edges of the C7. And another advantage: the C7 could be had as a new car! The old Corvettes were often not very reliable, and I wanted a car I could take to meets or drive on long tours.

When I again visited my brother in Dallas, I went looking at a Chevrolet dealership. Unfortunately, I couldn't buy a brand-new Corvette, because I could have had problems importing it into Germany. There was some kind of regulation that prevented that. I therefore got a used C7 convertible. With 600 miles on the odometer, it was virtually a new car. I was able to get the car to Germany without difficulty. I had it transported from Bremerhaven to the customs officer here in Kaiserslautern. That was 2017.

Driving a Corvette here in Germany is fabulous. Everyone here has experienced a BMW, a Mercedes, or even a VW. Even many taxis are Mercedes here. That is quite out of the ordinary to me as an American. In the rearview mirror, I often see people in other cars talking about the Corvette. They are puzzled about what kind of car it is, even though "Corvette" appears in large letters on the rear. But there just aren't that many of these sports cars in Germany. They have, however, become better known and more loved here because of the C7 and especially the C8. I am nevertheless frequently surprised by how many cars arrive at Corvette meets. Several hundred cars is by no means a rarity. There is a really great Corvette community here in Germany and Europe, with many clubs and shows and an exchange across borders. That is really worthy of mention.

With the C7, I have really fallen in love with the Corvette. I now also like the first three generations. But my next Corvette will be a C8, most definitely. General Motors has scored a major success with this car, and it can keep up with all the sports cars out there.

What is your all-time favorite Corvette model?
The C8 is my favorite. Its technology, performance, and reliability are simply impressive.

◀ **2017** Corvette C7, **Kaiserslautern**, Rhineland-Pfalz, **Germany** | September 5, 2021

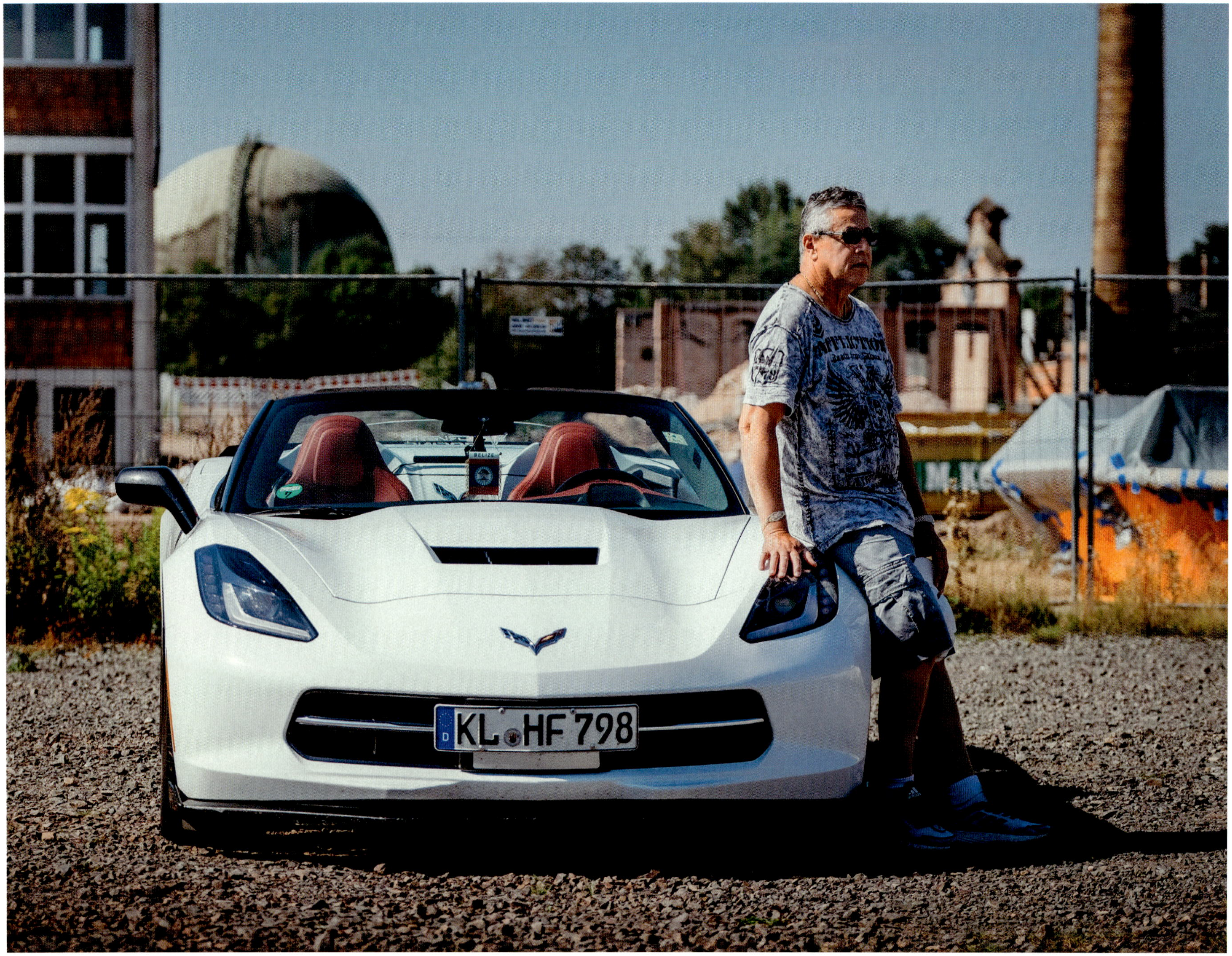
KL HF 798

TO EDDIE, CORVETTE MEANS:
EXCITING, DIFFERENT, AMERICAN

German way of life. Eddie Menzies came to Germany with the US Army. After his career in the military, he decided to remain in Germany. He did, however, bring a piece of American culture to Kaiserslautern: his Corvette.

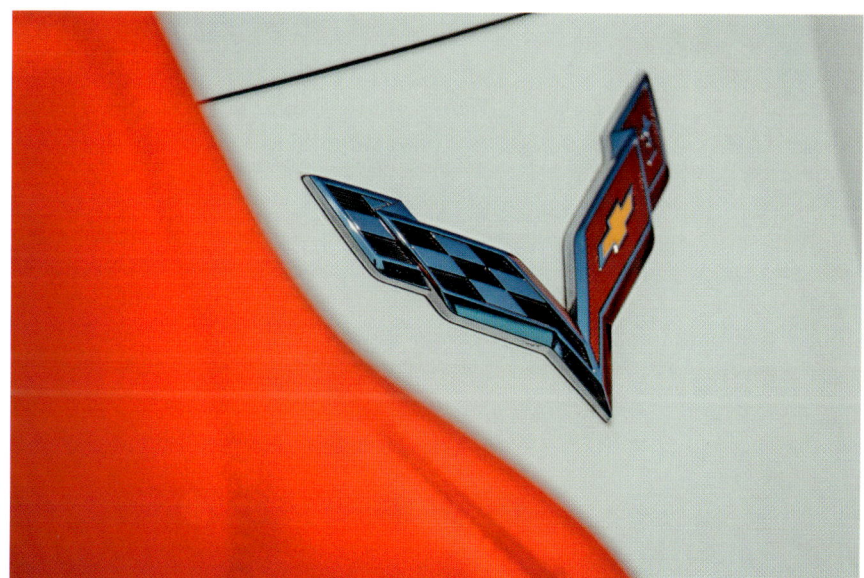

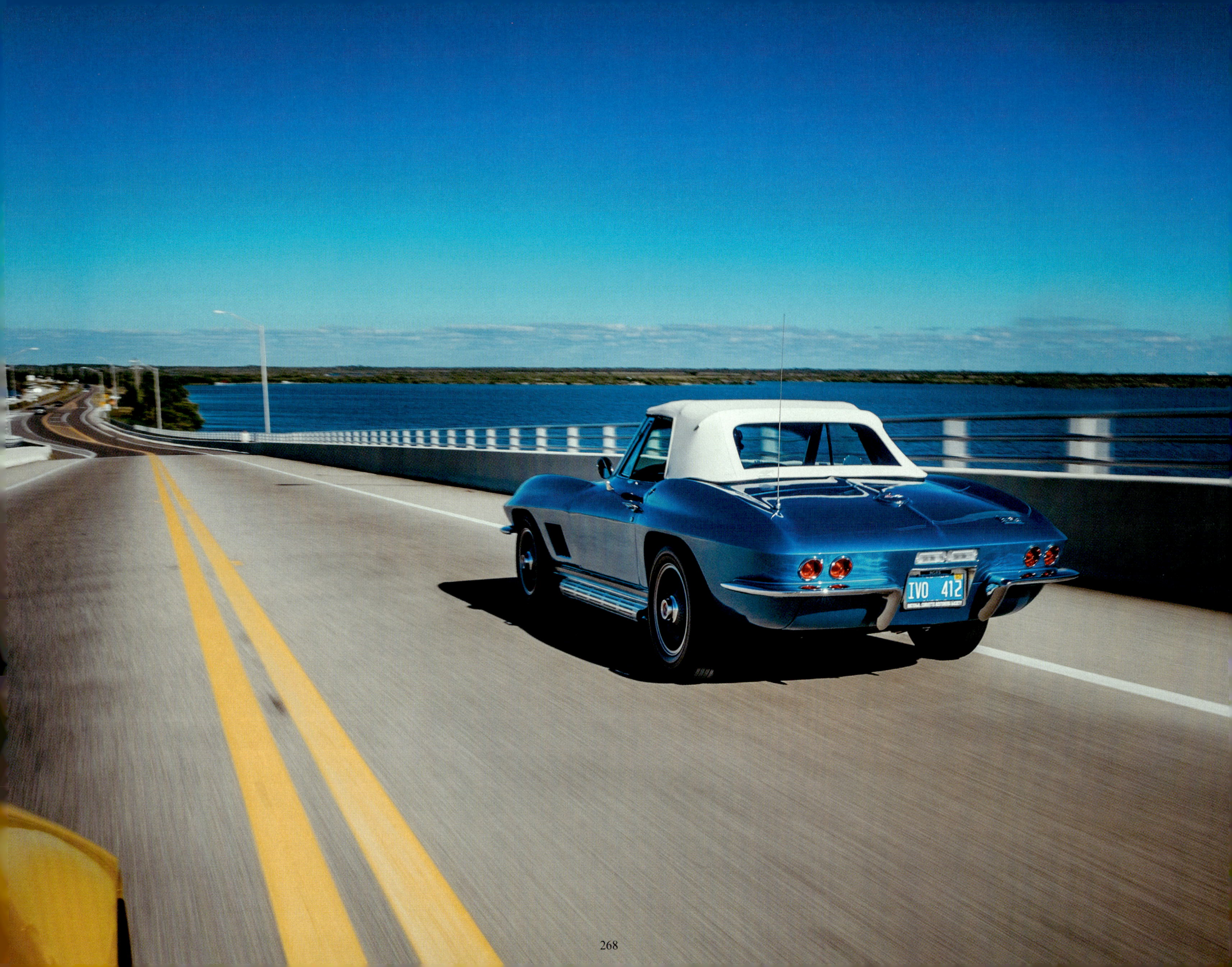
IVO 412

RIDE IN PEACE, JOHN

If you don't want a lot of people riding with you in the car all the time, buy a two-seater. That's what John Franklin did back in 1967, and he fell in love with his Corvette.

What's your Corvette story?
Well, when I was young, eons ago, I made an agreement with my parents after two of my friends were killed in car accidents when I was in high school. They told me that, if I didn't start driving as soon as I turned sixteen, and instead waited until I graduated, they would buy me a new car. That sounded good to me, so we made a deal.

I completed school and asked my parents about the car they had promised me. My father took me to a car dealership, and I got a '65 Chevrolet Impala Super Sport with a 396-cubic-inch V8, a crazy car. All of a sudden, everyone I knew was my best friend. Even before I got home from work, guys would be standing at our door. My mother would let them in, and they played pool until I got home. Then we all got in my car and drove somewhere. But to be honest, I really didn't like driving people around all the time. After a while, it really began getting on my nerves. I wanted to buy a new car, and I switched to a two-seater, a 1966 Corvette.

The car was just one and a half years old at the time and just the right thing for me. Suddenly I no longer had to be so social and friendly. I didn't have to drive anyone around the neighborhood, apart from my girlfriend. The Corvette was simply great; I loved that car. I kept it until I got married and had children. Then we unfortunately had to sell the Corvette and buy a larger family car.

At the first opportunity, after I no longer had to pay tuition fees and the children had left home, I began looking for another Corvette. I concentrated my search on a C2 that had the same color combination as my first Corvette, preferably with a 390hp big block engine. I often said to my wife, "Perhaps I'll come home some day and there will be a 427, 425 hp Corvette in our garage." After that didn't happen for twelve years, I gave up hope. But I did come across a '67 small block Corvette convertible. And I'm going to keep it. I love that car.

What is your all-time favorite Corvette model?
The C7. To me, the C7 is the best car General Motors ever made. It has real power, but it is easy to drive, and there so many choices when it comes to equipment and colors. All of the controls, like the hand brake, are in the right place. You get a 7-speed automatic transmission, and the design—the lines are simply outstanding. I must admit, however, that the C8 is even better looking from an aesthetic standpoint. Despite this, I would stay with the C7. It is simply the best total package. I can't think of anything I would criticize about the C7.

Thank you, John Franklin, who died in the summer of 2022:
Many thanks to John for the years we spent together and the memories I can look back on with a smile. I will always love him. —*Barbara Hurn*

I met John for the first time after I became a member of our Corvette club. We became friends immediately, spent a lot of time together, and laughed and talked about God and the world. I will always remember his hearty laugh. Rest in peace, my friend. —*Janice Green*

John was a wonderful friend and Corvette enthusiast. We will miss him. —*Jerry and Carol Walsh*

We met John at a Corvette show fifteen years ago. Thanks to his great sense of humor and his open manner, we became friends. From then on, we met once a week and went to Corvette shows year after year. We miss him and his legendary laugh. —*Jerry and Linda Paradise*

I miss John very much, especially his laugh and his wonderful stories. I still sometimes ask Neena if Barbara and John are going to the Corvette event we are going to. It was always good to know that John was there; it was always fun talking to him about Corvettes. John enriched my life in a way that I can't explain. I didn't know him as long as other members of the club, but his friendship left a lasting impression. May we one day see each other in heaven with our two black Corvettes. —*Pete and Neena Johnson*

John was a true friend with a big heart. Though we only knew each other four years, it felt as if we'd known each other forever. I will miss picking up the phone and hearing John's "Hey, how's it going?" John is now in heaven in his '67 big block Corvette, looking down on us and laughing as only John could laugh. —*Peter and Barbara Lenhard*

John Franklin was a true friend. His laughter was deep and contagious. His vast knowledge and love for the Corvette was never ending. We cherish the fun times we had together, whether at the Vette shows, at the Mecum Auction, or just out for a delicious meal with Barbara and him. His eyes sparkled when he spoke about his grandson, Johnny. Family was very important to John. John will forever remain in our hearts and is deeply missed today. —*Gary and Faye Leschitz*

◀ **1967** Corvette C2, **Titusville**, Florida, **USA** | November 16, 2021

TO JOHN, CORVETTE MEANT:
IT'S A LIFESTYLE

Never topless. This '67 Sting Ray still has a flawless top after 54 years. The first one, of course. Its owner John Franklin explained to us how: "Just don't pop the top. Here in Florida, you enjoy every moment in the shade anyway."

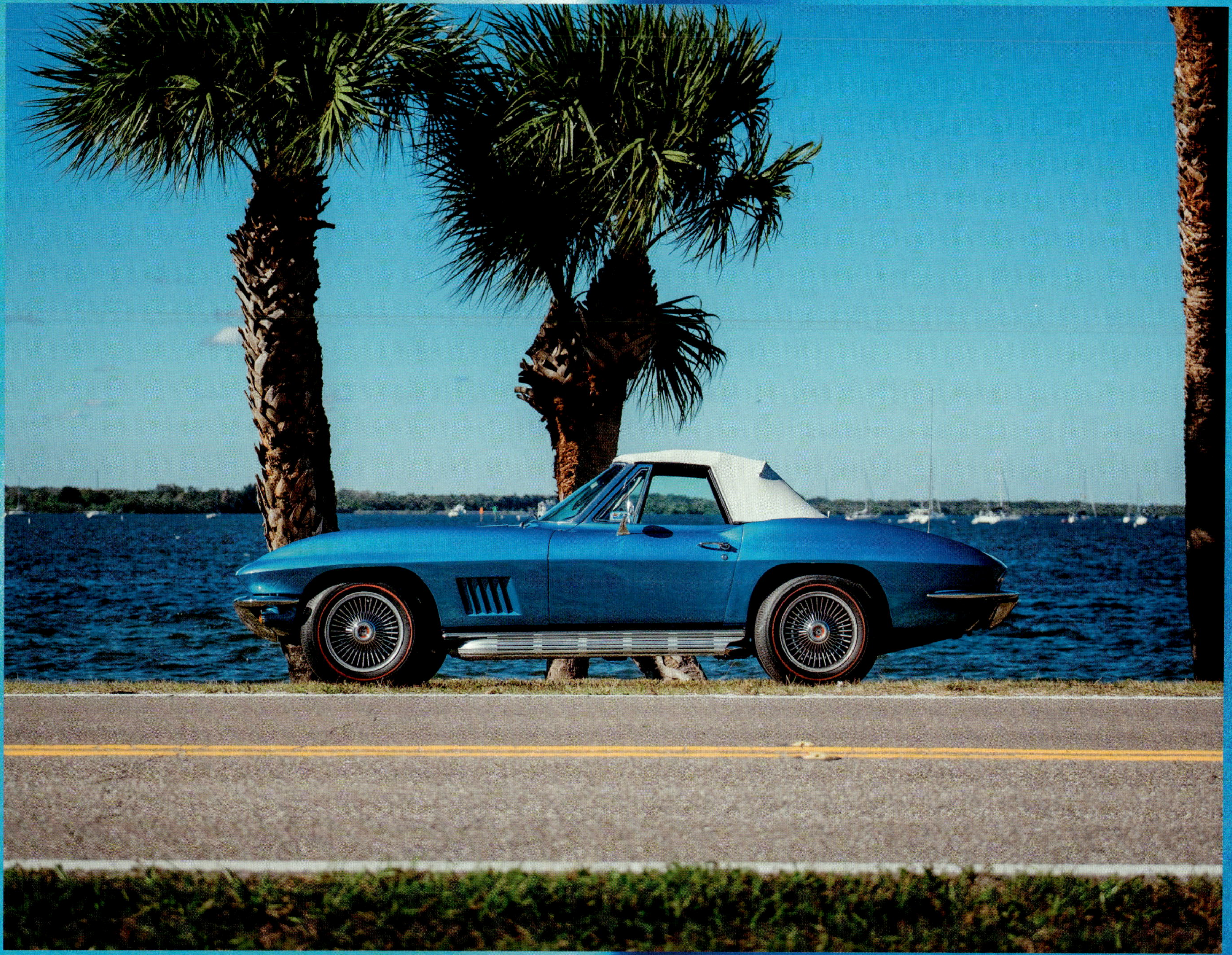

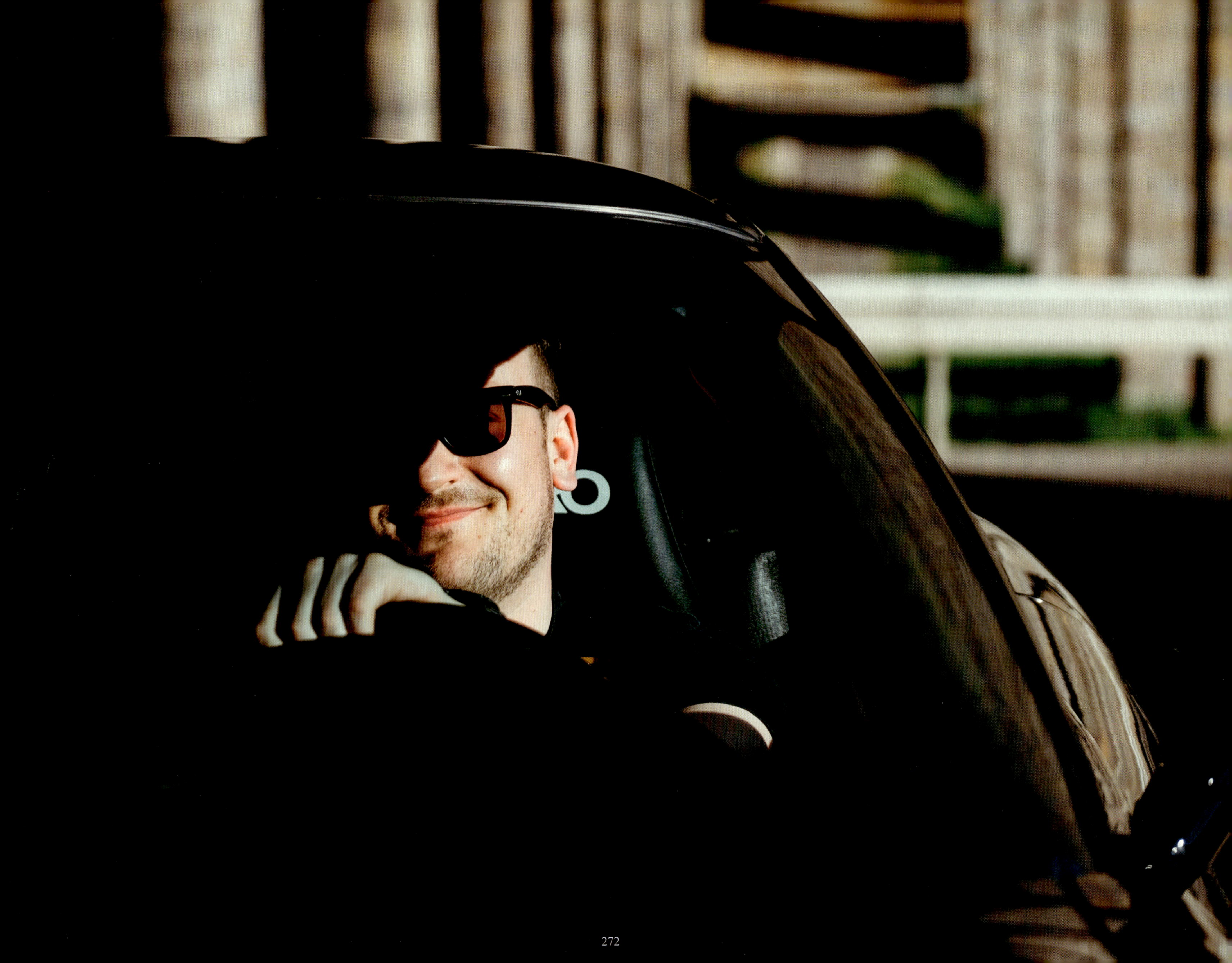

FIRST CAR, FIRST CORVETTE

To seriously look for a Corvette when you're fourteen years old is unusual. It is equally unusual to drive your own C5 in the company of an adult driver at the age of seventeen.

What's your Corvette story?
When I was about eight years old, I was driving down the autobahn with my parents and watching the passing cars from the back seat. At some point, a black flash shot past us. I immediately asked my father what kind of car it was, and he replied, "A Corvette." That was the first contact I remember. It immediately became clear that someday I would also need a Corvette.

As a teenager, I began learning about the Corvette, what models there were and how much one would have to expect to pay for one. By then, I had been working on cars with my Dad for a long time and definitely wanted my first car to be a Corvette. I initially focused on the C4. With my driver's license drawing ever closer, I also began looking more closely at the C5. I had been looking for Corvettes for three or four years already, but in the last twelve months before getting my license, I intensified my search. At the age of fourteen, I began looking on the internet every day, watching what went on there. How was the market? What are the differences between an American version and a European model? As a result, I was able to understand the facts quite well at an early stage.

When I was sixteen, my father and I began looking at several Corvettes all over Germany. This went on for about a year. At some point I found a C5 near Hamburg, in the Lüneburg Heath—one owner, first delivery to Germany with 19,000 kilometers (11,800 miles), standard transmission, black exterior and interior. Just as I had imagined it. The car was simply perfect for me. One weekend, we went to look at the C5. The owner was an older gentleman who had a small car collection. His treasures included cars like a Jaguar E Type, a Daimler Double Six, and the Corvette. He wanted to cut back a little and therefore decided to sell off his collection.

We came to an agreement, and a few days later, we returned on the Inter-City Express. It took six and a half hours to get there by train, while the drive back in the Corvette took just six. At that time, my father did the driving. That was in June 2013, and then in July or August, I got my driver's license. At seventeen! That meant that I could drive the Corvette if accompanied by my father. And that didn't happen every day.

For a few years, the Corvette was no more than a piece of jewelry, a pure Sunday car. At some point, I began improving and optimizing the car here and there; for example, with a MOV'IT braking system and Recaro sports seats. Of course, I kept all the original parts, bought two of everything I had to drill holes in, and put the spare away. My basement, meanwhile, became a huge parts warehouse. I believe that if I continue in this way, in a few years I'll be able to assemble a second Corvette from the parts.

I have now had the C5 for nine years, and I would never want to sell it. In that time, 45,000 kilometers (27,961 miles) have been put on the car. It's just going to stay; it will be with me all my life. But there would always be the possibility of putting everything back to original if I had to sell it.

What did your parents say when at 17, as a beginning driver, you told them that you wanted to buy a Corvette?
I must tell you that at that time, my Dad had a Cadillac SRX with the 4.6-liter Northstar V8 engine. He thus already had an affinity for American cars. Perhaps he would have been more skeptical about a Porsche 911 than a Corvette; I don't know. And I had worked on this project for four years. Everyone else my age was getting their moped license. I told myself that I would save the money and buy something sensible. I think that was more reasonable. If you really invest the last of your savings in this one car, then you will handle and care for it much more carefully and value it more highly. And with its 5.7-liter V8, the Corvette is ideal for a new driver; you won't stall the engine so quickly.

You often drive with two boys and two other Corvettes. How did that come about?
I had already had my Corvette for quite a while and driven with different groups. Somehow that wasn't for me, however. Then I met Gerry. He had a C6 ZR1. Then one day a guy wrote to me on Facebook. "I see that you are also from Munich and have a Corvette. Want to be friends?" At first, I thought, what kind of strange guy is this?

A month later, we met at Gerry's. We had planned a trip to Austria. At six in the morning, I was with him in the kitchen when suddenly a guy entered and said, "Hello, Kilian. It's me, Chris, from Facebook." That's how the whole thing started. Last year we went to Belgrade with Chris's Corvette and did a quick tour of the Balkans, including a party break. Now we are together at least twice a week, and we also work on our Corvettes together. Except for paintwork, we do everything ourselves.

What is your all-time favorite Corvette model?
If I could keep my C5, I would also get a C7 Z06 or ZR1. To me, that is the ultimate expression of the front engine concept. However, I wouldn't trade my C5 for any other Corvette.

◀ **2001** Corvette C5, **Geisenhausen**, Bavaria, **Germany** | May 15, 2022

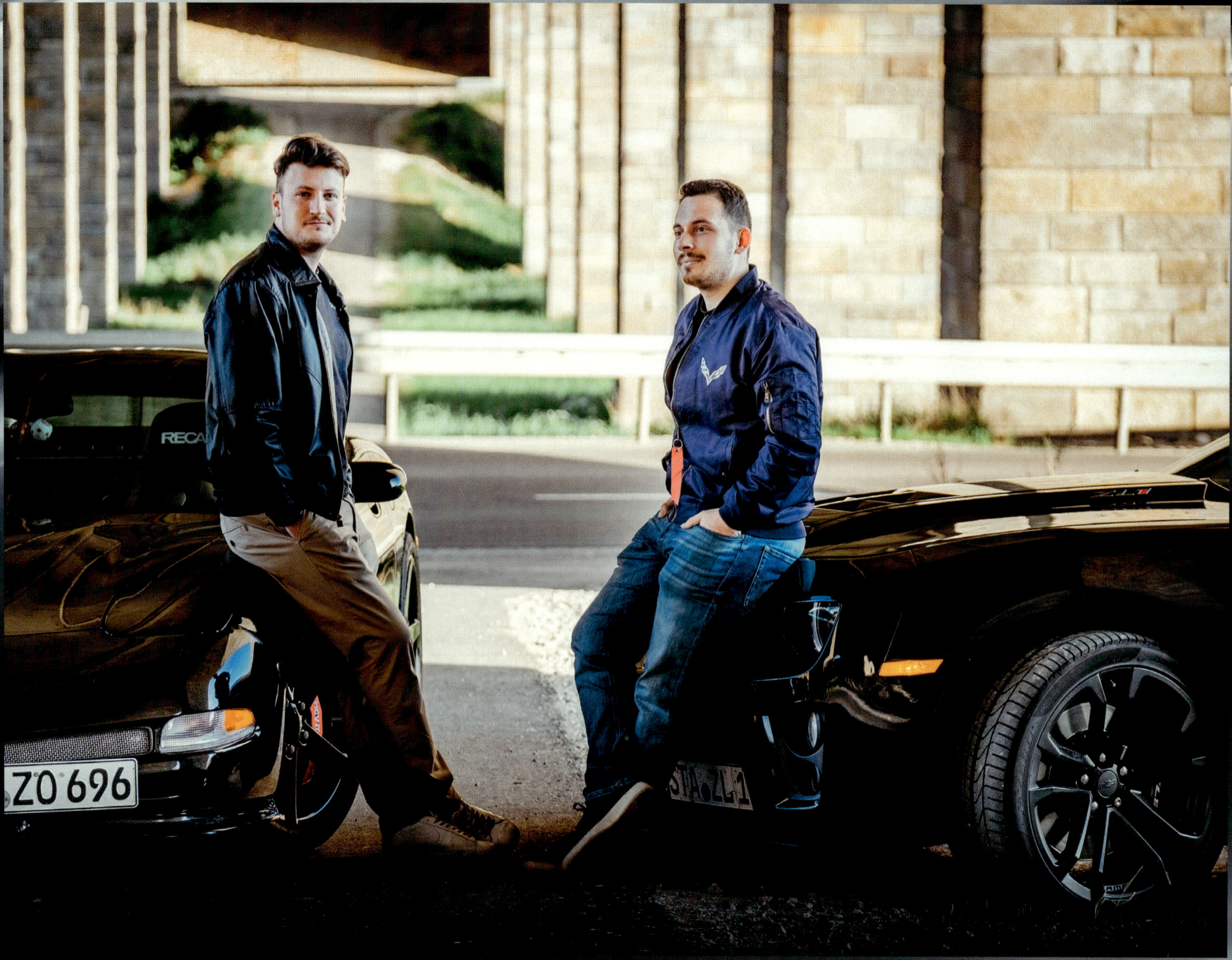
ZO 696

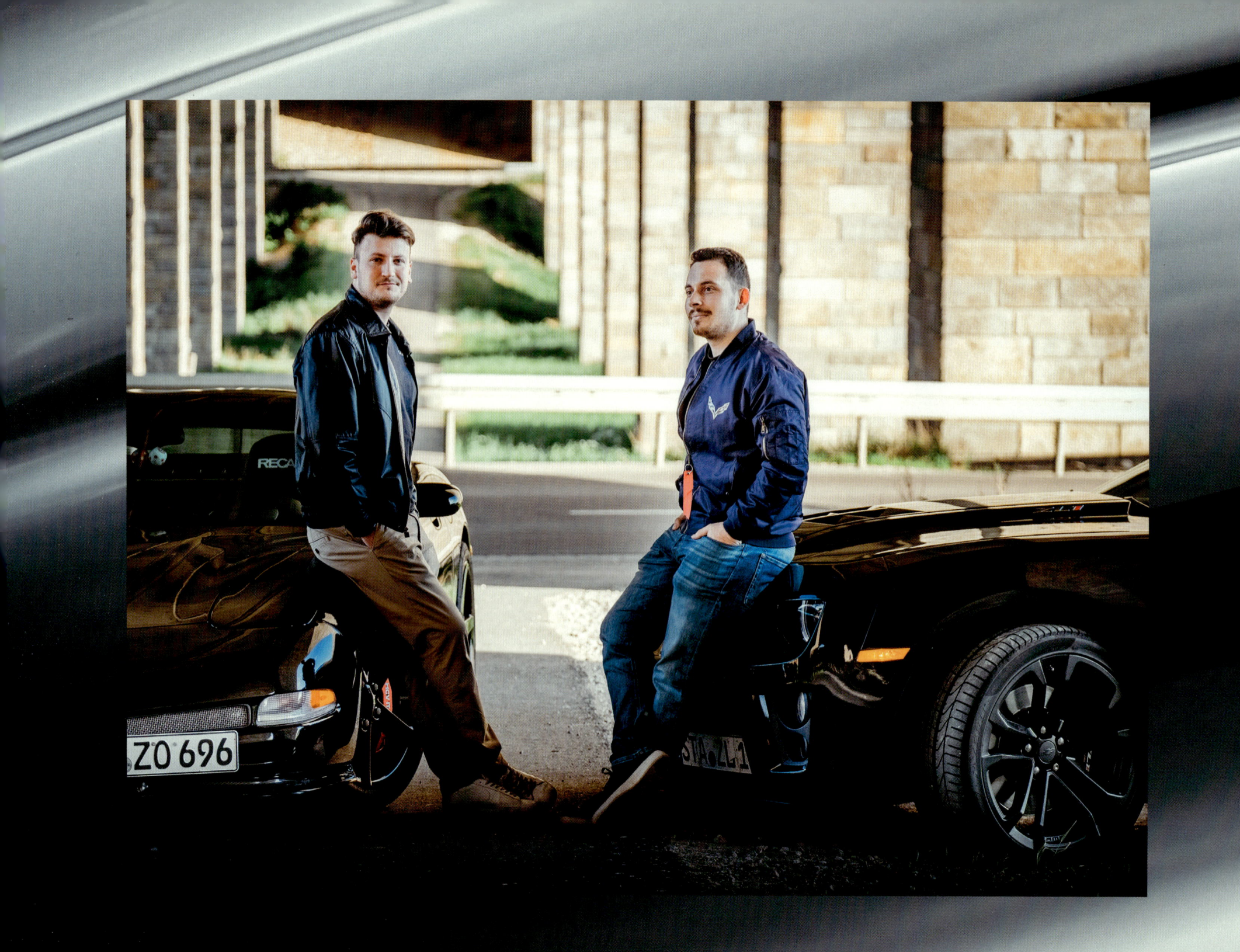

TO KILIAN, CORVETTE MEANS:
PERFORMANCE, LOVE, INDIVIDUALITY

Youth research. As you can see, the Corvette virus also infects young men who are still on the other side of 30. And if their own Corvette is being painted and is not available, they take out the spare car, a Camaro, to take part in meetings or outings.

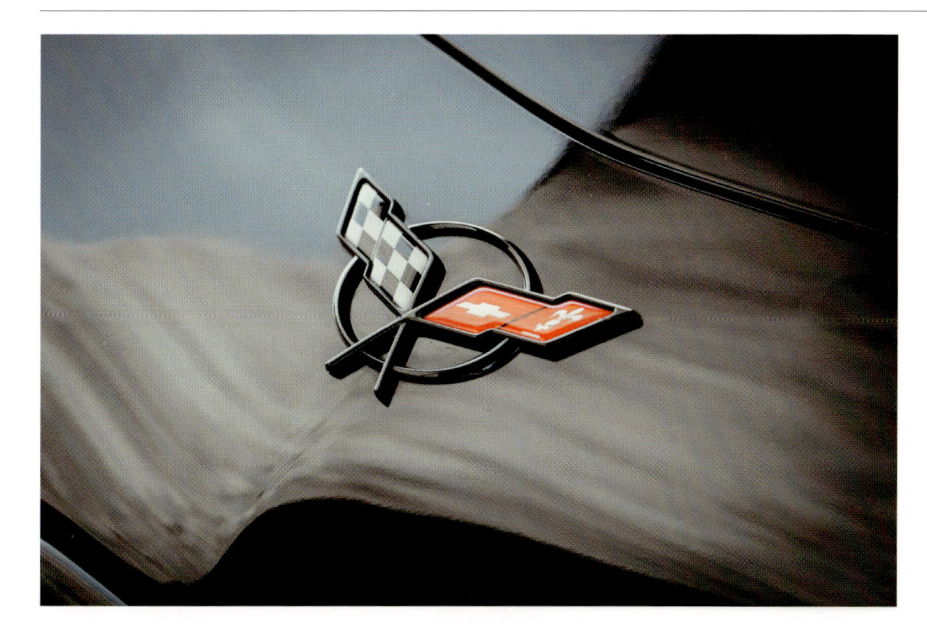

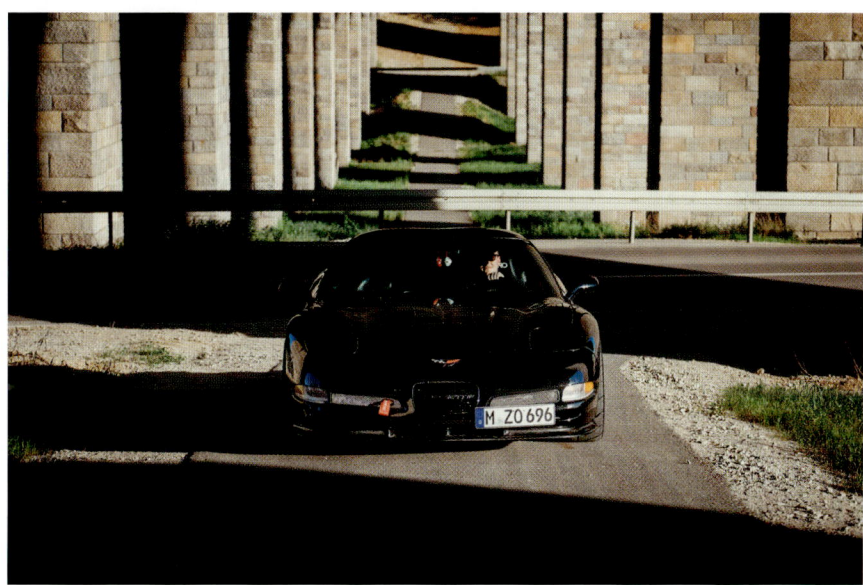

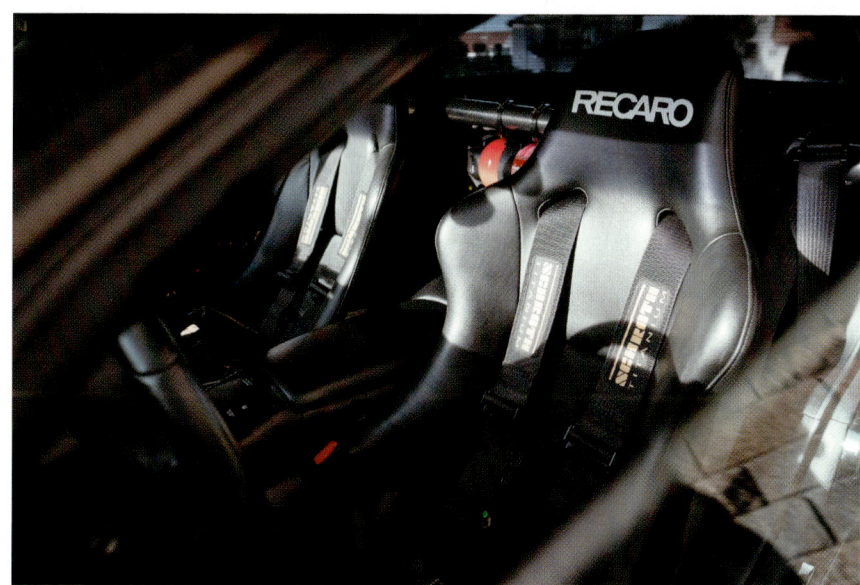

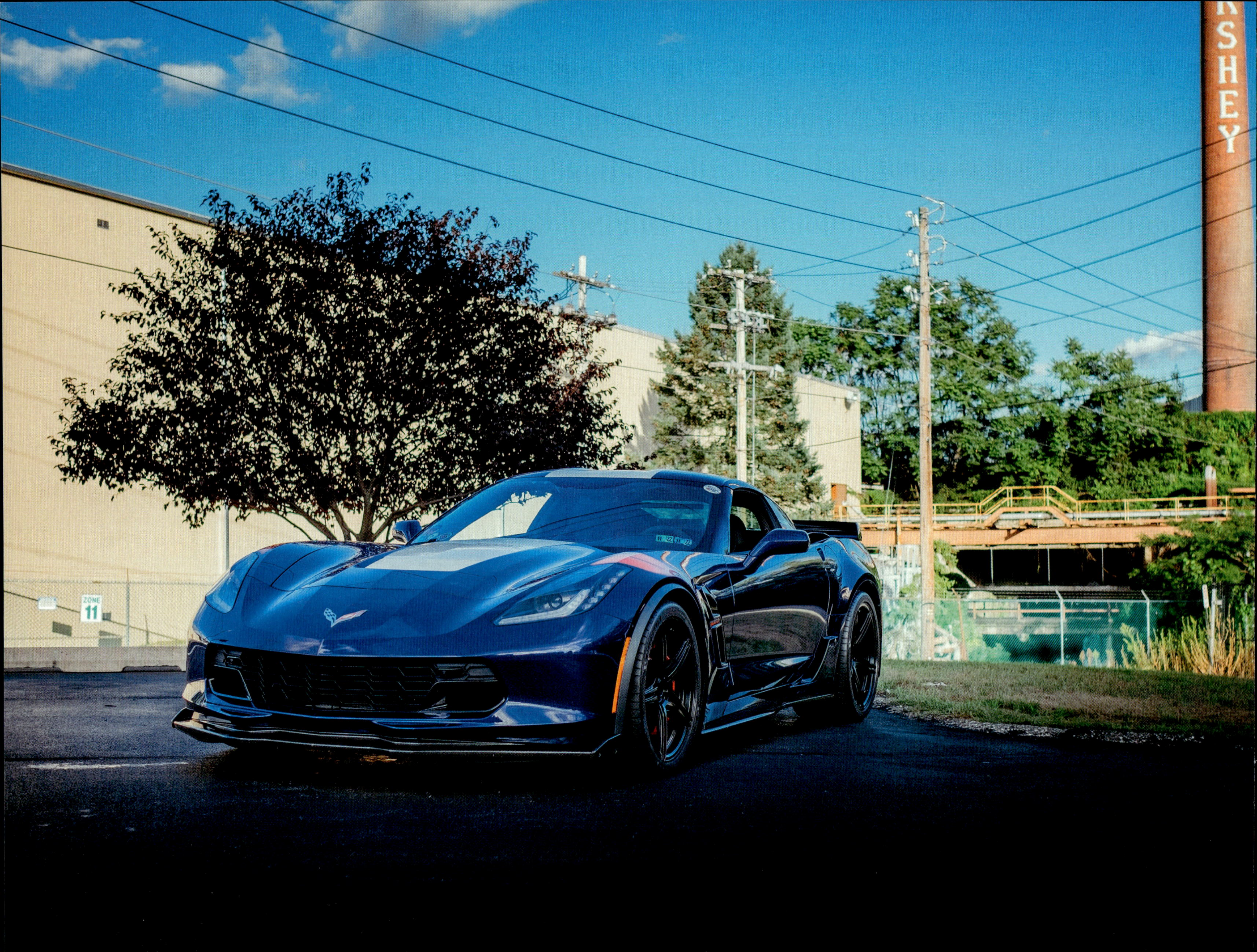
ZONE
11

MY ABSOLUTE FAVORITE PLACE

Some things just happen for a reason, including the meeting of David Allen Rodney and his C7.

What's your Corvette story?
Why Corvette? I would say car history. That began when I was a teenager, when everything with wheels and engines interested me. I had a subscription to *Road and Track*, read *Car and Driver* and *Motor Trend*, and on the pages of *Hemming Motor News*, I looked at the exotic vehicles that were for sale. I had fun learning more about cars. Of course, sports cars were my focus, but I had a general interest in the subject of automobiles.

The Corvette was always the only sports car from the US, and when the C4 came out, it looked different than everything else. I was excited, especially by the ZR-1. I remember in high school having an issue of *Road and Track* with me, and someone asked what I was reading. "An article about the Corvette ZR-1." I had to listen as people called it a grandpa car, but to me the ZR-1 was something special. I thought that this model made the Corvette into a world-class sports car. I didn't yet know if that was really true.

My enthusiasm for cars remained, but it changed over the years. I went to college and graduated as a civil engineer. I got married and we bought our first house. We had reached the point where one could acquire a car as a hobby—a vehicle one could tinker with and drive around on the weekend. My father-in-law was already a car lover; therefore, my wife liked the idea. I wanted to look for a C4 and began gathering information. I inhaled articles and blogs and made a checklist with all the important points for my purchase. Incidentally, I still have the list. I looked at about a dozen cars, until I realized that we didn't have a garage for the sports car. For the first time, I put the subject of a Corvette on ice.

A few years later, we moved into a new house with a garage. There was space that needed to be filled. I again began looking for something that would be fun. As by then we had a child, it was a sporty four-door, a 2008 Lexus IS350. It was a very small car with a big V6 and rear-wheel drive. It really was fun to drive and for the time being was a good substitute for a real sports car. When my son became older and no longer needed a car seat, I said to my wife that perhaps we could again look around for what we actually wanted: a two-seat sports car.

For some reason I didn't think of a Corvette straightaway. This time I wanted something rather exotic, one of the cars I had seen in magazines or on TV shows like *Magnum P.I.*, *Miami Vice*, *The A Team*, or *Nightrider*. Cars played a leading role in all these series.

And if I had to make a top ten list of my dream cars, probably five of them would have been Ferraris. I always liked the sports car from Modena: the Testarossa, the 308, and my absolute favorite, the 288 GTO. That was my absolute dream car. But I am a realist. The nearest Ferrari dealer is at least an hour away, and I also had the opportunity to sit in several Ferraris. Quite frankly, I didn't fit inside. I have no idea how Tom Selleck can sit in the 308, but I'm 5'11", and I can't do it. So my search went on, and the year was nearing its end. I had to completely rethink the idea several times and look at it from a different point of view. Somehow, I got no further. I firmly believed that some things happen for a specific reason and that there is a higher power. Therefore, perhaps I had just not found the right vehicle.

On a Saturday, I set off for my niece's to take a few things for her house. It was about an hour away. On the way there, I had to stop for gas and therefore took an earlier exit than planned. Then I took a different road to my niece's and on the way passed a car dealership that specialized in Corvettes. I saw all the used coupes and convertibles parked there and thought, "I have completely ignored the Corvette so far in my search. I'll stop on the way back and have a look."

On my way home, I stopped at the dealership. It had already closed, which was perfect for me. I was thus able to look at the cars in peace, without a salesman breathing down my neck. There were C5s, C6s, two C7 Corvettes, a Stingray, and a Z06. I had never taken a closer look at the C7 and had only seen them on the street now and then. Now I took plenty of time to examine the two C7s with their edgy design. The Z06 with its fender flares looked particularly aggressive, and I liked that look. I subsequently went home and immediately read about the C7 on the internet. There I discovered that the Grand Sport had come out in 2017. The plant was shut down early in 2018 to expand the paint shop. For this reason, there would be fewer 2018 models, and the dealers had therefore ordered more 2017 cars, which were now at the dealerships. There was therefore a large selection. At that time, one could go to a dealership with ten or twenty Corvettes on the lot, which one could take possession of immediately.

I had seen that there was a C7 Grand Sport in blue with white stripes and red hash marks on the fender. That immediately reminded me of the 1996 C4 Grand Sport. The C7 was precisely the car I wanted, and I immediately checked out all the dealerships within a radius of 180 miles for such a car. I found two coupes that weren't too far away. One was in Harrisburg and the other in Lancaster. I took an afternoon off. It was November and quite wintry, with sleet, freezing rain, and a little snow. I drove 45 minutes to the first dealership and bought the Corvette immediately. When the young salesman was taking my information, I said to him, "Today's not a very good day for a test drive, is it?" He looked at me and asked, "Have you ever driven a car like this?" My answer, "No, only a C4 years ago, but never a C7." He didn't want me to sign anything until I had driven one of these cars. I asked him if he was worried that I might not like the Corvette. "No, it's not that. I would just feel better if you drive it before you sign the contract." I took the car for a test drive the next weekend, and it was better than I had imagined.

Incidentally, the day I picked up the C7 was Veterans Day, very fitting for a Corvette in red, white, and blue. On the way home, I was surprised how many people gave us the thumbs up or waved. That still happens whenever I take the Corvette out.

With the C7 in my garage, I wanted to join a Corvette club, mainly to talk with other Corvette owners and learn even more about the sports car from Bowling Green. Our club, the Central PA Corvette Club, had its 50th anniversary in 2021. For some years, I have also held office in the club and was allowed to help organize the national event of the National Council of Corvette Clubs. The NCCC's slogan is "We joined for the car, we stay for the people." That's exactly how it was for me. I enjoy driving the car, but also getting together with the people from the club and sharing our passion. I am also a lifetime member of the Corvette Museum. The Corvette is not just any car; there is a lot of passion involved. When I climb into my C7, I feel that it was made for me. Definitely my favorite place to be.

What is your all-time favorite Corvette model?
That is a close race between the C7 and the C3. I see a lot of the old C3 Corvette in my C7. The lines of the fenders and the hood; there are several features both models have in common. If I were to get a second Corvette, it would definitely be a C3.

◂ 2017 Corvette C7, **Hershey**, Pennsylvania, USA | September 8, 2022

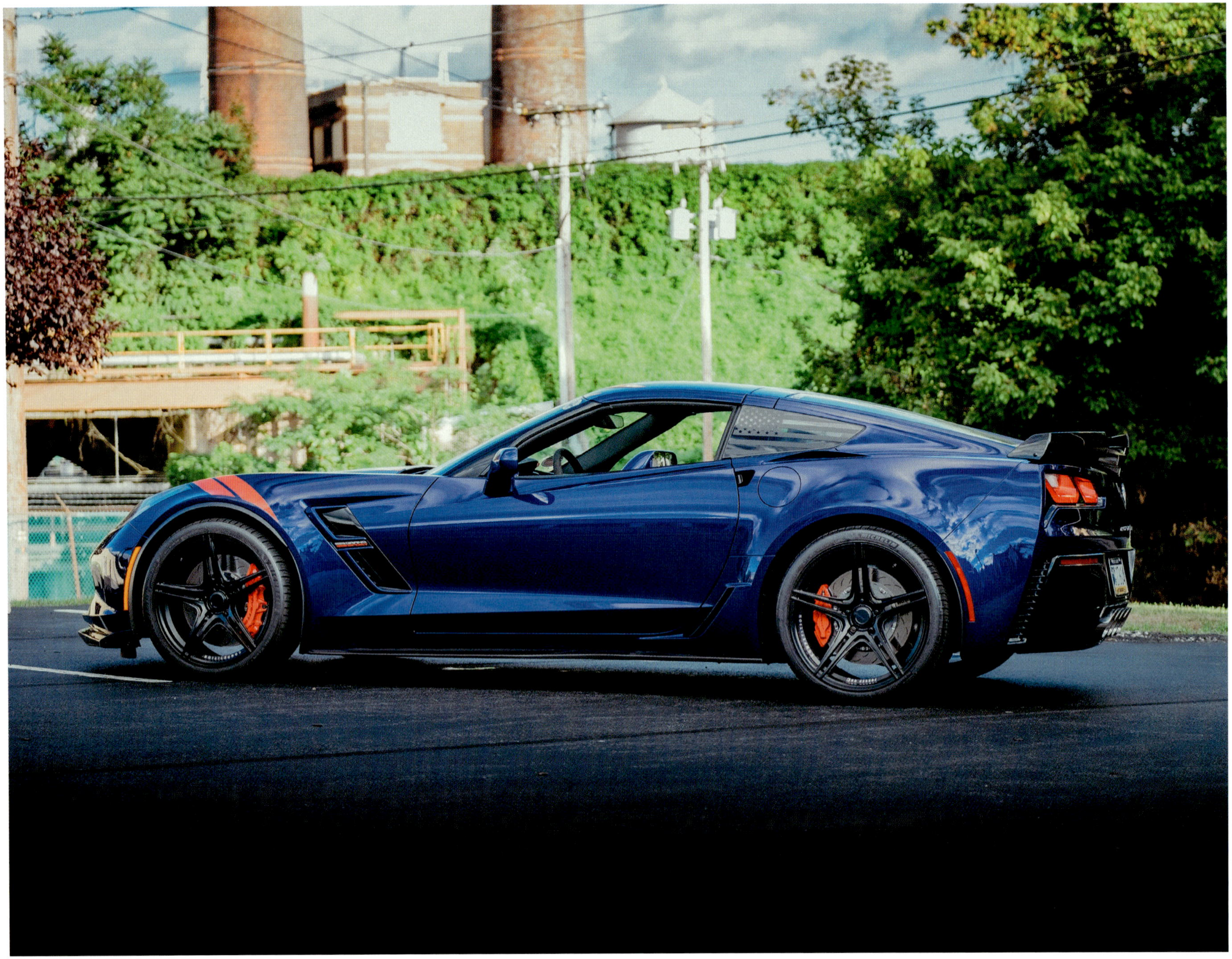

TO DAVE, CORVETTE MEANS:
HISTORIC, PASSION, PEOPLE

Chance acquaintance. David Allen Rodney has been a car fan since childhood. But for a long time, he didn't have the Corvette in particular on his radar—until he came into contact with the C7. The Grand Sport sparked a passion that continues to this day.

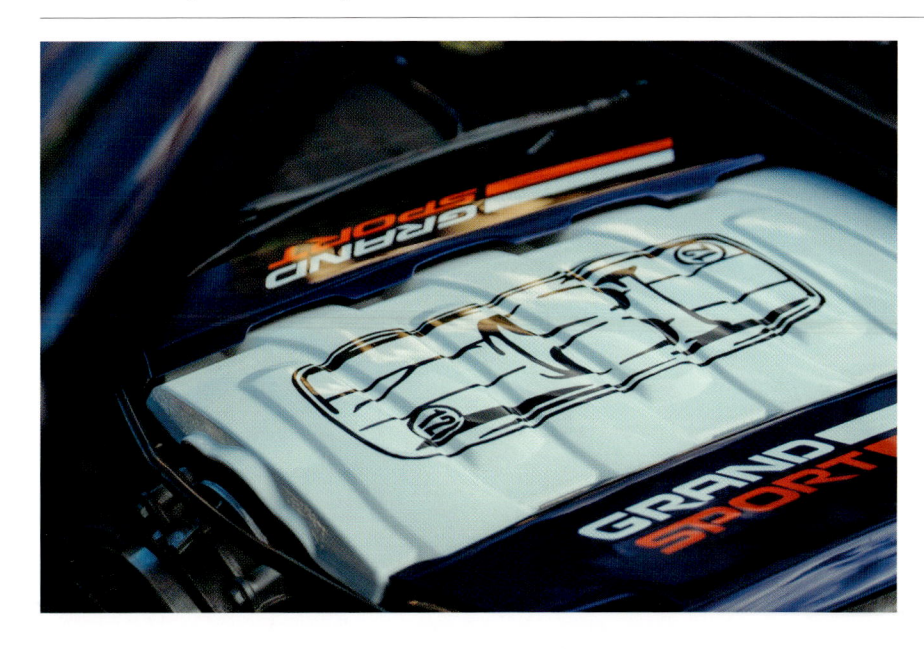

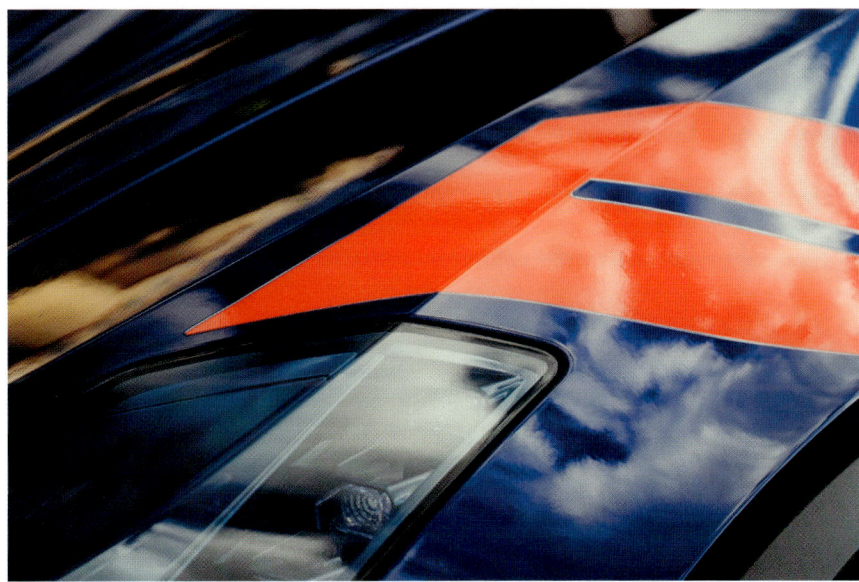

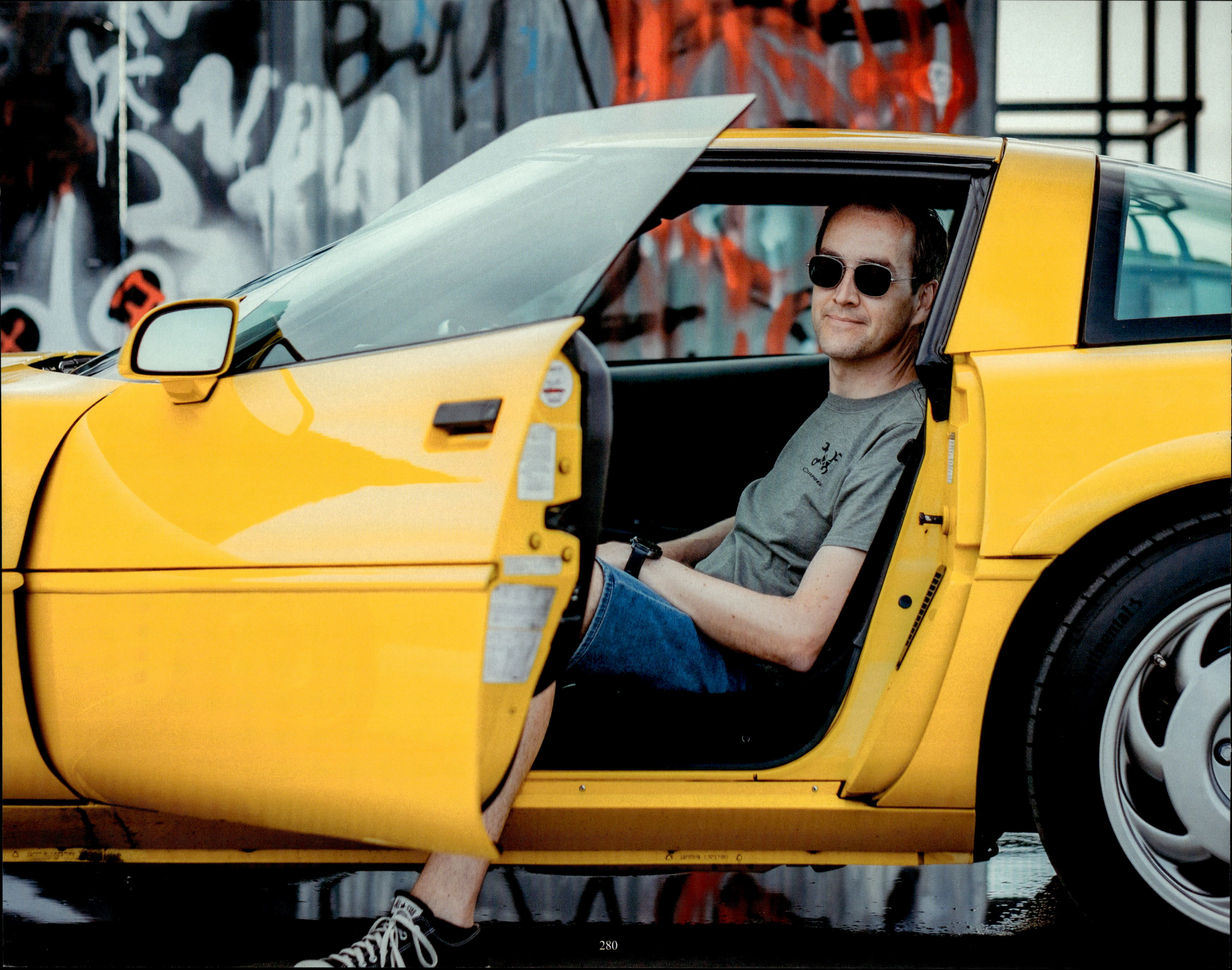

I DON'T CARE FOR A YELLOW PORSCHE

Even some Corvette fans don't know that there was in fact also an export version of the C4. The one shown here is one of a maximum of 150 units made for Europe in 1994. And perhaps the only yellow one.

What's your Corvette story?
It all began in 1966, when I made my first trip to the US. At that time, the Corvette wasn't even on my radar. I was traveling in Florida and saw them driving on the streets and thought to myself, "Wow, cool, what cars!" And since this vacation, it was clear to me that I wanted one. At that time in America, there was a small advertising booklet called *Corvette & Chevy Trader*, which I regularly had sent to me in Germany so that I could see what was for sale. For the first two years after my trip, my efforts here and in the US were fruitless.

I finally found one in Germany more or less right around the corner. I liked the yellow color, too, but the car didn't have a manual transmission. I didn't want an automatic. Despite that, I looked at the Corvette, which was owned by a tattoo artist, nicely covered in a garage. When he pulled the cover off the car, it looked like new. It was a 1994 model but had not been registered until 1995. The seller was the original owner, and he was selling it so that he could buy a C5. That was lucky for me. My search had come to an end. The Corvette looked cool, sounded cool, just the car I wanted. Two days later, I drove it to Switzerland to attend Europe's biggest Corvette meet, Super Corvette Sunday. On this first trip, I was forced to realize that my coupe felt more like an old Cadillac than a sports car. I subsequently optimized the suspension for German conditions, with better shocks and different stabilizers.

I also did not know prior to my purchase that my C4 was a rare EU export model. At first, all C5s looked the same to me. Optically, the 1994 Corvette also differed in that it had fender flares. They took some getting used to, but now I think they look classy. In 1996, GM also installed the rear flares on the Grand Sport coupes, because they had the wider ZR-1 rims.

Other differences included, for example, the lights. The running lights functioned as parking lights, and blinkers were mounted on the sides behind the front wheels. There were also different outside mirrors and a modified rear end. This resulted in space for larger labels, and the taillights were redesigned. If you look in the "black book," you will find that there were 830 yellow Corvette C4s made in 1994. Of the total of 23,330 examples built that year, 100 or 150 were export models. I don't know how many of them were yellow, probably just a few. In all the years I've had the Corvette, I haven't seen many more export models and to date no yellow ones.

Over the years, I have optimized the car a little, nothing extreme. In addition to the suspension, I have, for example, installed different brakes. The car drives well, but the standard brakes weren't good enough for me. Now you can brake from 150 mph several times without problems. I also mounted ZR-1 wheels. Because of the European model's previously mentioned fender flares, the standard light metal rims look rather too narrow on the car. The C4 now simply looks more harmonious.

In the past years, I have unfortunately not driven as much as before, last year just 720 miles. But I enjoyed each and every mile.

There is, by the way, a funny story about the yellow, a color that is not to everyone's taste. Once I was driving with my former girlfriend, now my wife, and in front of us was a yellow Porsche 911. At that time, she didn't know that I owned a yellow Corvette. And she simply said, "Wow, a yellow Porsche; I don't care for that." My answer, "Yes, I don't care for a yellow Porsche either." A few days later, I drove up with my Corvette; she looked a bit funny but thought the color looked cool on the C4. We have now been married for several years, and recently we saw another yellow Porsche. Remembering our past experience, we had to laugh.

On my first trip to Switzerland, I got to know the Swiss Corvette Club, joined the S.C.C.I., and was a member for ten years. There were different events each year; we went on outings, visited events, and rented racetracks. That was real fun. My car is much too good for full-throttle competition, but I have allowed myself a few regularity runs on one or other racetrack. At year's end, we always rent the Hockenheimring for the Corvette and Viper Shootout, also called the Corvette Euromeet. That was really a great event. At some point, however, the distance to Switzerland became too much for me and I dropped out, but it was a super time that I'll never forget.

I am now with the B.W.I.C.C. It is not a real club; rather, a loose association here in Baden-Württemberg. We get together more or less regularly and have fun with our Corvettes. No obligation, no executive; there is only a What's App group. The whole thing was created and sustained by the American soldiers who are stationed here. There was once a club in Kaiserslautern. I got in through them and found out that they are also often on the road in Heidelberg. There are still some Americans in the group, and only recently a few new ones joined. I have met so many new people and made so many friendships by way of the Corvette and the hobby, countless. Previously, I had never thought that possible, and I still like the Corvette community.

What's your all-time favorite Corvette model?
That's a tricky question. I find the C2 very beautiful, and of course the C4. But I also like the C6 and C7 very much. If I had to choose one, it would probably be the last year of the C7, the Grand Sport or the Z06.

◀ **1994** Corvette C4, **Ludwigsburg**, Baden-Wüttemberg, **Germany** | May 21, 2022

TO BERND, CORVETTE MEANS:
JOIE DE VIVRE, STYLE, DIFFERENT

Different from the others. Many small details distinguish the EU export variant of the C4 from its American siblings. Obvious differences are the fender flares, the side turn signals, the missing side markers, and the modified rear end design.

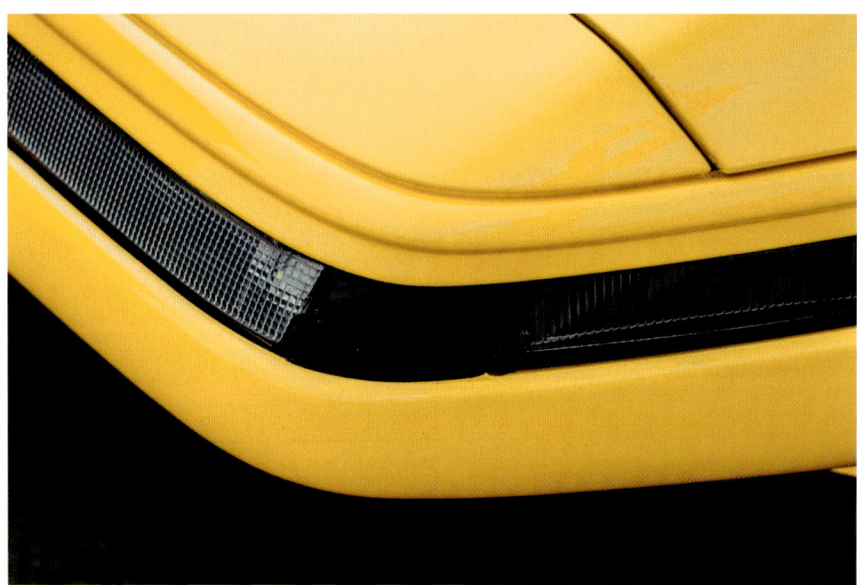

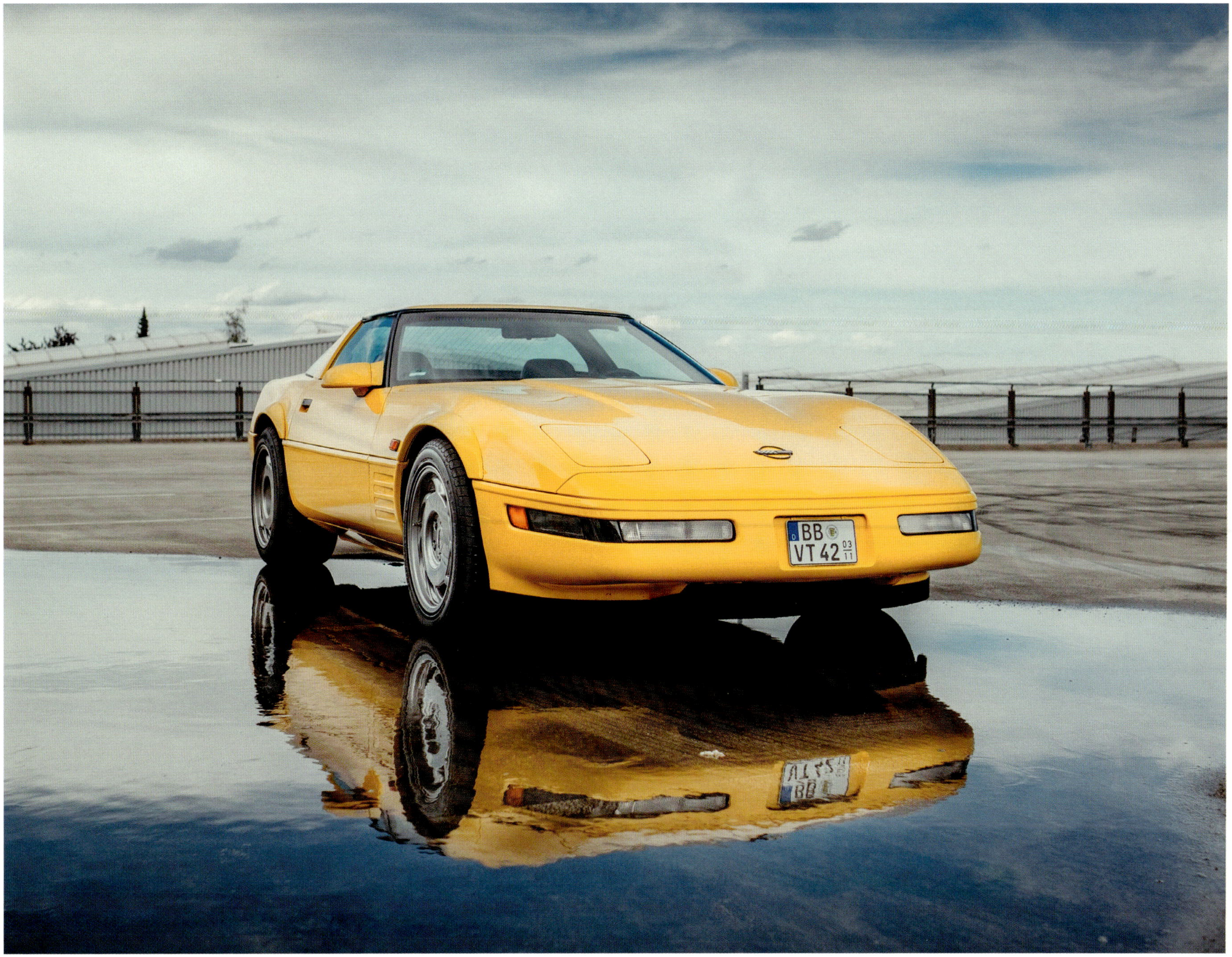
BB
VT 42

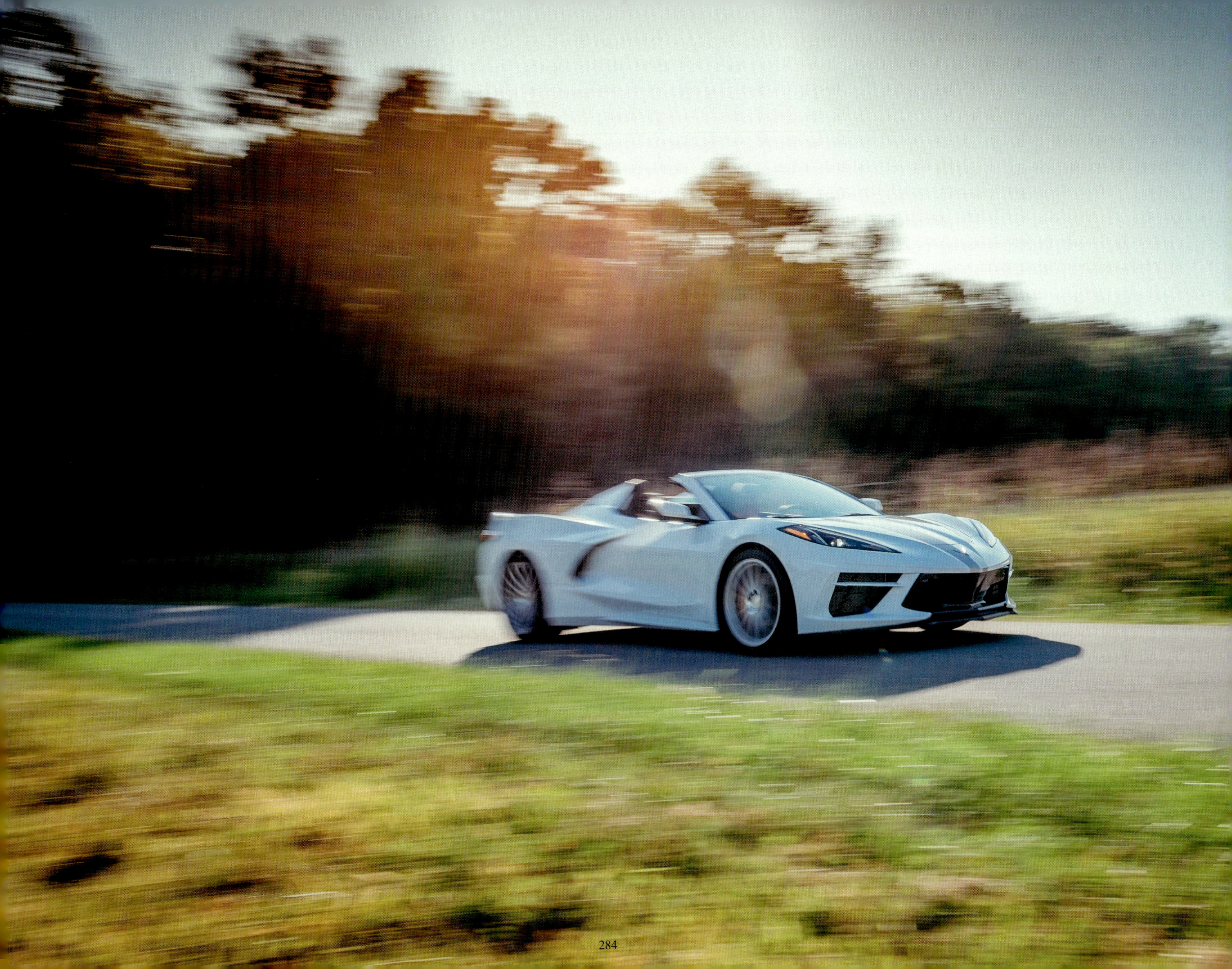

PLEASE, NOT A BLACK CORVETTE

Garry Luterek is a race driver and engineer. His passion for the Corvette began in the 1970s. Fifty years later, he is still enthralled by it.

What's your Corvette story?
I was a "gear head" in high school and mesmerized by cars and their technology. I had two friends in school who were equally enthusiastic about cars, one of whom became a master mechanic, the other a mechanical engineer, and I an engineer. One of them was always tinkering with his car, and I usually helped. In this way, I learned a lot about bodywork and painting. To us, the Corvette was simply the coolest. We couldn't afford one, unless we bought one that wasn't running or was in parts in someone's garage. We repaired such cars or put them together to sell them at a profit. Yes, that's how it was in the 1970s.

In junior college, I saved all my money so that I could finally buy a Corvette. I found a 1976 orange-colored C3. It was then two years old and was sitting on a dealer's lot. My friend and I looked at the car, and we were very impressed. I of course bought the car. I was twenty-one years old and for the first time owned a Corvette of my own.

After graduation, I got a job with John Deere in Iowa. That meant that I had to move. The Corvette was less than ideally suited for that. I therefore got an old, beat-up pickup truck. I packed it full of my things, and a friend drove my Corvette, and we set off from Buffalo to Iowa. At that time, I thought it was time for something new.

When it came to cars, I liked the old ones, and the C4 wasn't my thing. When the C5 came out, I was impressed by its advanced technology, but I believe that you should never buy the newest model of anything because of the inevitable teething troubles. I waited a few years before I switched to a C5 coupe, a 1999. A colleague also bought a C5, and we now had identical vehicles.

As I was already taking part in smaller rallies and autocross events, I wanted to get him interested too. He just said, "I don't think my car is fast enough for that." I looked at him uncomprehendingly. "You have the same Corvette as I do; what's wrong with it?" We therefore compared cars, started at about 5 mph, and at a given signal, stepped on the gas. Each time, he pulled away from me. The cars were identical, with the same engine, same year, and so on, but his was simply faster than mine. That wasn't what we had expected. And so I called the dealer and told him what had happened, and gave him my car's chassis number. We went back and forth for about six months, until they finally suggested that I buy a new 2000 Corvette and they would only charge me the difference compared to the new price of the C5. I could enter into the deal with peace of mind.

Then the new Z06 came on the market. I immediately knew that with my experience on the racetrack, it would be the perfect car for me. I went to a dealer in Illinois who had several of them sitting on his lot. All I had to do was pick a color, and then I could take one with me. I chose black. It looks really good, but it is frightfully care-intensive. I am really meticulous with my cars, and despite this, the Z06 very quickly looked dirty. I kept getting upset about it until at one point my wife said, "If you're going to be upset all the time, sell the thing." No sooner said than done.

When the C6 was introduced, I bought myself a silver one. The dirt didn't show as quickly. By the way, the 2005 Corvette had a really funny steering wheel. It had four spokes, and you could only put your hands in certain places. In 2006, there was a new and better version. I decided on that year. The Z06 arrived a year later, and everyone in the club said that it was just the car that I should have. Its seven-liter engine produced 505 hp. If one came out of a curve and applied full throttle, the crate oversteered like crazy. As a result of my experience, however, I knew what to expect and how to control the car. Otherwise, it would have been a very dangerous vehicle.

I had the Z06 until I bought a used ZR1 in 2011. The car had about 1,500 miles on the odometer, and I of course also took it on the racetrack. One weekend, I drove it on the Road America circular course in Elkhart Lake, Wisconsin. Once, in a curve the brakes didn't do what I expected; no idea why. I was driving too fast in the curve, 168 mph, and ended up in the stack of tires. The Corvette Racing Team was also on the track that weekend, and several team members signed a few pieces from the body of my wrecked Corvette. They included Jan Magnusson and Oliver Gavin, really nice boys.

The next Corvette on my list was a 2015 C7. It was Laguna Blue with silver stripes. It was a great car, and I still miss it. I had that C7 until the ZR1 was unveiled. I was back on the racetrack with it; after all, it was made to drive. You can also drive the Corvette in the rain, for after all, it isn't made of sugar! Then I got rid of the ZR1, because I thought that I would get the new C8 Z06 long before the year 2022. Today I feel some regret for having sold the car. With the Sebring Orange Design Package, the C7 ZR1 was simply perfect. It had just one disadvantage: with the large rear spoiler you can only load the trunk from the side.

I had to wait a really long time for the current Z06. After a year and a half, I wasn't really certain that it would ever come on the market. I therefore bought myself a C8 Stingray. My wife, Mary, and I had only had one convertible in our lives, a 2002 Camaro SS. We only had it for six months. With the soft top, it was simply too loud. We moved to Bowling Green, and I got a job in the Corvette factory and was part of the introduction of the C8. I saw all the new model colors and thought that a light paint would show off the shapes of the C8 much better. To my wife and me, the color of a car is a very important feature. We thought it over for a long time and finally decided on Arctic White. A small homage to the first Corvette from the year 1953, but with silver racing stripes.

Then we were at a Barrett Jackson auction, and Mary left me alone—a dangerous thing to do. She had actually promised me that she wouldn't do that. Then a 1968 big block Corvette came up, and I raised my hand. Before I knew it, the car belonged to me. A beautiful car that didn't need much work. Everyone loved the car whenever they drove it, but of course, its handling bore no comparison to that of the C8. Well, in the long run, two Corvettes were too much work for us, which is why we sold the C3.

What is your all-time favorite Corvette model?
My heart is attached to a silver '63 split-window coupe with red interior. I have hundreds of pictures of a Corvette like that. I love them. But I wouldn't buy one. More modern Corvettes are much more fun. I'm an engineer and I like to drive on racetracks. If you take that into account, you automatically end up with the latest Corvette with the best technology and the highest performance. I love the C8, but still miss my last ZR1. I was in engine development at John Deere, and when I heard about the new Z06 engine, I was immediately hooked. I wanted that engine! That's why the C8 Z06 is my absolute favorite

◀ 2022 Corvette C8, Oakland, Kentucky, USA | September 18, 2022

TO GARRY, CORVETTE MEANS:
FRIENDSHIP, RACING SPORT, ENGINEERING ART

Fact check. Garry Luterek worked as an engineer in engine development at John Deere. As a man of his trade, he was completely blown away when he heard about the C8's new LT2 powerplant. At that moment, he knew he had to have one of the new mid-engine Corvettes.

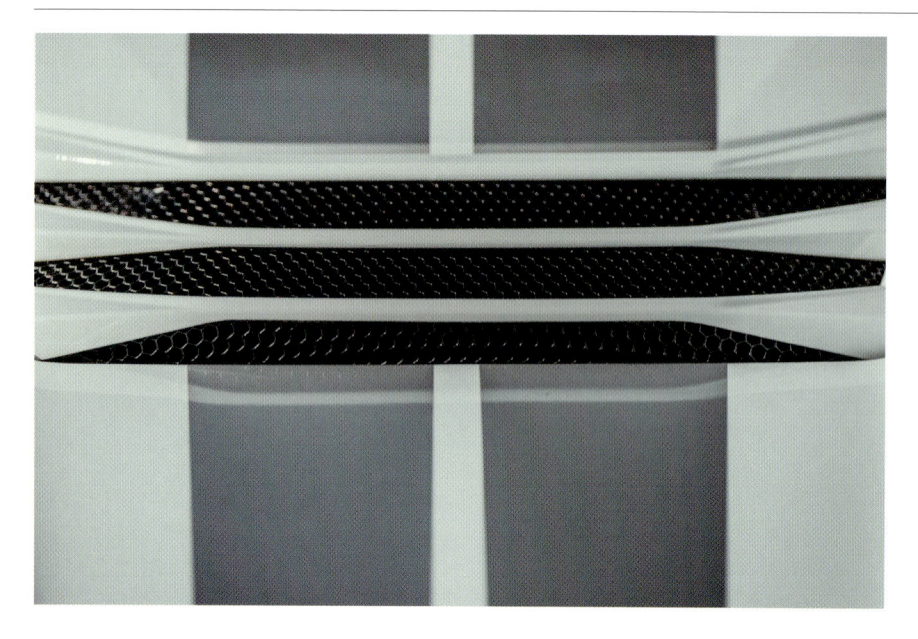

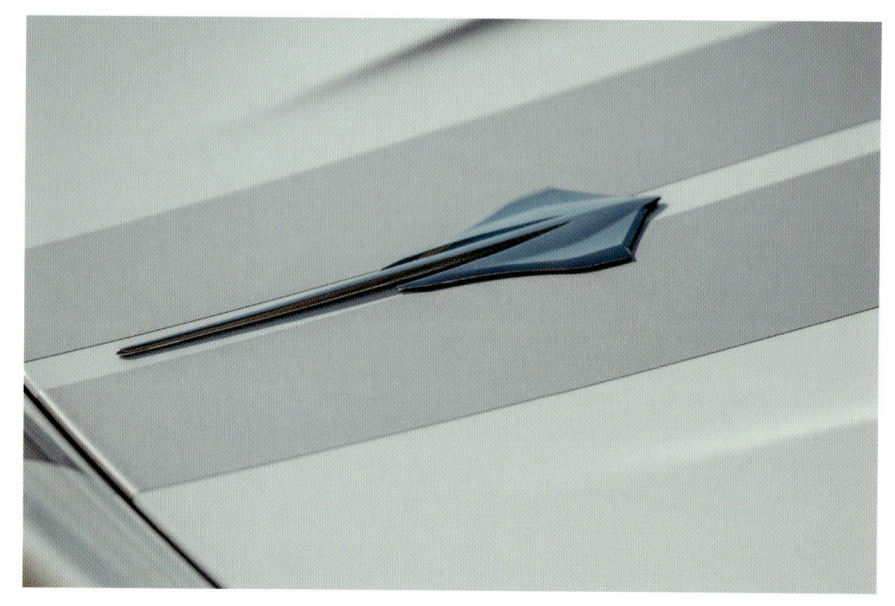

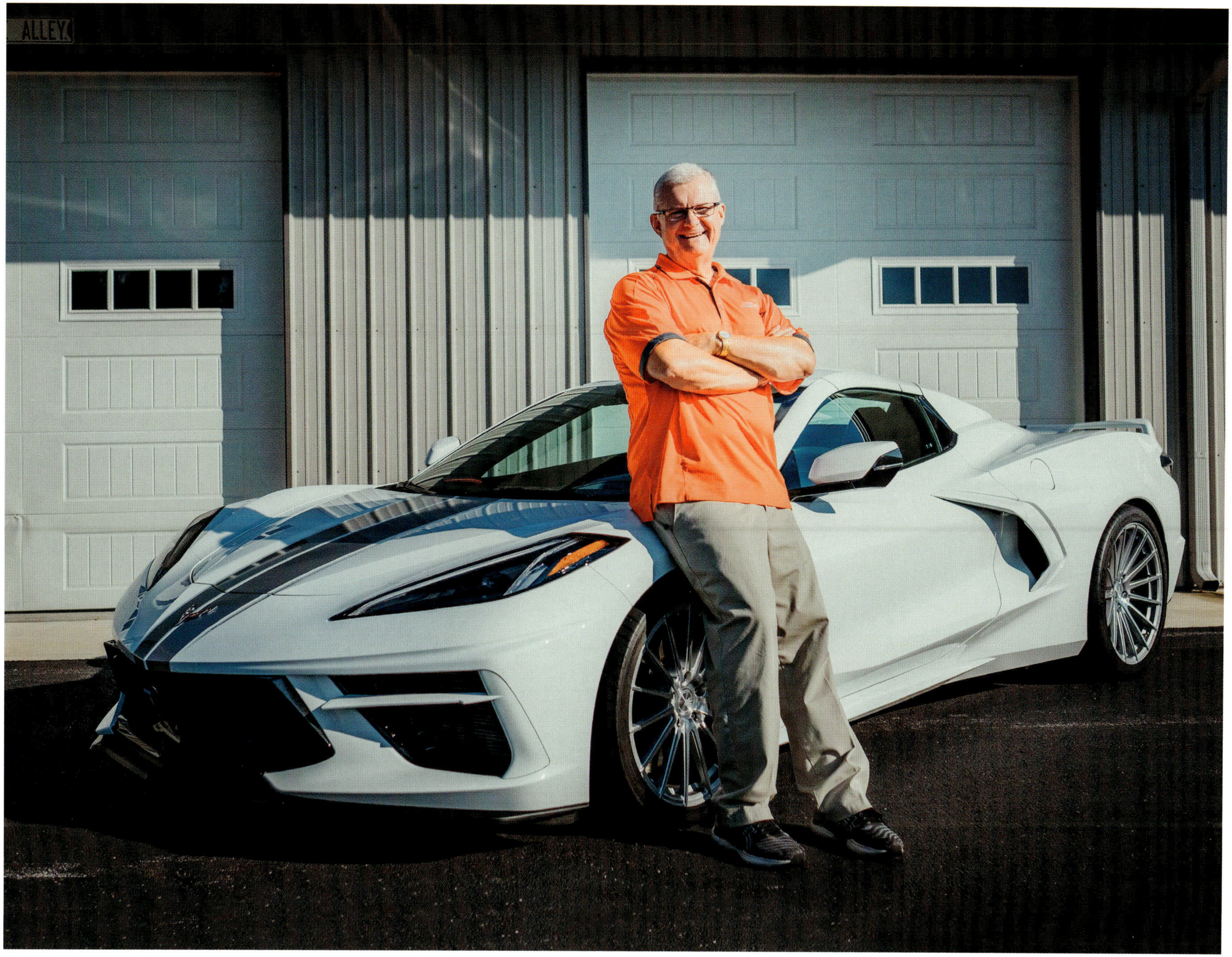
ALLEY

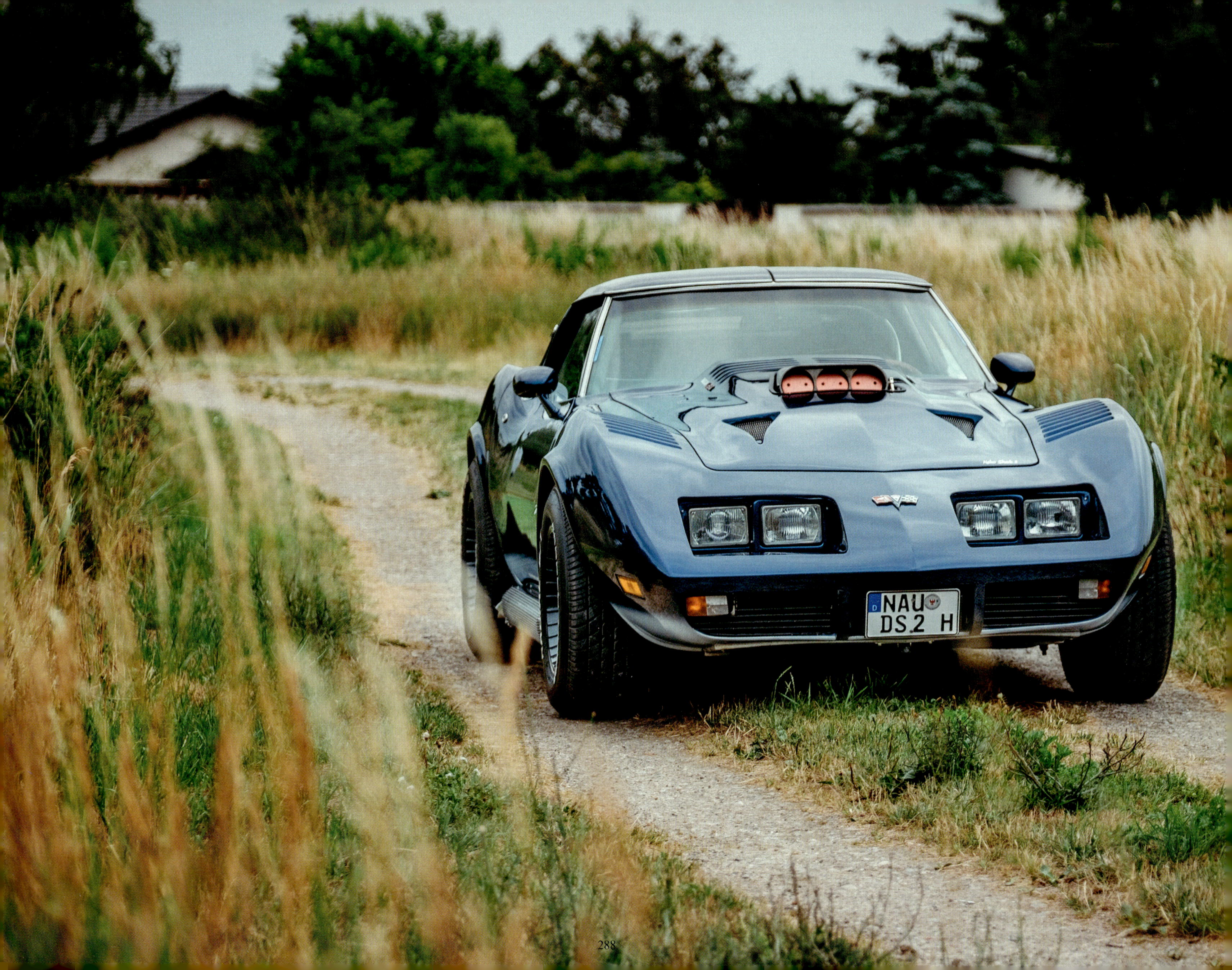
NAU
DS 2 H

THE SHARK HAS A V8

Tino Desens loves the Corvette, and he loves sharks. No wonder, then, that when he saw the Half Mako Shark II, he knew that the car was meant for him.

What's your Corvette story?
I came to the Corvette by way of the television series *Stingray*. The car in the series simply blew me away. All black, with that shape and the rims, magnificent. I decided that someday I would own a car like that. When I looked at the subject more closely, I quickly realized that one would have to pay a lot of money for a Corvette C2. And I didn't have it. That was the end of the idea for me for the next few decades.

That I nevertheless found a Corvette was in fact fate. I was still a fan of the Corvette, but also a lover of sharks. I had long had a soft spot for both. I was also involved in DB radio, and my radio call sign was of course Corvette.

Five years ago, I again began looking for a C2 on the net, watching how the price was developing. I also looked at C3 Corvettes, and I also found it very stylish. Then I stumbled upon a picture in an advertisement in which a mad rear end could be seen and below it the words "Half Mako Shark II." I just thought: "What is that? It looks unbelievable!" I had to immediately research further. I wanted to learn more about the car, but I couldn't find much. After twenty-five years of passion for the Corvette, I had never heard of the Mako Shark concept. It was a Corvette combined with a shark. That did it for me! Fate wanted me to stumble upon this car. Unfortunately, the ad disappeared again very quickly, as I had been too slow. As I then discovered, there were some conversion kits to change a normal Corvette into a Mako Shark. All right, I needed that. Luckily the advertisement for the Corvette in question appeared again, and I immediately pulled out all the stops to land her.

The car had several previous owners and had been used almost exclusively as an advertising medium and show car and consequently had been driven very little. Each owner had made improvements to the car to bring it closer to the original concept car. When the car was originally converted, it was all blue, but too light to be an accurate replica. The conversion took place between 1990 and 1992, and hidden beneath it was a '73 Corvette. When the C3 belonged to me, I contacted the original maker of the car. The gentleman was able to tell me about the car in detail, about the special intake manifold and the tires, for example. Due to its limited use, they were still on the car, since 1992! The engine was a 350, which according to the owner was supposed to be capable of 300 hp. He also installed the sequential 5-speed transmission. In total, he had probably invested about 200,000 marks in it, and everything had been very elaborately done. The man who owned the car in 2020 then had it painted in the Mako Shark design. The last owner applied the sharks on the fenders and the stickers on the sides. I replaced the light switch with a small shark.

I shared my Corvette on Instagram, simply to show people that there was such a Corvette and that there had been this unbelievable concept car in the Sixties. I am pleased that my conversion is not simply a fine-tuning job, but is based on the original Mako Shark II, which then became the C3. It is fascinating that the Mako Shark II, which had unleashed so much hype, was dismantled by GM and became unrecognizable as the Manta Ray.

Because so many people liked the Mako Shark, John Silva designed and sold conversion kits for the C3. According to my research, it is one of these kits, of which there were probably 125 examples. Other manufacturers also appear to have offered conversion kits, but few of them still exist. I know of five conversions in Germany, one in Norway, several in the USA, and of course Hanspeter Böhi's in Switzerland. To me the car is the realization of a dream, and driving it is indescribable.

What is your all-time favorite Corvette model?
If money were no object, then the C2. A black '65, to go with my Mako Shark.

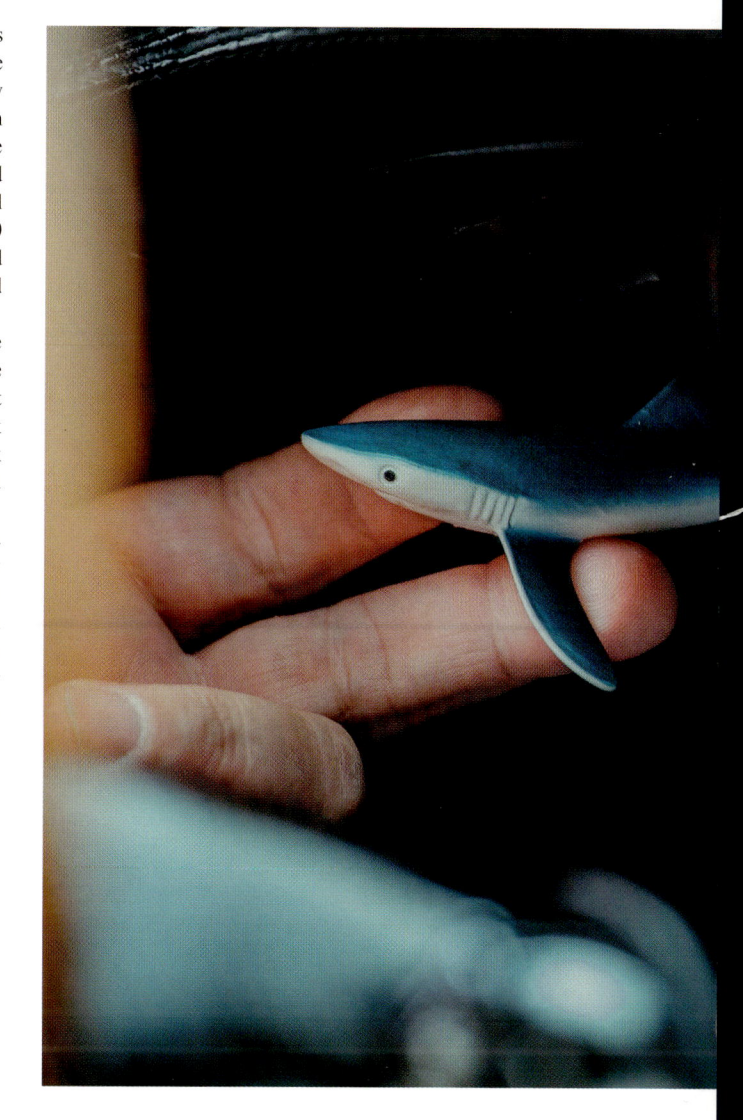

◀ **1973** Corvette C3, **Nauen**, Brandenburg, **Germany** | July 8, 2022

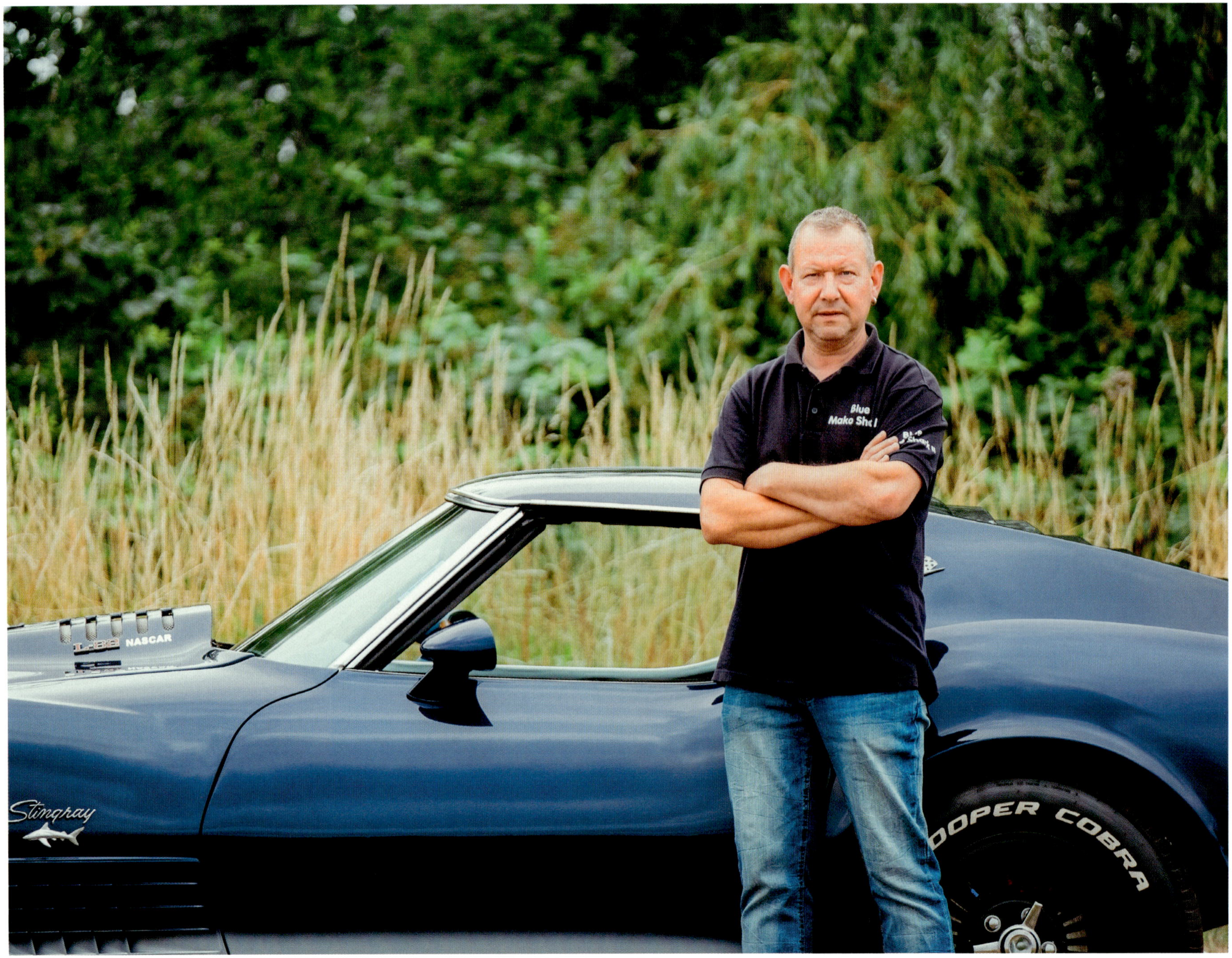
Blue
NASCAR
Stingray
OOPER COBRA

TO TINO, CORVETTE MEANS:
DESIGN, SOUND, DRIVING FUN

Deep blue sea. The Mako Shark was a concept car from 1965 that anticipated the shape of the C3. The design caused so much excitement that after the appearance of the third generation of the Corvette, several companies offered conversion sets. It is very likely that the kit used on this car was from John Silva.

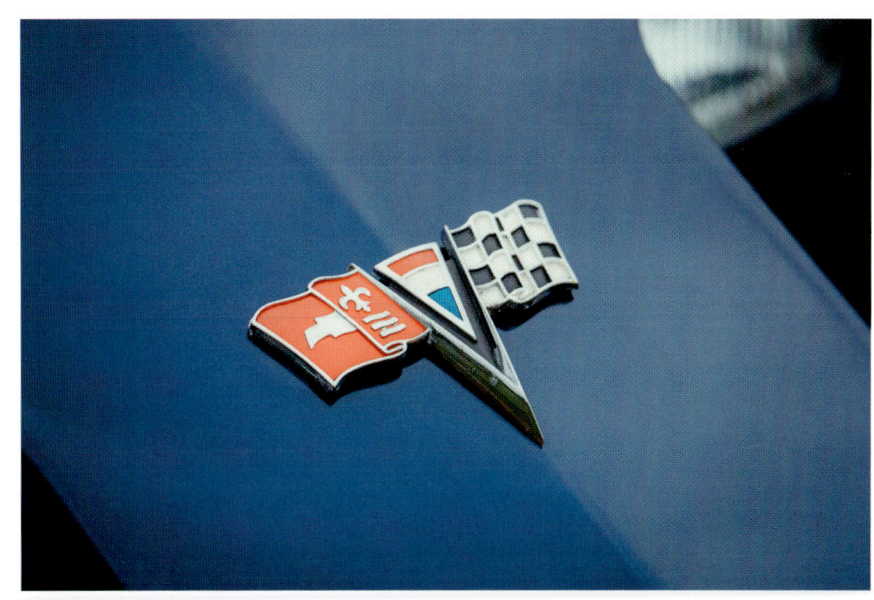

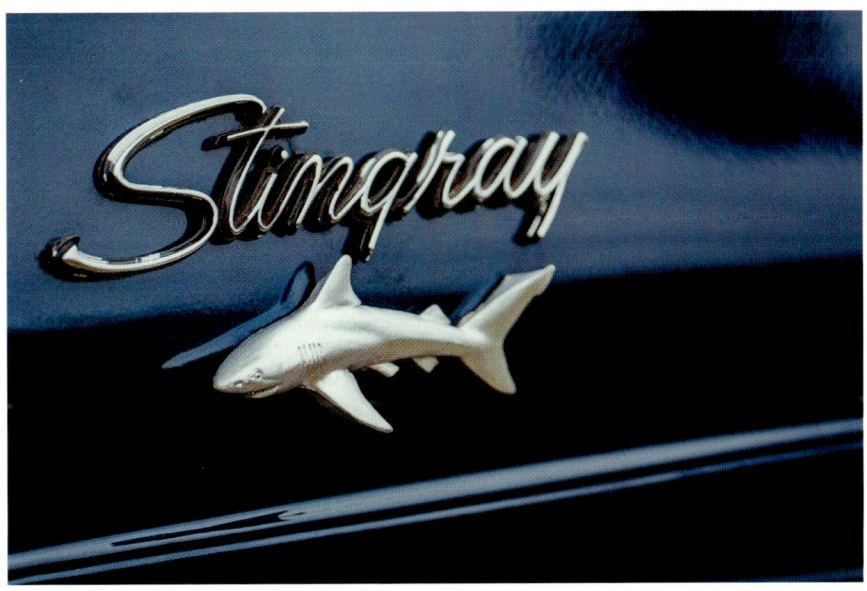

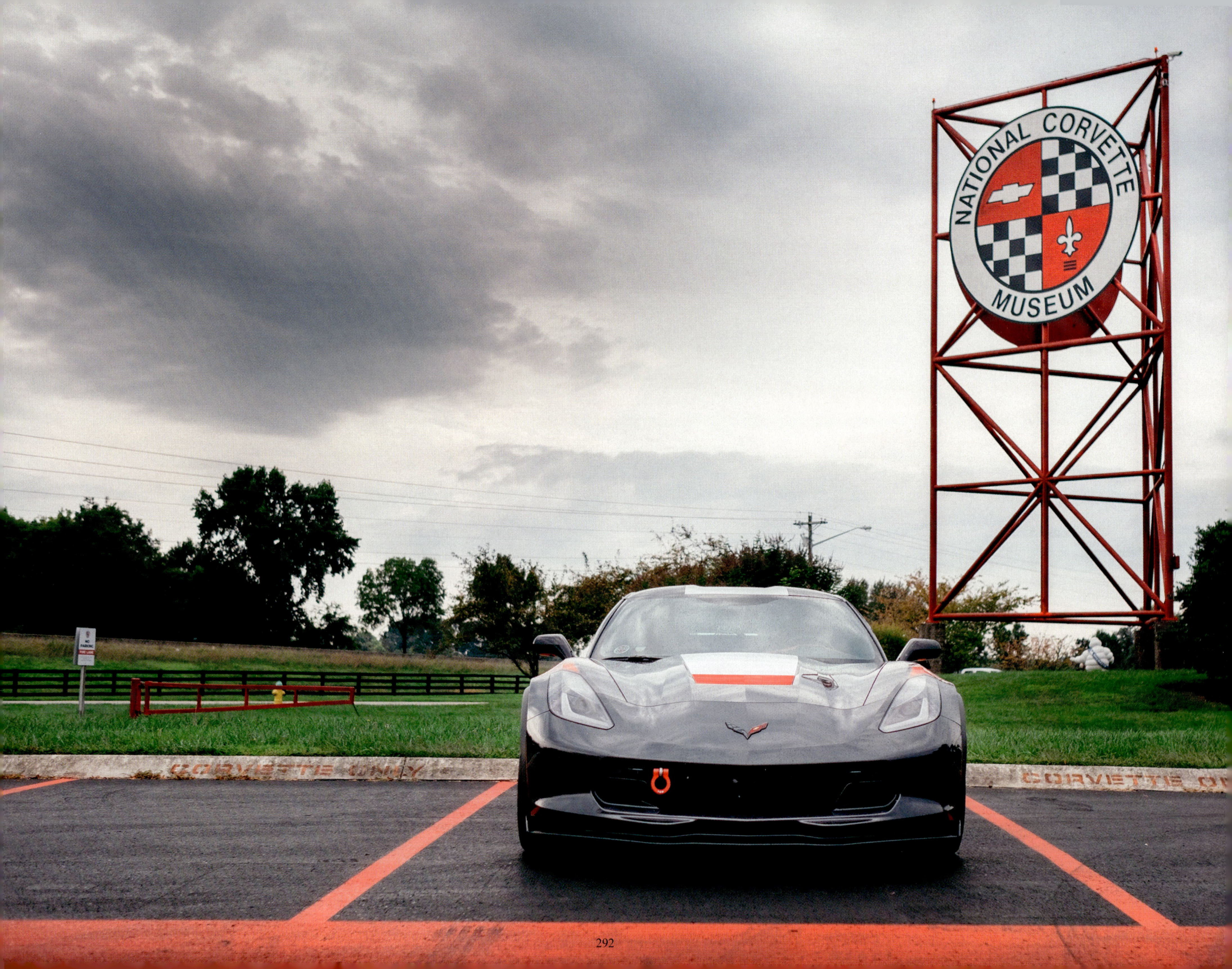
NATIONAL CORVETTE
MUSEUM
CORVETTE ONLY

LAST DAY AT BOWLING GREEN

John Cook is a big Corvette fan. When he was able to afford his first new Corvette in 2010, it was the beginning of his passion for the modern sports car from Bowling Green.

What's your Corvette story?
By far the coolest cars I saw as a child were Corvettes. There was no other comparable sports car here in the USA. That's what made the Corvette magical to so many people. If you are that excited as a child, it is obvious that you will want to buy one as soon as possible when you become a grown-up. I got my first Corvette, a '74 C3, when I was in my mid-twenties. Two or three years later, I upgraded to a '65 C2 convertible. After that, I bought another '65 convertible and then another. For some reason, I had several Corvette convertibles from the same year. At some point, I moved on and got myself a one-owner '64 Corvette. It was a great car. One should realize by now that I really like the C2. At some point, I began restoring C2 Corvettes, but only as a hobby.

In 2010, I finally had enough money to be able to afford my first new Corvette, a Grand Sport convertible. I was actually very pleased with the car, until the C7 came on the market. The thing looked much cooler than the C6! I simply had to have one. The C6 went; a standard C7 came. But as it happens, the manufacturer always comes up with something better, in this case the Grand Sport. I made the decision to buy a 2018 model. In fact, I ordered a 2017, at the beginning of June. It was made on June 6, and I was able to pick it up in the third week of the same month.

A 2019 ZR1 would also have been a good investment. One recently sold for a quarter of a million dollars at a Mecum auction in Harrisburg. It cost $110,000 new. I have a friend in Baltimore whom I meet once a year at Carlisle. His brother has a ZR1. I once said to him that if it was my car, I would have sold it long ago. I would immediately take the $250,000.

I take part in general car shows with my Corvette but also in special Corvette events. Twice I have been able to take part in Corvette driver training at the Spring Mountain Motor Resort in Nevada. There we are allowed to drive the C7 and C8, but on different tracks. It would have been cool to drive both generations on the same track for a better comparison. But even so, the driving experience there is really first-rate. There is an instructor, and he is followed by just three cars. As soon as the cars begin moving, the instructor begins driving. If you speed up, he also speeds up. You have to imagine: he sits with one hand on the wheel and talks to you over the radio, watching in the rearview mirror to see what you're up to. You should be able to keep up with him, as you only have to concentrate on driving, but that is easier said than done. If you are faster than the other two, then you are put in a new group. It was a challenge each time, and I learned a great deal. I had a really great time.

I have met many people from all over the country on Facebook. We meet at various events—at Carlisle, for example, at Corvettes at Carlisle. The car allows you to meet people you would not otherwise have met. Meanwhile, there are car shows, but I forget to look at the cars because it is so nice to talk with your friends. My friend Garry always says, "We meet, we eat." We all go out to eat after our Sunday meets, and there are usually twenty-five to thirty people. Of course, our club has more members, but they can't always all take part.

What is your all-time favorite Corvette model?
A C8 for the pure driving experience. And a C2 for everything else. There's nothing better than a second-generation Corvette.

◀ **2017** Corvette C7, **Bowling Green**, Kentucky, USA | September 19, 2022

TO JOHN, CORVETTE MEANS:
SIMPLY AN ATTITUDE TOWARD LIFE

Last but not least. John Cook's Corvette was the last one photographed for this book on American soil. The C7 is not only driven to meetings and car shows, but also on circuits. Just as its war paint suggests.

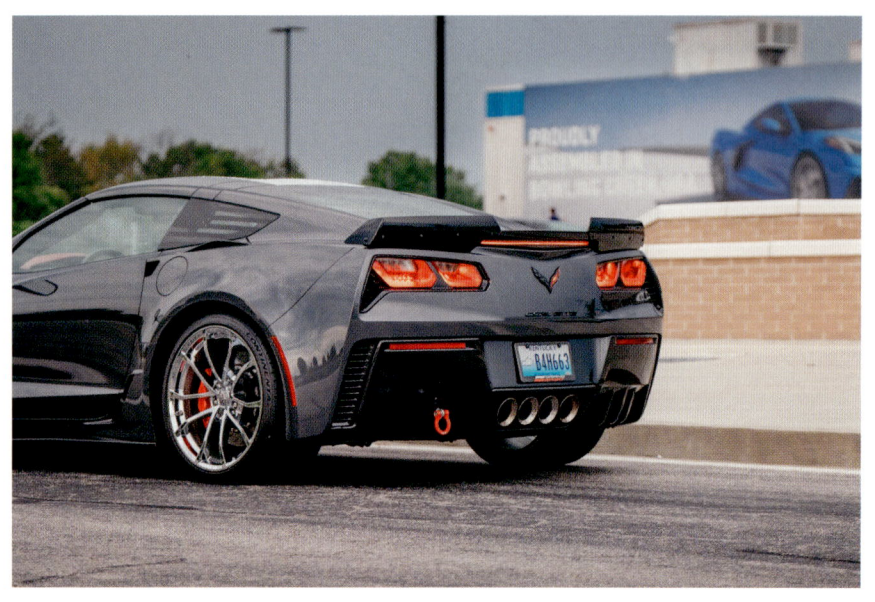

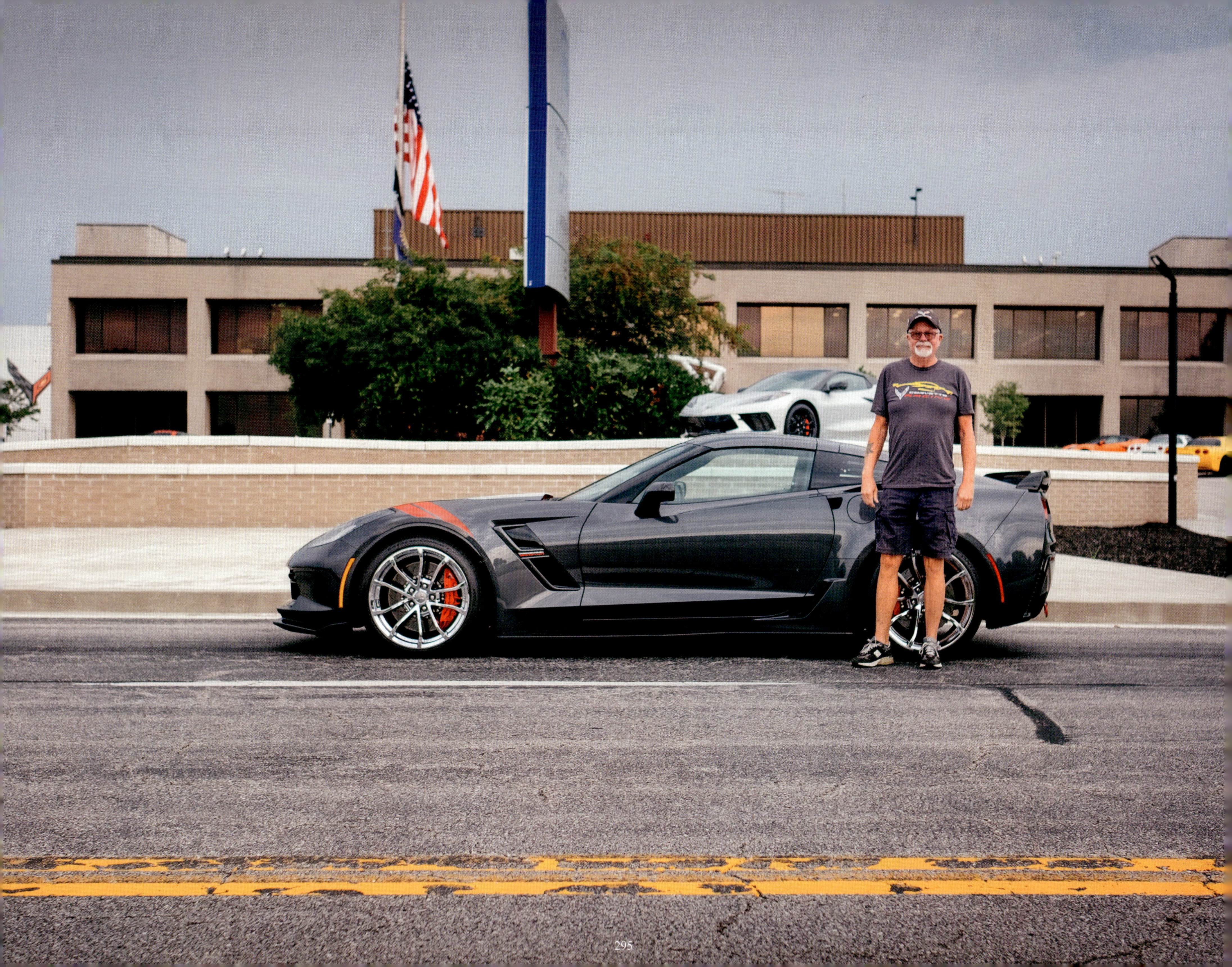

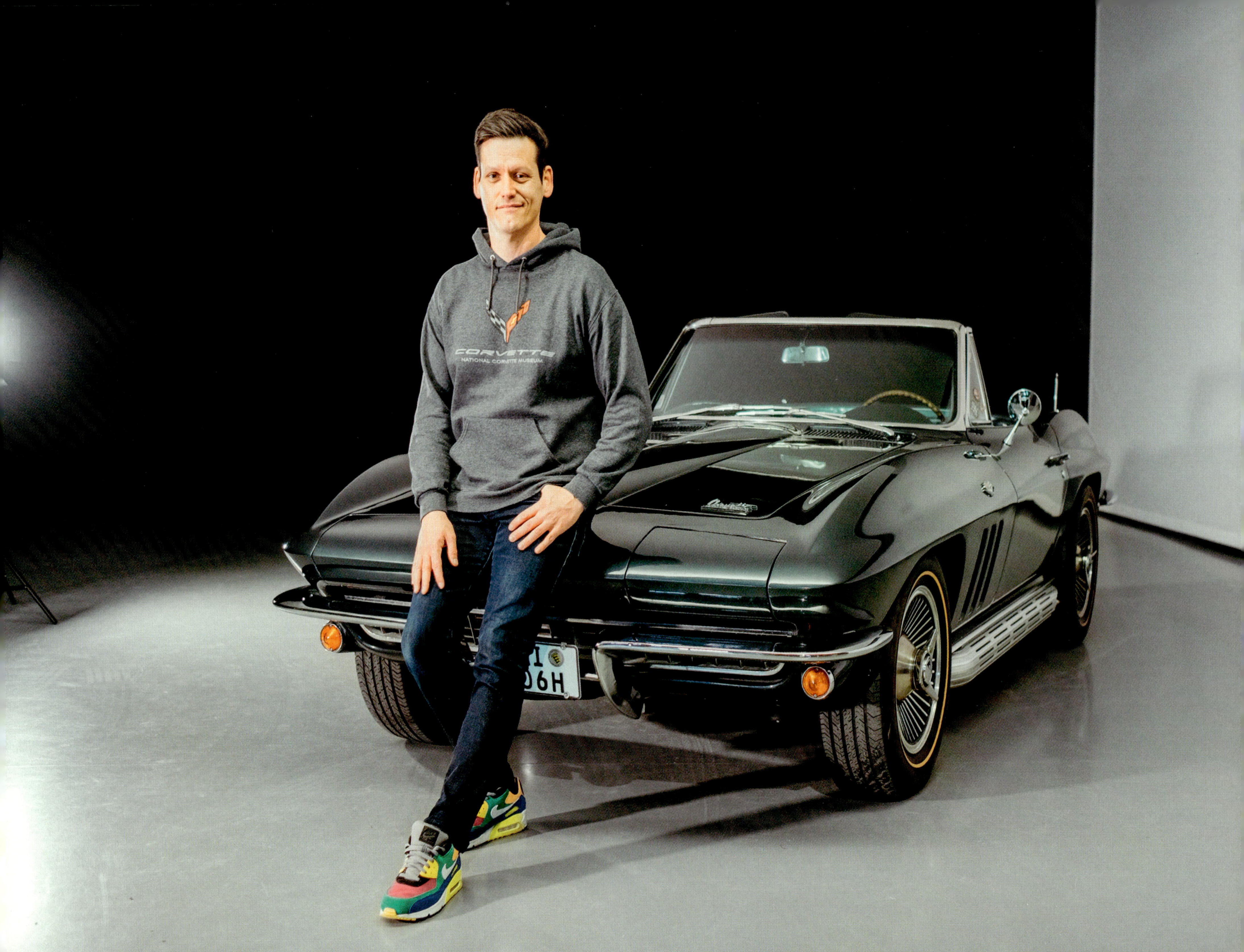
CORVETTE
NATIONAL CORVETTE MUSEUM

CORVETTE NUMBER 6

I am Mario Brunner, photographer and passionate Corvette fan. I not only fulfilled a great dream with this special C2; it was also the inspiration for this book on the 70th birthday of the American sports car icon.

What's my Corvette story?
My first word was car. My parents say that even as a young boy, I could identify all the types of cars driving on the road. And although I grew up in the Stuttgart area, I always had an affinity for American vehicles from the Sixties and Seventies. Generally, I find that the most beautiful cars were made at that time, and not just in the States. Porsches from that time are also very cool, but they have one problem: no V8.

My father died in late 2009 and left me some money. At the time, my mother said that it was time for me to fulfill a dream. The top three on my dream car list were the Corvette C2, a '68 or '69 Dodge Charger, and the '67 Chevrolet Camaro. Places one and two on my list were out of the question financially, so I went looking for a Camaro. I found a suitable car in the US—silver with a black vinyl roof, 383 Stroker engine, and the SS trim package. There was almost nothing original on the car. But it was magnificent and had a brutal V8 sound. An importer brought the car to Germany. My first American car, my first classic.

In the years that followed, my part-time job as a photographer continued to develop. I photographed more and more weddings, cars, people, and events. It was faring well, unlike my Camaro. It was the source of repeated problems, and at some point, I took it to OSCW in Weinstadt. That's what the store was called then; now the company goes by Detroit Performance Technologies, DPT for short. I often took photos for the boys for different trade magazines. My contact with the shop also allowed me to expand my motor pool. At some point, I had not just the Camaro, but also a '64 Impala convertible, a 1972 Ford van, and a small Suzuki as my everyday car. This was far beyond my means, and I knew that something had to change. I often thought about which car I would sell when, but I never made up my mind.

In the summer of 2019, my three American cars all went into the garage, one after another; consequently, the bill was higher than usual. When I picked up one of my cars in Weinstadt, another customer's blue C2 was sitting in the showroom. I asked Sönke Priebe, the head of the company, what the current cost of a C2 was. His answer spurred me into action.

A few days later, I put the Camaro and the Impala up for sale, and together with Sönke, I went looking for a Corvette. I had very firm ideas about what I wanted and what I didn't. The things I wanted included certain colors, the 350hp L-79 engine, and sidepipes. I restricted the year of construction to '65 to '67. Originality and matching numbers were a must. I had learned from the Camaro, on which little was original, what sort of problems that caused. The Impala had been restored and was no longer original, and it also proved difficult. In no way did I want to repeat these mistakes with the Corvette.

I brought Sönke on board as an expert, as I didn't want to make the decision to buy without the necessary expertise. Late in 2019, we drove together to the Netherlands to look at a '67 convertible. According to the seller, it had been finely restored, with many extras. The Corvette did in fact have many extras, but also a bend in the frame, which caused the left-to-right wheelbase to differ by almost an inch. It was therefore junk, expensive junk. With the ideas and wishes I had, there was nothing to be found in Germany and Europe, so I expanded my search to the US. In the evenings, I sat on the sofa with my laptop and clicked through Craigslist. Then an ad for a Corvette caught my eye. Wonderful color, plenty of extras, location Denver. According to its serial number 6 from 1966, it was a pilot car. I immediately sent the link to the ad to Sönke, who was immediately all for it. We contacted the seller and had him send us more pictures and information. We had a lengthy discussion about the serial number and the trim tag, for there were so many Corvettes around with falsified numbers. On the basis of the rivets, the position of certain letters, and traces of the embossing tools on the plates, you can tell whether they are genuine or not. The trim tag is a metal plate in the interior on which, for example, are found the codes for the car color and the interior systems. The pictures and details that we got to see made a good impression. Contact with the seller was also very promising and serious.

So far, so good. Sönke got in touch with Mark Reiss, his contact in the US. He was to fly to Denver and look at the car in person. I remember sitting in the dentist's waiting room and sending Mark the money for his flight and hotel by PayPal. On February 17, 2020, I was in Sönke's office. Mark was in Denver, and we examined the Corvette in detail by video call. We looked at everything that mattered: the underbody, suspension, engine compartment, interior details, and all the serial numbers. Ten years earlier, the owner had had the car repainted in the original Laguna Blue color. Otherwise, the car was unrestored and original, apart from a few parts subject to wear. The trim tag and the serial number plate looked like they did in the first photos, and all the numbers matched. It seemed that it was in fact serial number 6 from the year 1966, a rare pre-production vehicle, a pilot car. Sönke was excited, stating that such a car comes only once in a lifetime. I slept on it, checked my finances, and said yes. On February 19, I emptied my account and transferred the money to the US. I had a few sleepless nights; no one knew what was happening and what would happen next, when the next ship would leave port, and so on. In the end, however, all was well, and precisely three months later, on May 19, 2020, the Corvette was in Weinstadt. It was a very emotional moment for me; it was the fulfillment of a great dream.

The C2 looked like it did in the pictures. There were no unpleasant surprises, no damage, no scratches. A wonderful car with an unbelievably cool sound! The boys at DPT got the convertible ready for licensing, and I dug deeper into the subject of Corvettes and grappled with the topic of "pilot car." I began searching for serial numbers and date codes on the car, photographing them, recording them, and researching whether everything fit together. And the indications spoke a clear language; it was definitely a pilot car.

Production of the 1966 model year began in September 1965. My Corvette was built on July 9, 1965, two months before the official start of the '66 model year. The inner fender was changed slightly from the 1965 to 1966 model years. As the ultimate tools for it were not yet available in July 1965, the Corvette had handmade inner fenders. The engine block had the correct casting number for the '65 model year, but the correct serial number for '66. The serial numbers on the frame, transmission, and engine matched. The date codes on the glass, on parts in the engine compartment, and in the interior were all consistent, some dated to the winter or early spring of 1965. The engine, distributor, and cylinder head were all made on May 24, 1965, to name one more technical detail. I can have a so-called Shipping Data Report sent by the NCRS. The document tells you when and to where GM sent the Corvette, to the customer or dealer. There are no reports from that year for the serial numbers 1 to 8. That makes sense because the pilot cars could not be ordered by regular customers. Some of the pilot cars were

◀ **1966** Corvette C2, **Stuttgart**, Baden-Württemberg, **Germany** | February 10, 2023

scrapped, some remained at GM, and others went to car dealerships and were sold. By the way, the color Laguna Blue was only available in 1966 and was only ordered 2,054 times. It could well be that this is the first small block convertible ever produced in the color.

Of course, I also tried to get in touch with the former owner. He had probably had the vehicle for more than thirty years and came from the Denver area. I wrote two letters, but unfortunately, I have not received a reply. It would be nice to complete the car's history in this direction. As I said, the Corvette was produced on July 9, 1965. On July 9, 2020, I went with all the paperwork to the registration office, and on its fifty-fifth birthday, the Corvette received its German registration. What a lovely coincidence.

How did I come up with the idea for this book?
I have dealt very intensively with the Corvette, especially with the years 1965 and 1966, and have thus very quickly delved very deeply into the matter. As a result, my fascination grew even deeper. As a result of the pandemic, there wasn't as much photographic work to do as usual, and I thought to myself that I could use the time to tackle a photographic project. Just for me. Then I came up with the idea to meet 70 Corvette people on the Corvette's 70th birthday, to portray them and have them tell their personal Corvette stories. I wanted to put the whole thing into a book. I met with the first volunteers on June 11, 2021, and with the next the following day. I immediately felt that the idea had potential, for the people had exciting and individual stories. I asked everyone three questions. Why Corvette and how did you come to get your car? Which is your all-time favorite model? And what does the topic mean to you, summed up in three words. After this motivating beginning, I decided not only to interview people in Germany; instead, I decided on 35 people from Germany and 35 from the US. Meeting people in the US wasn't that simple, because at the time, I couldn't fly to the States thanks to the pandemic. By way of the Corvette Forum and social media, however, I quickly contacted many volunteers from both countries.

I then planned several trips through Germany which I had to make between jobs and weddings I had to photograph. In 2021, for example, I went to Munich, Heidelberg, Würzburg, Cologne, Essen, and Hamburg. In several cases, I met several people in one day. In 2022, I went to Rüsselheim, Frankfurt, Berlin, and the island of Rügen. After much planning, it was finally time, and on November 8, 2021, I flew to Los Angeles. I spent a total of 13 days in the US and during that time met with 18 people in California, Las Vegas, and Florida. One week after my arrival, I was in Florida, standing on the runway used by the Space Shuttle, where I photographed the C2 that had once belonged to Neil Armstrong. They even let me take a turn on the runway, just like James May in an episode of *The Grand Tour*. That was absolutely surreal, a goose bump moment. I also met Mark, Sönke's scout, in San Francisco and thanked him for his assistance in buying the Corvette by taking him to dinner. He is a very likeable fellow, and it was a great evening.

The following year, I traveled to the States for a second time for the project, visiting, among other places, Detroit and Bowling Green, sacred ground, so to speak. I had the honor of meeting Harlan Charles, Head of Marketing for Corvette, was given a private tour of the museum in Bowling Green, and was able to see what goes on behind the curtains there. In December 2022, I was in Hamburg as a guest on the *Two from Eleven* podcast and discussed my project with Frank Otero Molanes and Jens Seltrecht. In March 2023, I again met Frank and his 2023 C8 in the Hanseatic city and photographed his car for this book. His is the last story involving a C8, and in several places, one can find a reference to the 70th anniversary. The perfect ending.

There were so many highlights in my travels that I can't list them all here. I heard so many exciting stories, met so many great people, and was allowed to photograph wonderful cars. Even if I hadn't found a publisher for the book, it would have been worth every minute and every Euro. An absolute privilege and a unique adventure!

What is my all-time favorite Corvette model?
I have dealt really intensively with every Corvette generation. I have ridden in every generation as a passenger or behind the wheel. The C2 is still my favorite—the most beautiful Corvette ever built, to me the ultimate dream car. If I should win the lottery, I would also buy a 1953 C1, a C4, and a C8.

Here, I would like to thank all those who took the time to meet with me and tell me their personal stories. Many thanks for your trust and the great memories.
A very special thank you goes to:

my parents, for everything. Without the two of them, the Corvette would never have ended up in my garage and I would not have discovered photography.

Waltraud and Albert, for their support and the augmentation of my travel fund.

Sönke. His expertise and his friendship allowed me to delve deeper into the subject of American cars than I ever could have imagined. Without his enthusiasm and his counsel, I would surely have bought another car, and this book would never have been written.

Thomas Behringer, for his years of uncomplicated friendship, his creative input, constructive criticism, company while traveling, and technical support.

Thomas Pfromm, for the relaxed cooperation, his contacts, and our conversations on Lake Constance.

Mark Reiss, for his efforts in Colorado and the dinner with his Swabian father in San Francisco. An unforgettable evening.

Larry Courtney, for the contacts and his spontaneous assistance in Detroit. Without him, I would undoubtedly have had to spend a night in my car.

MY DEEPEST THANKS

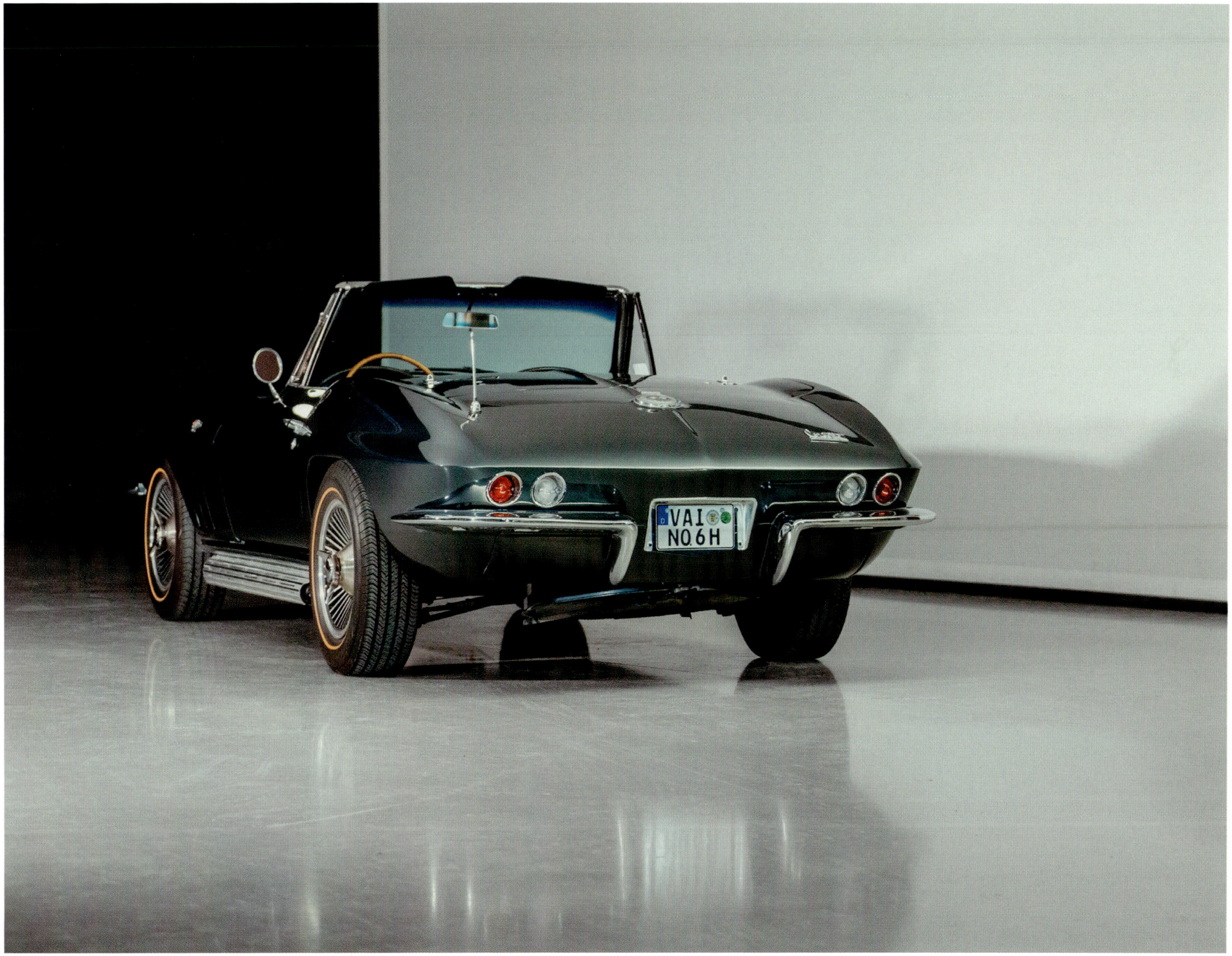
VAI
NO 6H

300

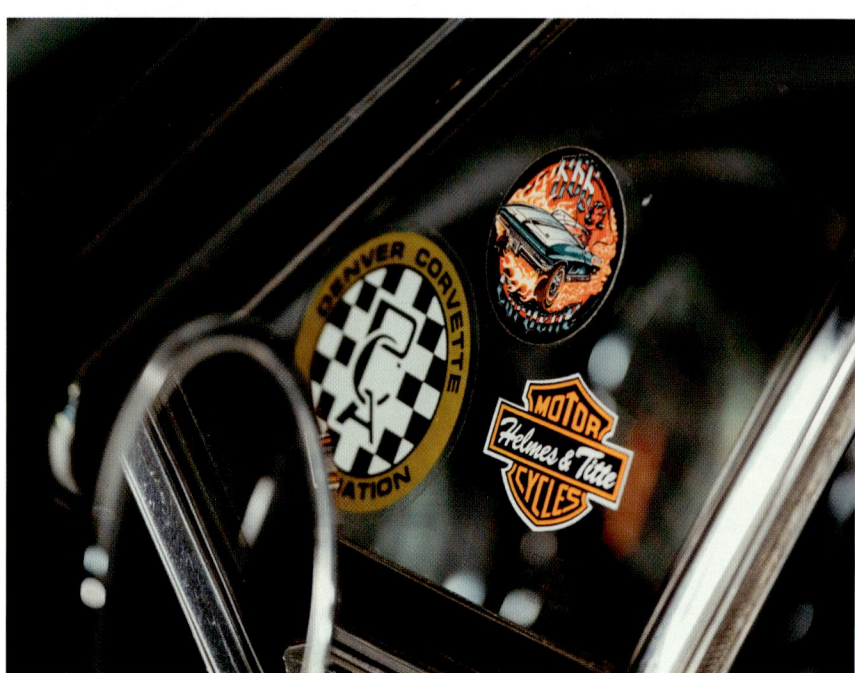

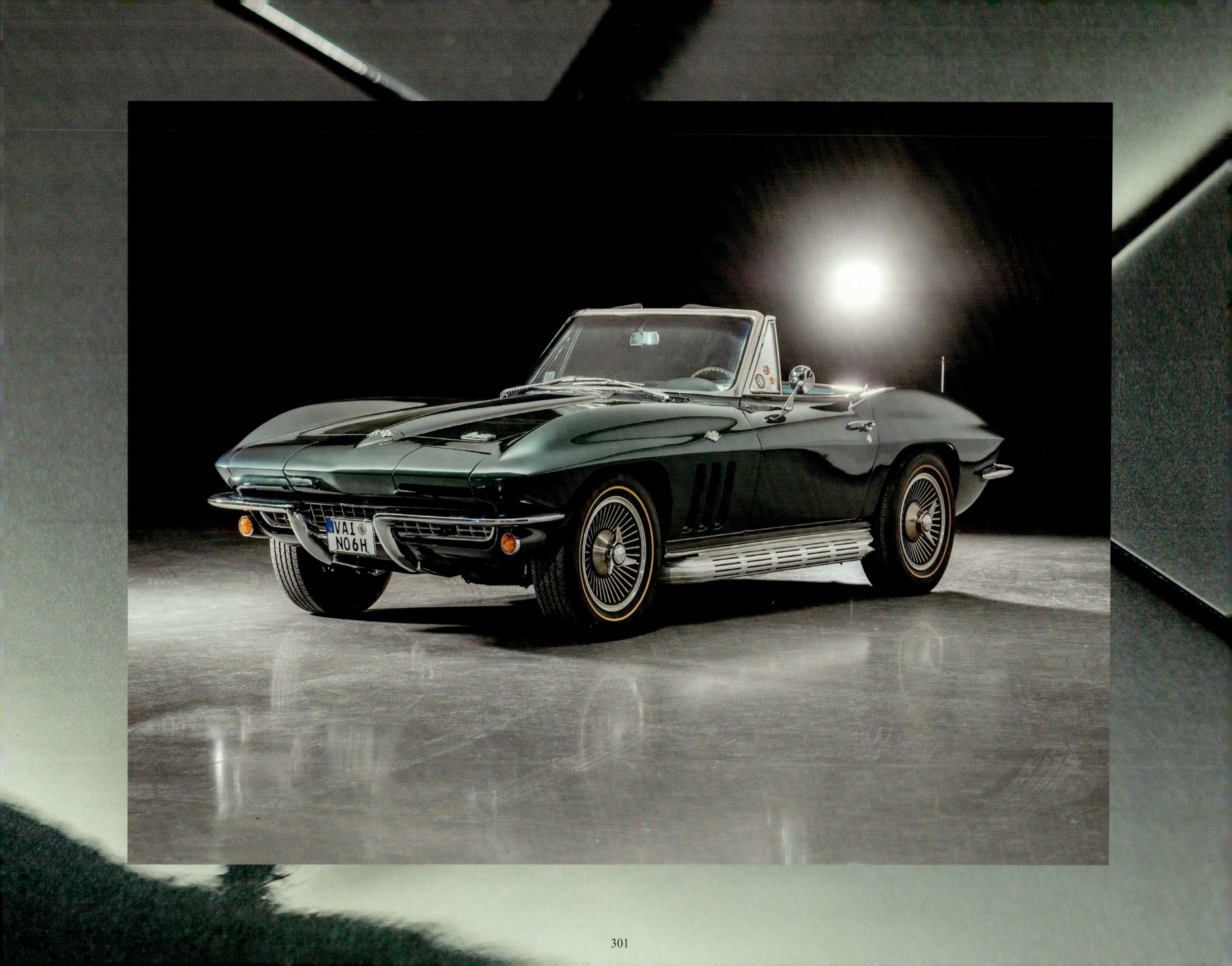
VAI
NO6H

CORVETTE STOPS

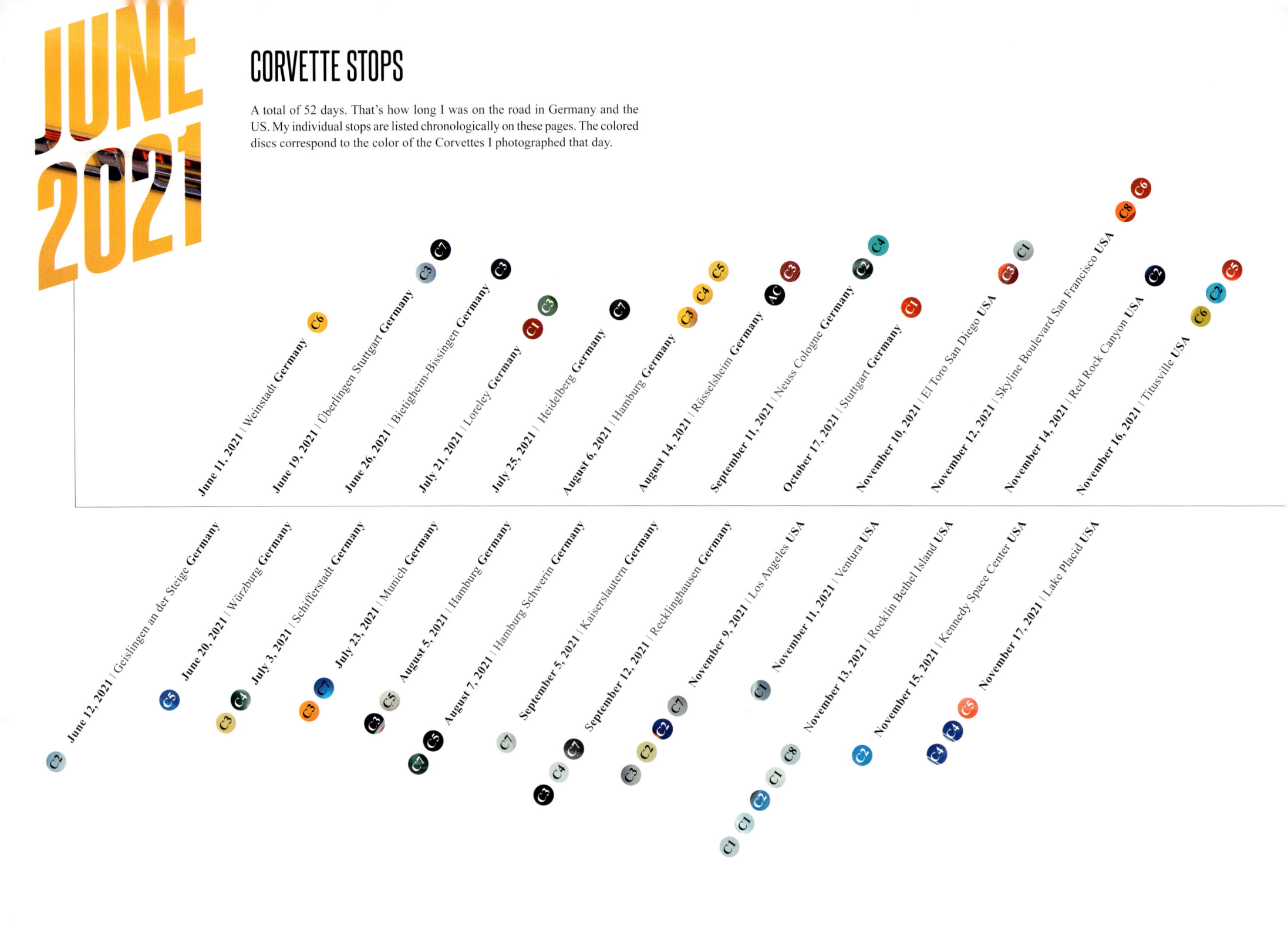

A total of 52 days. That's how long I was on the road in Germany and the US. My individual stops are listed chronologically on these pages. The colored discs correspond to the color of the Corvettes I photographed that day.

JUNE 2021

- June 11, 2021 | Weinstadt Germany — C6
- June 12, 2021 | Geislingen an der Steige Germany — C2
- June 19, 2021 | Überlingen Stuttgart Germany — C3, C7
- June 20, 2021 | Würzburg Germany — C5
- June 26, 2021 | Bietigheim-Bissingen Germany — C3
- July 3, 2021 | Schifferstadt Germany — C3, C4
- July 21, 2021 | Loreley Germany — C1, C3
- July 23, 2021 | Munich Germany — C7
- July 25, 2021 | Heidelberg Germany — C7
- August 5, 2021 | Hamburg Germany — C3, C5
- August 6, 2021 | Hamburg Germany — C3, C4, C5
- August 7, 2021 | Hamburg Schwerin Germany — C5, C7
- August 14, 2021 | Rüsselsheim Germany — AC, C3
- September 5, 2021 | Kaiserslautern Germany — C3, C4, C7
- September 11, 2021 | Neuss Cologne Germany — C2, C4
- September 12, 2021 | Recklinghausen Germany — C2, C3, C7
- October 17, 2021 | Stuttgart Germany — C1
- November 9, 2021 | Los Angeles USA — C1, C2, C8
- November 10, 2021 | El Toro San Diego USA — C1, C3
- November 11, 2021 | Ventura USA — C1, C2
- November 12, 2021 | Skyline Boulevard San Francisco USA — C1
- November 13, 2021 | Rocklin Bethel Island USA — C2
- November 14, 2021 | Red Rock Canyon USA — C2, C8, C6
- November 15, 2021 | Kennedy Space Center USA — C4, C4
- November 16, 2021 | Titusville USA — C2, C5, C6
- November 17, 2021 | Lake Placid USA — C4, C5

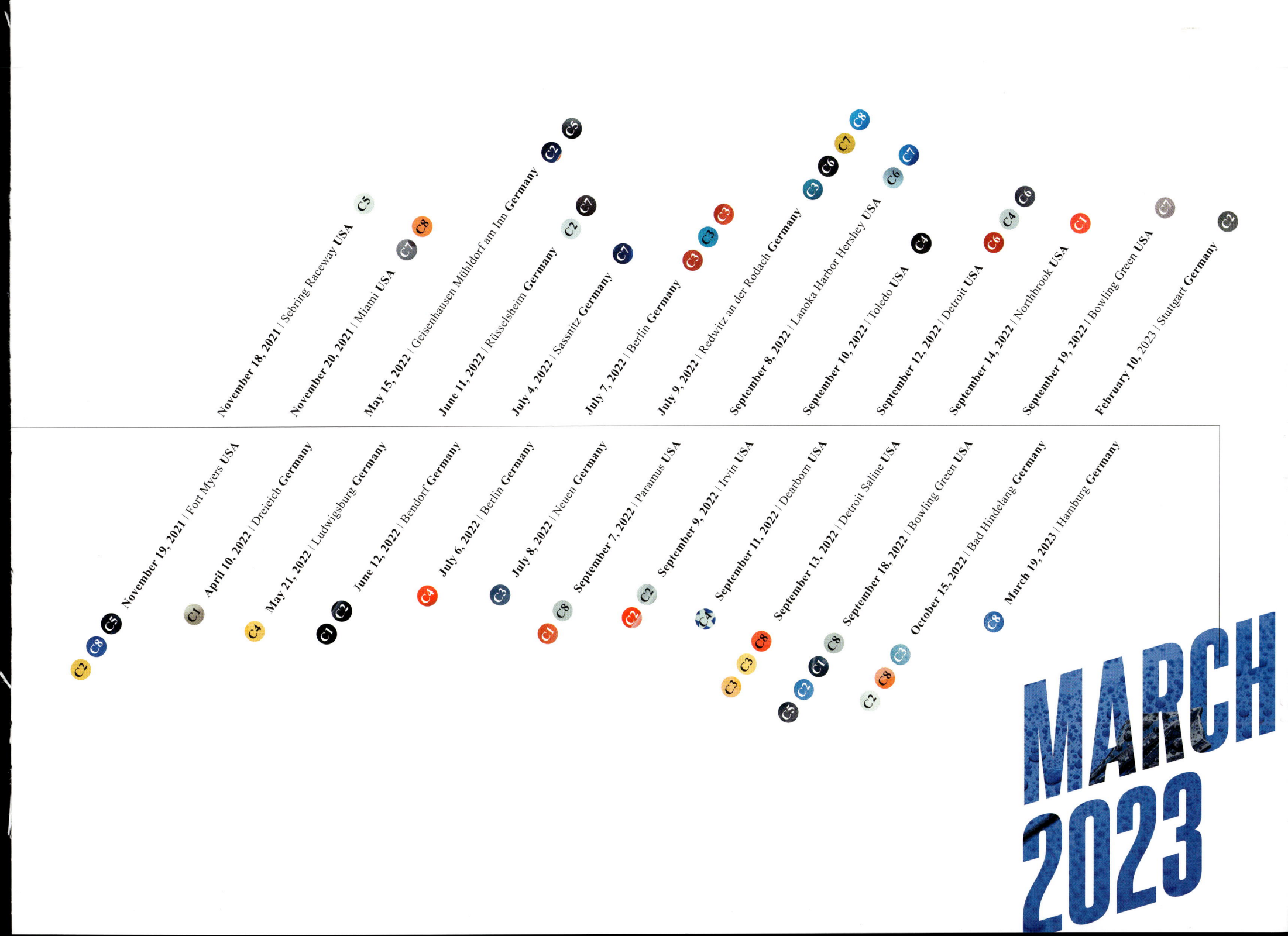

November 18, 2021 | Sebring Raceway USA
November 20, 2021 | Miami USA
May 15, 2022 | Geisenhausen Mühldorf am Inn Germany
June 11, 2022 | Rüsselsheim Germany
July 4, 2022 | Sassnitz Germany
July 7, 2022 | Berlin Germany
July 9, 2022 | Redwitz an der Rodach Germany
September 8, 2022 | Lanoka Harbor Hershey USA
September 10, 2022 | Toledo USA
September 12, 2022 | Detroit USA
September 14, 2022 | Northbrook USA
September 19, 2022 | Bowling Green USA
February 10, 2023 | Stuttgart Germany

November 19, 2021 | Fort Myers USA
April 10, 2022 | Dreieich Germany
May 21, 2022 | Ludwigsburg Germany
June 12, 2022 | Bendorf Germany
July 6, 2022 | Berlin Germany
July 8, 2022 | Neuen Germany
September 7, 2022 | Paramus USA
September 9, 2022 | Irvin USA
September 11, 2022 | Dearborn USA
September 13, 2022 | Detroit Saline USA
September 18, 2022 | Bowling Green USA
October 15, 2022 | Bad Hindelang Germany
March 19, 2023 | Hamburg Germany

MARCH 2023

For Dad & Leo